Drupal for Education and E-Learning

Second Edition

Create web-based, content-rich tools for teaching
and learning

James G. Robertson
Bill Fitzgerald

[PACKT] open source *
PUBLISHING community experience distilled

BIRMINGHAM - MUMBAI

Drupal for Education and E-Learning
Second Edition

First published: November 2008

Second Edition: June 2013

Production Reference: 1040613

Published by Packt Publishing Ltd.
Livery Place
35 Livery Street
Birmingham B3 2PB, UK.

ISBN 978-1-78216-276-6

www.packtpub.com

Cover Image by Žarko Piljak (zpiljak@gmail.com)

Credits

Authors
James G. Robertson
Bill Fitzgerald

Reviewers
János Fehér
Ron Simon

Acquisition Editor
Mary Jasmine Nadar

Lead Technical Editor
Susmita Panda

Technical Editors
Kaustubh S. Mayekar
Sharvari Baet
Akshata Patil

Project Coordinator
Leena Purkait

Proofreaders
Stephen Copestake
Amy Guest

Indexer
Rekha Nair

Production Coordinator
Manu Joseph

Cover Work
Manu Joseph

About the Author

James G. Robertson hasn't always been a developer. He started his long road to Drupal with a degree in history from Presbyterian College in Clinton, SC. After not being able to find a job that could use a history degree, he went to get his master's degree in journalism and public affairs from American University in Washington, DC. While working on his degree at AU, he worked as a teacher's assistant, taught himself Drupal, and developed his first website for The American Observer, American University's graduate journalism school publication. After internships at J-Lab and the Newseum, he worked for the National Geographic Society producing content and occasionally blogging for sections of `nationalgeographic.com`. After a year at National Geographic, he made the move to developing websites with Drupal full-time for Bravery Corporation, a public relations and marketing firm in Washington, DC. He now works at REI Systems, an IT services company in Sterling, VA.

There are many people I would like to thank for getting me here today. First, I would like to thank Bill Fitzgerald for writing this book, and for his clear and, often, humorous original text that I was lucky enough to inherit. Second, I would like to thank my grandparents, Gordon and Jacqueline Lewis, for letting me play on the IBM PS/2 in their basement as a kid and helping develop my love for computers. I would like to thank my parents, Jim and Michele Robertson, for always believing in and supporting me. I'd like to thank David Johnson at American University, who introduced me to Drupal by handing me a book and telling me to build him a website. David also introduced me to Max Brown at Bravery, who took a chance and let me get my career off the ground; for that, I am eternally grateful. I'd like to thank my team at REI Systems, who have been supportive and understanding through this process. And, last but not least, I'd like to thank my loving and eternally patient wife, Jessica, for everything.

Bill Fitzgerald was born in 1968, and worked as a teacher for 16 years. During that time, he taught English and history, and worked as a Technology Director at the K12 level. He began using technology in his own teaching in the early 90s; from there, he moved on to database design and systems administration. During that time, he began developing strategies to support technology integration in 1:1 laptop systems and in desktop computing environments.

In 2003, Bill founded FunnyMonkey, an open source development shop working primarily within education. He is active in various educational and open source communities. He blogs about education and technology at `http://funnymonkey.com/blog`.

When Bill is not staring deeply into computer screens, he can be found riding his fixed-gear bicycle through Portland, OR, or spending far too much time drinking coffee.

About the Reviewers

János Fehér, since 1996, has been involved in a wide variety of projects, including technical support for NATO operations, development for a high-performance computing grid, national TV and radio websites, Learning Management Systems (LMS) for university, and adult learning, news, and government websites. He has been heavily involved with Drupal for more than 8 years and is the lead of the Hungarian localization team, contributor of quite a few modules and the Drupal Core. He is currently a Senior Software Developer at Capgemini UK.

> I will always be thankful to the person who has been standing by me since our first meeting 10 years ago. To my love, Szilvi.

Ron Simon started working with computers in the early 1970s while working toward his degree in Computer Sciences and Business Administration. Much has changed from that point of punch cards and Cobol program languages. Presently, he is working on building a large interactive Historical Database Website using Drupal to let the community contribute to the History of a place called "Beckmaze", which has a fascinating interaction of history, maps, and stories.

He has been an editor of many technical and historical books, including three books on Drupal and two on historical documentation.

He finds that our past does define the direction we are moving toward and that, if we study history, we can learn from the advice and mistakes our ancestors have left us for guidance toward our future.

www.PacktPub.com

Support files, eBooks, discount offers and more

You might want to visit www.PacktPub.com for support files and downloads related to your book.

Did you know that Packt offers eBook versions of every book published, with PDF and ePub files available? You can upgrade to the eBook version at www.PacktPub.com and as a print book customer, you are entitled to a discount on the eBook copy. Get in touch with us at service@packtpub.com for more details.

At www.PacktPub.com, you can also read a collection of free technical articles, sign up for a range of free newsletters and receive exclusive discounts and offers on Packt books and eBooks.

http://PacktLib.PacktPub.com

Do you need instant solutions to your IT questions? PacktLib is Packt's online digital book library. Here, you can access, read and search across Packt's entire library of books.

Why Subscribe?

- Fully searchable across every book published by Packt
- Copy and paste, print and bookmark content
- On demand and accessible via web browser

Free Access for Packt account holders

If you have an account with Packt at www.PacktPub.com, you can use this to access PacktLib today and view nine entirely free books. Simply use your login credentials for immediate access.

Table of Contents

Preface

Drupal has its roots in building and supporting online communities. These roots have helped Drupal meet the needs of schools, teachers, and students in countless countries and in countless different learning contexts. Compared to a traditional Learning Management System, Drupal can feel less restrictive; Drupal has been designed to interact with the Web and to make the most of the array of possibilities offered by the Internet.

Drupal allows site administrators to set up as closed or as open a site as they desire. Using Drupal, a site administrator can create a learning environment where no content is visible outside the site and where all courses are entirely private. At the other end of the spectrum, a site administrator can create a learning environment where students and teachers have complete control over the content they share with classmates, other site members, and/or the entire Internet community. The purpose of this book is not to recommend one approach to teaching and learning over another, but rather to highlight the freedom that comes with having choices. In this text, we will cover the technical approaches to crafting the ideal social learning environment for your specific goals.

What this book covers

Chapter 1, Introducing Drupal, provides an overview of Drupal, including a brief section on Drupal terminology.

Chapter 2, Installing Drupal, covers how to install Drupal. This chapter takes you through the installation process and covers how to enable some of the core modules you will use in this book.

Chapter 3, Getting Started, begins by going through the options enabled in the core installation. From there, you will learn how to install additional modules and themes. Using these instructions, you will then install and configure two commonly used modules: the Chaos tool suite (Ctools) and Views. This chapter includes detailed instructions for creating new content types, adding fields to those content types, and displaying content using views. The foundation provided in this chapter is referenced extensively throughout the book.

Chapter 4, Creating a Teacher Blog, describes how to set up a blog. This chapter includes instructions for setting up a text editor (also known as a WYSIWYG editor) and for adding two new content types: one for blog posts and the second for assignments. The chapter continues by covering how to create custom views to display content and closes by showing how to clone an existing view in order to create a calendar to display assignments.

Chapter 5, Enrolling Students, covers how to add users to your site. This chapter provides details on creating roles and using roles to create granular permissions for the people who will use your site.

Chapter 6, Creating the Student Blog, includes more details on using roles effectively to structure your site. Additionally in this chapter more advanced techniques with views are covered, as we begin to use views to track student and teacher blog posts.

Chapter 7, Bookmarks, describes some of the classroom uses for social bookmarking. In *Chapter 3, Getting Started,* we created a content type for storing and categorizing bookmarks and this chapter goes through various methods of using bookmarks to support student learning.

Chapter 8, Podcasting and Images, covers how to use your site to publish audio and images. In addition to covering the technical details of publishing a podcast, this chapter covers various uses of audio in the classroom. In particular, the chapter focuses on skills that can be honed through creating podcasts.

Chapter 9, Video, describes how to embed media that is shared on the Web. As part of this chapter, we examine how to integrate video production into a curriculum, and how video production can relate to other types of content stored on the site. As with podcasts, the emphasis in this chapter is on what can be learned through video production and on how to use the medium of video effectively.

Chapter 10, Forums and Blogs, describes how to set up and configure forums in Drupal. The chapter also explains the similarities and differences between forums and blogs.

Chapter 11, Social Networks and Extending the User Profile, gives an overview of how to create user profiles, so users can share information about themselves with other users.

Chapter 12, Supporting Multiple Classes, describes how to set up the Organic Groups module to support formal and informal learning spaces. The chapter covers using different privacy settings, group wikis, e-mail notifications, and varying group types.

Chapter 13, Tracking Student Progress, shows how people can find content created by other users within the site. The chapter starts by examining the core Tracker module and then looks at using views and short code snippets to group users and make their work easier to find.

Chapter 14, Theming and User Interface Design, provides some introductory details of how to create an intuitive navigational structure. The techniques described in this chapter are predicated on keeping your site as simple as possible by using customized menus. The chapter also introduces Drupal's theming layer and describes how to get started with modifying a theme.

Chapter 15, Backup, Maintenance, and Upgrades, gets into one of the most commonly overlooked aspects of running a website: making sure that you have a working backup and keeping your codebase up-to-date. The goal of this chapter is to take the sting out of site maintenance. This chapter describes how to use the DB Maintenance module to automate the core tasks required for backup, as well as backing up using browser-based and command-line tools.

Chapter 16, Working Effectively in the Drupal Community, provides an overview of how to begin working with the Drupal community. One of the primary benefits of working with Drupal is the community of users and developers associated with the software. This chapter points out some of the methods for getting involved with and contributing back to the project.

What you need for this book

This book describes how to build websites using Drupal. To use this book effectively, you will need Internet access to be able to download Drupal and the contributed modules we describe in this book.

Additionally, you will need a place to host your website. Setting up a hosting environment is covered in *Chapter 2, Installing Drupal*.

Who this book is for

This book is intended for teachers building a website to support their classes and site administrators and technology integrators working within schools or training organizations. This book is also intended for technology directors at either the school or district level. The examples given in this book are appropriate for students and teachers at all levels, from elementary school, through higher education, to adult education and vocational training.

A secondary audience of this book includes people working to deliver curricula via online training or blended learning (a combination of online teaching and face-to-face meetings) or people interested in using social media in education. This text will also be of interest to general web developers looking to learn more about configuring Drupal without writing new code.

By design, this book is not a development manual. This text is intended to support people with little to no knowledge of PHP. No knowledge of development in PHP is required to use the explanations and tutorials in this text.

Conventions

In this book, you will find a number of styles of text that distinguish between different kinds of information. Here are some examples of these styles, and an explanation of their meaning.

Code words in text are shown as follows: "The blocks can be administered at `admin/structure/block`."

A block of code will be set as follows:

```
max_execution_time = 60;
max_input_time = 120;
memory_limit = 128M;
error_reporting = E_ALL & ~E_NOTICE
```

When we wish to draw your attention to a particular part of a code block, the relevant lines or items will be made bold:

```
$loaded_user = user_load(array('uid' => $u->uid));
$links[] = l($loaded_user->name, 'bygroup/'. $loaded_user->uid .'/'.
$gid) . $separator . $loaded_user->profile_last_name;
```

New terms and **important words** are shown in bold. Words that you see on the screen, in menus or dialog boxes for example, appear in the text like this: "The **Edit** tab allows users (or site administrators) to edit their profile information".

> [image] Warnings or important notes appear in a box like this.

> [image] Tips and tricks appear like this.

Reader feedback

Feedback from our readers is always welcome. Let us know what you think about this book—what you liked or may have disliked. Reader feedback is important for us to develop titles that you really get the most out of.

To send us general feedback, simply send an e-mail to feedback@packtpub.com, and mention the book title via the subject of your message.

If there is a topic that you have expertise in and you are interested in either writing or contributing to a book, see our author guide on www.packtpub.com/authors.

Customer support

Now that you are the proud owner of a Packt book, we have a number of things to help you to get the most from your purchase.

Errata

Although we have taken every care to ensure the accuracy of our content, mistakes do happen. If you find a mistake in one of our books—maybe a mistake in the text or the code—we would be grateful if you would report this to us. By doing so, you can save other readers from frustration and help us improve subsequent versions of this book. If you find any errata, please report them by visiting http://www.packtpub.com/submit-errata, selecting your book, clicking on the **erratasubmissionform** link, and entering the details of your errata. Once your errata are verified, your submission will be accepted and the errata will be uploaded on our website, or added to any list of existing errata, under the Errata section of that title. Any existing errata can be viewed by selecting your title from http://www.packtpub.com/support.

Piracy

Piracy of copyright material on the Internet is an ongoing problem across all media. At Packt, we take the protection of our copyright and licenses very seriously. If you come across any illegal copies of our works, in any form, on the Internet, please provide us with the location address or website name immediately so that we can pursue a remedy.

Please contact us at copyright@packtpub.com with a link to the suspected pirated material.

We appreciate your help in protecting our authors, and our ability to bring you valuable content.

Questions

You can contact us at questions@packtpub.com if you are having a problem with any aspect of the book, and we will do our best to address it.

1
Introducing Drupal

Welcome to the second edition of *Drupal for Education and E-Learning*!

In the last several years, we have seen an incredible upswing in the popularity and adoption of Drupal. The size of the Drupal community (as of June, 2013) is approaching 970,000 registered users, and Drupal is used to power everything from personal blogs to online stores to learning platforms to sites for record labels.

This book provides details of how to install Drupal and how to customize Drupal to support teaching and learning. This initial chapter provides a high-level overview of Drupal, along with details of how to get the most from this book.

What is Drupal?

A concise definition of Drupal is difficult to come by, as many people use Drupal for many different things. The following definitions provide an incomplete cross section of how different people use Drupal (our working definition is the final one in the list):

- Drupal is a database-driven web application written in PHP.
- Drupal is an open source **Content Management System (CMS)** freely available under the **GNU General Public License (GPL)**.
- Drupal is a community-building platform.
- Drupal is a web development framework. You can use Drupal as a platform to build a broad range of web applications.

> The previous definitions, however, can also benefit from further explanation. For those interested in additional reading and background, the following links provide a more detailed overview and some background information:
>
> - For PHP, visit `http://php.net/`.
> - For web content management system, visit `http://en.wikipedia.org/wiki/Web_content_management_system`.
> - For GPL, visit `http://www.gnu.org/licenses/licenses.html`. Drupal is covered under Version 2 of the GPL: `http://www.gnu.org/licenses/gpl-2.0.html`.
> - For web development framework, visit `http://en.wikipedia.org/wiki/Web_application_framework`.
> - For background information on open source, visit `http://www.opensource.org`.
> - For the overview section from the Drupal handbook, visit `http://drupal.org/documentation/concepts`.

Our definition: Drupal is a tool that helps people build interactive websites. It is free to download, install, customize, and use.

Drupal – a short historical overview

Drupal was started in 2000 by Dries Buytaert when he was a student at the University of Antwerp. Dries, along with some friends at the university, wanted a way to communicate about the various details of their lives. To meet that need, Dries wrote a web-based application that allowed people to share notes. In January 2001, Dries decided to release the source code, and the Drupal project was born.

The Drupal handbook provides a more detailed overview at `http://drupal.org/about/history`.

Drupal has gone through many improvements over the years, and as of the writing of this book, Drupal 7 is the most recent major version. It is the version we will be using in this book.

What Drupal can do for you

Drupal is not a traditional **Learning Management System** (**LMS**). Drupal started as a community-building platform and these community-centered roots form the range of possibilities available within Drupal today.

Drupal provides a wide variety of useful tools for educators. For the instructor, Drupal can serve as a blogging platform, allowing teachers to communicate directly with students, parents, and the larger school and Internet community.

Drupal also offers a flexible range of privacy options that allow users to keep some, or all, of the content within a site private. However, a Drupal site can be used for far more than a secure blogging platform. Within a single Drupal site, you can set up social bookmarking, podcasting, video hosting, formal and informal groups, rich user profiles, and other features commonly associated with social web communities. Building your site in Drupal allows you to start with precisely the features you want and expand as needed. This book provides the information needed to build, maintain, and grow your site.

Drupal terminology

Drupal, like most software applications, has a specific lexicon. Mastering Drupal jargon is useful for many reasons, not the least of which is that using Drupal-specific terminology can help you search for information more effectively. The glossary in this chapter will give you an overview of commonly used Drupal terms and what they mean.

This list of terminology will cover our common tasks and features. For a glossary that delves into some of the technical aspects of Drupal, the **Glossary** page in the Drupal handbook is a useful resource, which can be found at `http://drupal.org/glossary`:

- **Entity**: An entity is a new concept in Drupal 7 and it describes one instance of an entity type.
- **Entity type**: An entity type groups together fields and is used to store and display data. Examples of entity types are nodes, users, comments, and taxonomy terms.
- **Field**: A field is a reusable way to enter, store, and display information on the site, such as text, dates, and numbers.

- **Bundle**: A bundle is a certain kind of an entity type.

- **Node**: A node is a piece of content that has been created on your site. For example, if you create a page, you have created a node. A node is an entity type and each individual node you create is an entity.

- **Content type or node type**: On your Drupal site, you will have different types of nodes or content. The default installation comes with the two content types: the **Article** and **Basic** page. As we progress through this book, we will create a variety of other node types, such as bookmarks, student blogs, audio nodes, and so on. While all types of nodes are content, different node types can have different functions on your site. A content type is a bundle for the node entity type.

- **Post**: A post is a piece of content of any content type. For example, if a user creates a page node, they have created a post.

- **Core**: Core refers to the base installation of Drupal. The core installation consists of the essential modules and some basic themes for Drupal. Although any person who has an account on `drupal.org` can suggest a change to the core codebase, most changes to core are thoroughly reviewed by developers within the community and only a small number of people have the rights to actually make changes to core. As a result, the core codebase is stable and secure. The core codebase can be downloaded from `http://drupal.org/project/drupal`.

- **Contributed modules**: These have been written and shared by members of the Drupal community. Unlike core, which represents the work of several hundred contributors, most contributed modules have been written by individuals or small teams working together. The contributed modules extend the functionality of Drupal, and this book describes how to use various contributed modules effectively. However, you should be cautious when installing a new contributed module. The contributed modules have not been reviewed as thoroughly as core. An overview of all the contributed modules is available at `http://drupal.org/project/Modules`.

- **Theme**: The themes control the look and feel of your site. The core installation comes with several base themes and you can download a range of contributed themes from `http://drupal.org/project/themes`.

- **Menu**: The menus provide a lists of links and can be used to create an organizational and navigational structure for your site. All menus can be seen and edited at `admin/structure/menu`; additionally, all menus create blocks.

- **Block**: A block displays content within a specific place on the page. All menus create blocks but you can also embed HTML within a block. The blocks can be administered at `admin/structure/block`.

- **Region**: Every theme defines specific regions; blocks can be placed into these different regions using the administrative menu at `admin/structure/block`.

> Menus, blocks, and regions are covered in
> *Chapter 14, Theming and User Interface Design.*

- **Taxonomy**: Taxonomies can be used to organize content within a Drupal site. Drupal permits site administrators to create different taxonomy categories to organize posts. For example, when posting an assignment, an instructor might want to create two taxonomies: one for the type of assignment and another for the subject of the assignment.

- **Term**: Terms or tags are specific items within a taxonomy. For example: a physics instructor creates two taxonomies to organize assignments. The first is the type of assignment and the second is a subject. If the instructor assigns his or her students to read an explanation of the theory of relativity, this assignment could be tagged with **Reading** (for the type of assignment) and **Relativity** (for the subject).

- **User**: This is the technical term for people using your site.

- **Role**: All site users belong to one or more roles. The site administrators can assign different permissions to different roles.

- **Anonymous user**: Any person who visits your site and is not a member of your site is considered an anonymous user. The anonymous user role allows you to specify how people who are not site members can interact with content and members of your site.

> It is possible to remove all rights from the anonymous
> users, making the content of your site fully private or
> a walled garden.

- **Authenticated user**: All site members are authenticated users and belong to the default authenticated user role. This default role can be used to assign a base level of rights to all the site members. Then, other roles can be used to assign more advanced privileges to users.

> Roles and access control are covered in more detail in *Chapter 5, Enrolling Students.*

- **UID1 (User ID 1)**: This is the first user on a Drupal site. UID1, by design, has full rights over your entire site. As a matter of best practice and security, UID1 should only be used as a back-up administrator account. Often, problems with your configuration will not be visible when logged in as UID1, because UID1 has more rights than other users.

Taking notes

A final piece of advice before we launch into building your Drupal site: buy a notebook and keep it next to your computer. Use this notebook in the same way a ship's captain uses his/her log by taking brief notes on what you do and why.

In the process of building your site, you will make decisions about module configurations, user roles, design tweaks, and so on. As you are making these decisions, you will be fully convinced that you will remember each decision you made and why.

Unless you are the exception that proves the rule, however, you won't remember. And this is where your notebook comes in. Use the notebook to record the changes you make. A useful entry will include the URL where you made the change and a brief description of why you made the change.

For example, if I am adjusting user privileges for the authenticated user role, I would enter the following in my notes: *At admin/people/permissions/2 — adjust user privileges so that the authenticated user role needs to have comments approved.*

This way, when you are trying to remember why you made a specific change, you will have a record of your decision-making process.

Summary

This chapter provided an overview of Drupal and the functionality that you will be able to include on your site. Now that we have covered the general details, it's time to begin working directly with the software. In the next two chapters, we will install Drupal and start exploring the core functionality that you will use to build your learning community.

So, keep your notebook handy, and let's start building your site!

2
Installing Drupal

This chapter describes how to install the base Drupal application called **Drupal core**. By the end of this chapter, you will have a new Drupal site installed and ready to use.

Assumptions

To get Drupal up and running, you will need all of the following:

- A domain
- A web host
- Access to the web host's filesystem

    or

- You need a local testing environment, which takes care of the first three things

For building sites, either a web host or a local testing environment will meet your needs. A site built on a web-accessible domain can be shared via the Internet, whereas sites built on local test machines will need to be moved to a web host before they can be used for your course. The process of backing up and moving sites is covered in *Chapter 15, Backup, Maintenance, and Upgrades*.

> In these instructions, we are assuming the use of phpMyAdmin, an open source, browser-based tool, for administering your database. A broad range of similar tools exist, and these general instructions can be used with most of these other tools. Information on phpMyAdmin is available at http://www.phpmyadmin.net; information on other browser-based database administration tools can be found at http://en.wikipedia.org/wiki/PhpMyAdmin#Similar_products.

The domain

The domain is the address on the Web from where people can access your site. If you are building this site as part of your work, you will probably be using the domain associated with your school or organization. If you are hosting this on your own server, you can buy a domain for under US $10.00 a year. Enter `purchase domain name` in Google, and you will have a plethora of options.

The web host

Your web host provides you with the server space on which to run your site. Within many schools, your website will be hosted by your school. In other environments, you might need to arrange for your own web host by using a hosting company.

In selecting a web host, you need to be sure that they run software that meets or exceeds the recommended software versions.

Web server

Drupal is developed and tested extensively in an Apache environment. Drupal also runs on other web servers, including Microsoft IIS and Nginx.

PHP version

Drupal 7 will run on PHP 5.2.5 or higher; however, PHP 5.3 is recommended. The Drupal 8 release will require PHP 5.3.10.

MySQL version

Drupal 7 will run on MySQL 5.0.15 or higher, and requires the **PHP Data Objects (PDO)** extension for PHP. Drupal 7 has also been tested with MariaDB as a drop-in replacement, and Version 5.1.44 or greater is recommended.

> PDO is a consistent way for programmers to write code that interacts with the database. You can find out more about PDO and how to install it at `http://drupal.org/requirements/pdo`.

Drupal can technically use any database that PDO supports, but MySQL is by far the most tested and best supported. Third-party modules are required to use Drupal with other database systems. You can find these modules listed at `http://drupal.org/project/modules/?f[0]=im_vid_3%3A13158&f[1]=drupal_core%3A103&f[2]=bs_project_sandbox%3A0`.

FTP and shell access to your web host

Your web host should also offer FTP access to your web server. You will need FTP (or SFTP) access in order to upload the Drupal codebase to your web space. Shell access, or SSH access, is not essential for basic site maintenance. However, SSH access can simplify maintaining your site, so contracting with a web host that provides SSH access is recommended.

A local testing environment

Alternatively, you can set up a local testing environment for your site. This allows you to set up Drupal and other applications on your computer. A local testing environment can be a great tool for learning a piece of software. Fortunately, open source tools can automate the process of setting up your testing environment.

PC users can use XAMPP (`http://www.apachefriends.org`) to set up a local testing environment; Mac users can use MAMP (`http://www.mamp.info`).

If you are working in a local testing environment set up via XAMPP or MAMP, you have all the pieces you need to start working with Drupal: your domain, your web host, the ability to move files into your web directory, and phpMyAdmin.

Setting up a local environment using MAMP (Mac only)

While Apple's operating system includes most of the programs required to run Drupal, setting up a testing environment can be tricky for inexperienced users. Installing MAMP allows you to create a preconfigured local environment quickly and easily using the following steps:

1. Download the latest version of MAMP from `http://www.mamp.info/en/index.html`. Note that the paid version of the program will download as well. Feel free to pay for the software if you wish, but the free version will be sufficient for our needs.

2. Navigate to where you downloaded the `.zip` file, and double-click to unzip it. Once it is unzipped, double click on the `.pkg` file that was contained in the `.zip` file.

3. Follow the directions in the wizard until you reach the **Installation Type** screen. If you want to use only the free version of the program, click on the **Customize** button:

4. In the **Custom Install on "Macintosh HD"** window, uncheck the **MAMP PRO** option and click on the **Install** button to install the application:

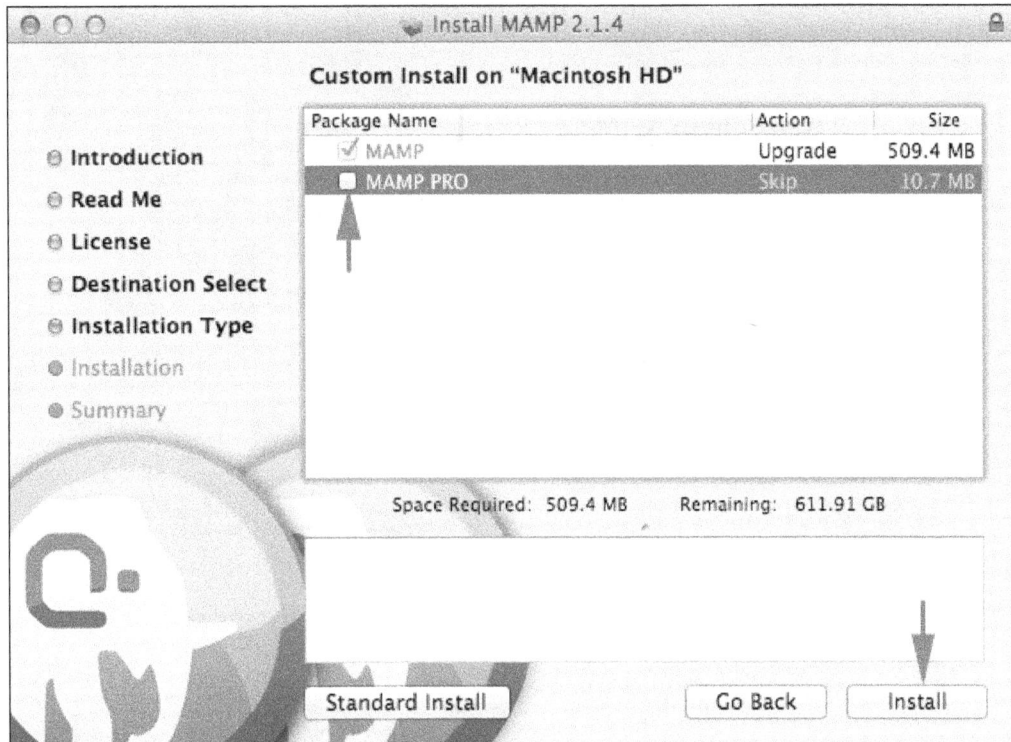

5. Navigate to /Applications/MAMP and open the **MAMP** application. The Apache and MySQL servers will start, and the start page will open in your default web browser. If the start page opens, MAMP is installed correctly.

Setting up a local environment using XAMPP (Windows only)

1. Download the latest version of XAMPP from http://www.apachefriends.org/en/xampp-windows.html#641. Download the .zip version.

2. Navigate to where you downloaded the file, right-click, and select **Extract All...**. Enter C:\ as the destination and click on **Extract**.

3. Navigate to C:\xampp and double-click the **xampp-control** application to start **XAMPP Control Panel Application**:

⊠ XAMPP Control Panel Application   ☐ ◻ ✕

⊠   XAMPP Control Panel | Service... | | SCM... |

Modules

				Status
☐ Svc	Apache	Start	Admin...	Refresh
☐ Svc	MySql	Start	Admin...	Explore...
☐ Svc	FileZilla	Start	Admin...	Help
☐ Svc	Mercury	Start	Admin...	Exit

```
XAMPP Control Panel Version 2.5 (9. May, 2007)
Windows 6.0 Build 6002 Platform 2 Service Pack 2
Current Directory: c:\xampp
Install(er) Directory: c:\xampp
Status Check OK
```

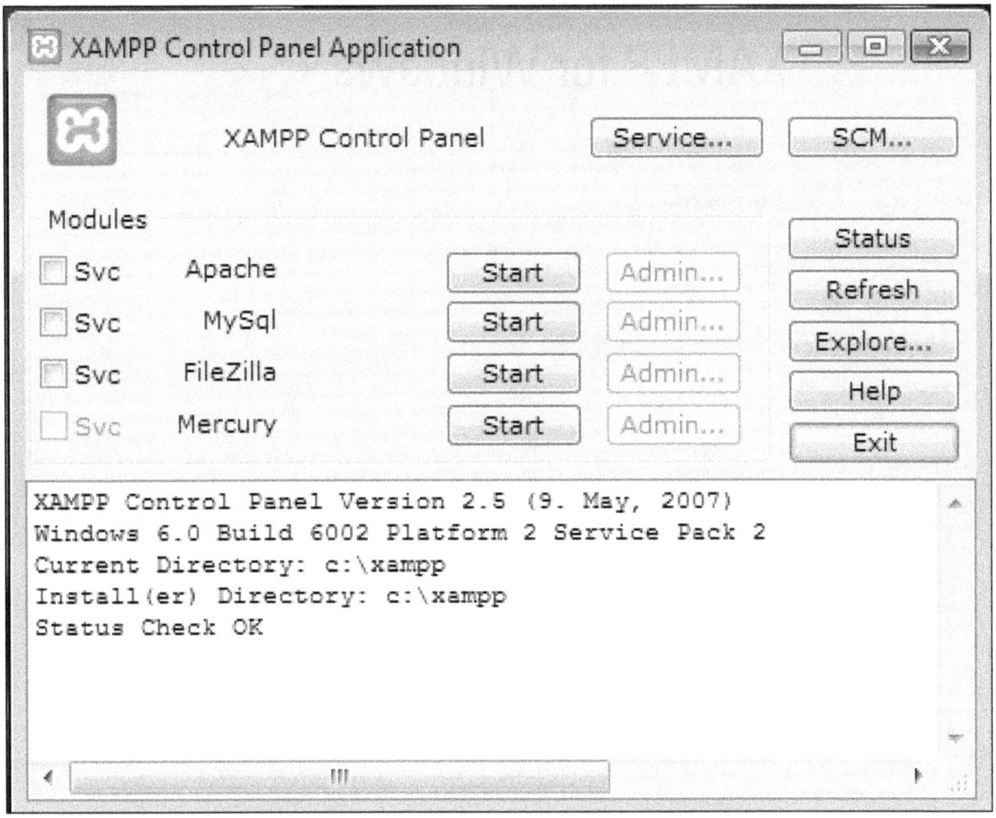

4. Click on the **Start** buttons next to **Apache** and **MySql**.

5. Open a web browser, and enter `http://localhost` or `http://127.0.0.1` in the address bar, and you should see the following start page:

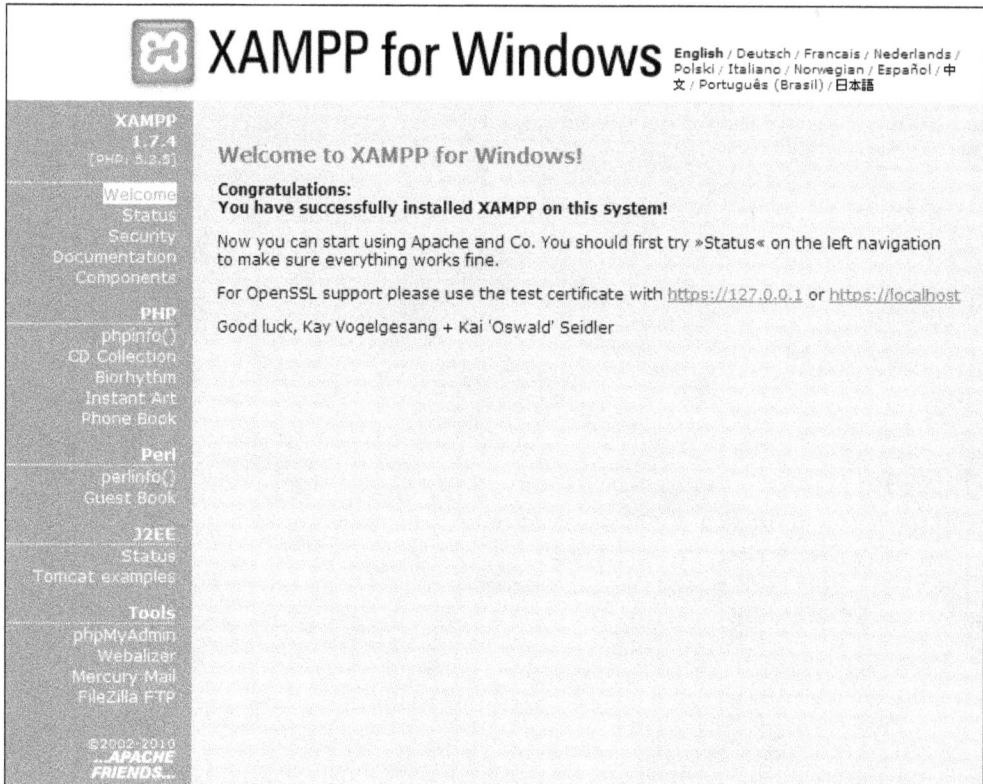

6. Navigate to `http://localhost/security/index.php`, and enter a password for MySQL's root user. Make sure to remember this password or write it down in your notebook because we will need it later.

Configuring your local environment for Drupal

Now that we have the programs required to run Drupal (Apache, MySQL, and PHP), we need to modify some of their settings to match Drupal's system requirements.

PHP configuration

As mentioned before, Drupal 7 requires Version 5.2.5 or higher, and as of the writing of this book MAMP includes Version 5.4.4 (or you can switch to Version 5.2.17) and XAMPP includes Version 5.4.7. PHP configuration settings are found in the program's `php.ini` file.

For MAMP, the `php.ini` file is located in `/Applications/MAMP/bin/php/[php version number]/conf`, where the `php version number` is either 5.4.4 or 5.2.17.

For XAMPP, the `php.ini` file is located in `C:\xampp\php`.

Open the file in a text editor (not a word processor), find the **Resource Limits** section of the file and edit the values to match the following values:

```
max_execution_time = 60;
max_input_time = 120;
memory_limit = 128M;
error_reporting = E_ALL & ~E_NOTICE
```

The last line is optional and is used if you want to display error messages in the browser, instead of only in the logs.

MySQL configuration

As mentioned before, Drupal 7 requires MySQL Version 5.0.15 or higher. MAMP includes Version 5.5.25 and XAMPP includes Version 5.5.27. MySQL's configuration settings are contained in a `my.cnf` or `my.ini` file.

MAMP does not use a `my.cnf` file by default, so we need to copy the `my-medium.cnf` file from the `/Applications/MAMP/Library/support-files` directory to the `/Applications/MAMP/conf` folder. After copying the file, rename it to `my.cnf`.

For XAMPP, the `my.ini` file is located in the `C:\xampp\mysql\bin` directory.

Open the `my.cnf` or `my.ini` file in a text editor, find the following settings and edit them to match the following values:

```
# * Fine Tuning
#
key_buffer = 16M
key_buffer_size = 32M
max_allowed_packet = 16M
thread_stack = 512K
thread_cache_size = 8
max_connections = 300
#
# * Query Cache Configuration
#
query_cache_type = 1
query_cache_limit = 15M
query_cache_size = 46M
join_buffer_size = 5M
# Sort buffer size for ORDER BY and GROUP BY queries, data
# gets spun out to disc if it does not fit
sort_buffer_size = 10M
innodb_flush_method = O_DIRECT
innodb_file_per_table = 1
innodb_flush_log_at_trx_commit = 2
innodb_log_buffer_size = 4M
innodb_additional_mem_pool_size = 20M
# num cpu's/cores *2 is a good base line for innodb_thread_concurrency
innodb_thread_concurrency = 4
```

After you have made the edits, you have to stop and restart the servers for the changes to take effect. Once you have restarted the servers, we are ready to install Drupal!

The most effective way versus the easy way

There are many different ways to install Drupal. People familiar with working via the command line can install Drupal very quickly without an FTP client or any web-based tools to create and administer databases.

The instructions in this book are geared towards people who would rather not use the command line. These instructions attempt to get you through the technical pieces as painlessly as possible, to speed up the process of building a site that supports teaching and learning.

Installing Drupal – the quick version

The following steps will get you up and running with your Drupal site. This quick-start version gives an overview of the steps required for most setups. A more detailed version follows immediately after this section.

Once you are familiar with the setup process, installing a Drupal site takes between five to ten minutes.

1. Download the core Drupal codebase from `http://drupal.org/project/drupal`.

2. Extract the codebase on your local machine.

3. Using phpMyAdmin, create a database on your server. Write down the name of the database.

4. Using phpMyAdmin, create a user on the database using the following SQL statement:

   ```
   GRANT SELECT, INSERT, UPDATE, DELETE, CREATE, DROP, INDEX, ALTER
   ON databasename.*
   TO 'username'@'localhost' IDENTIFIED BY 'password';
   ```

5. You will have created the `databasename` in step 3; write down the `username` and `password` values, as you will need them to complete the install.

6. Upload the Drupal codebase to your web folder.

7. Navigate to the URL of your site. Follow the instructions of the install wizard. You will need your `databasename` (created in step 3), as well as the `username` and `password` for your database user (created in step 4).

Installing Drupal – the detailed version

This version goes over each step in more detail and includes screenshots.

1. Download the core Drupal codebase from `http://drupal.org/project/drupal`.

2. Extract the codebase on your local machine.

> The Drupal codebase (and all modules and themes) are compressed into a tarball, or a file that is first tarred, and then gzipped. Such compressed files end in `.tar.gz`.
>
> On Macs and Linux machines, `tar.gz` files can be extracted automatically using tools that come preinstalled with the operating system. On PC's, you can use 7-zip, an open source compression utility available at `http://www.7-zip.org`.

3. In your web browser, navigate to your system's URL for phpMyAdmin. If you are using a different tool for creating and managing your database, use that tool to create your database and database user.

4. As shown in the following screenshot, create the database on your server. Click on the **Create** button to create your database.

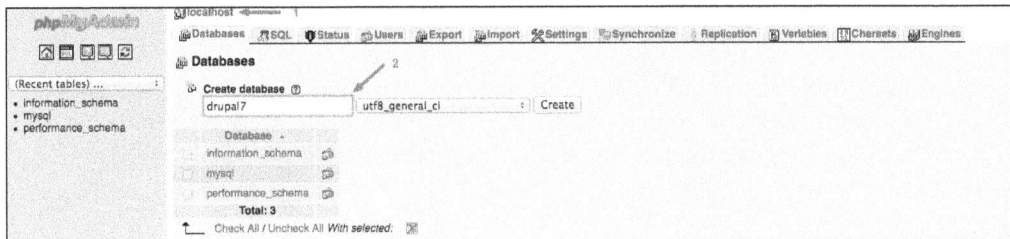

> Store your database name in a safe place. You will need to know your database name to complete your installation.

5. To create your database user, click on the **SQL** tab as shown in the following screenshot. In the text area, enter the following SQL statement:

```
GRANT SELECT, INSERT, UPDATE, DELETE, CREATE, DROP, INDEX, ALTER
ON databasename.*
TO 'username'@'localhost' IDENTIFIED BY 'password';
```

6. For `databasename`, use the name of the database you created in step 4. Replace the `username` and `password` with a username and password of your choice. Once you have entered the correct values, click on the **Go** button to create the user with rights on your database:

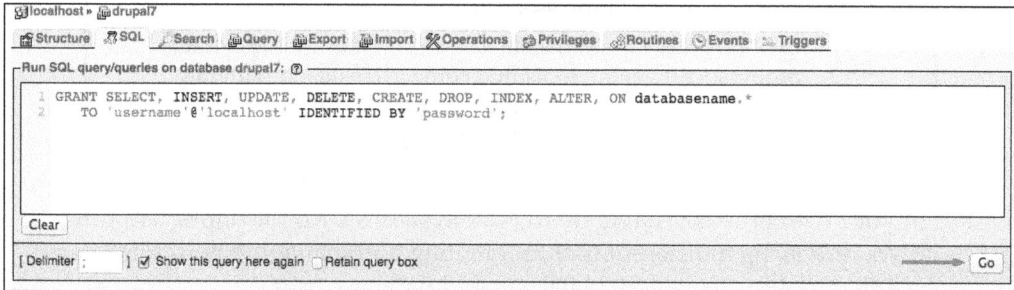

```
localhost »  drupal7
  Structure    SQL    Search    Query    Export    Import    Operations    Privileges    Routines    Events    Triggers
┌Run SQL query/queries on database drupal7: ⑦ ──────────────────────────────────────────────────────────────
│   1  GRANT SELECT, INSERT, UPDATE, DELETE, CREATE, DROP, INDEX, ALTER, ON databasename.*
│   2     TO 'username'@'localhost' IDENTIFIED BY 'password';
│
│
│
│
│
│
│ Clear
[ Delimiter  ;       ]  ☑ Show this query here again   ☐ Retain query box                          ──────▶  Go
```

> Store the username and the password of your database user in a safe place. You will need them to complete the installation.

7. Create and/or locate the directory from where you want Drupal to run. In this example, we are running Drupal from within a folder named `drupal7`; this means that our site will be available at `http://ourdomain.org/drupal7`.

> Running Drupal in a subfolder can make things a little trickier. If at all possible, copy the Drupal files directly into your web root.

8. Using your FTP client, upload the Drupal codebase to your web folder:

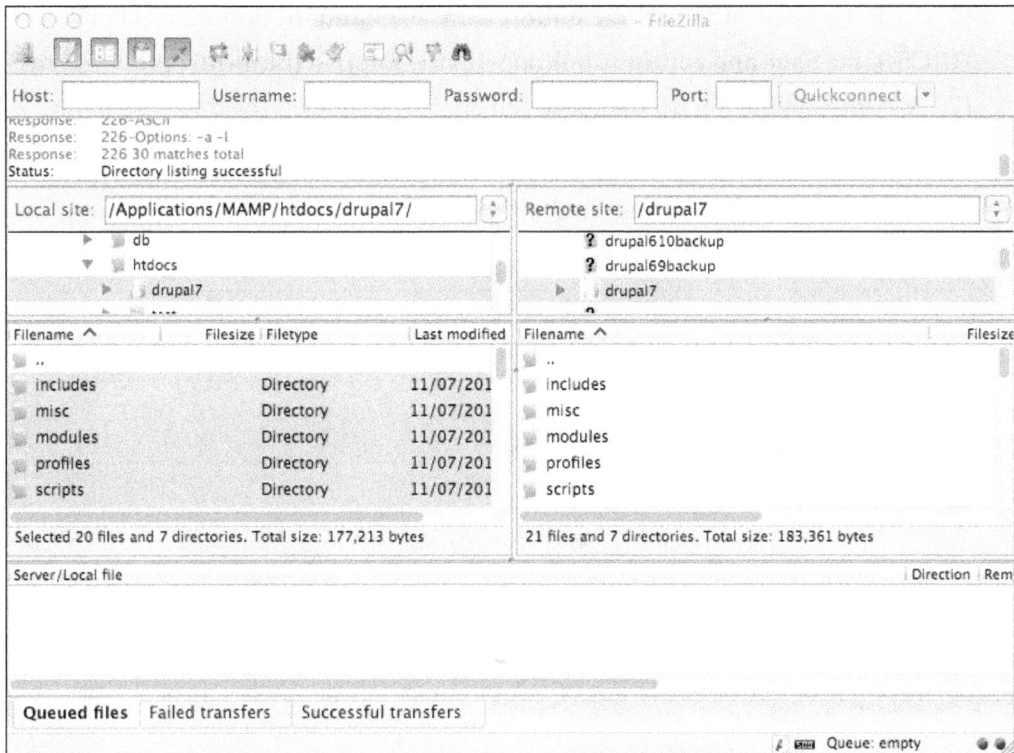

9. Navigate to the URL of your site. The automatic install wizard will appear on your screen:

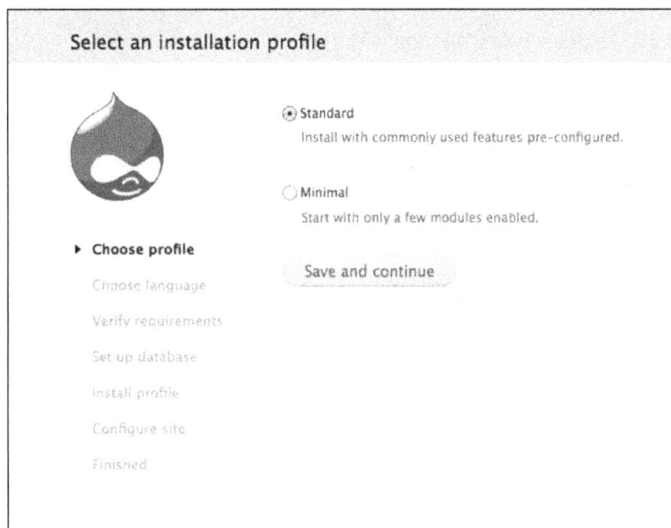

10. Click the **Save and continue** button with the **Standard** option selected.

11. Click the **Save and continue** button with the **English (built-in)** option selected.

12. To complete the **Set up database** screen, you will need the database name (created in step 4) and the database username and password (created in step 6). Select **MySQL, MariaDB, or equivalent** as the **Database type** and then enter these values in their respective text boxes as seen in the following screenshot:

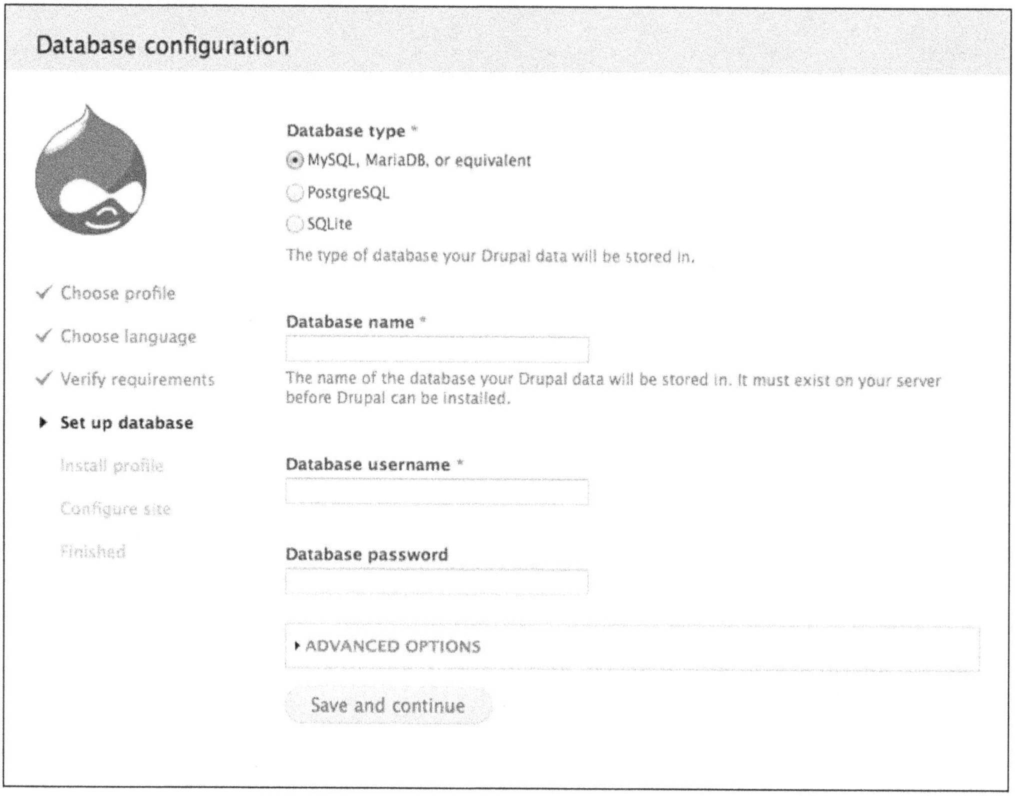

Database configuration

Database type *
- ◉ MySQL, MariaDB, or equivalent
- ○ PostgreSQL
- ○ SQLite

The type of database your Drupal data will be stored in.

✓ Choose profile

✓ Choose language

Database name *

[   ]

✓ Verify requirements

The name of the database your Drupal data will be stored in. It must exist on your server before Drupal can be installed.

▶ Set up database

Install profile

Database username *

[   ]

Configure site

Finished

Database password

[   ]

▶ ADVANCED OPTIONS

Save and continue

---

13. Most installs will not need to use any of settings under **ADVANCED OPTIONS**. However, if your database is located on a server other than localhost, you will need to adjust the settings as shown in the next screenshot.

In most basic hosting setups, your database is accessible at **localhost**.

To verify the name or location of your database host, you can use phpMyAdmin (as shown in the screenshot under step 4) or contact an administrator for your web server. For the vast majority of installs, none of the advanced options will need to be adjusted.

▾ADVANCED OPTIONS

These options are only necessary for some sites. If you're not sure what you should enter here, leave the default settings or check with your hosting provider.

Database host *

localhost

If your database is located on a different server, change this.

Database port

If your database server is listening to a non-standard port, enter its number.

Table prefix

If more than one application will be sharing this database, enter a table prefix such as *drupal_* for your Drupal site here.

14. Click on the **Save and continue** button. You will see a progress meter as Drupal installs itself on your web server.

Configure site

✓ Choose profile

✓ Choose language

✓ Verify requirements

✓ Set up database

✓ Install profile

▶ **Configure site**

Finished

SITE INFORMATION

Site name *

Site e-mail address *

Automated e-mails, such as registration information, will be sent from this address. Use an address ending in your site's domain to help prevent these e-mails from being flagged as spam.

SITE MAINTENANCE ACCOUNT

Username *

Spaces are allowed; punctuation is not allowed except for periods, hyphens, and underscores.

E-mail address *

Password *

Password strength:

Confirm password *

SERVER SETTINGS

Default country

United States ▾

Select the default country for the site.

Default time zone

America/New York: Sunday, November 11, 2012 - 13:39 -0500 ▾

By default, dates in this site will be displayed in the chosen time zone.

UPDATE NOTIFICATIONS

☑ Check for updates automatically

☑ Receive e-mail notifications

The system will notify you when updates and important security releases are available for installed components. Anonymous information about your site is sent to Drupal.org.

Save and continue

15. On the **Configure site** screen, you can enter some general information about your site, and create the first user account. The first user account has full rights over every aspect of your site. When you have finished with the settings on this page, click on the **Save and continue** button.

16. When the install is finished, you will see the following splash screen:

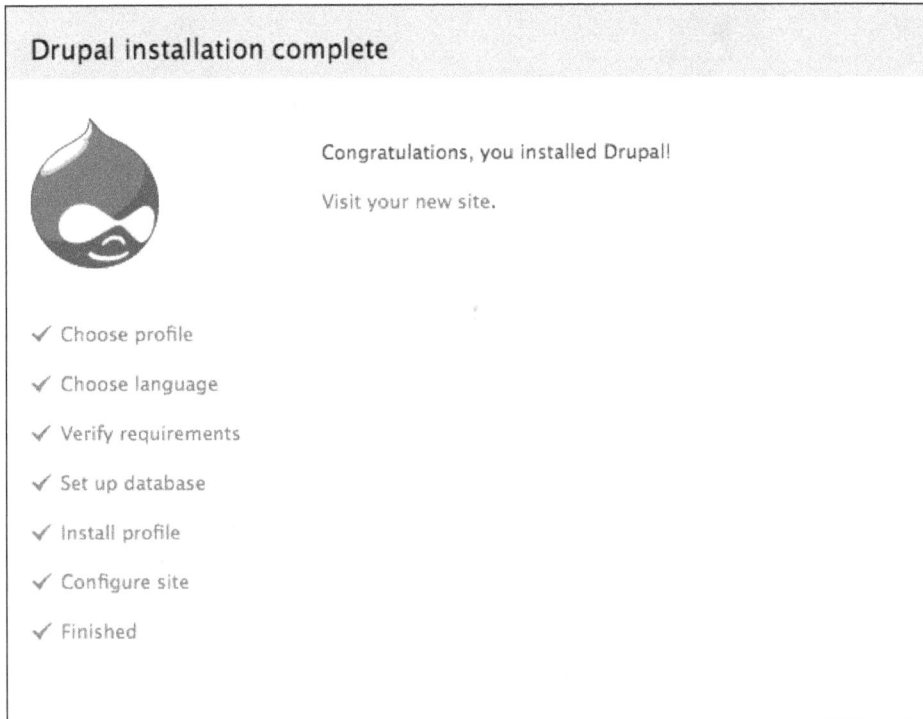

Drupal installation complete

Congratulations, you installed Drupal!

Visit your new site.

✓ Choose profile

✓ Choose language

✓ Verify requirements

✓ Set up database

✓ Install profile

✓ Configure site

✓ Finished

> Additional details on installing Drupal are available in the handbook at `http://drupal.org/documentation/install`.

Enabling core modules

In *Chapter 3, Getting Started*, we will look at the functionality of Core Drupal. In preparation for that section, we will look at the modules that come with core Drupal.

For a full description of the modules included in Drupal core, see `http://drupal.org/node/1283408`.

To see the modules included in Drupal core, navigate to **Modules** or `admin/modules`.

As shown in the following screenshot, the Standard installation profile enables the most commonly used core modules. (For clarity, we have divided the screenshot of the single screen in two parts.)

▼ CORE

ENABLED	NAME	VERSION	DESCRIPTION	OPERATIONS
☐	Aggregator	7.17	Aggregates syndicated content (RSS, RDF, and Atom feeds).	
☑	Block	7.17	Controls the visual building blocks a page is constructed with. Blocks are boxes of content rendered into an area, or region, of a web page. Required by: Dashboard (enabled)	Help Permissions Configure
☐	Blog	7.17	Enables multi-user blogs.	
☐	Book	7.17	Allows users to create and organize related content in an outline.	
☑	Color	7.17	Allows administrators to change the color scheme of compatible themes.	Help
☑	Comment	7.17	Allows users to comment on and discuss published content. Requires: Text (enabled), Field (enabled), Field SQL storage (enabled) Required by: Forum (disabled), Tracker (disabled)	Help Permissions Configure
☐	Contact	7.17	Enables the use of both personal and site-wide contact forms.	
☐	Content translation	7.17	Allows content to be translated into different languages. Requires: Locale (disabled)	
☑	Contextual links	7.17	Provides contextual links to perform actions related to elements on a page.	Help Permissions
☑	Dashboard	7.17	Provides a dashboard page in the administrative interface for organizing administrative tasks and tracking information within your site. Requires: Block (enabled)	Help Permissions Configure
☑	Database logging	7.17	Logs and records system events to the database.	Help
☑	Field	7.17	Field API to add fields to entities like nodes and users. Requires: Field SQL storage (enabled), Field (enabled) Required by: Drupal, Field SQL storage (enabled), Field (enabled), Text (enabled), Comment (enabled), Field UI (enabled), File (enabled), Options (enabled), Taxonomy (enabled), Forum (disabled), Image (enabled), List (enabled), Number (enabled), Tracker (disabled)	Help
☑	Field SQL storage	7.17	Stores field data in an SQL database. Requires: Field (enabled), Field SQL storage (enabled) Required by: Drupal, Field SQL storage (enabled), Field (enabled), Text (enabled), Comment (enabled), Field UI (enabled), File (enabled), Options (enabled), Taxonomy (enabled), Forum (disabled), Image (enabled), List (enabled), Number (enabled), Tracker (disabled)	Help
☑	Field UI	7.17	User interface for the Field API. Requires: Field (enabled), Field SQL storage (enabled)	Help
☑	File	7.17	Defines a file field type. Requires: Field (enabled), Field SQL storage (enabled) Required by: Image (enabled)	Help
☑	Filter	7.17	Filters content in preparation for display. Required by: Drupal	Help Permissions Configure
☐	Forum	7.17	Provides discussion forums. Requires: Taxonomy (enabled), Options (enabled), Field (enabled), Field SQL storage (enabled), Comment (enabled), Text (enabled)	
☑	Help	7.17	Manages the display of online help.	Help
☑	Image	7.17	Provides image manipulation tools. Requires: File (enabled), Field (enabled), Field SQL storage (enabled) Required by: Drupal (Field type(s) in use - see Field list)	Help Permissions Configure

	Module	Version	Description			
☑	List	7.17	Defines list field types. Use with Options to create selection lists. Requires: Field (enabled), Field SQL storage (enabled), Options (enabled)	⊙ Help		
☐	Locale	7.17	Adds language handling functionality and enables the translation of the user interface to languages other than English. Required by: Content translation (disabled)			
☑	Menu	7.17	Allows administrators to customize the site navigation menu.	⊙ Help	⚬ Permissions	⚙ Configure
✓	Node	7.17	Allows content to be submitted to the site and displayed on pages. Required by: Drupal	⊙ Help	⚬ Permissions	⚙ Configure
☑	Number	7.17	Defines numeric field types. Requires: Field (enabled), Field SQL storage (enabled)	⊙ Help		
☐	OpenID	7.17	Allows users to log into your site using OpenID.			
✓	Options	7.17	Defines selection, check box and radio button widgets for text and numeric fields. Requires: Field (enabled), Field SQL storage (enabled) Required by: Taxonomy (enabled), Forum (disabled), List (enabled)	⊙ Help		
☑	Overlay	7.17	Displays the Drupal administration interface in an overlay.			
☑	Path	7.17	Allows users to rename URLs.	⊙ Help	⚬ Permissions	⚙ Configure
☐	PHP filter	7.17	Allows embedded PHP code/snippets to be evaluated.			
☐	Poll	7.17	Allows your site to capture votes on different topics in the form of multiple choice questions.			
☑	RDF	7.17	Enriches your content with metadata to let other applications (e.g. search engines, aggregators) better understand its relationships and attributes.	⊙ Help		
☑	Search	7.17	Enables site-wide keyword searching.	⊙ Help	⚬ Permissions	⚙ Configure
☑	Shortcut	7.17	Allows users to manage customizable lists of shortcut links.	⊙ Help	⚬ Permissions	⚙ Configure
☐	Statistics	7.17	Logs access statistics for your site.			
☐	Syslog	7.17	Logs and records system events to syslog.			
✓	System	7.17	Handles general site configuration for administrators. Required by: Drupal	⊙ Help	⚬ Permissions	⚙ Configure
✓	Taxonomy	7.17	Enables the categorization of content. Requires: Options (enabled), Field (enabled), Field SQL storage (enabled) Required by: Drupal (field type(s) in use – see Field list), Forum (disabled)	⊙ Help	⚬ Permissions	⚙ Configure
☐	Testing	7.17	Provides a framework for unit and functional testing.			
✓	Text	7.17	Defines simple text field types. Requires: Field (enabled), Field SQL storage (enabled) Required by: Drupal (field type(s) in use – see Field list), Comment (enabled), Forum (disabled), Tracker (disabled)	⊙ Help		
☑	Toolbar	7.17	Provides a toolbar that shows the top-level administration menu items and links from other modules.	⊙ Help	⚬ Permissions	
☐	Tracker	7.17	Enables tracking of recent content for users. Requires: Comment (enabled), Text (enabled), Field (enabled), Field SQL storage (enabled)			
☐	Trigger	7.17	Enables actions to be fired on certain system events, such as when new content is created.			
☑	Update manager	7.17	Checks for available updates, and can securely install or update modules and themes via a web interface.	⊙ Help		⚙ Configure
✓	User	7.17	Manages the user registration and login system. Required by: Drupal	⊙ Help	⚬ Permissions	⚙ Configure

Assigning rights to the authenticated user role

Within your Drupal site, you can use roles to assign specific permissions to groups of users. As described in the brief glossary in *Chapter 1, Introducing Drupal*, Drupal comes with two default roles: the anonymous user and the authenticated user. Anonymous users are all people visiting the site who are not site members; all site members (that is, all people with a username and password) belong to the authenticated user role.

> Creating additional roles is covered in *Chapter 3, Getting Started*; assigning granular rights to users via roles is discussed in more detail in *Chapter 5, Enrolling Students*.

To assign rights to specific roles, navigate to **People | Permissions | Roles** or admin/people/permissions/roles.

As shown in the preceding screenshot, click on the **edit permissions** link for authenticated users.

Assign authenticated users the following rights:

- The **Comment** module: Authenticated users can see comments and post comments. These rights have the comments going into a moderation queue for approval, as we haven't checked the **Skip comment approval** box.

Comment	
Administer comments and comment settings	☐
View comments	☑
Post comments	☑
Skip comment approval	☐
Edit own comments	☑

- The **Node** module: Authenticated users can see published content.

Node	
Bypass content access control View, edit and delete all content regardless of permission restrictions. *Warning: Give to trusted roles only; this permission has security implications.*	☐
Administer content types *Warning: Give to trusted roles only; this permission has security implications.*	☐
Administer content *Warning: Give to trusted roles only; this permission has security implications.*	☐
Access the content overview page	☐
View published content	☑

- The **Search** module: Authenticated users can search the site.

Search	
Administer search	☐
Use search	☑
Use advanced search	☑

- The **User** module: Authenticated users can change their own username.

User	
Administer permissions *Warning: Give to trusted roles only; this permission has security implications.*	☐
Administer users *Warning: Give to trusted roles only; this permission has security implications.*	☐
View user profiles	☐
Change own username	☑
Cancel own user account Note: content may be kept, unpublished, deleted or transferred to the *Anonymous* user depending on the configured user settings.	☐
Select method for cancelling own account *Warning: Give to trusted roles only; this permission has security implications.*	☐

Once these options have been selected, click on the **Save permissions** button at the bottom of the page.

Summary

In this chapter, we installed the core Drupal codebase, enabled some core modules, and assigned rights to the **authenticated user** role. We are now ready to start building a feature-rich site that will help support teaching and learning. In the next chapter, we will take a look around your new site and begin to get familiar with how to make your site do what you want.

3
Getting Started

Now that you have installed your Drupal site, we need to take a look around and see exactly what we have at our disposal. The default Drupal installation is fairly minimalist and this base installation will be modified extensively as we progress through this book.

This chapter will cover the features enabled when the site is installed, and the Drupal-specific terminology used to describe those features.

In this chapter we will cover:

- The features of the standard Drupal installation
- Installing user-contributed modules to change the functionality of the core installation and themes to change the look and feel of the site
- Creating user roles and giving permissions to those roles
- Creating different types of content
- Using the Views module to create custom lists of content

The core installation

The core Drupal installation is a blank slate. Although the core installation contains the potential to become a powerful and flexible learning tool, much of this functionality needs to be enabled and configured. However, before we begin extending the features and functionality of your site, we will look at the functionality of the core Drupal installation and how the administrative sections are organized. The core installation provides the foundation on which we will build your site.

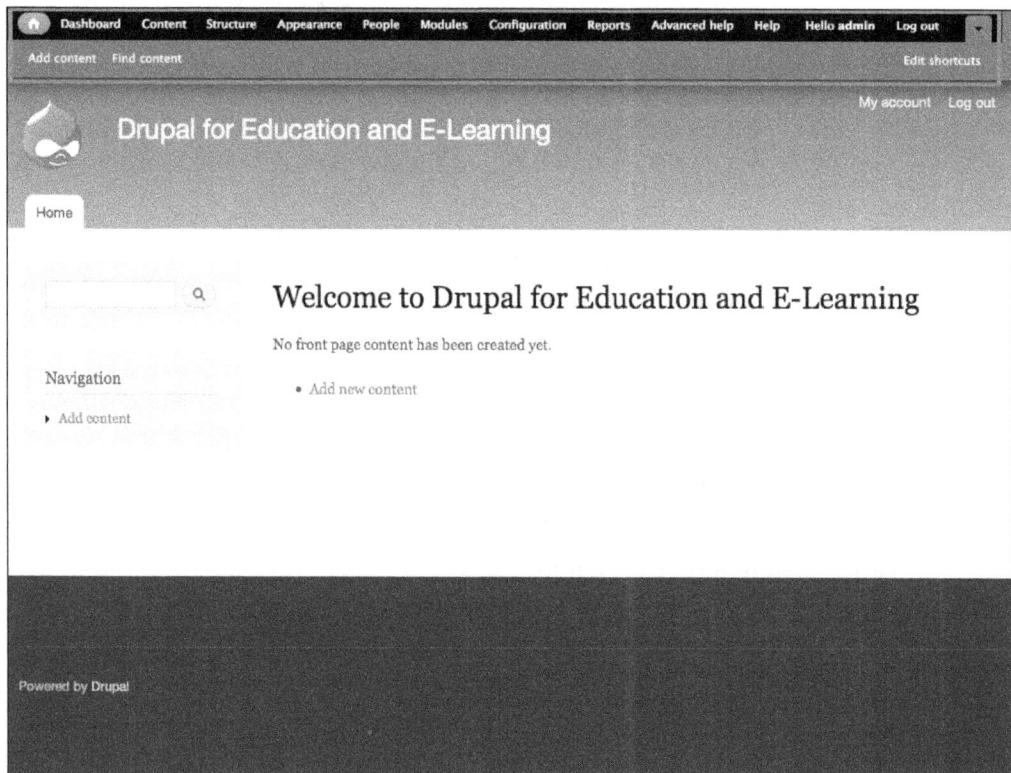

The default navigation menu seen in the preceding screenshot shows the options available in the core Drupal installation. In this explanation, we will break them down into core user functionality and administrative functionality.

Core user functionality

The options enabled in the default Drupal installation provide a starting point for creating your site. We will add to these options; however, before we begin making changes to the site, we will run through some of the features enabled by default.

My Account

The **My account** page, shown in the following screenshot, shows your user profile (all users have a profile page):

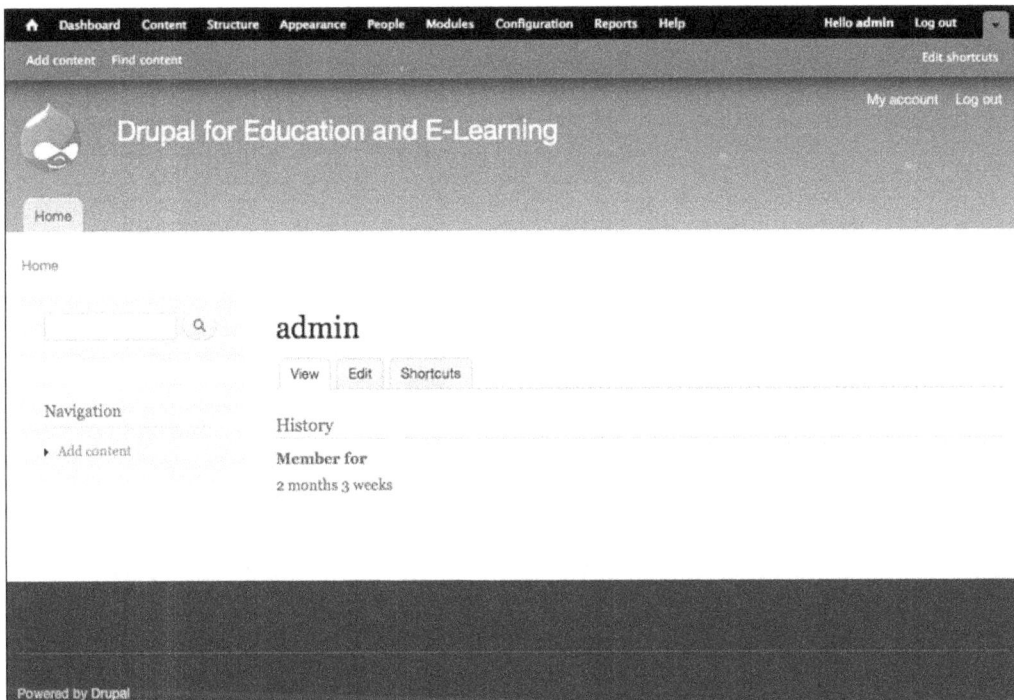

The **Edit** tab allows users (or site administrators) to edit their profile information. *Chapter 11, Social Networks and Extending the User Profile,* goes into more detail on how to extend the user profiles to introduce some of the common features of social networking sites.

Add content

The items in the **Add content** submenu allow you to add content to your site. To see the full list of content types that can be created, click on the **Add content** link or navigate to node/add:

In the core installation, the two content types are enabled by default: **Article page** and **Basic page**. The pages and articles provide two ways of adding content to your site. Functionally, they are interchangeable; however, because they are different content types, you can configure them differently and assign different access rights to them. For example, you can give one set of users the right to create pages and another set of users the right to create articles.

Log out

The **Log out** link logs you out of the site. When you click on this link, you will see the site as an anonymous user. This will be helpful when testing permissions later in this chapter.

Administrative functionality

You can see the **Administration** screen by clicking on any of the links in the navigation menu or by navigating to `admin`.

The administrative functionality is broken into nine sections:

- **Dashboard**
- **Content**
- **Structure**
- **Appearance**
- **People**
- **Modules**
- **Configuration**
- **Reports**
- **Help**

We will now explain each of these sections briefly. Most of these sections will be explained in greater detail in later chapters.

Dashboard

The **Dashboard** section provides a convenient and customizable place to access frequently used administrative functions. By default, it includes a list of recently added content, a site search form, and a list of recently added users.

By clicking on the **Customize dashboard** link, you can add, remove, or move other blocks of content that you use frequently. It works much like the **Blocks** section of Drupal, which will be covered in the **Structure** section and more in depth in *Chapter 14, Theming and User Interface Design*.

Content

The **Content** administrative section is accessed by clicking on the **Content** link or by navigating to `admin/content`.

The administrative features of this section provide a set of tools for managing content, including comments, on your site.

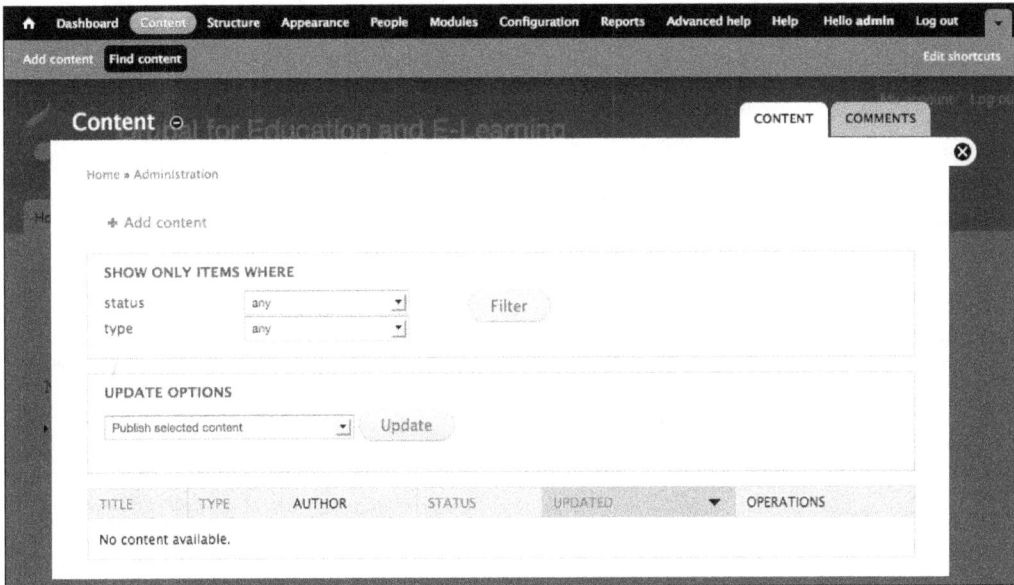

You can add content via a link on this page, filter content based on its status or type, or make certain updates to the filtered content in bulk.

You can access all the comments on the site by clicking on the **COMMENTS** tab or navigating to `admin/content/comment`. Here, you will find the comment moderation queue, where you can publish, unpublish, or delete comments in bulk. The comment settings will be covered later in this chapter. Refer to the following screenshot:

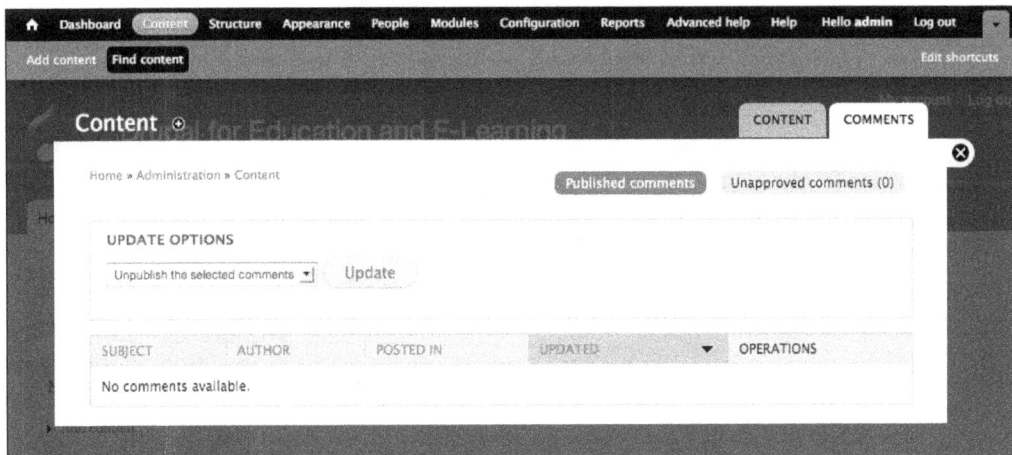

Structure

The **Structure** administrative section is accessed by clicking on the **Structure** link or by navigating to `admin/structure`.

The administrative features of this section allow you to add additional functionality and structure to your site. The **Menu** and **Block** sections, described in more detail in *Chapter 14, Theming and User Interface Design*, allow you to create a flexible navigational structure tailored to the specific roles within your site. Refer to the following screenshot:

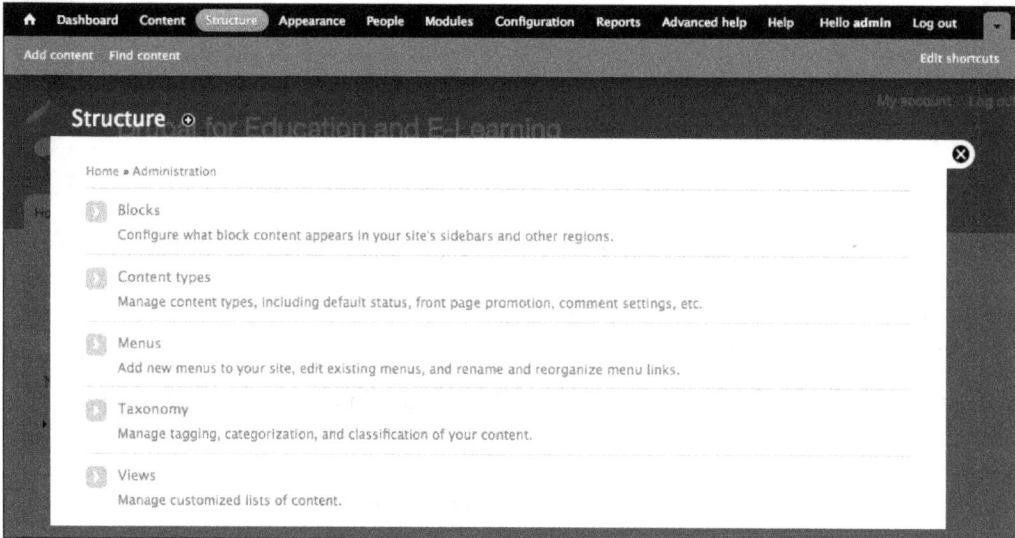

The **Content types** and **Taxonomy** sections will be covered later in this chapter, in the *Creating content types* section.

Appearance

The **Appearance** administrative section is accessed by clicking on the **Appearance** link or by navigating to `admin/appearance`.

The **Appearance** section allows you to change the look and feel of the whole site. Whenever you need to enable or disable a theme, you will do so in this section. Installing themes will be covered later in this chapter, and the topic of theming will be addressed in greater detail in *Chapter 14, Theming and User Interface Design*.

People

The **People** administrative section is accessed by clicking on the **People** link or by navigating to `admin/people`.

The administrative features of this section let you filter your list of users, make bulk updates to users, add roles, and assign rights to those roles.

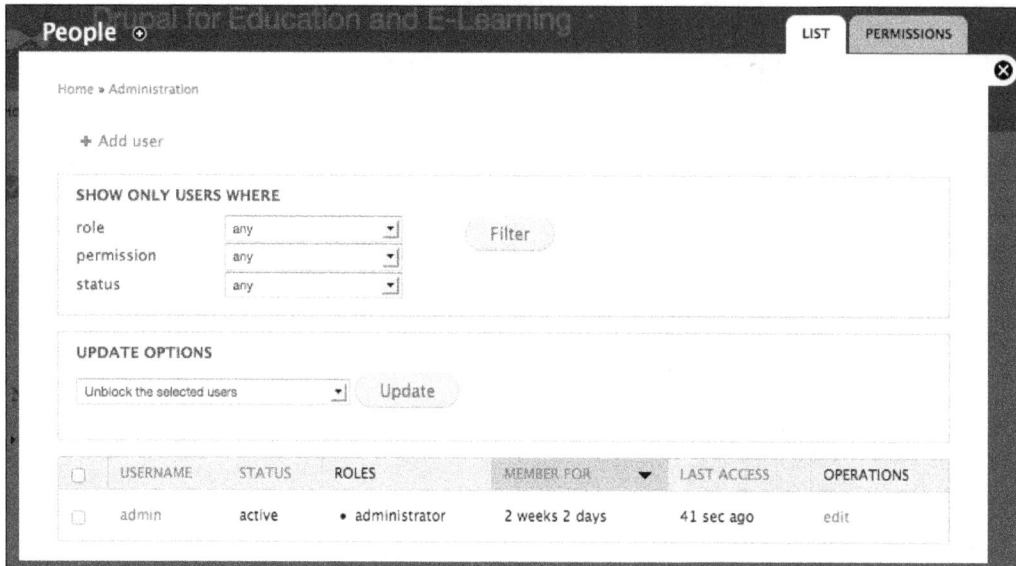

The details of user management are covered in more detail in *Chapter 5, Enrolling Students*.

Modules

The **Modules** page is accessed by clicking on the **Modules** link or by navigating to `admin/modules`:

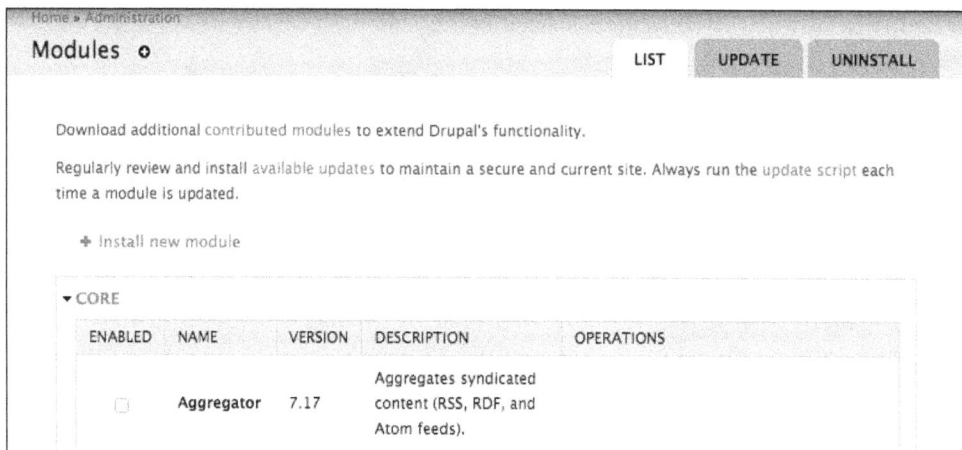

The **Modules** page gives an overview of all modules installed and enabled on your site. Whenever you need to enable or disable a module, you will need to go to this page. Installing and enabling modules will be covered later in this chapter.

Configuration

The **Configuration** administrative section is accessed by clicking on the **Configuration** link or navigating to `admin/config`:

The administrative features of this section allow you to fine-tune various features of the site. In most cases, the default values will work perfectly well. In subsequent chapters, we will adjust the settings in this section to fine-tune the functionality to run your site.

Reports

The **Reports** administrative section is accessed by clicking on the **Reports** link or navigating to admin/reports.

The options in this section provide different report logs of activity on your site.

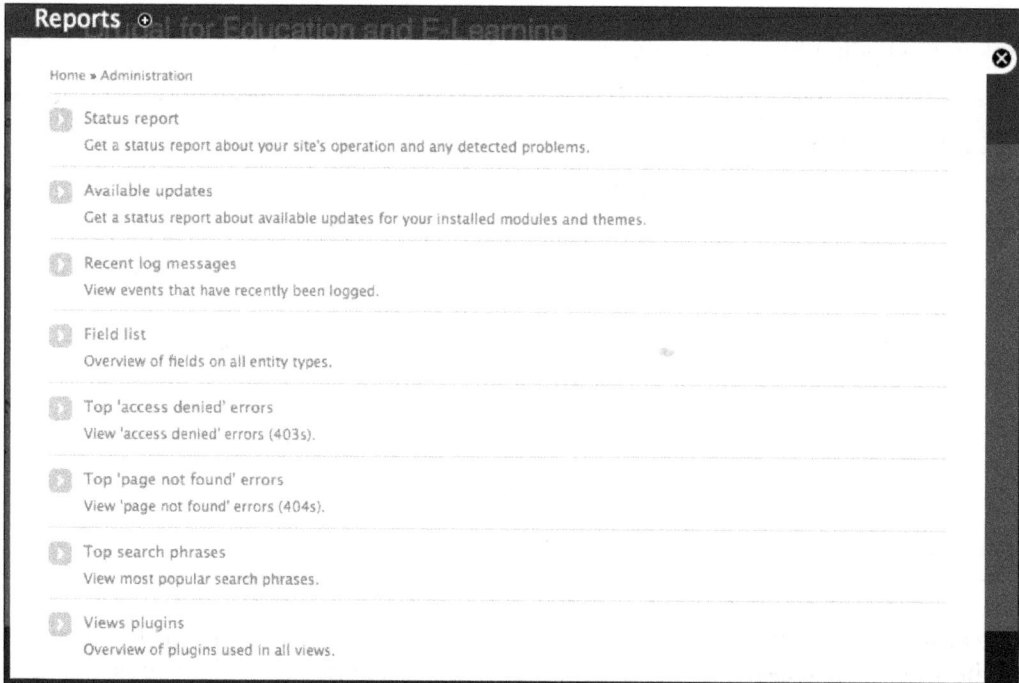

Reports ⊕

Home » Administration

Status report
Get a status report about your site's operation and any detected problems.

Available updates
Get a status report about available updates for your installed modules and themes.

Recent log messages
View events that have recently been logged.

Field list
Overview of fields on all entity types.

Top 'access denied' errors
View 'access denied' errors (403s).

Top 'page not found' errors
View 'page not found' errors (404s).

Top search phrases
View most popular search phrases.

Views plugins
Overview of plugins used in all views.

The information logged in this section gives you an overview of how your site is running. In particular, the **Available updates** section at admin/reports/updates (covered in more detail in *Chapter 15, Backup, Maintenance, and Upgrades*) gives you an at-a-glance overview of any modules in need of upgrading.

Dashboard	Content	Structure	Appearance	People	Modules	Configuration	Reports	Advanced help	Help	Hello **admin**	Log out

Add content   Find content   Edit shortcuts

Home » Administration » Reports

Status report ⊙

Here you can find a short overview of your site's parameters as well as any problems detected with your installation. It may be useful to copy and paste this information into support requests filed on drupal.org's support forums and project issue queues.

Drupal	7.17
Access to update.php	Protected
CTools CSS Cache	Exists
Configuration file	Protected
Cron maintenance tasks	Last run 43 min 47 sec ago
You can run cron manually. To run cron from outside the site, go to http://localhost:8888/drupal7 /cron.php?cron_key=d5jicgsrdLACuf1QSQ9_1VHKbm1TGGd4kXz_Jy1Rrfs	
Database system	MySQL, MariaDB, or equivalent
Database system version	5.5.25
Database updates	Up to date
⚠ Drupal core update status	No update data available
No update information available. Run cron or check manually.	
File system	Writable (*public* download method)
GD library PNG support	bundled (2.0.34 compatible)
GD library rotate and desaturate effects	bundled (2.0.34 compatible)
Node Access Permissions	Disabled
If the site is experiencing problems with permissions to content, you may have to rebuild the permissions cache. Rebuilding will remove all privileges to content and replace them with permissions based on the current modules and settings. Rebuilding may take some time if there is a lot of content or complex permission settings. After rebuilding has completed, content will automatically use the new permissions. Rebuild permissions	
PHP	5.4.4 (more information)
PHP extensions	Enabled
PHP memory limit	32M
PHP register globals	Disabled
Unicode library	PHP Mbstring Extension
Update notifications	Enabled
Upload progress	Not enabled
Your server is capable of displaying file upload progress through APC, but it is not enabled. Add apc.rfc1867 = 1 to your php.ini configuration. Alternatively, it is recommended to use PECL uploadprogress, which supports more than one simultaneous upload.	
Web server	Apache/2.2.22 (Unix) mod_ssl/2.2.22 OpenSSL/0.9.8r DAV/2 PHP/5.4.4

The **Status report** admin screen at `admin/reports/status`, as shown in the preceding screenshot, gives you useful technical information about your Drupal codebase and the hosting environment. Frequently, when troubleshooting issues with your site, the information from this page can be invaluable. For those users with a technical inclination, the more information link after the PHP version number links to a page that gives you an overview of how PHP is configured.

Help

The administrative section also includes a brief **Help** section, which is accessible by clicking on the **Help** link or by navigating to `admin/help`. The help texts in this section provide an overview of the modules and functionality within your site and link to any relevant handbook pages:

Next steps – building the foundation

Now that we have examined the core Drupal installation and its default settings, we are ready to begin building our additional functionality. The rest of this chapter covers the steps you will be using repeatedly as you design your site.

Although some details will vary depending on the context, the details in this chapter will provide a point of reference as you build out your site.

The elements of this foundation include:

- Installing modules and themes
- Adding roles
- Creating content types
- Creating views

Installing modules and themes

As you run and administer your Drupal site, you will need to install and enable different contributed modules and themes. To understand how to install contributed modules and themes, we will need to take a brief look at the Drupal's directory structure, as pictured in the following screenshot:

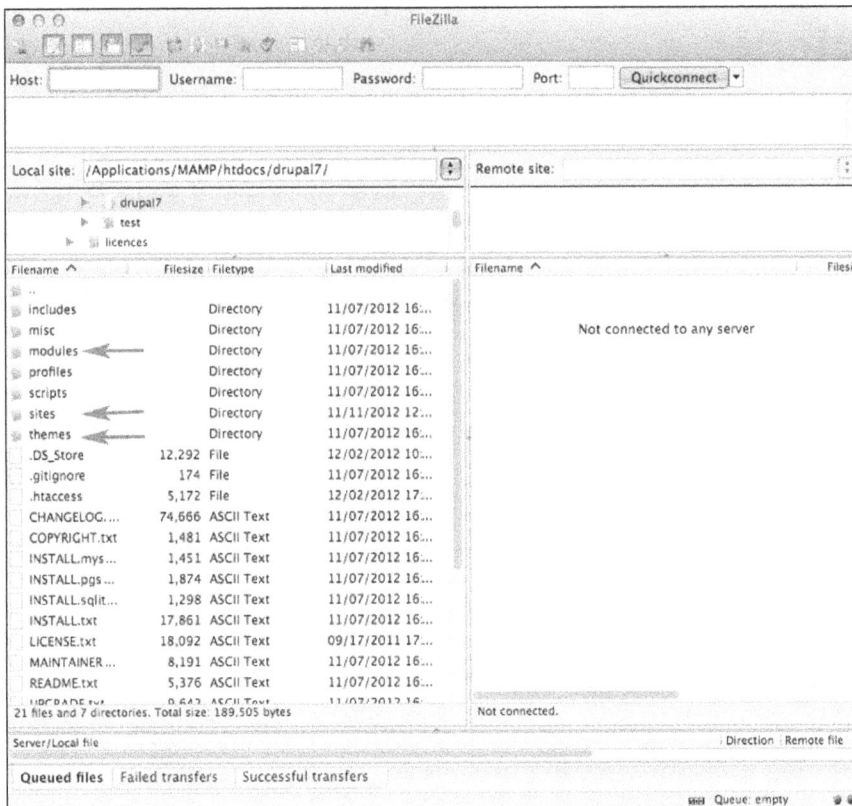

As seen in the preceding screenshot, the directory structure contains seven directories, in addition to 20 files in the base folder of the Drupal installation.

Files

On looking at the files in the base folder of the Drupal installation, we will see three different types of files: an .htaccess file, a series of .txt files, and a series of .php files. The .htaccess file contains specific settings that help ensure that your site runs smoothly; the .txt files (with the exception of robots.txt) contain all the information about Drupal and the .php files are all part of the codebase that allows your site to run.

For most sites, you will never need to open or edit any of these files. Of all the files in the base directory of your Drupal installation, the only two that could ever require editing are the .htaccess and robots.txt files. However, tweaks to these files should only be done when absolutely necessary, and you should always back up these files before attempting any modifications to them.

Directories

On looking at the directories of the Drupal installation, we will focus on three directories: modules, themes, and sites.

Core modules and themes

The modules and themes directories of the core Drupal installation, indicated by the first and last arrows in the preceding screenshot, contain the core modules and themes.

> Under no circumstances should anything ever be added into these directories.

The sites directory

The `sites` directory, indicated by the middle arrow in the preceding screenshot, contains the directories into which we install the additional modules and themes. The default Drupal installation, as shown in the following screenshot, comes with two subfolders in the `sites` directory: `all` and `default`.

The `default` directory contains our `settings.php` file; the `all` directory is where we will put contributed themes and modules. Refer to the following screenshot:

Steps for adding modules and themes

To add a module or a theme, follow these four steps:

1. Download the theme or module from `http://drupal.org`.
2. Decompress the theme or module. They are packaged on `drupal.org` as `tar.gz` files and needed to be extracted before they can be installed.
3. Upload the theme or module to your site.
4. Enable modules at `admin/modules` or themes at `admin/appearance`.

Step 1 – downloading

All modules and themes are downloaded from their project page. In this example, we will download and install the Views module, the Chaos tool suite (Ctools), and the Advanced Help module. To get the source code, we will navigate to the **Views** project page at http://drupal.org/project/views, (as shown in the following screenshot), the Ctools project page at http://drupal.org/project/ctools, and also the Advanced help project page at http://drupal.org/project/advanced_help:

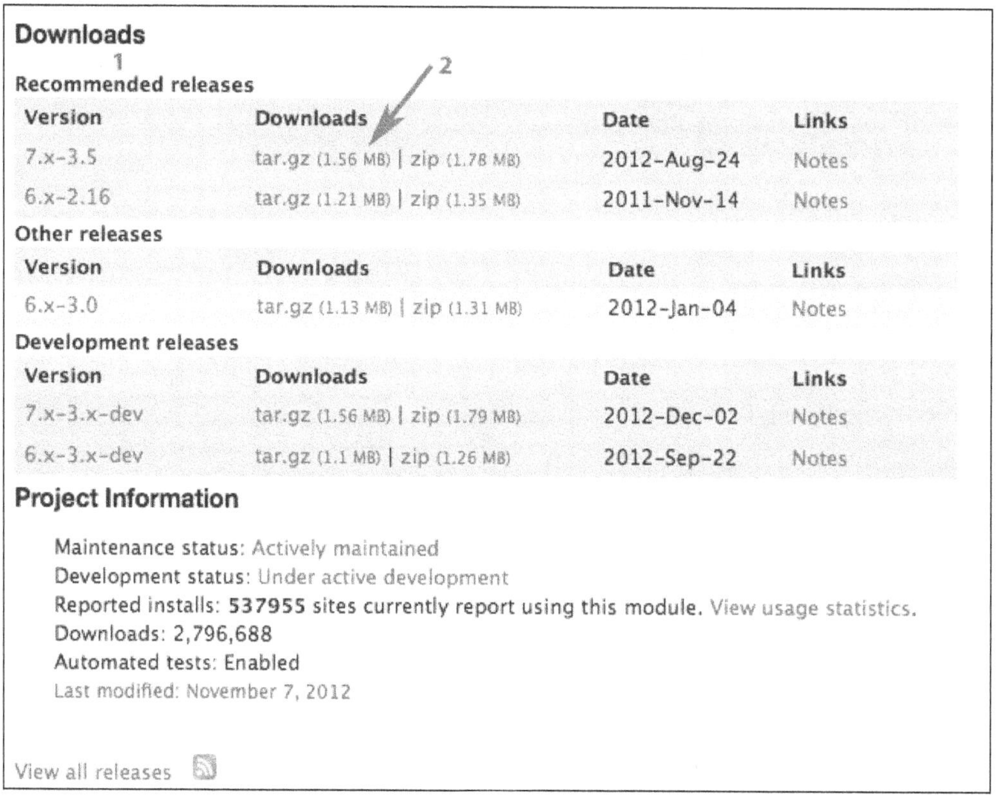

Downloads

Recommended releases

Version	Downloads	Date	Links
7.x-3.5	tar.gz (1.56 MB) | zip (1.78 MB)	2012-Aug-24	Notes
6.x-2.16	tar.gz (1.21 MB) | zip (1.35 MB)	2011-Nov-14	Notes

Other releases

Version	Downloads	Date	Links
6.x-3.0	tar.gz (1.13 MB) | zip (1.31 MB)	2012-Jan-04	Notes

Development releases

Version	Downloads	Date	Links
7.x-3.x-dev	tar.gz (1.56 MB) | zip (1.79 MB)	2012-Dec-02	Notes
6.x-3.x-dev	tar.gz (1.1 MB) | zip (1.26 MB)	2012-Sep-22	Notes

Project Information

Maintenance status: Actively maintained
Development status: Under active development
Reported installs: **537955** sites currently report using this module. View usage statistics.
Downloads: 2,796,688
Automated tests: Enabled
Last modified: November 7, 2012

View all releases

> The Drupal 7 version of Views requires the Ctools module to function. The Drupal 6 version of the module did not require this module. Views has been moved into Drupal's core for Drupal 8.

The **Views** project page shows the official releases as well as other stable releases and development versions. The **Status** column, indicated by section **1** in the preceding screenshot, gives you information about the different versions that are available. In most cases, you should only use official releases that have a status of **Recommended**. Also, the version of the module needs to match up with the version of Drupal; for example, only the 7.x Versions of modules work with Drupal 7.

In this case, we want to install Views for Drupal 7, so we click on the **Download** link, indicated by section **2** in the preceding screenshot, to download the module.

Then, repeat these steps for the Ctools module at `http://drupal.org/project/ctools` and the Advanced help module at `http://drupal.org/project/advanced_help`.

> To keep your downloaded code organized, create a folder to use specifically for this purpose.

Step 2 – decompressing

Once you have downloaded the code from `drupal.org` to your computer, decompress the file. On a Mac or Linux machine, this will occur automatically; on a PC, use 7-zip (an open source utility available at `http://www.7-zip.org`) to decompress the tarball into the `Views` directory.

Step 3 – uploading

Open your FTP client and upload the directory containing the module (in our case, Views) to the `sites/all/modules` directory, as shown in the following screenshot:

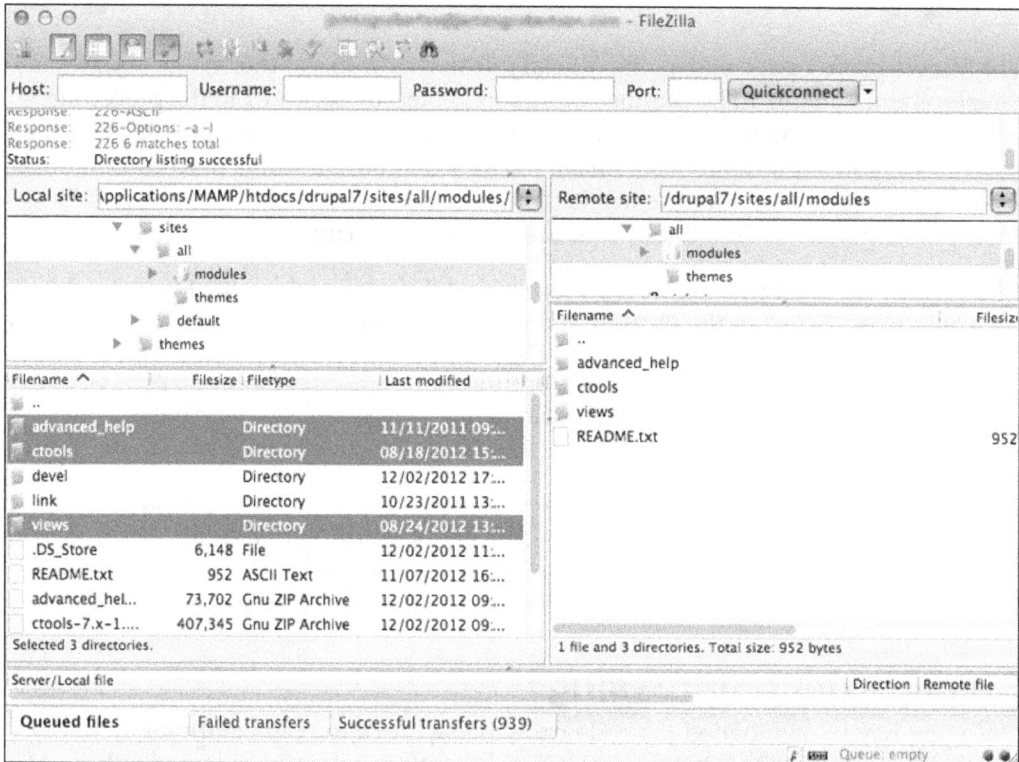

If you were uploading a theme, you would upload the theme folder into the `sites/all/themes` directory.

Step 4 – enabling

Once the modules have been successfully uploaded into your `sites/all/modules` directory, click on the **Modules** link or navigate to `admin/modules`, as shown in the following screenshot:

▼ OTHER

ENABLED	NAME	VERSION	DESCRIPTION	OPERATIONS	
☑	Advanced help	7.x-1.0	Allow advanced help and documentation. Required by: Chaos Tools (CTools) Plugin Example (disabled), Advanced help example (disabled)	Help	Permissions
☐	Advanced help example	7.x-1.0	A example help module to demonstrate the advanced help module. Requires: Advanced help (enabled)		

▼ VIEWS

ENABLED	NAME	VERSION	DESCRIPTION	OPERATIONS	
☑	Views	7.x-3.5	Create customized lists and queries from your database. Requires: Chaos tools (enabled) Required by: Views content panes (disabled), Views UI (enabled)	Help	Permissions
☑	Views UI	7.x-3.5	Administrative interface to views. Without this module, you cannot create or edit your views. Requires: Views (enabled), Chaos tools (enabled)		Configure

Save configuration

This screen gives a breakdown of the modules that you have uploaded into your `sites/all/modules` folder.

To enable the Advanced help module, select the checkbox next to **Advanced help**. To enable the Ctools module, select the checkbox next to **Chaos tools**. To enable the Views module, select the checkboxes next to the **Views** and **Views UI** modules. Click on the **Save configuration** button to save your settings and enable your modules. You will receive a confirmation message at the top of the screen.

▼ CHAOS TOOL SUITE

ENABLED	NAME	VERSION	DESCRIPTION	OPERATIONS
☐	**Bulk Export**	7.x-1.2	Performs bulk exporting of data objects known about by Chaos tools. Requires: Chaos tools (enabled)	
☑	**Chaos tools**	7.x-1.2	A library of helpful tools by Merlin of Chaos. Required by: Bulk Export (disabled), Custom rulesets (disabled), Chaos Tools (CTools) AJAX Example (disabled), Custom content panes (disabled), Page manager (disabled), Chaos Tools (CTools) Plugin Example (disabled), Stylizer (disabled), Views (enabled), Views content panes (disabled), Views UI (enabled)	ⓘ Help

Many projects are actually a collection of related modules. For example, the Views module comes with two related modules. Before you install any module, you should read the README.txt and INSTALL.txt files that come with most modules. These files are usually located in the base directory of the project download.

Configuring modules and themes

Now that we have finished installing modules and themes, we need to configure them.

Modules

Once you have enabled a new module, you should check to see if there are any configuration options for the module. To do this, look in the **OPERATIONS** column of the **Modules** page.

By looking at the page, we see that both the Views module and the Advanced help module have links to **Permissions**. These permissions are covered in more detail later in this chapter, in the *Creating views* section.

Themes

After you have uploaded a theme into the `sites/all/themes` directory, you will need to enable it via the **Appearance** link or by navigating to `admin/appearance`. The themes and their different settings are covered in more detail in *Chapter 14, Theming and User Interface Design*.

Modules and themes – a summary

As described in this section, installing modules and themes involves four steps:

- Downloading
- Decompressing
- Uploading
- Enabling

Modules are uploaded into `sites/all/modules` and themes are uploaded into `sites/all/themes`.

Modules, once uploaded, are enabled at `admin/modules`. Themes, once uploaded, are enabled at `admin/appearance`. Although different modules and themes will have the varying configuration settings, the previous steps will remain constant for any module or theme you use on your site.

Creating roles

Although roles are covered in more detail in *Chapter 5, Enrolling Students* and *Chapter 6, Creating the Student Blog*, we will briefly cover how to create roles here.

To create a new role, click on **People | Permissions | Roles** or navigate to admin/people/permissions/roles, as shown in the following screenshot:

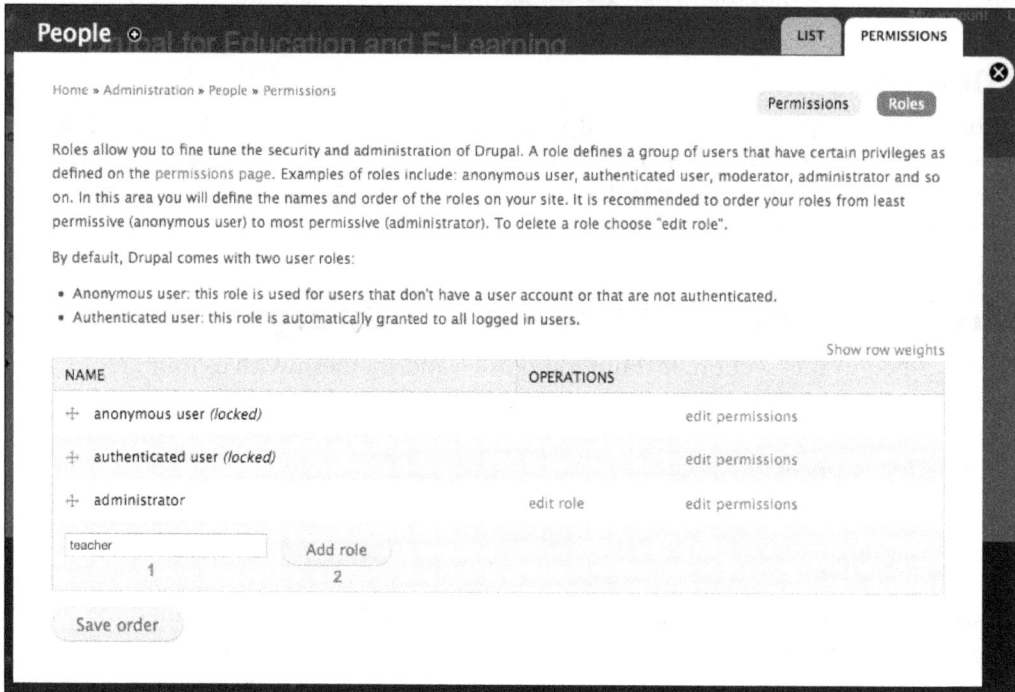

As seen in section **1**, you need to enter the name of the role. Once you have entered the name, click on the **Add role** button. Add two roles: teacher and student.

Creating content types

As we build this site, we will build a range of content types for different functions. Although these different content types will have varied uses throughout the site, the basic process for creating content types remains consistent.

> A content type and a node type mean the same thing.
> In most situations, a node is a piece of content.

For this example, we will create a content type for storing and sharing bookmarks.

Adding new content types requires the following steps:

1. Create the content type.

2. Add fields to the content type (this is optional: not all content types require additional fields).

3. Assign a taxonomy to the content type (this is optional: not all content types will be organized using taxonomy).

4. Assign permissions to the content type.

Of these four steps, only step one and two need to happen for all the new content types. As we will discuss, some content types do not require additional fields and some content types are not associated with a taxonomy.

Step 1 – creating the content type

To create a content type, follow these steps:

1. Click on **Structure | Content types** or navigate to `admin/structure/types`.

2. Click on the **Add content type** link as shown in the following screenshot:

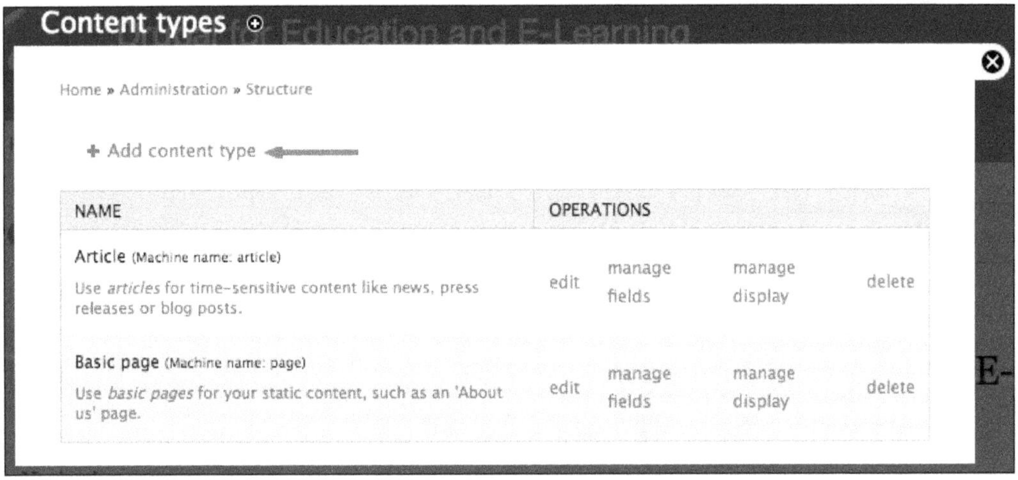

This brings you to the administrative screen to add a content type, accessible at `admin/structure/types/add`. As shown in the following screenshot, this screen has six sections:

- **Name** and **Description**
- **Submission form settings**
- **Publishing options**
- **Display settings**
- **Comment settings**
- **Menu settings**

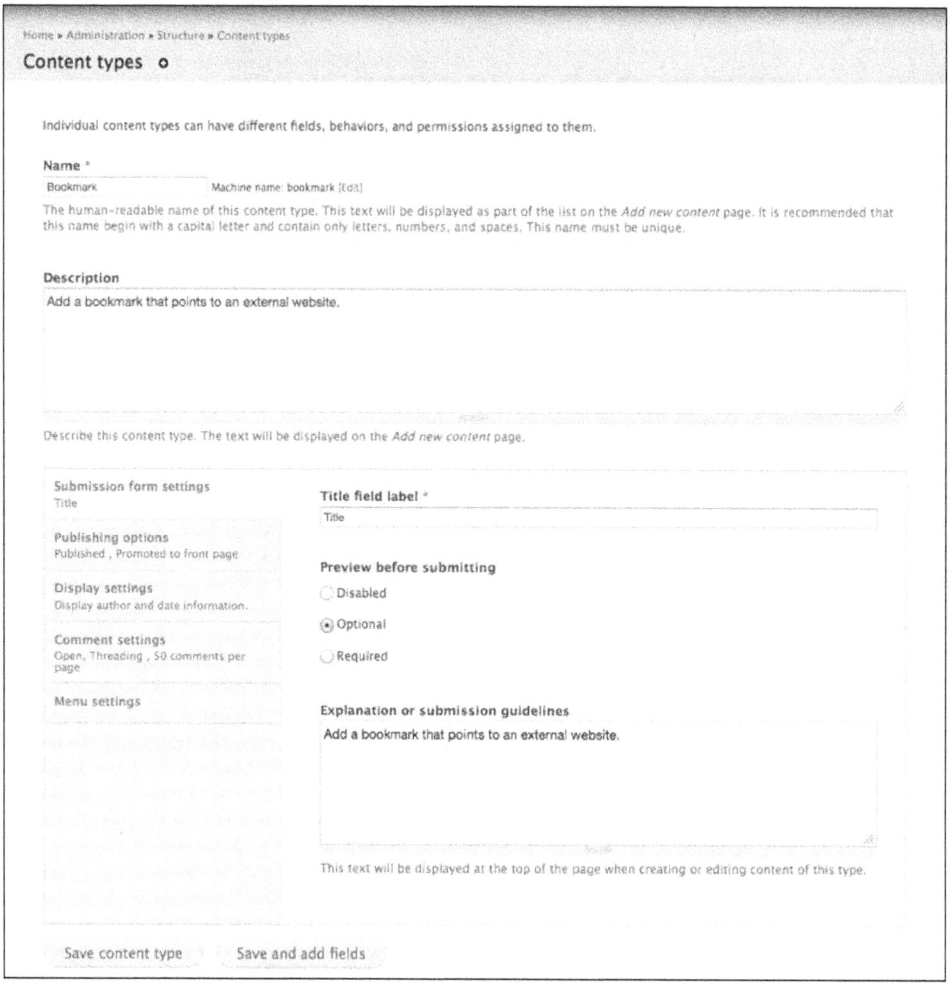

The Name and Description sections

As seen in the preceding screenshot, the **Name** and **Description** section contains two fields:

- **Name**: This field provides a human-readable name for the content type. The name for a content type should provide a general sense of what the content type will be used for. In this example, as we are creating a node type that will store bookmarks, we will name the content type `Bookmark`.

- **Description**: This field holds a more detailed description of what the content type is used for. It field can hold HTML, so a description can contain, for example, links to external pages. Typically, a good description is brief. For the bookmark, we will use: `Add a bookmark that points to an external website.`

The Submission form settings page

You can view the different fields on the **Submission form settings** page as shown in the following screenshot:

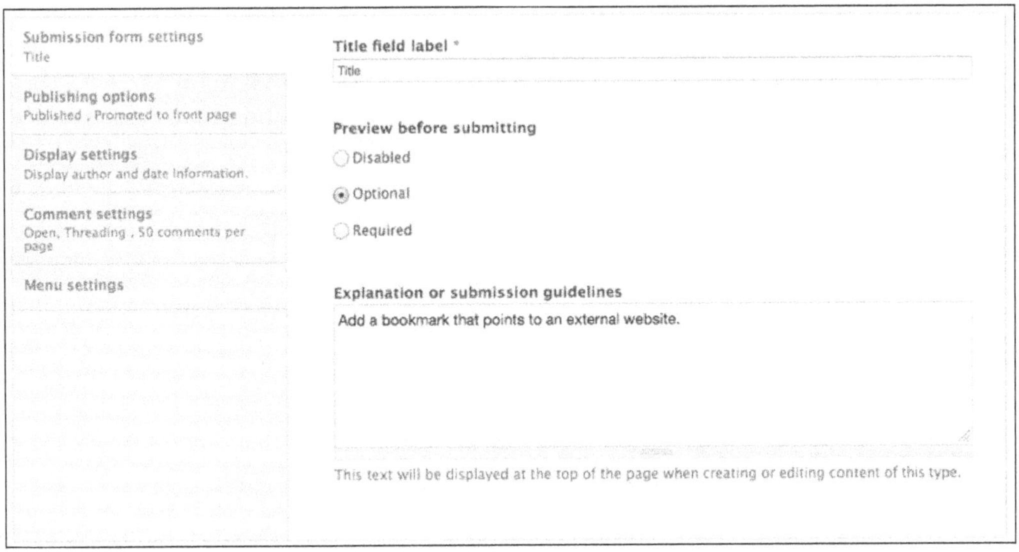

The values in the various **Submission form settings** fields allow you to customize what appears to people as they add content on your site. The following screenshot shows where these values appear when people are adding content:

Compare this form with the previous **Submission form settings** screenshot to see the relationship between the two pages.

When creating new content types, the only value that requires changing is the **Explanation or submission guidelines** field. In this example and in many cases, we can use the same text that we used for the **Description** field: `Add a bookmark that points to an external website`.

The Publishing options page

You can view the different fields on the **Publishing options** page as shown in the following screenshot:

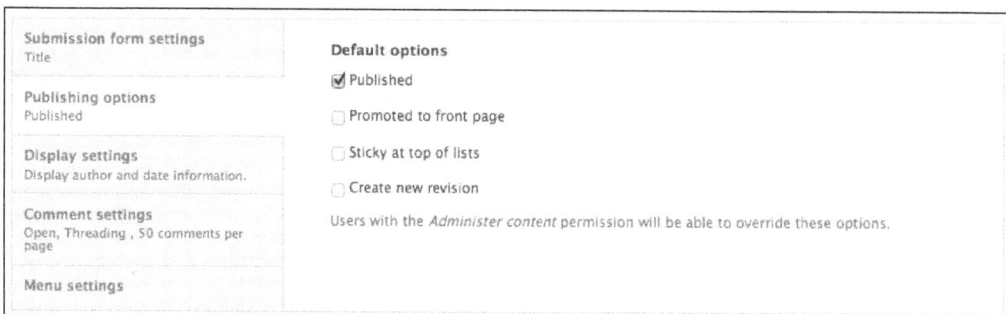

The **Publishing options** section covers the basic rules for what happens to a piece of content when it is created and edited. Under the **Default options** section, you will want to select **Published**; without this, regular users will not be able to see your content.

Of the other options, the most commonly used is the **Create new revision** feature. Selecting this option allows you to create wiki-like functionality; each time a piece of content is edited and saved, it creates a revision and users with sufficient permissions can view and manage older revisions.

The other two flags (**Promoted to front page** and **Sticky at top of lists**) are useful if you are using Drupal's default home page or default organization. In most cases, however, we will be organizing our content using the Views module, and these flags will be of limited use.

The Display settings page

The **Display settings** section covers whether you want author and date information shown on posts, as shown in the following screenshot:

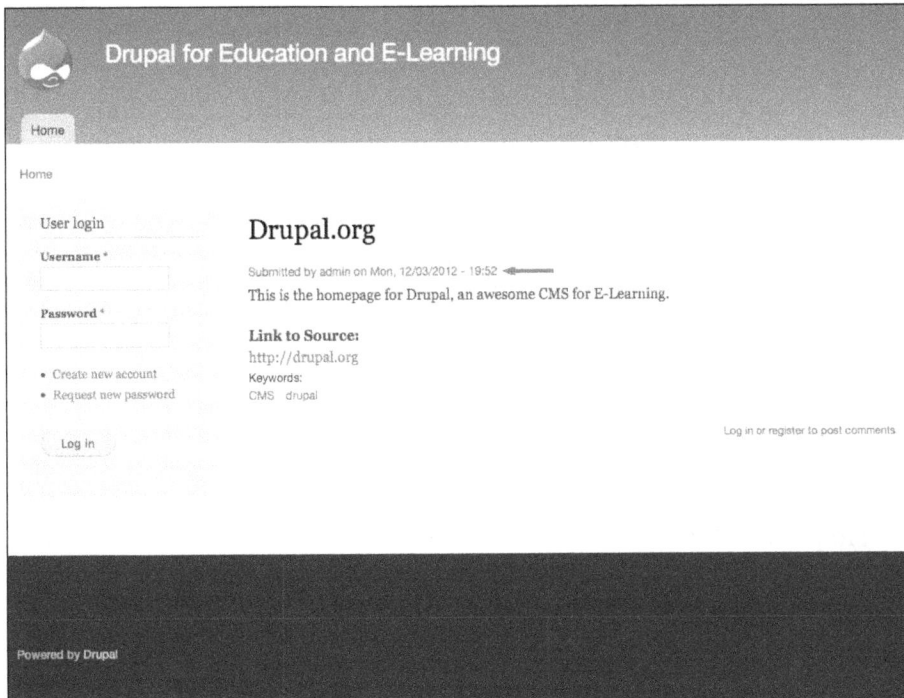

This setting is a matter of personal preference; we'll leave it enabled for now, so we can easily see who created the bookmark and when it was created:

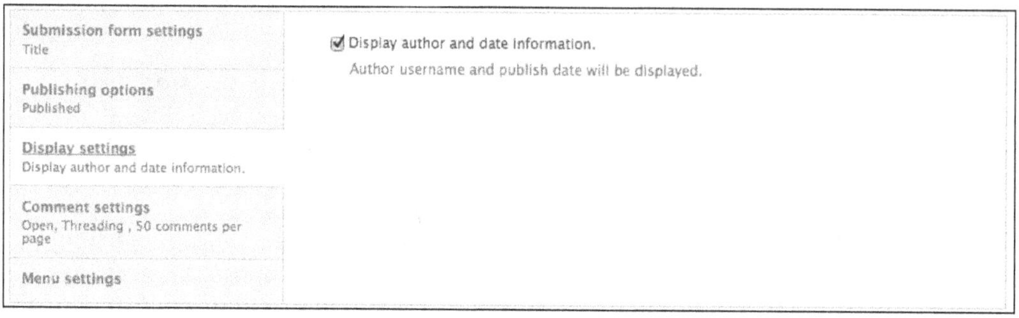

The Comment settings page

You can view the different fields on the **Comment settings** page as shown in the following screenshot:

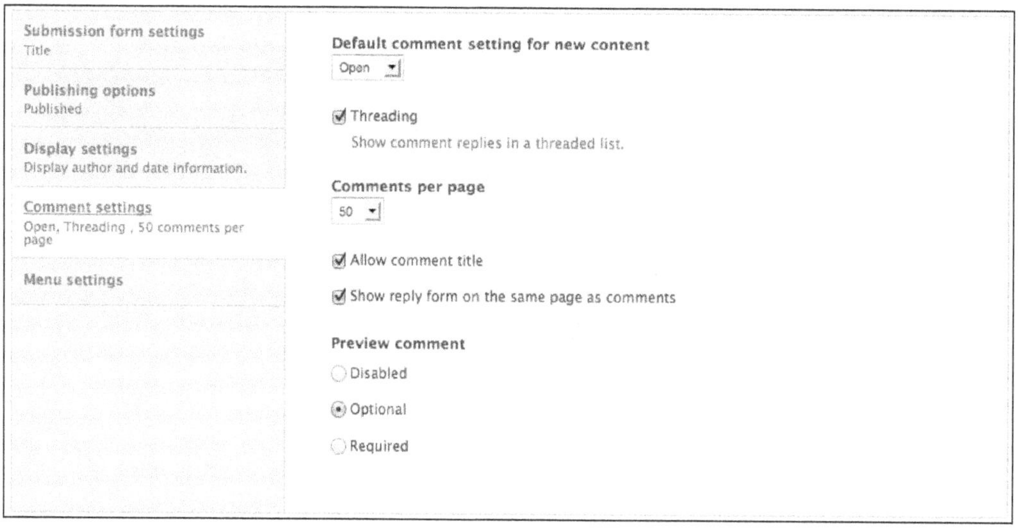

The most important setting in this section is the first one, **Default comment setting for new content**. If you want to allow comments, set this to **Open**. If you don't want to allow comments on this node type, select **Hidden**.

The second most important setting is **Preview comment**. Set this to **Optional**, as requiring users to preview their comments is an added step that can inhibit interaction on your site.

The remaining settings in this section are largely cosmetic, and the correct settings here tend to be a matter of taste. The settings shown in the preceding screenshot are sensible defaults that get you a nested comment thread, with earlier posts at the top of the thread.

The Menu settings page

You can view the different fields on the **Menu settings** page as shown in the following screenshot:

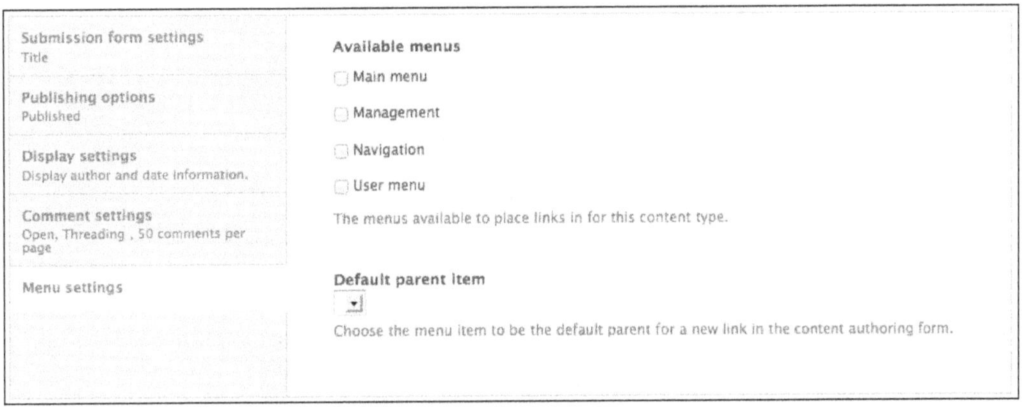

The **Menu settings** section allows the content type to be available to certain menus generated by Drupal. Users can add individual posts to menus on the site by using these settings. Since we won't be adding individual bookmarks to menus on this site, we will not make it available to any menus by unchecking all the boxes under **Available menus**. The menus will be covered in more detail in *Chapter 14, Theming and User Interface Design*.

Once you have set the defaults, click on the **Save and add fields** button to create your new content type.

Step 2 – adding fields

Once the content type has been created, we need to add fields. In Drupal 6, adding fields required the CCK module, but this functionality was added to Drupal's core in Drupal 7 with the field API. Because we are creating a bookmark and need to store a link, which is not one of Drupal's default field types, we do need to install the Link module.

The Link module can be downloaded from `http://drupal.org/project/link`.

Once you have downloaded and extracted the module, upload it into `sites/all/modules` as described earlier in this chapter, and then click on the **Modules** link or navigate to `admin/modules` to enable it.

Drupal's field API allows you to add fields to content types, and the project includes several submodules. In this section, we will enable the various field-related modules we will use throughout this book. In later chapters, we will install the additional modules that will further extend the functionality of fields via the field API.

ENABLED	NAME	VERSION	DESCRIPTION	OPERATIONS
✓	Link	7.x-1.0	Defines simple link field types. Required by: Drupal (Field type(s) in use – see Field list)	

▼ FIELDS

Of all the modules shown in the preceding screenshot, only the **Link** module is not a part of the core fields. Enable the modules as shown. Once you have enabled the modules, navigate to **Structure | Content types** or navigate to `admin/structure/types`.

Content types ⊕

Home » Administration » Structure

✚ Add content type

NAME	OPERATIONS				
Article (Machine name: article) Use *articles* for time-sensitive content like news, press releases or blog posts.	edit	manage fields	manage display	delete	
Basic page (Machine name: page) Use *basic pages* for your static content, such as an 'About us' page.	edit	manage fields	manage display	delete	
Bookmark (Machine name: bookmark)	edit	manage fields	manage display	delete	

Then, click on the **MANAGE FIELDS** link to get to the screen shown in the following screenshot:

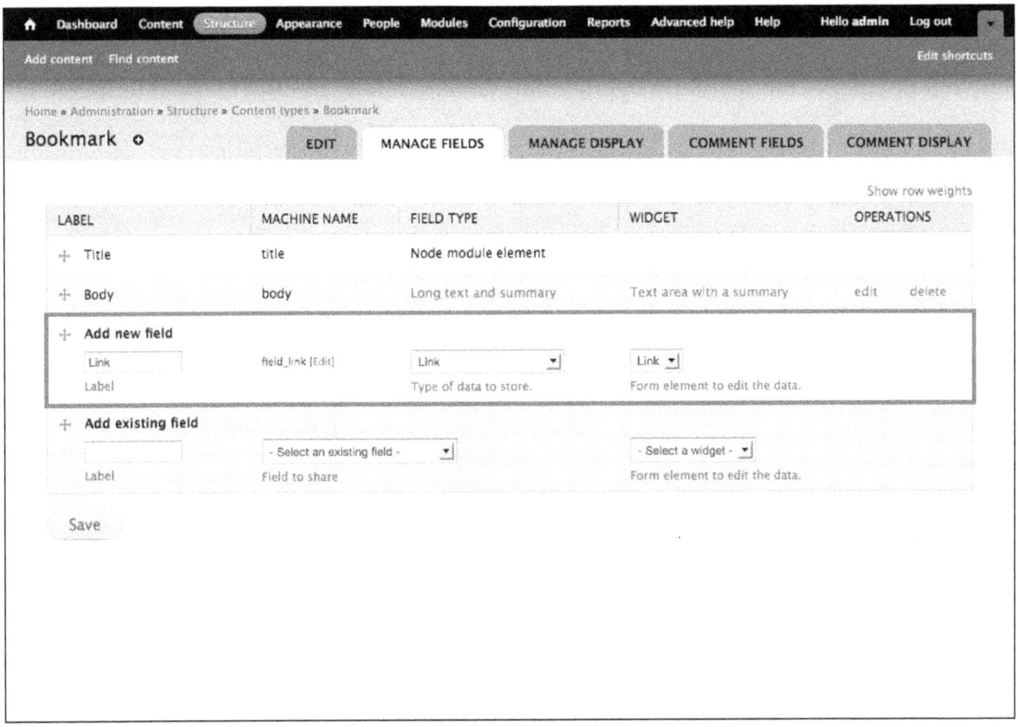

As shown in the previous screenshot, when adding your new field, you need to enter the following information:

- **LABEL**, in this example, **Link to source**
- **FIELD TYPE**, in this example, **Link**

Then, depending on the type of data to be stored in the field, you will be presented with some widget options for the form element used to edit the data. While some field types have many different widgets, the **Link** field only offers one option: **Link**.

After selecting the appropriate options, click on the **Save** button to save your field and move on to the configuration screen:

Home » Administration » Structure » Content types » Bookmark » Manage fields

Link to Source ✿

| | EDIT | FIELD SETTINGS | WIDGET TYPE | DELETE |

BOOKMARK SETTINGS

These settings apply only to the *Link to Source* field when used in the *Bookmark* type.

Label *

Link to Source

1 ☑ Required field

Help text

Enter a link to an external web site. Most links will start with http://

2

Instructions to present to the user below this field on the editing form.
Allowed HTML tags: `<a> <b> <big> <code> <del> <em> <i> <ins> <pre> <q> <small> <span> <strong>`
`<sub> <sup> <tt> <ol> <ul> <li> <p> <br> <img>`

☑ Validate URL

If checked, the URL field will be verified as a valid URL during validation.

☐ Optional URL

If checked, the URL field is optional and submitting a title alone will be acceptable. If the URL is omitted, the title will be displayed as plain text.

Link Title

○ Optional Title

○ Required Title

3

○ Static Title

◉ No Title

If the link title is optional or required, a field will be displayed to the end user. If the link title is static, the link will always use the same title. If token module is installed, the static title value may use any other node field as its value. Static and token-based titles may include most inline XHTML tags such as *strong*, *em*, *img*, *span*, etc.

During configuration of the **Link** field, in most cases, the default settings will work. For the bookmark, we make three changes, marked 1 to 3 in the preceding screenshot.

The first marked option is **Required**; given that the purpose of this content type is to store bookmarks, the **Link** field is a required field.

The second marked option **Help text**. As the name implies, this text can be used to give instructions to the person filling out the form.

The third marked option removes the title from the **Link** field. Given that the node already has a title, requiring a title for the link as well would be redundant.

Once the settings have been adjusted, click on the **Save settings** button. This returns you to the **Manage fields** administrative screen. On this page, you can order your fields by dragging-and-dropping; click on the **Save** button to record any changes.

Step 3 – assigning taxonomies

Once you have created a node type, you need to decide whether or not you will use taxonomy to organize or categorize the posts made with that content type. For bookmarks, we want users to be able to use tags to categorize their links.

To add a taxonomy, click on **Structure | Taxonomy link** or navigate to admin/ structure/taxonomy. Click on the **Add vocabulary** link shown in the following screenshot:

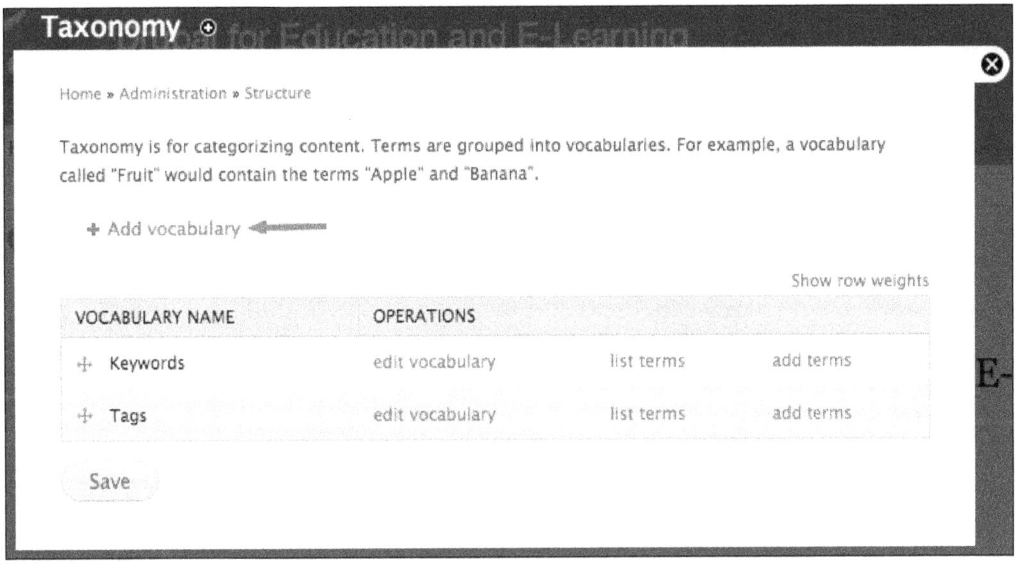

Clicking on the **Add Vocabulary** link brings you to the screen shown in the following screenshot:

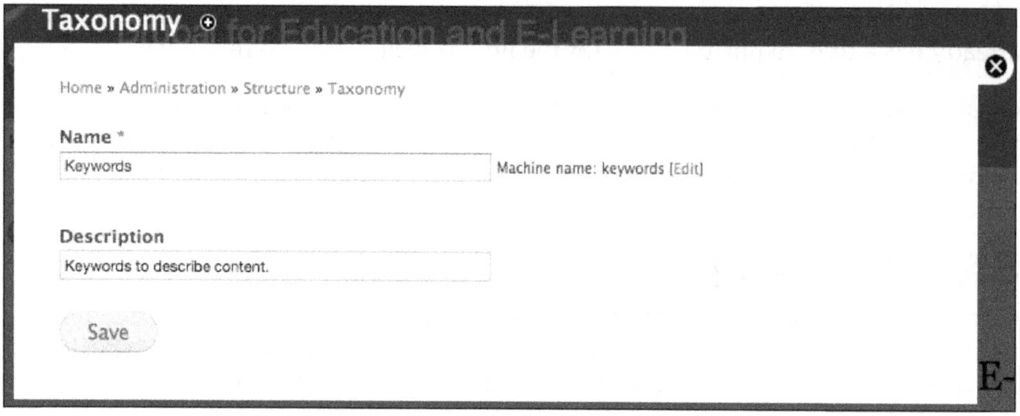

Here you need to provide a vocabulary name and a description. The name should be somewhat intuitive, and as this vocabulary will be used to describe posts, we will call it Keywords. The description of the vocabulary is more for administrative purposes, as it is not displayed anywhere on the site by default. Click on **Save** to create the vocabulary.

After saving, you will be redirected to the **Taxonomy** page. To edit the vocabulary's other options, you must add it to a content type.

Adding a taxonomy to a content type

Navigate to **Structure** | **Content types** | **MANAGE FIELDS** or admin/structure/types/manage/bookmark/fields to add the **Keywords** vocabulary to the **Bookmark** content type:

Add a new field called `Keywords`, and select **Term reference** as the field type.
Since we want this to be a vocabulary where the options are not controlled by a site
administrator, choose **Autocomplete term widget (tagging)** as the widget type.

Click on **Save** to edit the field's options.

On the next screen you will see options for the taxonomy on the **Bookmark** content type. Most of the default options are fine for our purposes, except for the two numbered fields in the following screenshot:

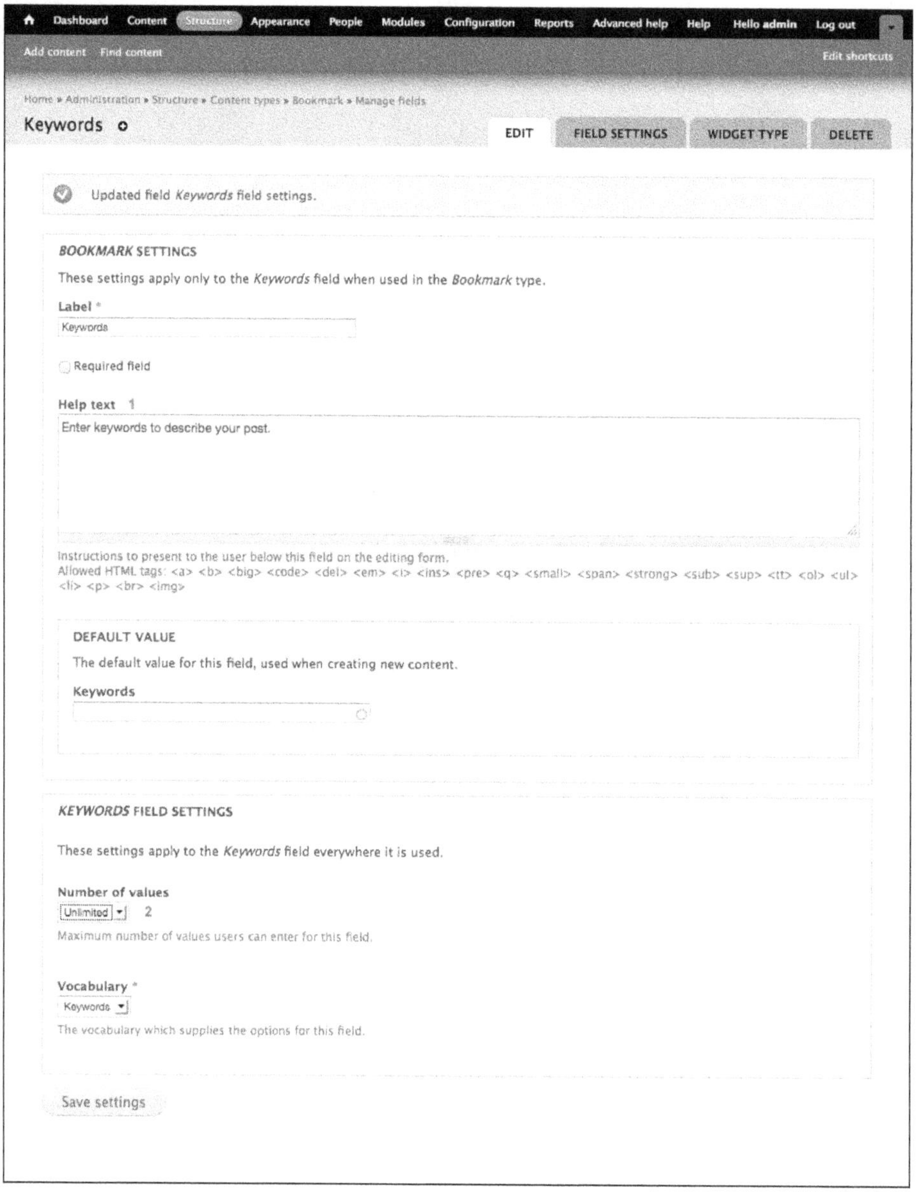

In the first marked item, you can add an explanatory text for the end user.

In the second marked item, you can set how many terms can be added to the post. Since we don't want to impose a limit on our users, we will select **Unlimited**.

Once you have adjusted the settings, click on the **Save settings** button to save your preferences.

Step 4 – assigning permissions

The final step in preparing content types for use on your site is to assign permissions via user roles. To do this click on **People | Permissions | Roles link** or navigate to `admin/people/permissions/roles`.

For this example, we will assign permissions to the teacher role.

> For more information on roles and how to use them effectively within your site, see *Chapter 4, Creating a Teacher Blog* and *Chapter 5, Enrolling Students*.

To assign rights for teachers, click on the **edit permissions** link that is on the right-hand side of the entry for teacher, as shown in the following screenshot:

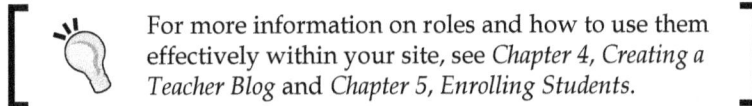

Then, on the **Permission** page, scroll down to the section titled **Node**. As pictured in the following screenshot, give the teacher role the rights to administer content, access the content overview page, view published content, create bookmark content, edit own bookmark content, and delete own bookmark content.

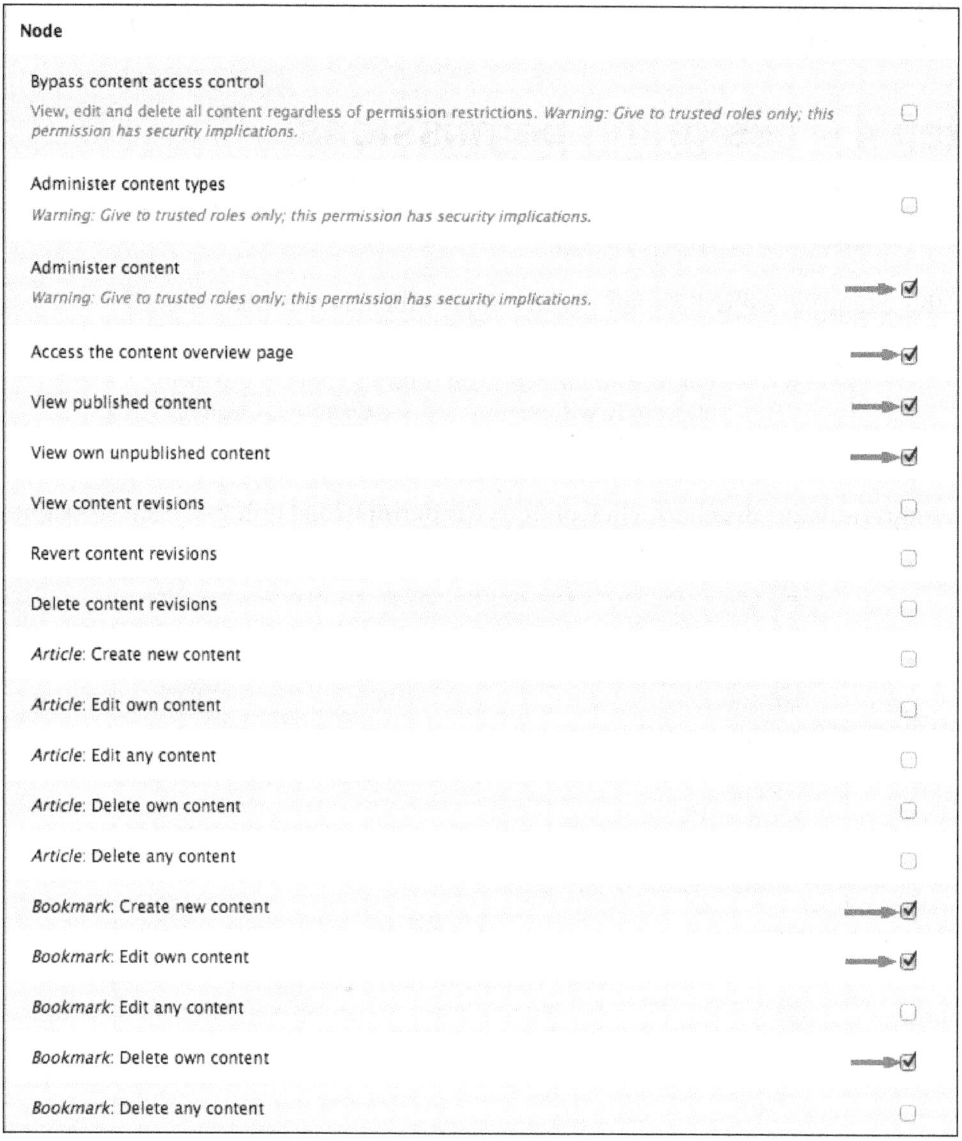

Node	
Bypass content access control	
View, edit and delete all content regardless of permission restrictions. *Warning: Give to trusted roles only; this permission has security implications.*	☐
Administer content types	
Warning: Give to trusted roles only; this permission has security implications.	☐
Administer content	
Warning: Give to trusted roles only; this permission has security implications.	☑
Access the content overview page	☑
View published content	☑
View own unpublished content	☑
View content revisions	☐
Revert content revisions	☐
Delete content revisions	☐
Article: Create new content	☐
Article: Edit own content	☐
Article: Edit any content	☐
Article: Delete own content	☐
Article: Delete any content	☐
Bookmark: Create new content	☑
Bookmark: Edit own content	☑
Bookmark: Edit any content	☐
Bookmark: Delete own content	☑
Bookmark: Delete any content	☐

Click on the **Save permissions** button to save your settings.

The result

Click on the **Create content** link or navigate to node/add. Click on the **Bookmark** link, which brings you to node/add/bookmark.

Enter the required information and then click on the **Save** button to save your new bookmark.

Creating content types – summary

Creating content types has four steps:

1. Create the content type.
2. Add fields (optional).
3. Assign taxonomy (optional).
4. Assign permissions.

These steps will apply to all new content types created on the site. In some cases, new content types will not require additional fields or taxonomy; however, these steps will guide you through the general process of creating new content types.

Creating views

The Views module allows site administrators to sort and display content created on the site. The Views module is incredibly flexible, but initially the process of creating views can seem daunting.

In this section, we will examine the basic steps that you will follow as you create different views on your site. Although each view will vary depending on what you are trying to show, the steps outlined here provide the basis for getting started.

To create a view, follow these steps:

1. Add a view and follow these steps:
    1. Describe the view.
    2. Select the type of data and filters.
    3. Select a display type.
    4. Set display type options.
    5. Set the display format.

2. Edit the view and follow these steps:
    1. Add fields.
    2. Add/edit filters.
    3. Add/edit contextual filters (optional).
    4. Edit display format (optional).
    5. Set additional configuration options (optional).

3. Define multiple display types (optional) and follow these steps:
    1. Override the default values (optional).

In this example, we will create a view that displays bookmarks, and all taxonomy terms connected with those bookmarks.

Step 1 – adding a view

To add a view, click on **Structure | Views link** or navigate to `admin/structure/views`:

The **Views** administration page, shown in the preceding screenshot, provides tools for finding, creating, and organizing views. The first marked item provides the links for adding and importing views. The field set indicated by the second marked item lists and describes the different views saved on the site, as well as provides a way to sort the views on the site.

Click on the **Add new view** link; this brings you to `admin/structure/views/add`.

Step 1 (a) – describing the view

The section **a** on this screen is the name of the view and can only contain letters, numbers, and underscores. The optional **Description** field holds a brief description that is displayed on the view's administrative page.

Step 1 (b) – selecting the type of data and filter

You can use views to display different collections of information; the view type (section **b**) specifies what type of data you'll be collecting. The most significant setting on this screen is the view type, as this determines what type of information will be shown in the view. Although views can be used to collect and display a broad array of information, in this book we will focus largely on using views to display nodes or content created by site members.

Step 1 (c) – selecting a display type

The sections **c** and **f** allow you to choose a display type for the view. A page display type allows you to display all your data on a full page on the site, while a block display type allows you to create a block of information from the view that can be placed in a region of the site. Check the box next to **Create a page** for now, and we will add a block to the view later.

Step 1 (d) – setting display type options

The display type options allow you to set options that will help the data make more sense to your users.

The following is the description of the sections mentioned in the previous screenshot:

- **Title**: This section lets you set a title for your view. For this example view, we will set the title to `All Bookmarks`.

- **Path**: A page display type requires a path where you can see the page on the site. For this example, set the path to `bookmarks/all`, which will cause the page to be visible at `http://yoursite.org/bookmarks/all`.

- **Items to display**: This setting lets you adjust the number of items to display on a single page. The default is **10**; for table views, you can show more content by setting it higher. For this example view, we will set it to `30`.

- **Use a pager**: A pager allows you to show multiple pages of data and controls if the data shown by the view are more than the number set under **Items to display**. We will leave this option unchecked for now.

- **Create a menu link**: This option allows you to easily add the page created by the view to a menu on the site. The menus will be covered in *Chapter 14, Theming and User Interface Design*. Leave this option unchecked for now.

- **Include an RSS feed**: **Really Simple Syndication** (**RSS**) allows other websites and programs to access the data from your site in a standardized way. Since this is more of an advanced option, we will leave it unchecked for now.

Step 1 (e) – setting the display format

The **Display format** settings allow you to specify how the view will be displayed on the page. The default style is an unformatted list; this allows for the view to be adjusted via CSS. In this example, we want to create a table view by following these steps:

1. Choose **Table** from the select box under **Display format**.
2. Click on **Continue & edit** to continue creating the view.

Step 2 – editing the view

The **Page display** type now holds the defaults for the view. The settings stored in the defaults are used in step 3, where we will add another **Display type**. The initial screen allows us to edit the default values for the view.

Step 2 (a) – adding fields

To add fields to your view, click on the **add** link next to the **FIELDS** option, as indicated by section **1** in the following screenshot:

This brings up the list of available fields. These fields can be organized by group, as shown in the following screenshot:

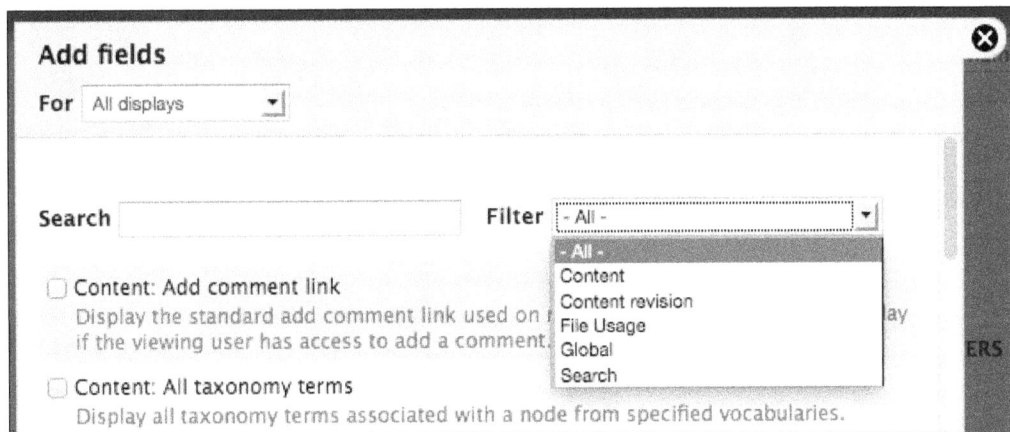

You can select a specific group to limit the number of fields you see, thus making the field list easier to navigate. For our example—creating a view showing all saved bookmarks—all of our fields will be under the **Content** group.

The Views module automatically selected the **Content: Title** field when we selected the **Table display** format.

Add the **Content: Updated date** field as shown in the following screenshot:

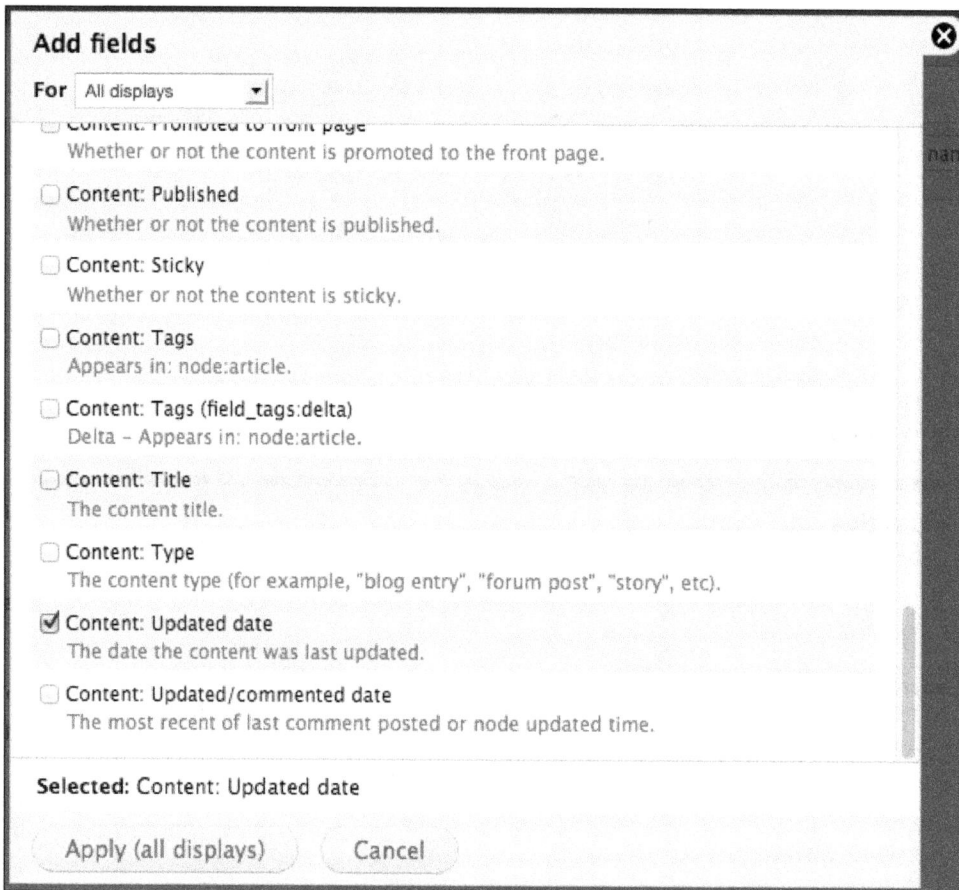

Add fields

For All displays

Content: Promoted to front page
Whether or not the content is promoted to the front page.

☐ **Content: Published**
Whether or not the content is published.

☐ **Content: Sticky**
Whether or not the content is sticky.

☐ **Content: Tags**
Appears in: node:article.

☐ **Content: Tags (field_tags:delta)**
Delta – Appears in: node:article.

☐ **Content: Title**
The content title.

☐ **Content: Type**
The content type (for example, "blog entry", "forum post", "story", etc).

☑ **Content: Updated date**
The date the content was last updated.

☐ **Content: Updated/commented date**
The most recent of last comment posted or node updated time.

Selected: Content: Updated date

Apply (all displays)   Cancel

Select the **Content: Link to source** field as shown in the following screenshot:

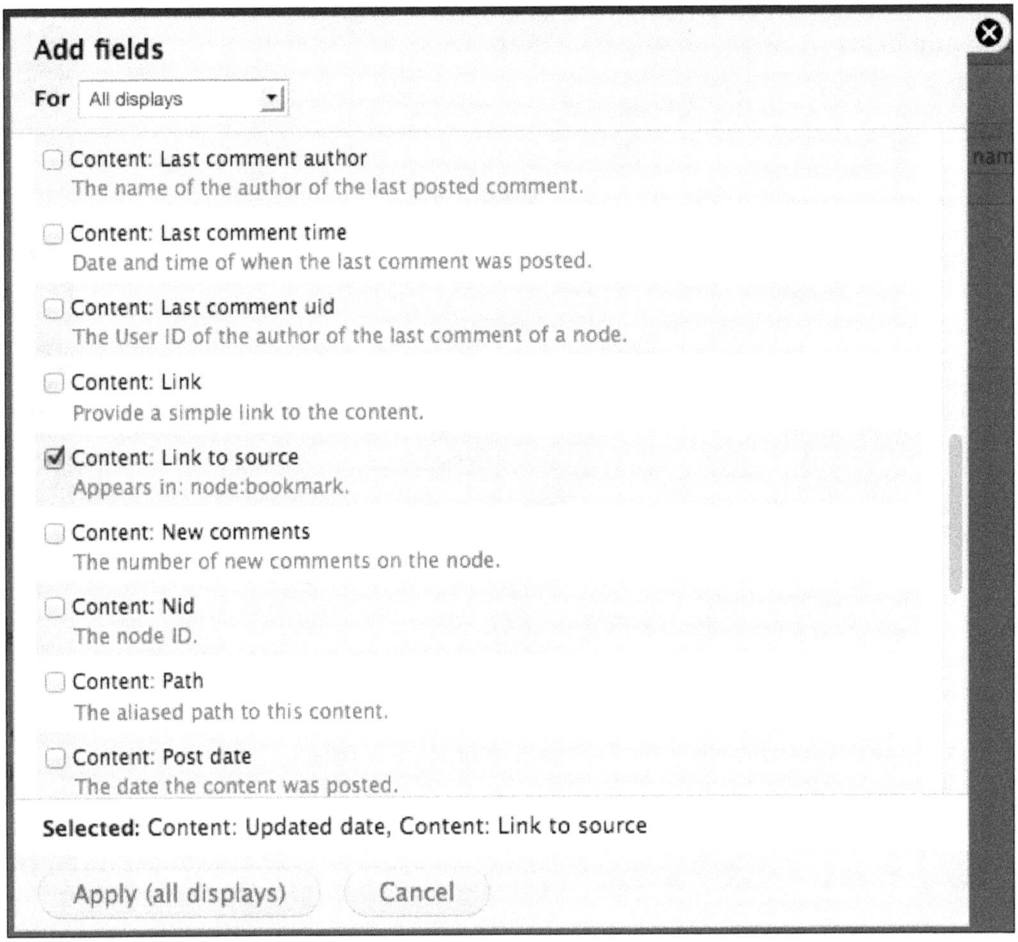

Add fields

For   All displays ▾

☐ Content: Last comment author
The name of the author of the last posted comment.

☐ Content: Last comment time
Date and time of when the last comment was posted.

☐ Content: Last comment uid
The User ID of the author of the last comment of a node.

☐ Content: Link
Provide a simple link to the content.

☑ Content: Link to source
Appears in: node:bookmark.

☐ Content: New comments
The number of new comments on the node.

☐ Content: Nid
The node ID.

☐ Content: Path
The aliased path to this content.

☐ Content: Post date
The date the content was posted.

Selected: Content: Updated date, Content: Link to source

(Apply (all displays))   (Cancel)

Select the **Content: All taxonomy terms** field as shown in the following screenshot:

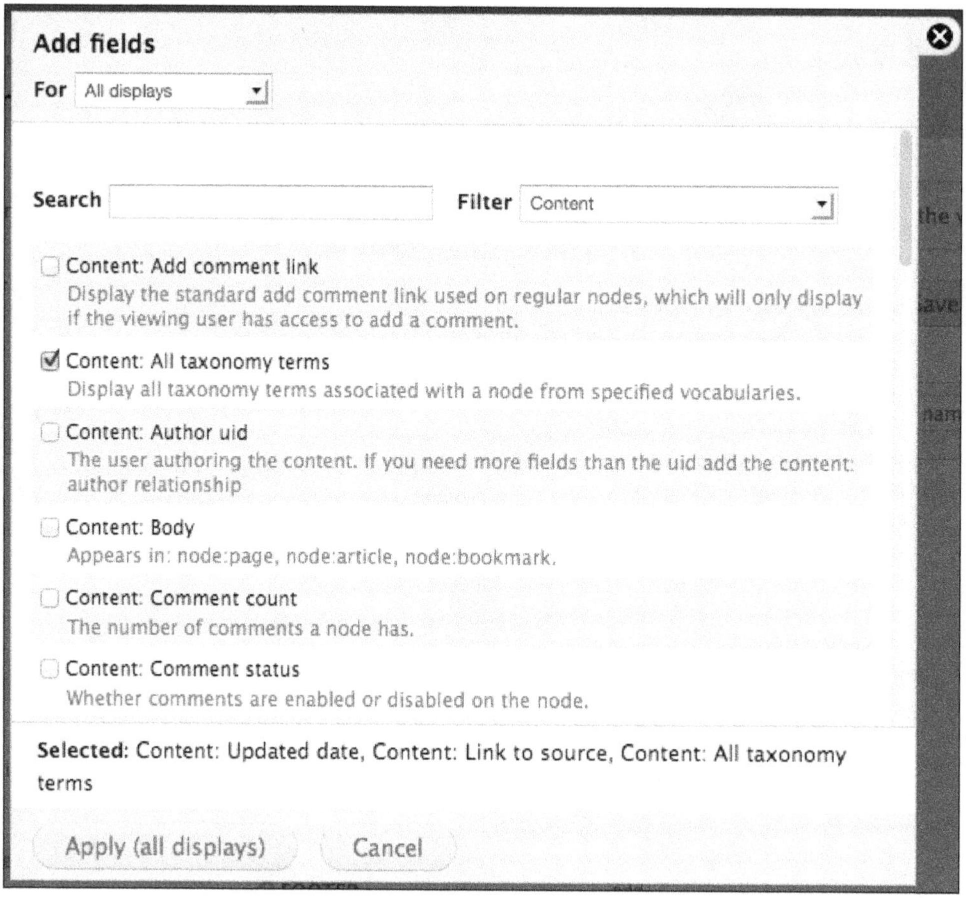

As this is the last field we need to add, click on **the Apply (all displays)** button. This will automatically bring us to the wizard that walks us through configuring some display options for these fields.

Configuring fields

Once you choose to add fields to your view, you will automatically be prompted to configure your newly added fields. The fields will be presented to you alphabetically based on the field group. After you have configured them, you will be able to order them as you want, as described later in this section.

The first field we are presented with is the **Content: All taxonomy terms** field, as shown in the following screenshot:

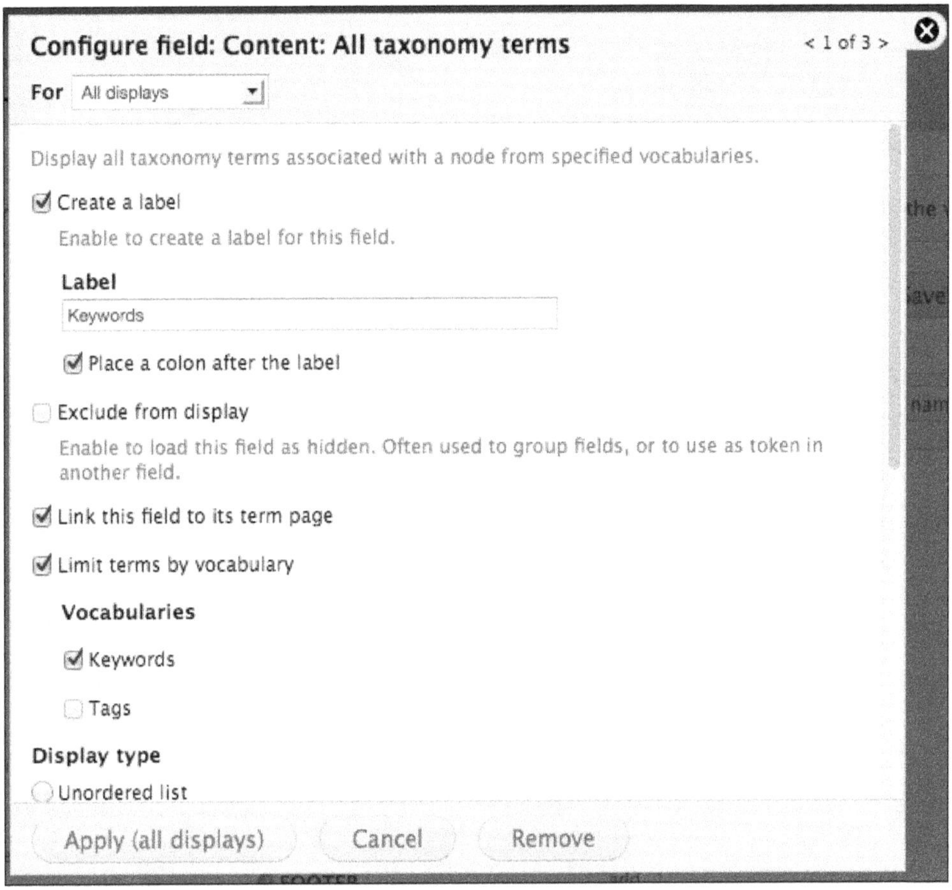

```
Configure field: Content: All taxonomy terms            < 1 of 3 >    ⊗

For  All displays        ▼

Display all taxonomy terms associated with a node from specified vocabularies.

☑ Create a label
   Enable to create a label for this field.

   Label
   Keywords

   ☑ Place a colon after the label

☐ Exclude from display
   Enable to load this field as hidden. Often used to group fields, or to use as token in
   another field.

☑ Link this field to its term page

☑ Limit terms by vocabulary

   Vocabularies

   ☑ Keywords

   ☐ Tags

Display type
○ Unordered list

   Apply (all displays)        Cancel        Remove
```

When configuring this field, we will make the following changes from the default values. The preceding screen is a screenshot after these changes have been made:

- Set **Label** to **Keywords**; this field will show terms from the **Keywords** vocabulary

- **Empty list text** under the **No Results Behavior** link will read **No terms available for this post**

- **Limit terms by vocabulary** and the **Keywords** vocabulary is selected

Then, click on **Apply (all displays)** to continue. The second field we are presented with is the **Content: Link to source** field, as shown in the following screenshot:

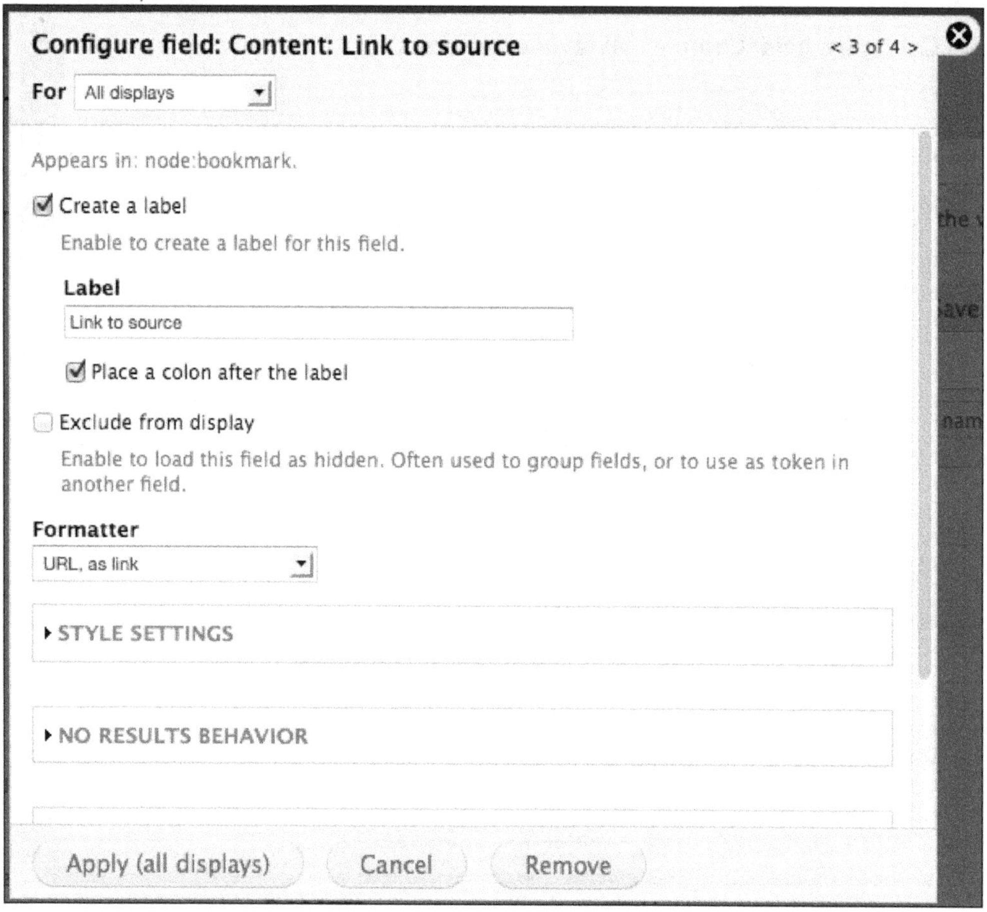

Configure field: Content: Link to source   < 3 of 4 >   ⊗

For All displays ▾

Appears in: node:bookmark.

☑ Create a label
   Enable to create a label for this field.

   Label
   Link to source

   ☑ Place a colon after the label

☐ Exclude from display
   Enable to load this field as hidden. Often used to group fields, or to use as token in
   another field.

Formatter
URL, as link ▾

▸ STYLE SETTINGS

▸ NO RESULTS BEHAVIOR

(Apply (all displays))   (Cancel)   (Remove)

In the **Formatter** drop-down menu, we select the **URL, as link** option. This specifies that the URL will work as a link to the stored location. For **Label**, we will use the same value we created when we added the node type earlier in this chapter.

Click on the **Apply (all displays)** button to configure the next field type.

The third field we are presented with is the **Node: Updated/commented date** field, as shown in the following screenshot:

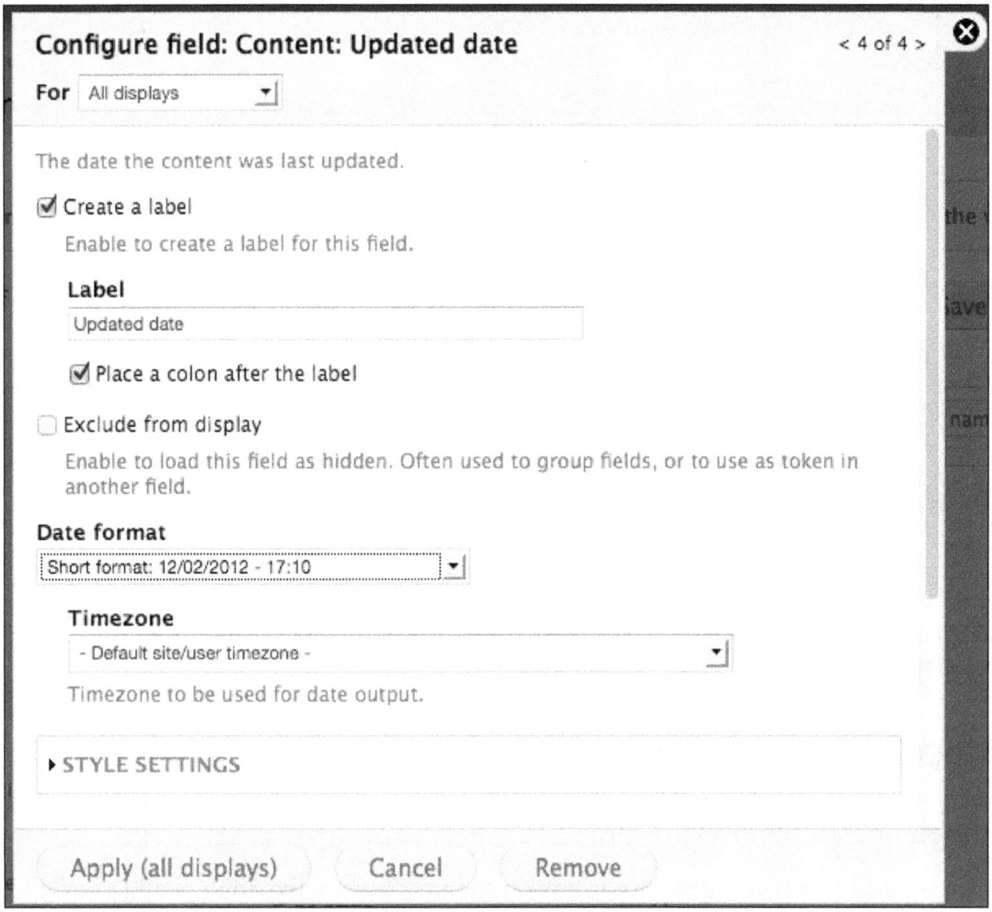

For this field, change **Date format** to **Short format**.

Click on the **Apply (all displays)** button to finish configuring these fields.

Then, click on the **Rearrange** icon as shown in the following screenshot. This allows us to reorder the fields within the view:

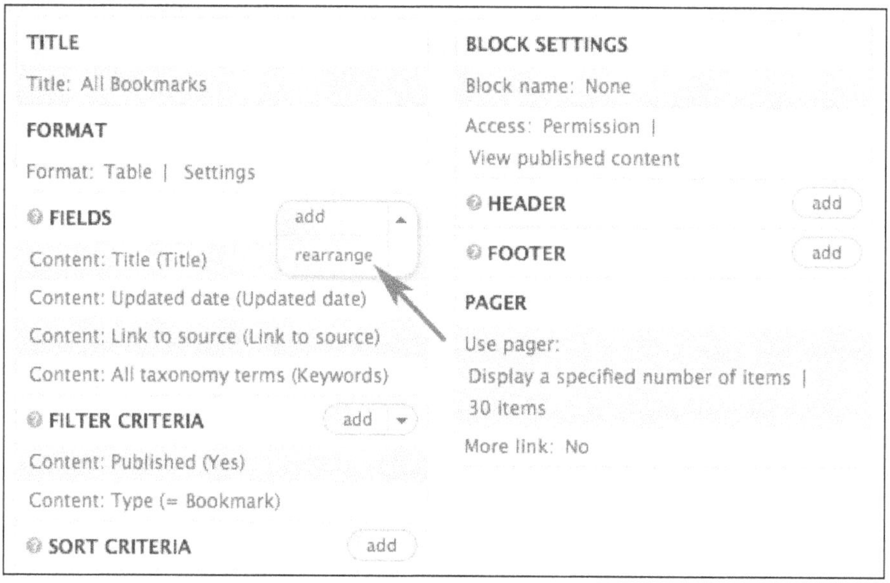

```
TITLE                                      BLOCK SETTINGS

Title: All Bookmarks                       Block name: None

FORMAT                                     Access: Permission |
                                           View published content
Format: Table | Settings
                                           ⊙ HEADER                    add
⊙ FIELDS                    add      ▲
                                           ⊙ FOOTER                    add
Content: Title (Title)      rearrange

Content: Updated date (Updated date)       PAGER

Content: Link to source (Link to source)   Use pager:

Content: All taxonomy terms (Keywords)     Display a specified number of items |
                                           30 items
⊙ FILTER CRITERIA           add      ▼
                                           More link: No
Content: Published (Yes)

Content: Type (= Bookmark)

⊙ SORT CRITERIA             add
```

Reorder the fields as shown in preceding screenshot, then click on the **Apply (all displays)** button to save the changes.

Step 2 (b) – adding/editing filters

Once we have finished configuring the fields for our views, you can see the **Auto preview** option of the view.

Since we added all our necessary filters on the first screen, we don't need to add or change any filters now. Adding filters will be covered again in *Chapter 4, Creating a Teacher Blog* and *Chapter 6, Creating the Student Blog*.

Step 2 (c) – adding/editing contextual filters (optional)

The contextual filters allow you to filter the content returned in a view through a value in the URL; for example, using arguments you can filter for content created by a specific user based on their username (http://yoursite.org/your-custom-view/harry would give you all posts by user harry and http://yoursite.org/your-custom-view/tom would give you all posts by user tom).

Adding arguments is not necessary for all views, and views can function perfectly well without arguments. Used effectively, however, arguments can add a level of flexibility that is not possible with the filters. The arguments are covered in *Chapter 13, Tracking Student Progress*.

Step 2 (d) – editing display format (optional)

Although we set the display format on the first screen, we need to change some of the default options for our example view.

Click on the **Settings** link next to **Table** in the **Format** section, as shown in the following screenshot by section **1**:

TITLE

Title: All Bookmarks

FORMAT

Format: Table | Settings   **1**

⚙ **FIELDS**   add   ▾

Content: Title (Title)

Content: Updated date (Updated date)

Content: Link to Source (Link to Source)

Content: All taxonomy terms (Keywords)

⚙ **FILTER CRITERIA**   add   ▾

Content: Published (Yes)

Content: Type (= Bookmark)

⚙ **SORT CRITERIA**   add

As shown in the following screenshot by section **1**, you need to select **DEFAULT SORT** for the **Updated date** field, and select **Descending** for the **DEFAULT SORT** order. This will show the most recently added or commented on bookmarks at the top of the table.

Page: Style options

For All displays ▾

Place fields into columns; you may combine multiple fields into the same column. If you do, the separator in the column specified will be used to separate the fields. Check the sortable box to make that column click sortable, and check the default sort radio to determine which column will be sorted by default, if any. You may control column order and field labels in the fields section.

FIELD	COLUMN	ALIGN	SEPARATOR	SORTABLE	DEFAULT ORDER	DEFAULT SORT	HIDE EMPTY COLUMN
Title	Title ▾	None ▾		☐		○	☐
Updated date	Updated date ▾	None ▾		☑	Descending ▾	⦿	☐
Link to source	Link to source ▾	None ▾		☐		○	☐
Keywords	Keywords ▾	None ▾					☐
None						○	

Grouping field Nr.1

- None - ▾

You may optionally specify a field by which to group the records. Leave blank to not group.

Apply (all displays)   Cancel

You also want to check the **Enable Drupal style "sticky" table headers (Javascript)** checkbox. This setting makes it such that the heading of the table scrolls down the page if the list goes longer than one screen.

☑ Enable Drupal style "sticky" table headers (Javascript)

(Sticky header effects will not be active for preview below, only on live output.)

2

Click on the **Apply (all displays)** button to save your settings. To see the effect of the new settings, look at the **Auto preview** pane shown in the following screenshot:

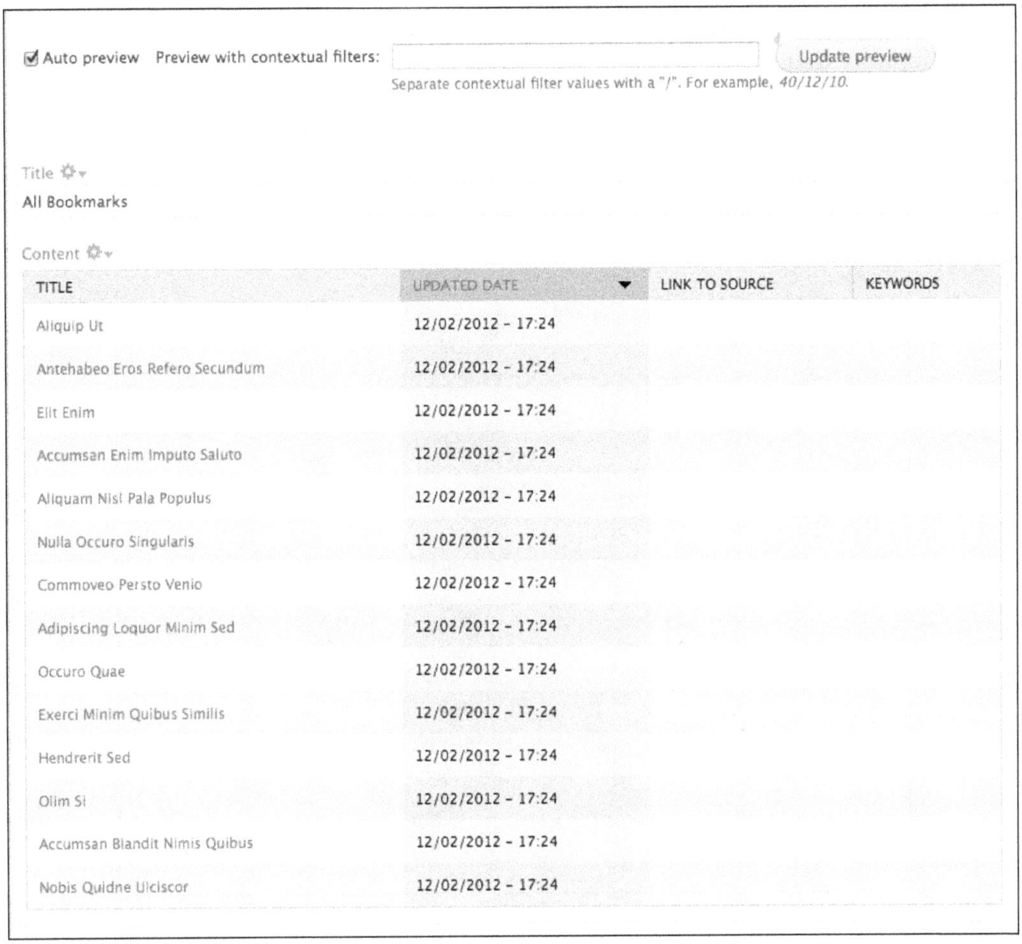

At this point, the view is functionally complete. However, there are some additional configuration options that can be used to fine-tune and enhance views.

Step 2 (e) – setting additional configuration options (optional)

As it is probably clear at this point, the Views module exposes an enormous amount of functionality that can be accessed via different configuration options. Although views can function perfectly well without adjusting these last few settings, these options help you to create views that make more sense for people using your site.

PAGE SETTINGS		▼ Advanced		
Path: /bookmarks/all		⊚ CONTEXTUAL FILTERS		add
Menu: No menu		⊚ RELATIONSHIPS		add
Access: Permission | View published content	1	NO RESULTS BEHAVIOR	3	add
⊚ HEADER	add	EXPOSED FORM		
	2	Exposed form in block: No		
⊚ FOOTER	add	Exposed form style: Basic | Settings		
PAGER		OTHER		
Use pager:		Machine Name: page		
Display a specified number of items |		Comment: No comment		
30 items		Use AJAX: No		
More link: No		Hide attachments in summary: No		
		Hide contextual links: No		
		Use aggregation: No		
		Query settings: Settings		
		Field Language: Current user's language		
		Caching: None		
		CSS class: None		
		Theme: Information		

- **Access**: This setting allows you to control access to the view based on user roles or user permissions.

- **HEADER** and **FOOTER**: These settings allow you to set headers and footers for your view.

- **NO RESULTS BEHAVIOUR**: This setting allows you to set a message if the view does not return any data. Setting empty text is recommended when you expose filters to end users, as user can potentially set filters that do not return any data.

Step 3 – defining multiple display types (optional)

When you add a display type to your view, you provide a method of displaying the data returned by your view. The most commonly used display types are pages and blocks. Any display types added to a view inherit the default settings; however, the display types can override the default settings if needed. In this way, for example, we can create a page display type that shows full nodes and a block display type that shows a table view of just the title. This section covers adding display types and overriding the values set in the default display.

To add a display type, click on the **Add** button under the **Displays** heading. The most commonly used options are **Page** and **Block**, and the different options will be discussed throughout the text as they become relevant. Refer to the following screenshot:

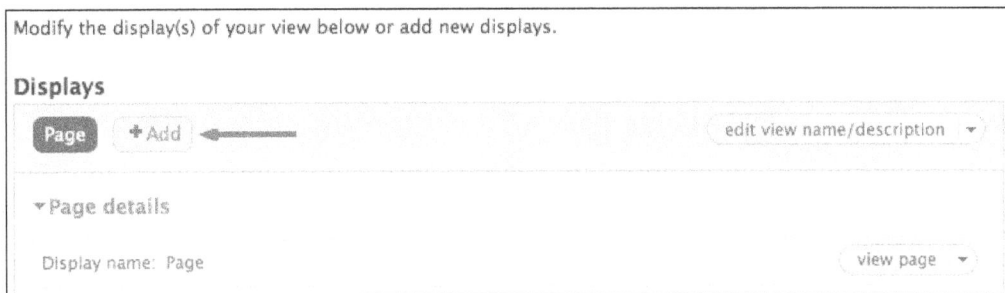

Modify the display(s) of your view below or add new displays.

Displays

| Page | + Add | ←——————— | | edit view name/description ▼ |

▾ Page details

Display name: Page   view page ▼

To begin, we will add a block display by selecting **Block** from the drop-down menu. This will create a block that we can then enable via **Administer | Structure | Blocks** or via the `admin/structure/block` page.

> The blocks are covered in more detail in *Chapter 14, Theming and User Interface Design*.
>
> To emphasize, the block we will create in this section will not be visible until we enable it via the `admin/structure/block` page.

Step 3 (a) – overriding the default values (optional)

For the next step, we need to remove some fields from the block view.

> Given that most blocks are displayed in the sidebar and that the width of a sidebar is limited, you usually want to limit the number of fields in blocks to three or fewer.

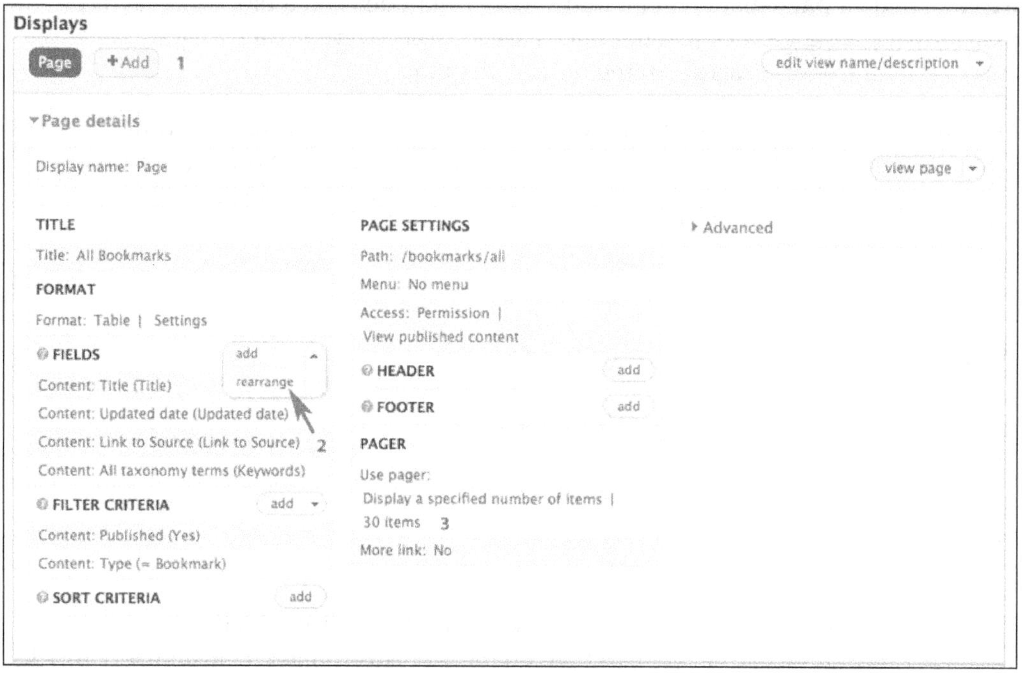

Displays

Page   + Add   1   edit view name/description ▾

▾ Page details

Display name: Page   view page ▾

TITLE   **PAGE SETTINGS**   ▸ Advanced

Title: All Bookmarks   Path: /bookmarks/all

FORMAT   Menu: No menu

Format: Table | Settings   Access: Permission |
                                   View published content
ℹ **FIELDS**   add   ▲
                                   ℹ **HEADER**   add
Content: Title (Title)   rearrange
                                   ℹ **FOOTER**   add
Content: Updated date (Updated date)

Content: Link to Source (Link to Source)   2   **PAGER**

Content: All taxonomy terms (Keywords)   Use pager:

ℹ **FILTER CRITERIA**   add   ▾   Display a specified number of items |

Content: Published (Yes)   30 items   3

Content: Type (= Bookmark)   More link: No

ℹ **SORT CRITERIA**   add

To remove fields, click on the rearrange icon as shown by section **2** in the preceding screenshot.

This will show the options shown in the following screenshot:

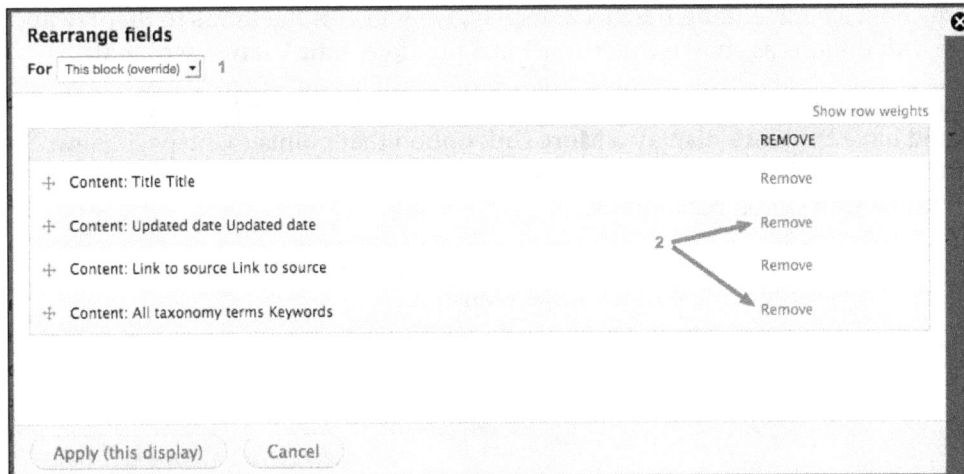

First, select **This block (override)** as indicated in section **1**; this sets specific values for the block display separate from the default display. Then, remove the **Node: Update/commented date** and **Taxonomy: All terms Keywords** fields by clicking on the icons indicated in section **2**.

A successful edit will look like the following screenshot:

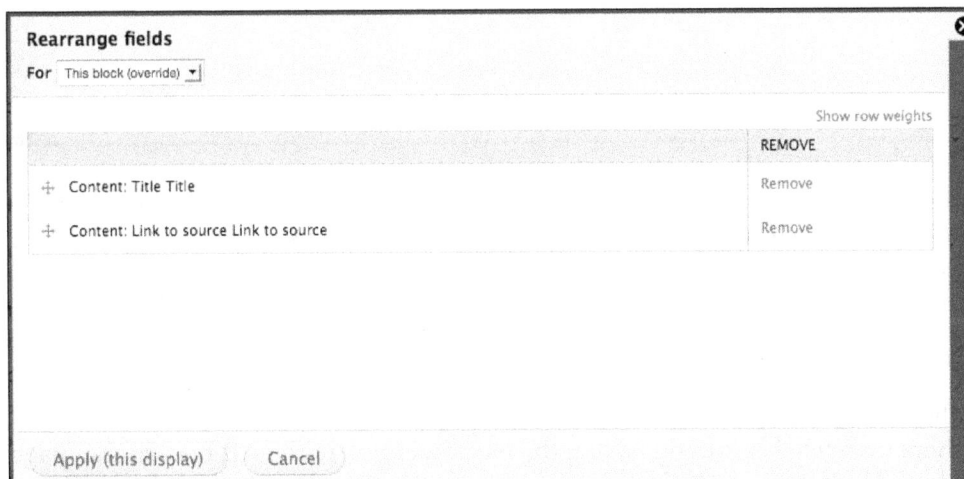

Click on the **Apply (this display)** button to make your changes.

For the final step in editing the block display, we will edit the **Items to display** and **More link** options as shown in section **3** in a previous **Edit View** screenshot.

In order to minimize the size of the block, we will set the **Items to display** option to **5** and have the block display a **More link** option that points to the page view. These settings will display the five most recent bookmarks and a link to the page that displays all stored bookmarks.

To start, click on the link next to **Display a specified number of items**. This brings up the options shown in the following screenshot:

As you can see in the preceding screenshot in section **1**, after you elect to override the default settings, the **Apply (all displays)** button switches to a **Apply (this display)** button. Once you have elected to override the default values, set the **Items to display** option to **5**, as shown in section **2**.

Click on the **Apply (this display)** button to make your changes.

For the final step, we will add a **More link** option to the block. This way, if there are more than five bookmarks saved, the block will link to the **All bookmarks** page. To add the link, click on the link as shown in section **1** in the following screenshot:

Displays

| Page | **Block*** | **+ Add** | | | edit view name/description ▾ |

▾ Block details

Display name: Block | | clone block ▾

TITLE

Title: All Bookmarks

FORMAT

Format: Table | Settings

⊚ *FIELDS* add ▾

Content: Title (Title)

Content: Link to source (Link to source)

⊚ **FILTER CRITERIA** add ▾

Content: Published (Yes)

Content: Type (= Bookmark)

⊚ **SORT CRITERIA** add

BLOCK SETTINGS

Block name: None

Access: Permission |
View published content

⊚ **HEADER** add

⊚ **FOOTER** add

PAGER

Use pager:

*Display a specified number of items |
5 items*

More link: No ◀━━━ 1

▸ Advanced

As we did earlier, select **This display (override)** as shown in section **2**. Then, select the option **Create more link** as shown in section **3** and click on the **Apply (this display)** button to save your changes.

Block: Add a more link to the bottom of the display. ⊗

For [This block (override) ▾] 2

☑ Create more link ◀━━━ 3

This will add a more link to the bottom of this view, which will link to the page view. If you have more than one page view, the link will point to the display specified in 'Link display' section under advanced. You can override the url at the link display setting.

☑ Display 'more' link only if there is more content

Leave this unchecked to display the 'more' link even if there are no more items to display.

More link text

more

The text to display for the more link.

(Apply (this display)) (Cancel)

Saving your view

Once you have set your defaults and specified the view display, you need to do the most important thing, that is, to save the view. None of the changes, settings, or configuration options are permanently stored until you click on the **Save** button. When you are building a view, you should get in the habit of regularly saving the view and then returning to it. This ensures that you don't lose any work.

Creating views – a summary

The Views module exposes an incredible range of functionality. At first glance, the amount of options exposed by views can seem overwhelming. At its core, though, using the Views module involves three central steps:

1. Add a view.
2. Set up the default view, including adding fields, filters, and arguments.
3. Add the display types.

Summary

In this chapter, we began by exploring our core Drupal installation. After taking a look around, we began to build our site.

The process of building our site included examining some steps that we will be revisiting frequently as we build our site. These steps include installing contributed modules and themes, adding user roles, adding and configuring content types, and adding views. Although these tasks have varying levels of complexity, the different aspects of site development have some steps that will be repeated as we design the site.

Now, with the foundation in place, we are ready to begin building our a flexible platform to support teaching and learning. The first three chapters of this book covered the details of making a site live, how the site is organized, and also introduced some general Drupal concepts and terminology.

In the coming chapters, we will continue working with the Drupal core and selected contributed modules, as we build a student and teacher blog. Brew some coffee and turn off the phone; it's time to get into it!

4
Creating a Teacher Blog

This chapter covers the details of creating a teacher blog. In this chapter, you will:

- Set up a text (WYSIWYG) editor
- Create two content types: one named **teacher blog** and another named **assignments**
- Assign rights to use the text editor and the new content types
- Create views to display the teacher blog posts and assignments

As a part of this chapter, we will cover adding content into the instructor blog. Once finished, this blog can be used to communicate notes, facts, assignments, and other information to students, parents, and colleagues.

It should be noted that the instructions in this chapter cover many administrative details required in the setup that, once completed, are rarely touched while using the site. The steps covered in this chapter create the tools that will power the instructor blog. Many of these steps are done once and are never carried out again. However, taking the time to do them right, and understanding how to go back and adjust them, as needed, will ensure that you have the ability to make your site do what you need it to do.

Installing the text editor

To get started using the text editor, navigate to the CKEditor project page at `http://drupal.org/project/ckeditor`.

Uploading and enabling CKEditor

To use the CKEditor module, we need to follow these steps:

1. As described in *Chapter 3*, *Getting Started*, download the module, extract the code, and then upload it into the `sites/all/modules` directory.

> In this site, we are using CKEditor for the text editor. The support for CKEditor within the Drupal community is solid, which is one of the factors to consider when selecting a module. With that said, other options that can be used include the WYMeditor, TinyMCE, and BUI editors.

2. Unlike most modules, installing the CKEditor has one additional step: you need to download the text editor from the CKEditor site `http://ckeditor.com/download`. You want to get the current release, which will be listed as shown in the following screenshot:

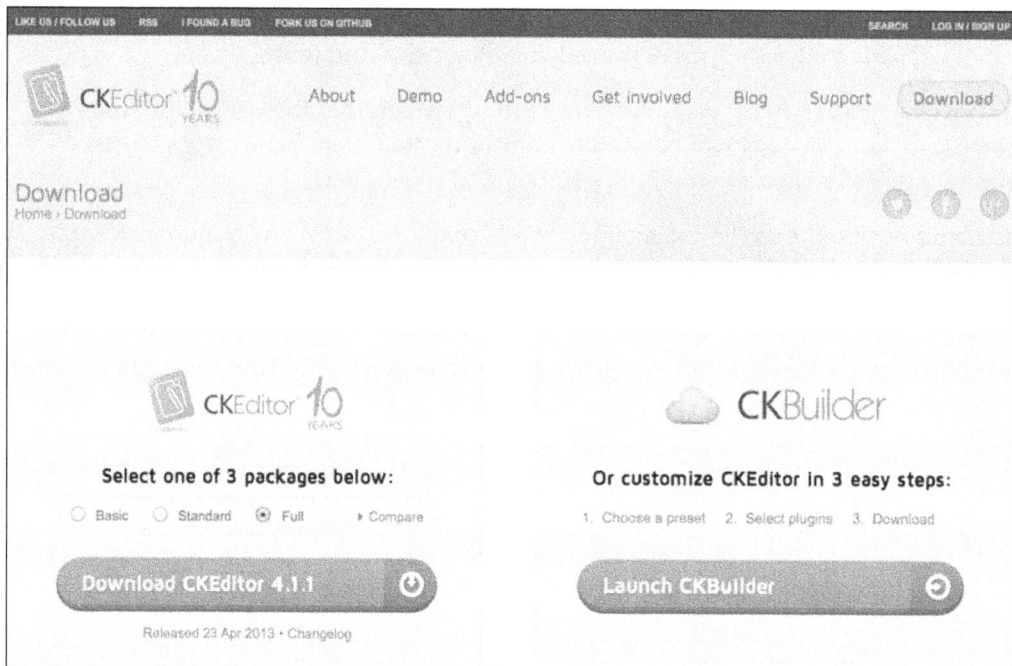

3. Download the files from the CKEditor site and extract them. Then, as shown in the following screenshot, add the new folder to the site's `libraries` folder. You will probably need to create this directory.

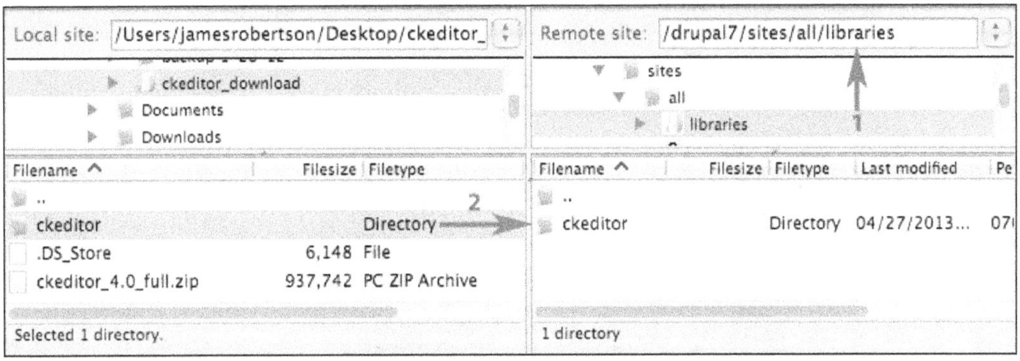

Local site:	/Users/jamesrobertson/Desktop/ckeditor_	‡	Remote site:	/drupal7/sites/all/libraries	‡

			▼ sites
▶ ckeditor_download			▼ all
▶ Documents			▶ libraries	↑
▶ Downloads				1

Filename ^	Filesize	Filetype		Filename ^	Filesize	Filetype	Last modified	Pe
..			2	..				
ckeditor		Directory →		ckeditor		Directory	04/27/2013...	07
.DS_Store	6,148	File						
ckeditor_4.0_full.zip	937,742	PC ZIP Archive						

Selected 1 directory.		1 directory

4. As in the previous screenshot, the code downloaded from `http://ckeditor.com/download` goes into `sites/all/libraries`.

5. Once you have uploaded the code, click the **Modules** link, or navigate to `admin/modules` and enable the CKEditor module, as shown in the following screenshot:

▼ USER INTERFACE

ENABLED	NAME	VERSION	DESCRIPTION	OPERATIONS
☑	CKEditor	7.x-1.11	Enables CKEditor (WYSIWYG HTML editor) for use instead of plain text fields.	🔘 Help 🔍 Permissions ⚙ Configure

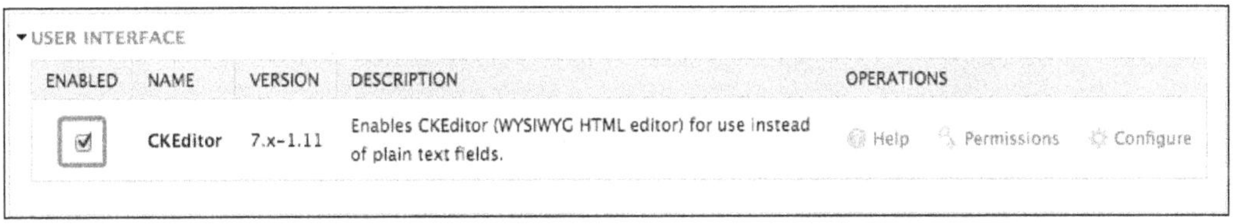

6. Click on the **Save** configuration button to finish enabling the module:

Home » Administration » Configuration » Content authoring
CKEditor ✿

The CKEditor module allows Drupal to replace textarea fields with CKEditor. CKEditor is an online rich text editor that can be embedded inside web pages. It is a WYSIWYG editor which means that the text edited in it looks as similar as possible to the results end users will see after the document gets published. It brings to the Web popular editing features found in desktop word processors such as Microsoft Word and OpenOffice.org Writer. CKEditor is truly lightweight and does not require any kind of installation on the client computer.

Useful links: CKEditor website | Developer's Guide | User's Guide.

Profiles are linked with input format types. A CKEditor profile defines which buttons are available in the editor, how the editor is displayed, and a few other editor functions. The Global Profile stores some general information about CKEditor.

Profiles

PROFILE	INPUT FORMAT	OPERATIONS
Advanced	Filtered HTML	edit clone delete
Full	Full HTML	edit clone delete

Create a new profile

Global settings

PROFILE	OPERATIONS
CKEditor Global Profile	edit

7. By default, the CKEditor module creates two **Profiles** based on **Text formats**. The CKEditor will be added to all text fields that use that text format. You can change the CKEditor options based on the text format, but the default options are sufficient for our needs in this case. We will set the permissions for who will be allowed to use the CKEditor by setting permissions on the text formats.

> The CKEditor has many settings that can be adjusted, and addressing the full range of settings goes beyond the scope of this book. For more information, including links both to a *Developer's Guide* and a *User's Guide*, see `http://docs.cksource.com/Main_Page`.

Setting the proper text formats

Text formats control the HTML tags and other text handling that people can use when creating content on your site. Setting your text formats is an essential part of running your site securely.

> Drupal allows you to grant some users permission to enter either PHP code or full HTML tags directly into a post. If these rights are granted at all, they should only be granted to a small number of very trusted users, as sloppy or malicious use of PHP code or certain HTML tags could compromise a site.

To set the text formats, click the **Configuration | Text formats** link, or navigate to `admin/config/content/formats`:

Home » Administration » Configuration » Content authoring

Text formats ⚙

Text formats define the HTML tags, code, and other formatting that can be used when entering text. **Improper text format configuration is a security risk.** Learn more on the Filter module help page.

Text formats are presented on content editing pages in the order defined on this page. The first format available to a user will be selected by default.

➕ Add text format

Show row weights

NAME	ROLES	OPERATIONS	
⊹ Filtered HTML	anonymous user, authenticated user, administrator	configure	disable
⊹ Full HTML	administrator	configure	disable
⊹ Plain text	All roles may use this format	configure	

Save changes

As shown in the preceding screenshot, click the configure link for **Filtered HTML**.

This brings you to the **Filtered HTML** input format page at `admin/config/content/formats/filtered_html`.

Home » Administration » Configuration » Content authoring » Text formats

Filtered HTML ⚙

A text format contains filters that change the user input, for example stripping out malicious HTML or making URLs clickable. Filters are executed from top to bottom and the order is important, since one filter may prevent another filter from doing its job. For example, when URLs are converted into links before disallowed HTML tags are removed, all links may be removed. When this happens, the order of filters may need to be re-arranged.

Name *

Filtered HTML   Machine name: filtered_html

Roles

☐ anonymous user

☑ authenticated user   1

☑ administrator

☐ teacher

☐ student

Enabled filters

☑ Limit allowed HTML tags

☐ Display any HTML as plain text

☑ Convert line breaks into HTML (i.e.
 and <p>)

☑ Convert URLs into links

☑ Correct faulty and chopped off HTML

Filter processing order

Show row weights

✛ Convert URLs into links

✛ Limit allowed HTML tags

✛ Convert line breaks into HTML (i.e.
 and <p>)

✛ Correct faulty and chopped off HTML

Filter settings

Limit allowed HTML tags
Enabled

Convert URLs into links
Enabled

2 ➡ **Allowed HTML tags**

<a> <b> <blockquote>
 <caption> <center> <code> <col> <colgroup> <d

A list of HTML tags that can be used. JavaScript event attributes, JavaScript URLs, and CSS are always stripped.

☑ Display basic HTML help in long filter tips

☐ Add rel="nofollow" to all links

Save configuration

Assigning user rights via roles

Within a Drupal site, individual users can be granted different roles. Within each role, the site administrator can assign different privileges. Some of these privileges relate to access control, while other privileges relate to accessing functionality.

> In *Chapter 3, Getting Started*, you created the **teacher** role. In this chapter, we will assign privileges to that role to allow teachers to access CKEditor and create assignments and teacher blog posts for the teacher blog as needed. Once these rights have been tuned, any user granted the **teacher** role will have the rights to run an effective teacher blog.

Understanding roles and how they work

In a Drupal site, role assignments are cumulative. If a user is a member of two or more roles, they have the collected rights of all of these roles.

Additionally, all users belong to the **authenticated user** role; this role is frequently used to establish basic rights for all users, with more advanced privileges being granted via other roles. In this site, we will only assign basic privileges to the **authenticated user** role. The majority of users of the site will belong to either of the **teacher** or **student** roles that we created in *Chapter 3, Getting Started*.

Home » Administration » Configuration » Content authoring » Text formats

Filtered HTML ✷

A text format contains filters that change the user input, for example stripping out malicious HTML or making URLs clickable. Filters are executed from top to bottom and the order is important, since one filter may prevent another filter from doing its job. For example, when URLs are converted into links before disallowed HTML tags are removed, all links may be removed. When this happens, the order of filters may need to be re-arranged.

Name *

Filtered HTML   Machine name: filtered_html

Roles

☐ anonymous user

☑ authenticated user

☑ administrator

☐ teacher

☐ student

As shown in the previous screenshot, assign the authenticated user role permissions to access the **Filtered HTML** text format.

For our purposes, the default options under **Enabled filters** are adequate.

In the **Allowed HTML** tags field under the **Limit allowed HTML** tags, as indicated by **2** in the screenshot that showed the Filtered HTML input format page, enter the following list of HTML tags:

```
<a> <b> <blockquote> <br> <caption> <center> <code> <col>
<colgroup> <dd> <del> <div> <dl> <dt> <em> <font> <h1> <h2> <h3>
<h4> <h5> <h6> <hr> <i> <img> <li> <ol> <p> <span> <strong> <sub>
<sup> <table> <tbody> <td> <tfoot> <th> <thead> <tr> <u> <ul>
```

Click on the **Save configuration** button to save your changes.

This list of tags is fairly permissive and will allow users a great degree of freedom over the page layout. It will also work well with the text editor and will not pose any security risks.

> Input filters mostly exist for security reasons, and security is generally balanced against ease of use. Some modules add input filters that make adding their features to content easier. The previous list does not contain any of the tags that can be used to run malicious code (also known as hacking your site); using these HTML tags, you can create tables, change font appearance, and do many more things.

Now that we have enabled the CKEditor and created a safe input format, we are ready to create the first two content types that will power the Teacher blog.

> For a full list and explanation of HTML tags, look at the tag list from W3Schools: http://www.w3schools.com/tags/default.asp. For an overview of HTML tags and security, visit: http://www. feedparser.org/docs/html-sanitization.html.

Creating content types for the teacher blog

In this section, we will outline how to create two content types used in the teacher blog. This section will refer to the process outlined in *Chapter 3, Getting Started*. When creating a content type you will need to:

- Create the content type
- Add fields to the content type (optional—not all content types require additional fields)
- Assign a taxonomy to the content type (optional—not all content types will be organized using taxonomy)
- Assign permissions to the content type

The blog post content type

The blog post content type will be one of the publishing tools available to users in this site. To create this content type, click on the **Structure | Content types** link, or navigate to `admin/structure/types`.

As described in *Chapter 3, Getting Started*, to create a new content type, click on the **Add content type** link.

For the **Identification** section, use the following values:

- **Name**: `Blog post`
- **Description**: `Create a blog post`

In the **Submission form** settings section, the **Explanation or submission guidelines** can be set to: **Create your blog post. Enliven your post with relevant details, and describe these details with sumptuous prose.**

> The values of the **Explanation or submission guidelines** section are somewhat arbitrary; while this section can be used to give instructions, it can also be used to have fun. Obviously, the rules of civil and appropriate discourse apply but you can use these instructions to add a touch of unexpected flavor.

In the **Workflow** settings, set default settings to **Published**. In the **Comment** settings section, set the default to **Open** and configure the comment displays as described in *Chapter 3, Getting Started*. Click on the **Save and add fields** button to create the content type.

Adding fields and assigning a taxonomy

On the **Manage Fields** tab, you can add a copy of an existing field to the content type. Choose **Term reference: field_keywords (Keywords)** from the **Field to share** drop-down list. Click on the **Save** button, and you can configure the field in the same way you did in *Chapter 3, Getting Started*.

Home » Administration » Structure » Content types » Blog post

Blog post ⚙

| EDIT | MANAGE FIELDS | MANAGE DISPLAY | COMMENT FIELDS | COMMENT DISPLAY |

Show row weights

LABEL	MACHINE NAME	FIELD TYPE	WIDGET	OPERATIONS
✛ Title	title	Node module element		
✛ Body	body	Long text and summary	Text area with a summary	edit delete
✛ **Add new field**				
Label		- Select a field type - ▼ Type of data to store.	- Select a widget - ▼ Form element to edit the data.	
✛ **Add existing field**				
➡ Keywords Label		Term reference: field_keywords (Keywords) ▼ Field to share	Autocomplete term widget (tagging) ▼ Form element to edit the data.	

Save

Assigning permissions

Click on **People** | **Permissions** | **Roles** link or navigate to `admin/user/rolesadmin/people/permissions/roles`. Click on the **edit permissions** link for the **teacher** role.

> 💡 Every time we create a new content type, we will need to assign user roles permissions to use the content type. The permissions for content types are usually assigned via the node module.

PERMISSION		TEACHER
Blog post: Create new content	◀▬▬▬▬	☑
Blog post: Edit own content	◀▬▬▬	☑
Blog post: Edit any content		☐
Blog post: Delete own content	◀▬▬▬	☑
Blog post: Delete any content		☐

> Assigning a role the **Administer nodes** permission will allow all users in that role to add, edit, or delete all posts of all content types. Administer nodes permissions should only be assigned to *highly-trusted* users. The permissions described in this section need to be assigned individually for all content types.

Content types usually have five permissions. For every individual content type, the following permissions can be assigned:

- **Create new**: This permission allows a user to create nodes of a specific content type
- **Edit own**: This permission allows user to edit posts they have authored
- **Edit any**: This permission allows users to edit any post, regardless of who authored it
- **Delete own**: This permission allows users to delete posts they have authored
- **Delete any**: This permission allows users to delete any post, regardless of who created it

As shown in the preceding screenshot, we want to assign the **teacher** role permissions to **Create new content**, **Edit own content**, and **Delete own content** for the blog post. Click the **Save permissions** button to save the permissions.

Hey! Why not use the blog module?

Drupal comes with a blog module. Although it could be used for this site, we are opting not to use it because of how we are structuring the blog. Unlike more traditional blogs, we will be configuring this blog to make it easy to include audio, video, and images, as well as text. A person's blog will contain the full range of content they create.

Additionally, Drupal's blog module has some features that work better for single user or multiple-user blogs than for this site. These features include some default displays that list all blog posts. For this site, we will be using views to create displays for our content; this allows for a greater degree of flexibility than the blog module. So, rather than trying to override the default behavior of the blog module, we will sidestep the issue entirely.

Creating the assignment content type

To create assignments, we will create another content type. This content type will be very similar to the blog post content type we just created, with one exception: assignments will contain a **Date** field to allow teachers to specify a due date. As described earlier in this chapter and in *Chapter 3, Getting Started*, we need to follow these four steps:

1. Create the content type
2. Add fields to the content type
3. Assign a taxonomy to the content type
4. Assign permissions to the content type

Getting started – installing modules

To add and display date fields, we need to download and install the **Date** and **Calendar** modules. Navigate to the project pages for **Date** and **Calendar** at `http://drupal.org/project/date` and `http://drupal.org/project/calendar`.

1. As described in *Chapter 3, Getting Started*, upload the modules into the `sites/all/modules` directory. Then, click on the **Modules** link, or navigate to `admin/modules` as shown in the following screenshot:

▼ DATE/TIME

ENABLED	NAME	VERSION	DESCRIPTION	OPERATIONS
☑	Calendar	7.x-3.4+1-dev	Views plugin to display views containing dates as Calendars. Requires: Views (enabled), Chaos tools (enabled), Date API (enabled), Date Views (disabled)	
☑	Date	7.x-2.6	Makes date/time fields available. Requires: Date API (enabled) Required by: Date All Day (disabled), Date Context (disabled), Date Migration (disabled), Date Repeat Field (disabled), Date Migration Example (disabled), Date Tools (disabled)	
☐	Date All Day	7.x-2.6	Adds 'All Day' functionality to date fields, including an 'All Day' theme and 'All Day' checkboxes for the Date select and Date popup widgets. Requires: Date API (enabled), Date (disabled)	
☑	Date API	7.x-2.6	A Date API that can be used by other modules. Required by: Date Views (disabled), Calendar (disabled), Date (disabled), Date All Day (disabled), Date Context (disabled), Date Migration (disabled), Date Repeat API (disabled), Date Repeat Field (disabled), Date Migration Example (disabled), Date Popup (disabled), Date Tools (disabled)	
☐	Date Context	7.x-2.6	Adds an option to the Context module to set a context condition based on the value of a date field. Requires: Date (disabled), Date API (enabled), Context (missing)	
☐	Date Migration	7.x-2.6	Provides support for importing into date fields with the Migrate module. Requires: Migrate (missing), Date (disabled), Date API (enabled) Required by: Date Migration Example (disabled)	
☑	Date Popup	7.x-2.6	Enables jquery popup calendars and time entry widgets for selecting dates and times. Requires: Date API (enabled)	
☐	Date Repeat API	7.x-2.6	A Date Repeat API to calculate repeating dates and times from iCal rules. Requires: Date API (enabled) Required by: Date Repeat Field (disabled), Date Migration Example (disabled)	
☐	Date Repeat Field	7.x-2.6	Creates the option of Repeating date fields and manages Date fields that use the Date Repeat API. Requires: Date API (enabled), Date (disabled), Date Repeat API (disabled) Required by: Date Migration Example (disabled)	
☐	Date Tools	7.x-2.6	Tools to import and auto-create dates and calendars. Requires: Date (disabled), Date API (enabled)	
☑	Date Views	7.x-2.6	Views integration for date fields and date functionality. Requires: Date API (enabled), Views (enabled), Chaos tools (enabled) Required by: Calendar (disabled)	

2. Enable the **Calendar, Date, Date API, Date Popup**, and **Date Views** modules. These modules are all part of the **Date** and **Calendar** modules.

3. Click on the **Save configuration** button to save the settings, and enable the modules.

4. You will receive a message stating that you need to set up the site's time zone and first day of the week settings and date format settings. These were set when you installed Drupal, but you may follow the links to further customize if you wish.

The assignment content type

Navigate to **Structure | Content types**, or `admin/structure/types`. Click on the **Add content type** link.

For the **Identification** section, use the following values:

- **Name**: Assignment
- **Description**: Add an assignment

In the **Submission form settings** section, the **Explanation or submission guidelines** can be set to: **Create an assignment. Remember to set a due date**.

In the **Workflow settings** section, set default settings to **Published**. In the **Comment settings** section, set the default to **Open**, and configure the **Comment Display** section as described in *Chapter 3, Getting Started*. Click on the **Save and add fields** button to create the content type.

Adding fields

Now that we have created the **Assignment** content type, we need to add a **Date** field to specify a due date for assignments.

We will then a add a new field, as shown in the following screenshot:

Home » Administration » Structure » Content types » Assignment

Assignment ⚙

| EDIT | MANAGE FIELDS | MANAGE DISPLAY | COMMENT FIELDS | COMMENT DISPLAY |

✅ The content type *Assignment* has been added.

Show row weights

LABEL	MACHINE NAME	FIELD TYPE	WIDGET	OPERATIONS
✛ Title	title	Node module element		
✛ Body	body	Long text and summary	Text area with a summary	edit delete
✛ **Add new field**				
Due date	field_due_date [Edit]	Date ▾	Pop-up calendar ▾	
Label		Type of data to store.	Form element to edit the data.	
✛ **Add existing field**				
		- Select an existing field - ▾	- Select a widget - ▾	
Label		Field to share	Form element to edit the data.	

Save

Enter the following values:

- **Label**: Due date
- **Field name**: due_date
- **Field type**: Date

Selecting the field type exposes the form element to edit the data option; select the **Pop-up calendar** option.

Click on the **Save** button. This brings up the final settings screen for Date fields, pictured in the following screenshot:

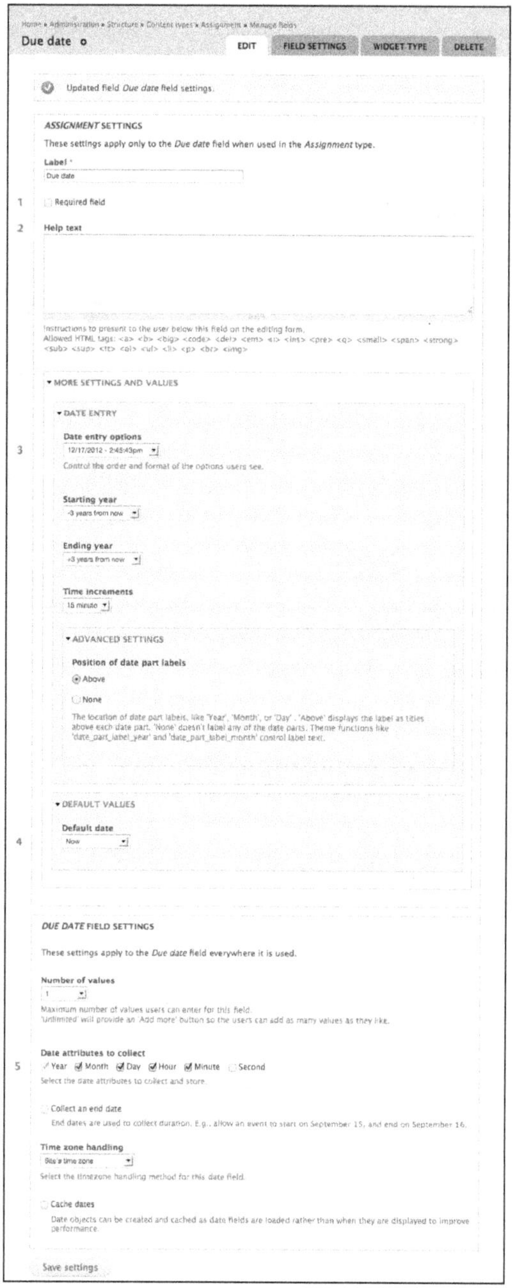

For most uses, including this one, the default settings will work perfectly well. However, we want to highlight five places on this screen that allow you to customize the **Date** fields in order to make them do exactly what you want. In the preceding screenshot, you will see that we have divided the **Edit** section into five sections namely, **1**, **2**, **3**, **4**, and **5**. Let's review these sections:

- **Required field** (**1**): As all assignments have due dates, we set this to required.
- **Help text** (**2**): The text here will be shown to users as they are creating assignments. For this example, we can use `Enter the date and time when the assignment will be due`.
- **Date entry options** (**3**): The default value is in military, or 24 hour, time. In some cases, users are more comfortable using A.M./P.M. to indicate times.
- **Default date**: Set to **Now** (**4**). This will autofill the form with the current time, which helps guide users as they fill it out.
- **Date attributes to collect** (**5**): The items specified here will be presented to users as options when they create content. For example, if you only want to collect a day, you would set the granularity to **Year**, **Month**, and **Day**. In this example, as we want to set a specific time when assignments are due, we opt to include **Hours** and **Minutes**.

Once you have adjusted the settings, click on the **Save settings** button in order to save your changes.

Ordering fields

After saving your field settings, you will be returned to the **MANAGE FIELDS** page.

The fields can be adjusted via drag-and-drop. Drag the **Due date** label to be second on the page. Click on the **Save** button in order to submit the form and save the changes.

Assigning a taxonomy

As described in *Chapter 3, Getting Started,* and earlier in this chapter, use the **Keyword** taxonomy to categorize assignments.

For a greater degree of control, we can create an additional taxonomy for assignments named **Type of Assignment**. This would allow teachers to apply keywords to the assignments separate from the keywords used for other content. While this is not necessary, increased organization can be useful in larger sites.

Assigning permissions

As described earlier in this chapter, assign the **Teacher** role permissions to **Create new content**, **Delete own content**, and **Edit own content** for the **Assignment** content type.

Click on the **Save permissions** button to save the permissions.

Sample users and testing

Now, we have installed and configured the CKEditor, created two content types for the instructor blog, and assigned permissions to those content types. The next steps involve creating a test user for the instructor role and creating some sample content.

Adding new users

Click on the **People** link, or navigate to admin/people. Click on the **Add user** link, which brings you to admin/people/create.

Home » Administration » People

People ○

LIST   PERMISSIONS

This web page allows administrators to register new users. Users' e-mail addresses and usernames must be unique.

Username *

test_teacher

Spaces are allowed; punctuation is not allowed except for periods, hyphens, apostrophes, and underscores.

E-mail address *

test_teacher@yourdomain.com

A valid e-mail address. All e-mails from the system will be sent to this address. The e-mail address is not made public and will only be used if you wish to receive a new password or wish to receive certain news or notifications by e-mail.

Password *

....   Password strength: Weak

Confirm password *

....   Passwords match: yes

> To make your password stronger:
> - Make it at least 6 characters
> - Add uppercase letters
> - Add numbers
> - Add punctuation

Provide a password for the new account in both fields.

Status

○ Blocked

◉ Active

Roles

☑ authenticated user

☐ administrator

☑ teacher

☐ student

☐ Notify user of new account

(Create new account)

When adding a new user, you will need to provide **Username**, **E-mail address**, and **Password**. You will also have the opportunity to add the user to a role. When adding users, you can also opt to send them an introductory e-mail; the content of this e-mail can be edited by clicking **Configuration | Account settings** link, or by navigating to `admin/config/people/accounts`.

Click on the **Create new account** button to submit the form and create the new user account.

> Drupal does not put restrictions on usernames or passwords by default, although it will estimate the strength of your password. Users can use their real name or a screen name. There are contributed modules, such as Password Policy (http://drupal.org/project/password_policy) and Real Name (http://drupal.org/project/realname) that can enforce your chosen policies.

Section summary

In the first section of this chapter, we have set up the basic functionality that will power the teacher blog. We have:

- Installed and configured CKEditor and the text editor
- Installed the modules required to create the teacher blog
- Created two content types for the teacher blog
- Assigned permissions to allow users in the teacher role to use the assignment and blog content types
- Added a test user to the teacher role

To finish creating the Teacher blog, we need to complete two remaining steps:

1. Add some sample blog posts and assignments.
2. Create two views: one to display all posts from users in the teacher role and a second view to display assignments.

Adding sample content

To begin adding sample content, log in as test_teacher, the sample user we created earlier in this chapter.

Once you have logged in as test_teacher, click on the **Create Content** link as shown in the following screenshot:

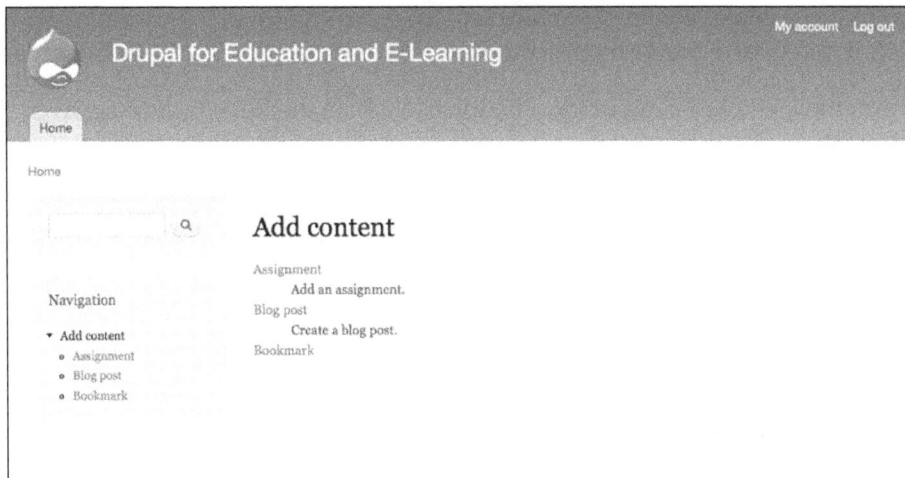

To add an assignment, click on the **Assignment** link. To add a blog post, click on the
Blog post link. For this example, we will create an assignment.

To add an assignment, we need to complete the form shown in the preceding screenshot; the **Create assignment** form is what we created earlier in this chapter.

When you have entered content into the form, click on the **Save** button to save your content.

Add two additional assignments and two or three sample blog posts. These sample posts will allow us to see how the views that we will create in the next section will organize and display our content.

Views for the teacher blog and assignments

Now that we have created some sample content, we are ready to complete the final step in creating the teacher blog: adding a view to display the content types in one place. As discussed in detail in *Chapter 3, Getting Started*, we need to complete the following three main steps to create a view:

1. Add a view. We need to do the following:
    - Describe the view
    - Select the type of data and filters
    - Select a display type
    - Set display type options
    - Set the display format

2. Edit the view. We need to do the following:
    - Add fields
    - Add/edit filters
    - Add/edit contextual filters (optional)
    - Edit display format (optional)
    - Set additional configuration options (optional)

3. Define multiple display types (optional)
4. Override the default values (optional)

> *Chapter 3, Getting Started*, provides a detailed overview of adding views.

In this section, we will create two views: one for the teacher blog and a second for assignments.

The teacher blog view

To get started, click on the **Structure | Views** link, or navigate to admin/structure/ views.

Adding a view

Click on the **Add new view** link to add a view. Enter the following values:

- **View name**: teacher_blog
- **Description**: All posts to be displayed in the teacher blog.
- The next section after **Description** should read: Show Content of type Blog post tagged with [blank] sorted by Newest first
- Check the box next to **Create a page**
- **Path**: teacher-blog
- **Items to display**: 10
- Check the box next to **Use a pager**
- Click on the **Continue and edit** button to continue

Editing the view

Once we have selected the view type and named the view, we can begin setting the values for the default view.

Adding fields to the view

This view will display full nodes; therefore, we don't actually need to add any fields to it. Next, we will begin adding filters.

Adding filters

For this view, we have already added two filters. The first filter selects only published nodes; the second filter selects specific content types; and the final view will select only content created by users in the teacher role.

To add this last filter, we have to add a Relationship. **Relationships** make other kinds of information about a node available to a view. In this case, we need to make information about the author of the node available to the view.

1. Under the **Advanced** options, click on the **add** link next to the **RELATIONSHIPS** heading as shown in the following screenshot:

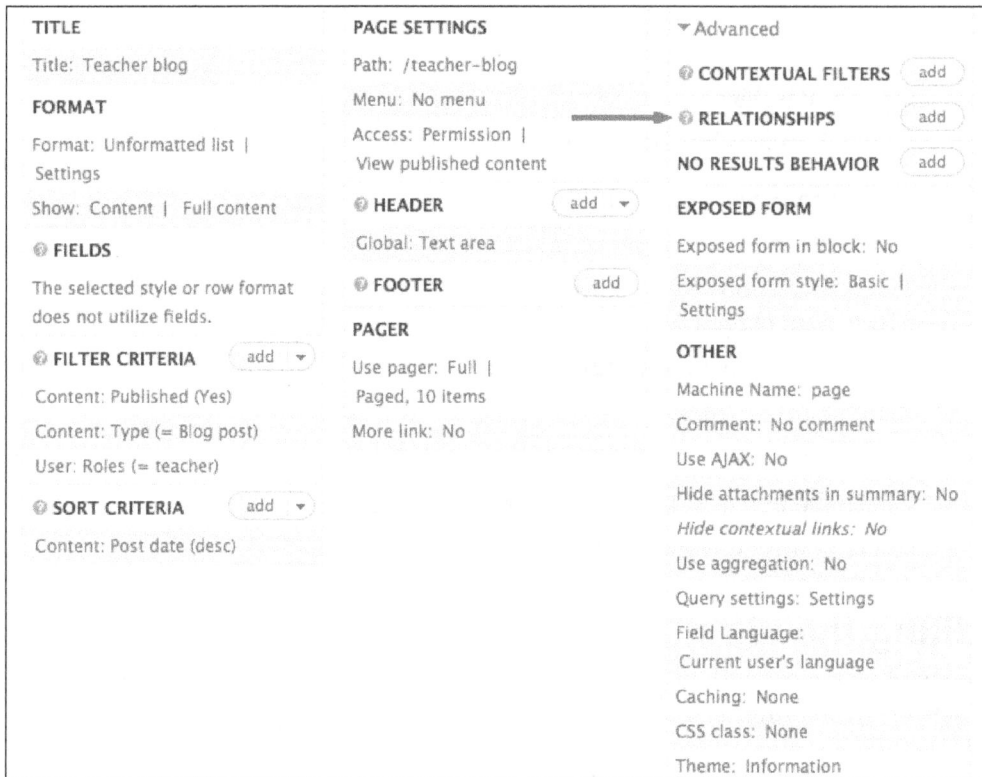

TITLE	PAGE SETTINGS	▾ Advanced
Title: Teacher blog	Path: /teacher-blog	⊚ CONTEXTUAL FILTERS (add)
FORMAT	Menu: No menu	⊚ RELATIONSHIPS (add)
Format: Unformatted list | Settings	Access: Permission | View published content	NO RESULTS BEHAVIOR (add)
Show: Content | Full content	⊚ **HEADER** (add ▾)	**EXPOSED FORM**
⊚ **FIELDS**	Global: Text area	Exposed form in block: No
The selected style or row format does not utilize fields.	⊚ **FOOTER** (add)	Exposed form style: Basic | Settings
⊚ **FILTER CRITERIA** (add ▾)	**PAGER**	**OTHER**
Content: Published (Yes)	Use pager: Full | Paged, 10 items	Machine Name: page
Content: Type (= Blog post)	More link: No	Comment: No comment
User: Roles (= teacher)		Use AJAX: No
⊚ **SORT CRITERIA** (add ▾)		Hide attachments in summary: No
Content: Post date (desc)		*Hide contextual links: No*
		Use aggregation: No
		Query settings: Settings
		Field Language: Current user's language
		Caching: None
		CSS class: None
		Theme: Information

2. Check the box next to **Content: Author**, and put **Author** in the **Identifier** box. Then, click on **Apply (all displays)**.

3. Next, we'll add the **User: Roles** filter.

4. When configuring this filter, select **Is one of** under the **Operator** radio buttons, and **teacher** in the **Options** select box. Click on **Apply (all displays)** to save your choices.

5. Click on the **Save** button to store these values.

Adding contextual filters

This view will not require any contextual filters; we can move on to setting the display format.

Setting the display format

We set the display format when creating the view, so there is no need to change anything. We do want to set a pager for this view, however. To set a pager, click on the **Use pager** link as shown in the following screenshot:

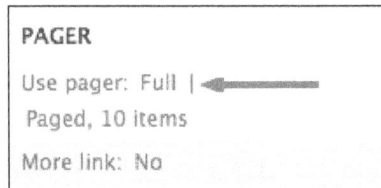

PAGER

Use pager: Full | ◀━━━━━━━

Paged, 10 items

More link: No

The difference between a **Full** and **Mini** pager is primarily cosmetic; select the option that looks best to you and click on the **Apply (all displays)** button. We are now ready to complete the settings for the default view.

Setting additional configuration options

For this view, we want to provide a meaningful title and some text in the header to provide some context.

As described in *Chapter 3, Getting Started*, add a title by clicking on the link next to the label **Title**. As shown in the following screenshot, titles are displayed in the browser title bar. For this example, use **Teacher blog** for the title:

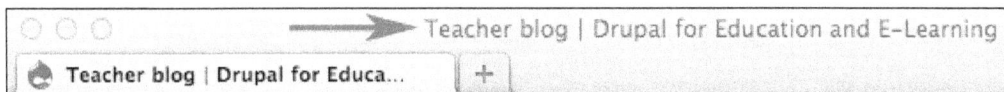

○ ○ ○ ━━━━━━━▶ Teacher blog | Drupal for Education and E-Learning

🔴 Teacher blog | Drupal for Educa...   +

Next, add some text for the views header by clicking on the link next to **HEADER**. Select **Global: Text area** and click on **Apply (all displays)**. For this view, a simple header will suffice: **Hello! You are viewing posts from the teacher blog. Enjoy your reading, and comment frequently.**

The final option we would need to set for the view default is the **Sort Criteria** option. Since this was set when we created the view, we don't need to do anything else right now. Click on the **Save** button to save the view.

To see the **teacher blog**, navigate to the path you defined earlier; in this example, the path is `http://yoursite.org/teacher-blog`.

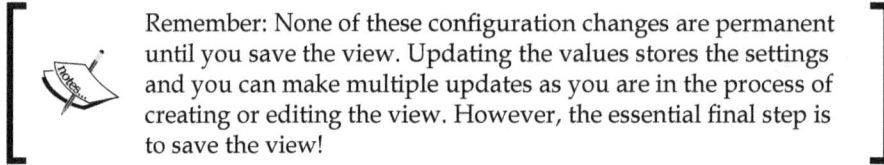

> Remember: None of these configuration changes are permanent until you save the view. Updating the values stores the settings and you can make multiple updates as you are in the process of creating or editing the view. However, the essential final step is to save the view!

The assignment view

To get started, click on the **Structure | Views** link, or navigate to `admin/structure/views`.

To create this view, we are going to take a shortcut: we are going to clone an existing calendar view that comes as part of the calendar module.

Cloning a view allows us to make an exact copy of it, thus saving us the time and effort of having to build the entire view from scratch.

Some modules come with default views or templates; cloning them and studying how they are put together can be a useful method of understanding more about how views work.

Home » Administration » Structure

Views ○

LIST   SETTINGS

✦ Add new view   ✦ Add view from template   ✦ Import

VIEW NAME	DESCRIPTION	TAG	PATH	OPERATIONS
bookmarks_all Displays: *Block, Page* In database Type: Content	All bookmarks created on the site.	default	/bookmarks/all	edit ▾
teacher_blog Display: *Page* In database Type: Content	All posts to be displayed in the teacher blog.	default	/teacher-blog	edit ▾

Click on the **Add view from template** link on the **Views** screen. You can see, in the list in the following screenshot, that there is a view template for the **'field_due_date' field in the 'node' base table** option. Click on the **add** link next to it:

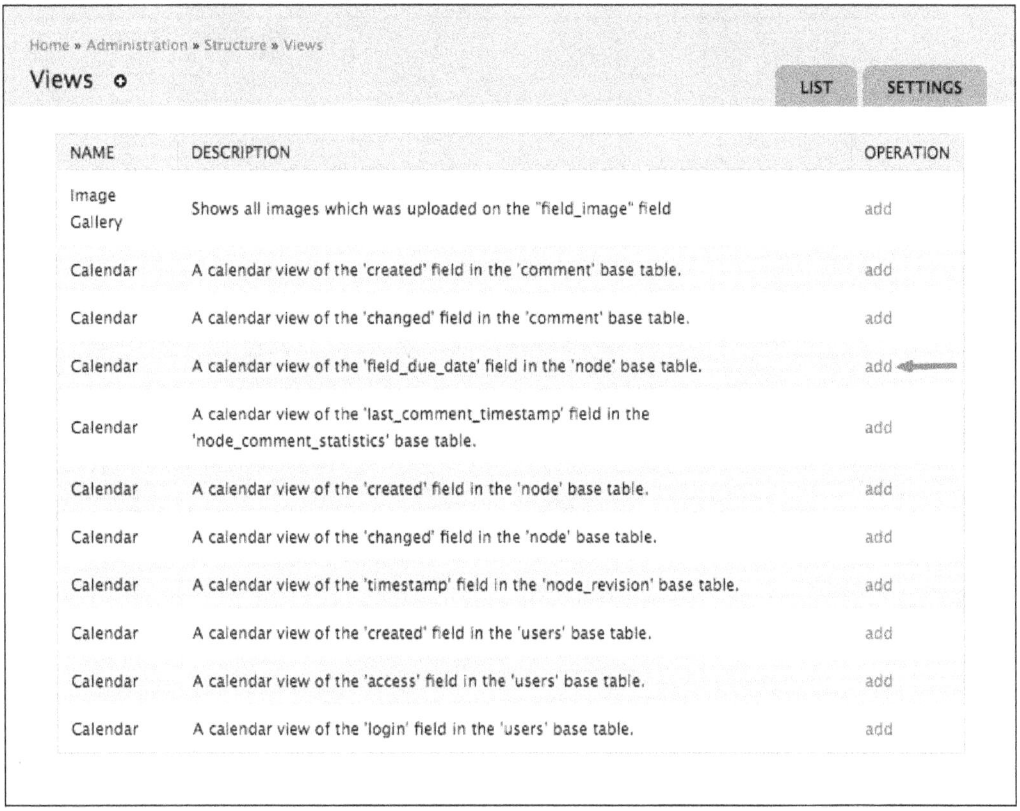

Once you have chosen to clone the view, you need to rename the cloned copy of the view and give it a new description—the first step in adding a new view. For this example, we will name the view `assignment_calendar`; then, we will click on the **Continue** button to begin editing the view.

Editing the default values

To get the functionality we need, we need to make changes in three sections:

- Add filters in the filters section
- Add a title and header
- Edit the calendar page display

Adding filters

To add filters, click on the **add** icon in the **FILTER CRITERIA** section, as shown in the following screenshot:

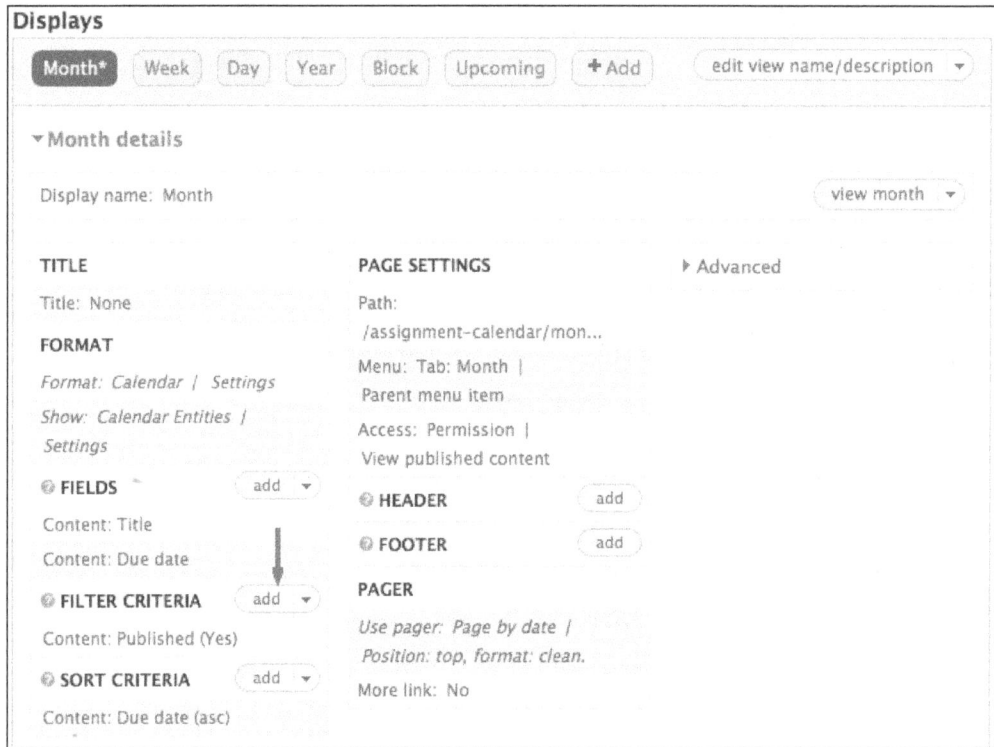

Displays

| Month* | Week | Day | Year | Block | Upcoming | **+Add** | edit view name/description ▾ |

▾ **Month details**

Display name: Month   view month ▾

TITLE

Title: None

FORMAT

Format: Calendar | Settings

Show: Calendar Entities | Settings

🔘 **FIELDS**   (add ▾)

Content: Title

Content: Due date

🔘 **FILTER CRITERIA**   (add ▾)

Content: Published (Yes)

🔘 **SORT CRITERIA**   (add ▾)

Content: Due date (asc)

PAGE SETTINGS   ▸ Advanced

Path:
/assignment-calendar/mon...

Menu: Tab: Month |
Parent menu item

Access: Permission |
View published content

🔘 **HEADER**   (add)

🔘 **FOOTER**   (add)

PAGER

*Use pager: Page by date |
Position: top, format: clean.*

More link: No

We need to add one filter to this view that is **Content: Type**. Set **Content: Type** to be one of **Assignment**; click on the **Apply (all displays)** button to store your changes.

Adding a title and header

As described earlier in this chapter, and in *Chapter 3, Getting Started*, we can customize the title and header. For this view, the title should read **Assignment Calendar**. The header should give the user information about what they are seeing; for this view, a good header would be: **This page shows all assignments. Get to work!**

Editing the calendar display

In this section, we will edit two settings: the URL path where the view is displayed, and the menu settings.

Displays

Month* | Week | Day | Year | Block | Upcoming | **+** Add | edit view name/description ▾

▾ Month details

Display name: Month   view month ▾

TITLE   **PAGE SETTINGS**   ▸ Advanced

Title: None   ➡ Path:

FORMAT   /assignment-calendar/mon...

Format: Calendar | Settings   ➡ Menu: Tab: Month |

Show: Calendar Entities | Parent menu item

Settings   Access: Permission |
                             View published content

Setting the path and menu

Both the **Path** and the **Menu** can be adjusted within the **PAGE SETTINGS** section.

To edit the path, click on the link next to **Path**. Set the new path to **assignment-calendar/month**. Repeat this step with the **Week**, **Day**, and **Year** displays, substituting the correct amount of time at the end of the URL (that is, **assignment-calendar/week** for the **Week** display). As described earlier in this chapter, and in *Chapter 3, Getting Started*, this means that the view will be visible at `http://yoursite.org/assignment-calendar`. Click on the **Apply (all displays)** button to store your settings.

Then, to set the menu, click on the **Parent menu item** link next to **Menu** on the **Month** display. Set the menu to **Normal menu item**, and give it a **Title** of **Assignment Calendar**. Click on the **Apply (all displays)** button to store your changes.

> Remember: None of these configuration changes are permanent until you save the view. Updating the values stores the settings and you can make multiple updates as you are in the process of creating or editing the view. However, the essential final step is to save the view!

To see the newly-created assignment calendar, navigate to the path we defined earlier. In this example, we set the path to `http://yoursite.org/assignment-calendar`.

Summary

In this chapter, the site began to take shape. From an administrative place, we installed and configured the CKEditor, our full text editor. We also got more familiar with installing modules and extended our use of fields to add the date field for the **Assignment** content type. We also continued to use and experiment with views, creating a new view for the **teacher blog** and cloning an existing view for the assignment calendar.

You also began to familiarize yourself with roles and access control, an area you will explore more fully in the next chapter.

In the next chapter, we will build on this foundation by adding students into the site.

5
Enrolling Students

Now that you have created your instructor blog, you are nearly ready to make your course interactive. At the risk of stating the obvious, interactions can't happen if you are the only member of the course. In this chapter, we will begin enrolling students into your class site and assigning rights to users via roles.

This process involves two steps:

- Assigning rights to the student role
- Creating student user accounts

This chapter covers these two steps and other details related to personalizing your site to create a more welcoming learning environment.

Understanding roles and assigning rights

The default Drupal installation comes with three standard roles: anonymous user, authenticated user, and administrator. The anonymous user is used for any nonmembers visiting the site and has limited rights on a site used for a learning environment. All site members belong to the authenticated user role; consequently, any permission granted to the authenticated user role is given to every site member. The administrator user is given all permissions by default, much like the first user created on the site; as new content types are created and modules are enabled, you will have to continue to update its permissions. In *Chapter 2, Installing Drupal*, we assigned privileges to the authenticated user role. As discussed in *Chapter 4, Creating a Teacher Blog*, the rights assigned to user roles are cumulative; therefore, if a single user is assigned to multiple roles, that user has the accumulated permissions of all the roles.

On small sites, some site administrators use the authenticated user role to assign permissions to students. From a technical perspective, this will work, but creating a specific student role (as we did in *Chapter 3, Getting Started*) provides an additional level of security and flexibility. Later in this chapter we will assign specific rights to the student role.

We will leave the authenticated user role with relatively few rights and assign more rights to the student role. When working with students under the age of 18, this added level of security can be reassuring to concerned parents. The practice of assigning limited rights to the authenticated user role means that even if someone outside of the course creates an account on the site, they still won't have the ability to do anything until their account has been vetted and approved by a site administrator.

Additionally, as the site grows, it can be useful to use roles to organize users into groups. As an example, let's examine the possibility of inviting parents into the site. If the authenticated user role was being used to control the access rights of students, then all parents would be able to behave exactly like students within the site. By using a separate student role and leaving the authenticated user role untouched, parents can be given a different set of rights from those granted to their children.

Unfortunately, Drupal's access rules cannot be similarly extended to govern parent behavior in the brick and mortar classroom.

Assigning rights

To assign rights to specific roles, click on **People** | **Permissions** | **Roles** or navigate to `admin/people/permissions/roles`.

Rights for the student role

Click on the **edit permissions** link for the student role.

The rights we will assign to this role will allow us to get students into the site. In *Chapter 6, Creating the Student Blog*, we will begin to assign greater rights to the student role to allow them to participate in a broader range of activities.

As we add the ability to create different types of content on the site, we will assign rights to add, edit, and delete that content. In most cases, this will be done via the node module, as described in *Chapter 3, Getting Started*. This description will not cover assigning rights to specific content types, as these permissions will be discussed in the chapters devoted to these specific content types.

Assign the following rights to the student role:

- The **Comment** module: Students do not need approval to post comments

As mentioned earlier, assigned rights are cumulative. The student role does not need rights to access or post comments, because these permissions have already been assigned to authenticated users; all users in the student role (and in the entire site) will always be authenticated users.

PERMISSION	STUDENT
Comment	
Administer comments and comment settings	☐
View comments	☐
Post comments	☐
Skip comment approval	☑
Edit own comments	☐

In some sites, teachers want to set up an approval queue for student comments. To do that, simply leave the **Skip comment approval** checkbox (as shown in the preceding screenshot) unchecked. However, students are more likely to actively participate in an activity when you remove barriers to their participation. The students are used to sites where they can publish instantly, and sites that don't meet that expectation are more likely to be underused. So, although the permissions allow you to moderate comments on a role-by-role basis, in practice, moderating comments can chill the conversation.

- The **User** module: Students can view their classmates' profiles and change their own username

PERMISSION	STUDENT
User	
Administer permissions *Warning: Give to trusted roles only; this permission has security implications.*	☐
Administer users *Warning: Give to trusted roles only; this permission has security implications.*	☐
View user profiles	☑
Change own username	☑
Cancel own user account *Note: content may be kept, unpublished, deleted or transferred to the Anonymous user depending on the configured user settings.*	☐
Select method for cancelling own account *Warning: Give to trusted roles only; this permission has security implications.*	☐

Once these options have been selected, click on the **Save permissions** button at the bottom of the page.

Creating student accounts

For students to be able to participate fully in the course, they need to have accounts on the site. The students can either create their own accounts, or a site administrator can create these accounts for them (in this case, you can create one for them).

Creating accounts for the students, as opposed to having students create their own accounts, requires more work when setting up your course. However, once your course is up and running, there is no difference between these methods. The best way is largely a matter of personal preference.

These instructions cover the default enrollment process and then describe how to customize that process. Details of how to expand and customize student profiles are covered in more detail in *Chapter 11, Social Networks and Extending the User Profile.*

Method 1 – students creating their own accounts

For the following directions, students will complete the initial steps. Once the students have created their accounts, you will need to promote them into the student role.

Student sign-in

Follow these steps:

1. On the navigation block, click on the **Create new account** link as shown in the following screenshot:

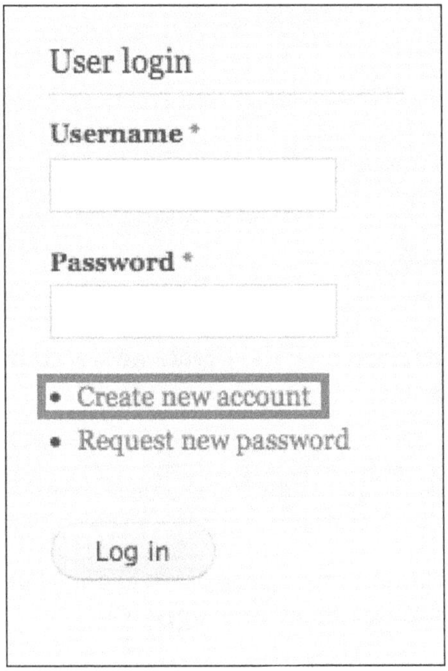

User login

Username *

Password *

- Create new account
- Request new password

Log in

2. Students will enter a username and an e-mail address. For this example, we will create a sample user named `jimmy`. Once they have entered the appropriate values, they should click on the **Create new account** button.

Once a student has clicked on the **Create new account** button, they will see the following message:

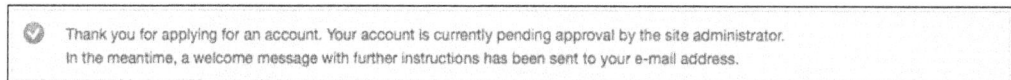

The user is then placed in the user approval queue and receives an e-mail stating that their account is pending approval.

Promoting new members into the student role

Follow these steps:

1. As students join the course, you will need to promote them into the student role. Click on the **People** link or navigate to `admin/people`.

2. As shown in the following screenshot, select the student(s) you want to promote:

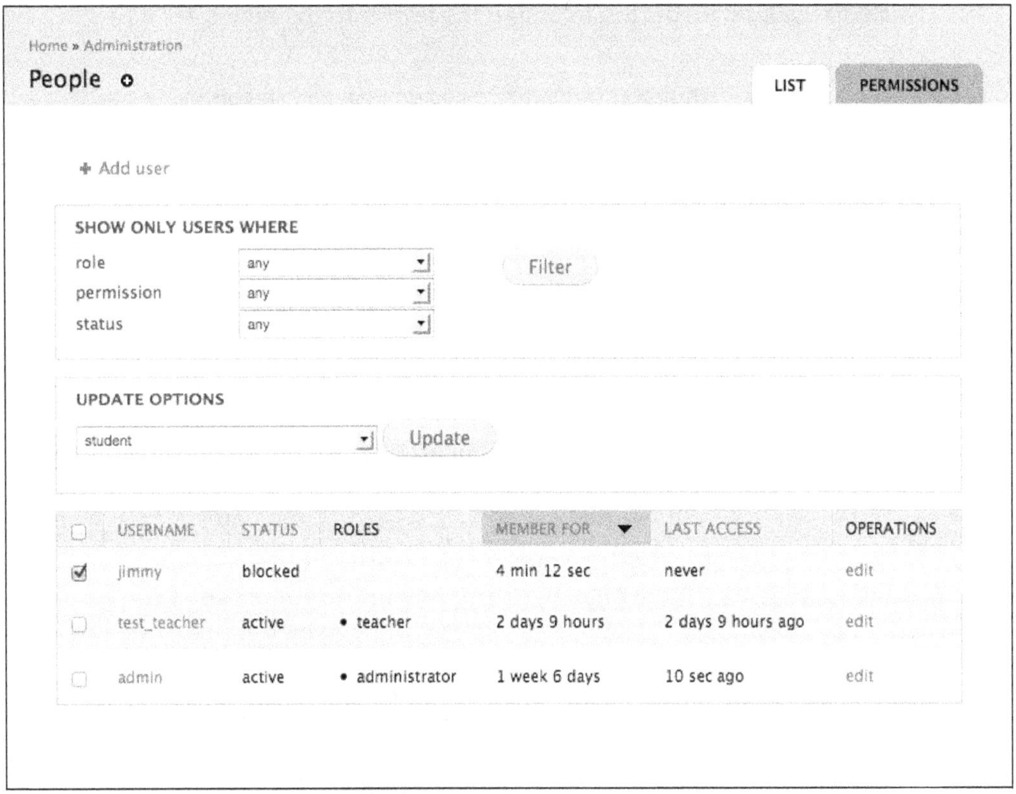

3. Use the drop-down box to select the **student** role:

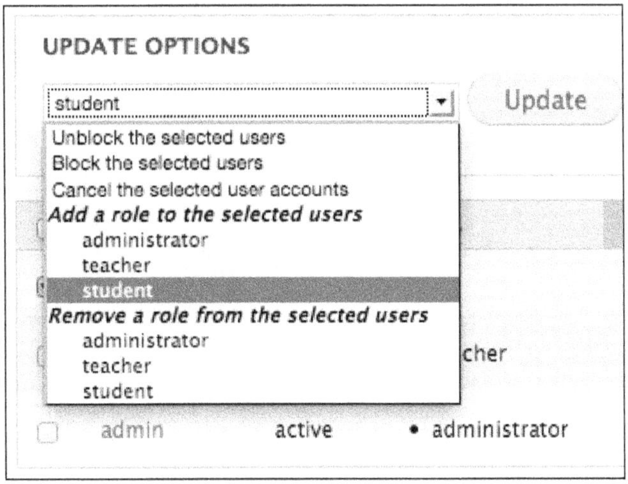

4. Click on the **Update** button to assign the user into the new role.

> The registration process can be customized and streamlined, as described later in this chapter. For example, you can allow your students to skip the e-mail confirmation. Although e-mail confirmation is a useful tool to prevent unwanted people from joining your site, in a controlled setting it can be an additional and unnecessary step.

Retrieving the confirmation e-mail

Follow these steps:

1. Students will need to access their e-mail account to retrieve the confirmation e-mail. This e-mail contains an autogenerated password and a link to their account page where they can change the password to whatever they want.

2. Using the information in the e-mail, students can then log in to the site. The students should change their password to something they will remember. They can access their account page by following the **My account** link (shown in the following screenshot for jimmy):

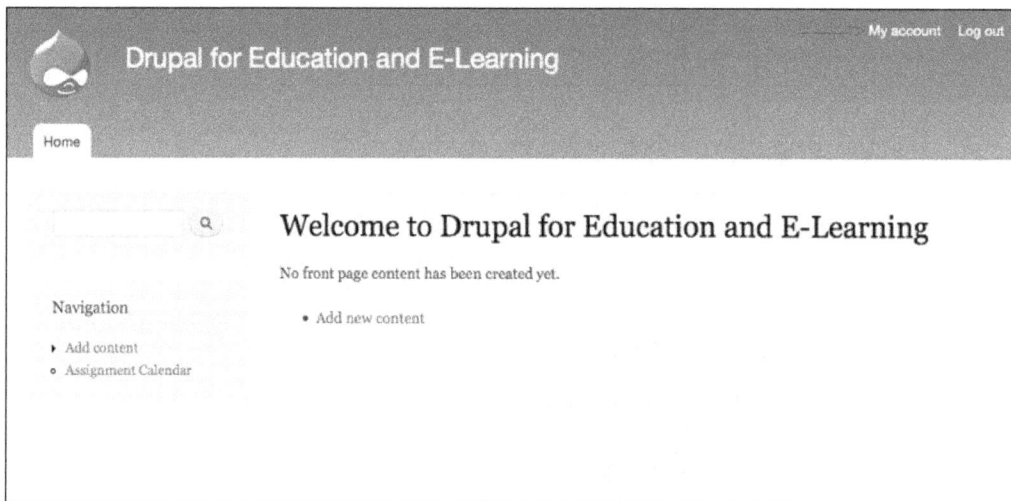

Method 2 – creating the student accounts

To manually create student user accounts, follow these steps:

1. Click on the **People** link or navigate to `admin/people`. Then, click on the **Add user** link, which brings you to `admin/people/create`.

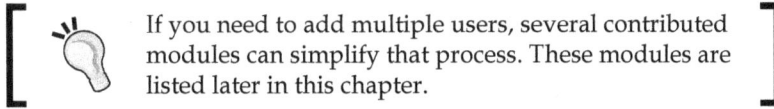

> If you need to add multiple users, several contributed modules can simplify that process. These modules are listed later in this chapter.

2. Fill out the form with the appropriate values.

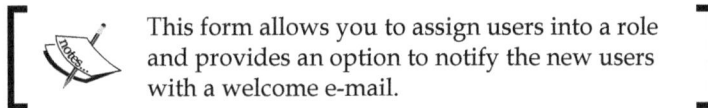

> This form allows you to assign users into a role and provides an option to notify the new users with a welcome e-mail.

3. Click on the **Create new account** button to submit the form and create the account.

Customizing the registration process

As you are running your course, you will want to control how people join your online course. For example, during the beginning of the term, you might want to allow anyone to join the site. Then, once the academic year has gotten underway, you might want to change the site to only allow new users with site administrator approval. These changes are available on the **Account settings** page. The settings on this page do not require any changes to run your course effectively. However, these settings allow you to create a more personal feel to your course.

The Account Settings page

To access the **Account settings** page, click on **Configure | Account settings** or navigate to `admin/config/people/accounts`.

This page has five sections:

- **ANONYMOUS USERS**
- **ADMINISTRATOR ROLE**

- **REGISTRATION AND CANCELLATION**
- **PERSONALIZATION**
- **E-mails**

The ANONYMOUS USERS section

This section simply allows you to choose the name for anonymous users.

The ADMINISTRATOR ROLE section

This section allows you to set which role is considered the administrator role. By default, this role is given all permissions for a module once it is enabled.

ANONYMOUS USERS

Name *

Anonymous

The name used to indicate anonymous users.

ADMINISTRATOR ROLE

Administrator role

administrator ▼

This role will be automatically assigned new permissions whenever a module is enabled. Changing this setting will not affect existing permissions.

The REGISTRATION AND CANCELLATION section

You can use these settings to turn registration off after an initial enrollment period. If you are allowing students to create their own accounts, you can enable account creation with no administrator approval required and/or no e-mail verification. Then, once the initial enrollment period has ended, you can change this setting to only allow new users to be added by the site administrator.

Additionally, you can use these settings to decide what to do with a user's content once their account has been canceled. Certain roles can override this behavior by giving them the **Select method for cancelling account** or **Administer users** permissions.

REGISTRATION AND CANCELLATION

Who can register accounts?

○ Administrators only

○ Visitors

◉ Visitors, but administrator approval is required

☑ Require e-mail verification when a visitor creates an account.

New users will be required to validate their e-mail address prior to logging into the site, and will be assigned a system-generated password. With this setting disabled, users will be logged in immediately upon registering, and may select their own passwords during registration.

When cancelling a user account

◉ Disable the account and keep its content.

○ Disable the account and unpublish its content.

○ Delete the account and make its content belong to the *Anonymous* user.

○ Delete the account and its content.

Users with the *Select method for cancelling account* or *Administer users* permissions can override this default method.

The PERSONALIZATION section

This section allows you to enable some basic features of user profiles. Adding more advanced features to user profiles will be covered in *Chapter 11, Social Networks and Extending the User Profile*.

Signatures

Often, in community sites, users can create a customized signature (similar to those in e-mail programs) that will automatically be added to the end of any comments they post.

Pictures

Within the site, students can be allowed to upload small pictures or avatars.
This feature can be allowed or disallowed from the **Account settings** page.

PERSONALIZATION

☐ Enable signatures.

☑ Enable user pictures.

Picture directory

    pictures

Subdirectory in the file upload directory where pictures will be stored.

Default picture

URL of picture to display for users with no custom picture selected. Leave blank for none.

Picture display style

    thumbnail ▾

The style selected will be used on display, while the original image is retained. Styles may be configured in the Image styles administration area.

Picture upload dimensions

    1024x1024 pixels

Pictures larger than this will be scaled down to this size.

Picture upload file size

    800 KB

Maximum allowed file size for uploaded pictures. Upload size is normally limited only by the PHP maximum post and file upload settings, and images are automatically scaled down to the dimensions specified above.

Picture guidelines

This text is displayed at the picture upload form in addition to the default guidelines. It's useful for helping or instructing your users.

The E-mails section

The settings in this section allow you to customize the various notification e-mails that are sent out when users register for the site, forget their password, and so on. Customizing these e-mails helps to create a more personal feel to your course, as the original e-mail text is fairly bland. The full range of e-mails is shown in the following screenshot:

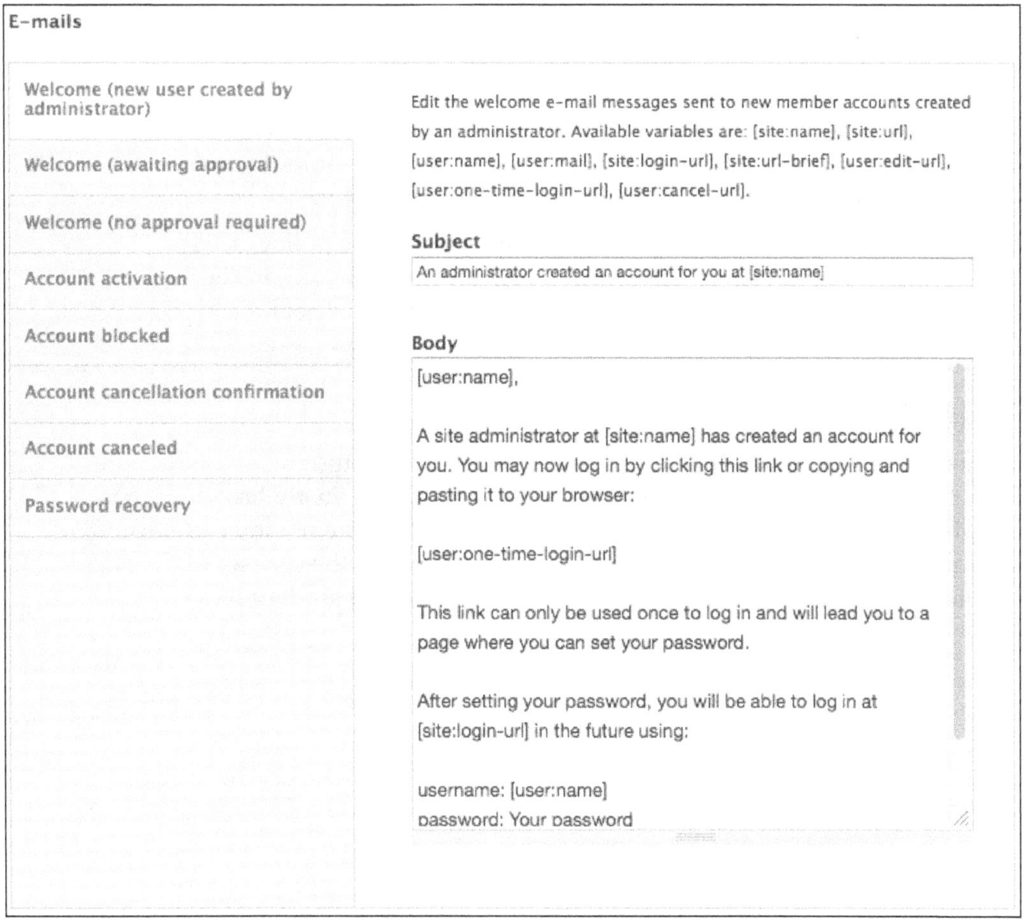

E-mails

Welcome (new user created by administrator)

Welcome (awaiting approval)

Welcome (no approval required)

Account activation

Account blocked

Account cancellation confirmation

Account canceled

Password recovery

Edit the welcome e-mail messages sent to new member accounts created by an administrator. Available variables are: [site:name], [site:url], [user:name], [user:mail], [site:login-url], [site:url-brief], [user:edit-url], [user:one-time-login-url], [user:cancel-url].

Subject

An administrator created an account for you at [site:name]

Body

[user:name],

A site administrator at [site:name] has created an account for you. You may now log in by clicking this link or copying and pasting it to your browser:

[user:one-time-login-url]

This link can only be used once to log in and will lead you to a page where you can set your password.

After setting your password, you will be able to log in at [site:login-url] in the future using:

username: [user:name]
password: Your password

Additional modules for creating user accounts

Several other modules exist for streamlining the account creation process. If you have a large number of users to manage or if you are a system administrator at a school, you might want to look at these options:

- Import users from a CSV file, such as User Import (http://drupal.org/project/user_import) or Feeds (http://drupal.org/project/feeds).

- Integrate with **Lightweight Directory Access Protocol (LDAP)** (http://drupal.org/project/ldap). These modules include support for mapping LDAP groups to Drupal roles.

- To add terms and conditions or an acceptable use policy, see the Legal module (http://drupal.org/project/legal) or Terms of Use (http://drupal.org/project/terms_of_use).

Summary

In this chapter, you looked at the main ways of adding students into your site. Now that students are in your online course, you have a vastly broader range of options available to you. Again, at the risk of stating the obvious, you can't interact within your course if you are the only person in the course. In the next chapter, we will start these interactions by setting up the student blog.

6
Creating the Student Blog

In the preceding chapters, we built the framework for our teaching and learning platform.

In *Chapter 3, Getting Started*, we set up the ability for users to share categorized bookmarks. We also added a view that collects and displays these bookmarks in one central location. The instructions in that chapter provided a baseline set of instructions for two frequently-repeated administrative activities, such as creating new content types and creating new views to organize and display content.

In *Chapter 4, Creating a Teacher Blog*, we created the beginning of the teacher blog. We built on the instructions laid out in *Chapter 3, Getting Started*, to create two new content types, and to create the view to organize and display teacher blog posts. To create an assignment calendar for the assignments, we covered how to use a convenient shortcut: *cloning a view*.

These site-building techniques will be used and referenced to as we build out the rest of our site. In this chapter, we will add the functionality to power the student blog; in *Chapter 7, Bookmarks*, we will take a look at how these different pieces fit together. Then, in *Chapter 8, Podcasting and Images* to *Chapter 13, Tracking Student Progress*, we will look at more advanced functionality: adding images, audio, video, tracking student responses to assignments, and managing multiple classes. This chapter will entail the following:

- Cloning and modifying the teacher_blog view created in *Chapter 4, Creating a Teacher Blog*, to create the student_blog view
- Enabling, cloning, and modifying the Backlinks view to track student discussion

As discussed in *Chapter 4, Creating a Teacher Blog,* blogging in Drupal encompasses a range of learning activities. When incorporated into a course as a regular part of the coursework, blogs provide an incredibly powerful means of tracking student growth. For students who are disorganized (that is, students whose backpacks resemble tumbleweed), the blog can also be an organizational tool. Most importantly, though, blogs create a record of student work that can be accessed at any time. As such, blogs provide a convenient window into both process (how students work) and product (the end results of student work).

Setting up the student blog

In *Chapter 4, Creating a Teacher Blog,* as we set up the teacher blog, we created a blog post content type, and a view to display the teacher blog posts. To create the student blog, we need to do the following two things:

- Give users in the **student** role permissions over the **blog post** content type
- Clone the **teacher_blog** view, and edit it to display student blog posts

Assigning permissions

To allow students to blog in the site, we need to allow users in the student role the ability to create blog posts. Click on **People | Permissions | Roles** link, or navigate to admin/people/permissions/roles. Click on the link to **edit permissions** for the student role.

> For additional reference on assigning rights to content types, see *Chapter 3, Getting Started* and *Chapter 4, Creating a Teacher Blog.*

Navigate down to the section for the node module. Select the options for **Create new content**, **Delete own content**, and **Edit own content** for the blog post content type.

Click on the **Save permissions** button to save the settings. Students can now blog in the site.

Cloning the teacher blog

Now that the students have the ability to create blog posts, we now need to create a central place where people can read these posts. We have already set up this structure for the teacher blog; cloning this pre-existing view will allow us to quickly replicate this structure for the student blog.

The process of cloning a view is also discussed in *Chapter 4, Creating a Teacher Blog*.

To begin, click on **Structure | Views**, or navigate to admin/structure/views. Scroll down to the teacher_blog view and click on the **clone** link:

VIEW NAME	DESCRIPTION	TAG	PATH	OPERATIONS
teacher_blog Display: *Page* In database Type: Content	All posts to be displayed in the teacher blog.	default	/teacher-blog	edit ▲ disable delete clone export
Archive Displays: *Block, Page* In code Type: Content	Display a list of months that link to content for that month.	default	/archive	

Change the view name to student_blog. Click on the **Continue** button to continue.

In the default settings, we want to change the **User: Roles** filter. To edit the **User: Roles** filter, click on the link as indicated by section **1**; and to edit the **Title**, click on the link indicated by section **2**.

Displays

Page ＋Add   edit view name/description ▼

▼ Page details

Display name: Page   view page ▼

TITLE

Title: Teacher blog ◀——— 2

FORMAT

Format: Unformatted list | Settings

Show: Content | Full content

FIELDS

The selected style or row format does not utilize fields.

FILTER CRITERIA   add ▼

Content: Published (Yes)

Content: Type (= Blog post)

(Author) User: Roles (= teacher) ◀——— 1

SORT CRITERIA   add ▼

Content: Post date (desc)

PAGE SETTINGS

Path: /teacher-blog

Menu: No menu

Access: Permission | View published content

HEADER   add ▼

Global: Text area

FOOTER   add

PAGER

Use pager: Full | Paged, 10 items

More link: No

▶ Advanced

Change the **User: Roles** setting to **student**; this will only select content posted by users in the student role. Change the **Title** setting to **Student blog**.

> As we add more content types (audio, video, and images), we will need to revisit this view to update the **Content: Type** filter. At this stage, this filter only selects **blog posts** and **bookmarks**.

Then, as shown in the following screenshot, click on the **Page** link (indicated by section **1**) to change the settings for the **Page** display for this view. We need to edit both of the options under **PAGE SETTINGS** (indicated by section **2**). We also need to edit the **HEADER** (indicated by section **3**).

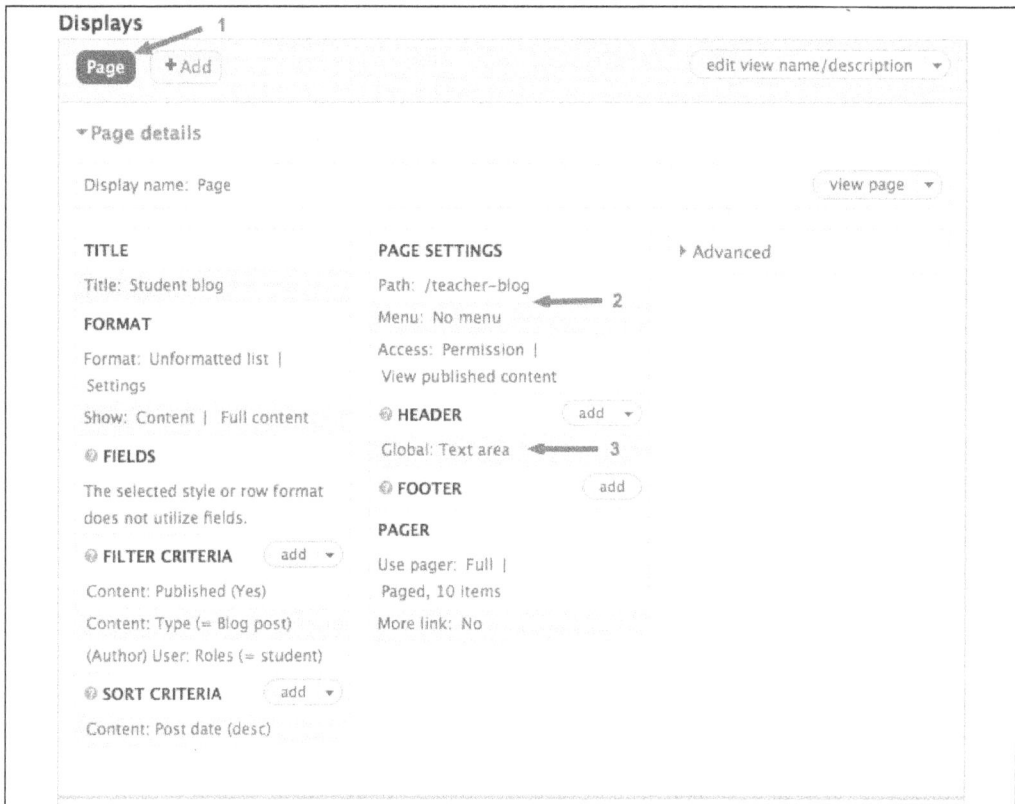

Under **PAGE SETTINGS**, change the **Path** to **student-blog**, and change **Menu** to **Normal: Student blog**.

Edit the **HEADER** to read the following:

```
Hello! You are viewing posts from the student blog. Enjoy your
reading, and comment frequently.
```

Click on the **Save** button to save the view. All student blog posts are now visible at `http://yoursite.org/student-blog`.

Getting interactive

Now that students can create blogs in the site, you have the ability to foster dialogue within your class. The easiest way, of course, is simply through commenting. Students have the rights to comment on assignments, and on teacher and student blog posts. However, students might also want to reference other pieces of content in their work. In this section, we will set up a mechanism that will keep track of when one post within the site references another post within the site. This way, people can see when exchanges are occurring about different posts, and it provides another way (in addition to comment threads) for people to hold discussions within the course.

These ideas (including tracking student responses to assignments) are covered in more detail in *Chapter 13, Tracking Student Progress*.

Seeing who's discussing what

Within the site, we will want to see who is discussing what posts. In web parlance, this is referred to as a **backlink**. Fortunately, the Views module comes with a means of tracking backlinks by default. We will clone and customize this existing view to get exactly the functionality we want.

The process of cloning this view includes the following steps:

1. The default **backlinks** view needs to be enabled and cloned.
2. In the cloned view, the different displays need to be edited:
   - In the **Page** display, a **RELATIONSHIP** needs to be added to the view, **FIELDS** need to be added to the view, the **CONTEXTUAL FILTERS** need to be adjusted, and the **Empty text** needs to be deleted.

° As the new view will only generate a block, the **Page** display should be removed.

° In the **Block** display, the **Items per page** needs to be decreased, the **More** link needs to be removed, and the **Block** settings needs to be changed.

3. Then, once the new view has been saved, the block created by this view needs to be enabled.

Enabling and cloning the backlinks view

To get started, click on the **Structure | Views** link, or navigate to admin/structure/views. As shown in the following screenshot, enable the default backlinks view:

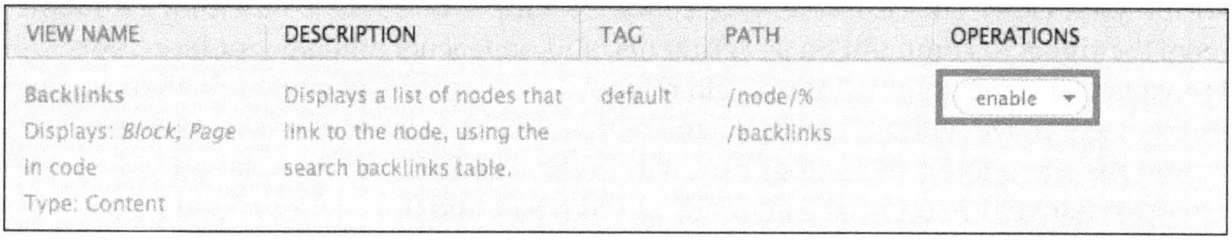

VIEW NAME	DESCRIPTION	TAG	PATH	OPERATIONS
Backlinks Displays: *Block, Page* In code Type: Content	Displays a list of nodes that link to the node, using the search backlinks table.	default	/node/% /backlinks	enable ▾

Once we have enabled the **Backlinks** view, we want to clone it. So, we click on the **clone** link. Change the **VIEW NAME** to **conversations**. Click on the **Continue** button, which brings us to the **Edit** page for the view.

Editing the page display

As shown in the following screenshot, we will make four main edits to this view. We will add a relationship, add fields, adjust the contextual filters, delete the empty text, and remove the page display.

Displays

| Page | What links here | **+** Add | | edit view name/description ▾ |

5

▾ Page details

Display name: Page   clone page ▾

TITLE

Title: None

FORMAT

Format: HTML list | Settings

Show: Fields | Settings

◎ **FIELDS**   2   add ▾

Content: Title

◎ **FILTER CRITERIA**   add ▾

Content: Published (Yes)

◎ **SORT CRITERIA**   add

PAGE SETTINGS

Path: /node/%/backlinks

Menu: Tab: What links here

Access: None

◎ **HEADER**   add

◎ **FOOTER**   add

PAGER

Use pager: Full | Paged, 30 items

More link: No

▾ Advanced

◎ **CONTEXTUAL FILTERS**   3   add ▾

Search: Links to

◎ **RELATIONSHIPS**   1   add

NO RESULTS BEHAVIOR   add ▾

Global: Text area 4

EXPOSED FORM

Exposed form in block: No

Exposed form style: Basic | Settings

OTHER

Machine Name: page

Comment: No comment

Use AJAX: No

Hide attachments in summary: No

Hide contextual links: No

Use aggregation: No

Query settings: Settings

Field Language: Current user's language

Caching: None

CSS class: None

Theme: Information

> Adding views is introduced in *Chapter 3, Getting Started*, and cloning views is introduced in *Chapter 4, Creating a Teacher Blog*.

To add a relationship, click on the **Advanced** link, then the **add** link next to **RELATIONSHIPS**, as shown by section **1**. Add the **Content: Author** relationship, and click on the **Apply (all displays)** button.

To add fields, click on the **add** link as indicated in the preceding screenshot by section **2**. Add three fields: **Content: Post Date**; **Content: Type**; and **User: Name**. Click on the **Apply (all displays)** button, and then configure the new fields to your preferences.

Next, edit the **Contextual Filters** by clicking on the **Search: Links** to link as indicated in the preceding screenshot by section **3**. We will edit the argument handling as shown in the following screenshot:

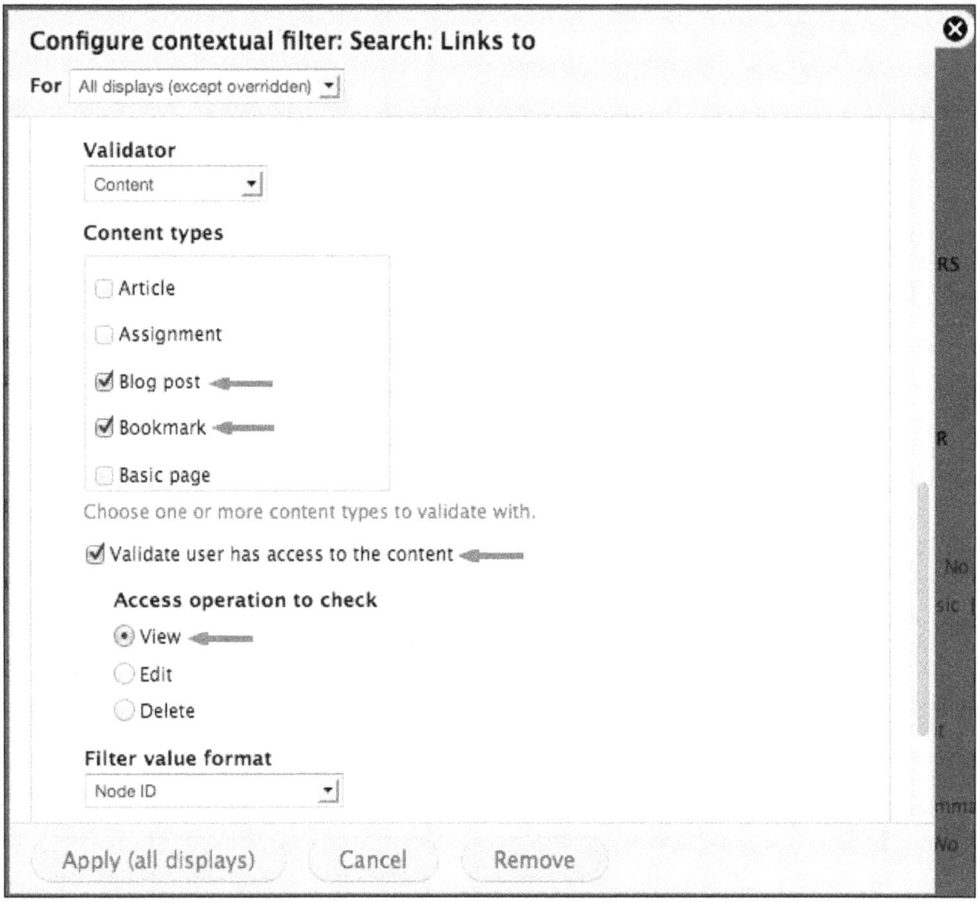

Select the options to only validate for **Blog post** and **Bookmark**. Additionally, check the option for **Validate user has access to the content**.

> These argument settings confirm that we are only checking for backlinks on blog posts and bookmarks. As we add more content types (for audio, video, and images), we will need to update this view to check for backlinks on these additional content types as well. We will also use a version of this view in *Chapter 13, Tracking Student Progress*.

Click on the **Apply (all displays)** button to store these changes.

Then, we will remove the **Empty text** by clicking on the **Global: Text area** link as indicated by section **4** in the screenshot just above the preceding one. Delete the existing empty text string, and click on the **Apply (all displays)** button to store the changes.

Deleting the empty text makes it so the view will not be displayed if the view returns no content. Although this would not be useful on a **Page** display, it is useful for a **Block** display, as this hides the block when there is nothing to show.

Removing the page display

As shown by section **5** in the screenshot just before the preceding one, click on the link to show the **Page display** type.

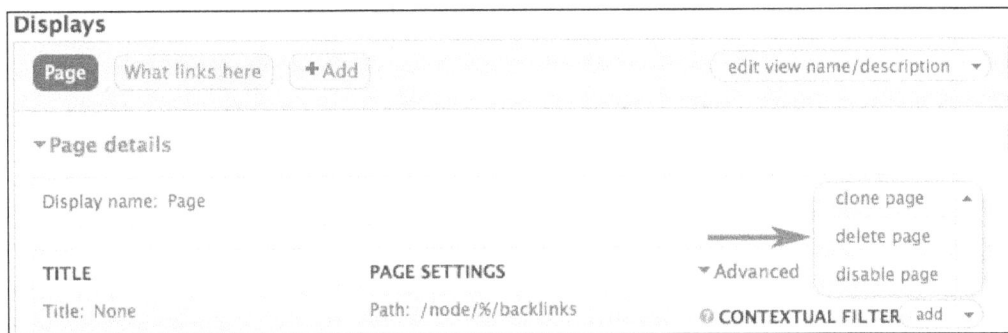

We are going to be displaying the backlinks in a block, and will not need the **Page** display. Therefore, we want to remove it by clicking on the **delete page** link as shown in the preceding screenshot.

Once we have clicked the **delete page** link, click on the **What Links Here details** link to edit the block display.

Editing the block display

When we are editing the **Block** display, we will need to edit three values as follows:

▾What Links Here details

Display name: What links here   **3**

TITLE

Title: None

FORMAT

Format: HTML list | Settings

Show: Fields | Settings

⊚ **FIELDS**   (add ▾)

Content: Title

Content: Post date (Post date)

Content: Type (Type)

(author) User: Name (Name)

⊚ **FILTER CRITERIA**   (add ▾)

Content: Published (Yes)

⊚ **SORT CRITERIA**   (add)

BLOCK SETTINGS

Block name: None

Access: None

⊚ **HEADER**   (add)

⊚ **FOOTER**   (add)

PAGER

Use pager: Full | Paged, 30 items   **1**

More link: Yes   **2**

- Change the **Items per page** option (as indicated by section **1** in the preceding screenshot) to **10**
- Change the **More** link option (indicated by section **2**) to **No** by unchecking the **Create more link** checkbox
- Change the **Display** name (indicated by section **3**) to **conversations**
- Click on the **Save** button to save the view

Then, return to **Structure | Views** link, or navigate to `admin/structure/views`, and disable the default **backlinks** view. Although we used it as a starting point, we now have no further need for it; therefore, we can disable it.

Enabling the block

As a result of the modifications, we have just completed for our new view, we created a block that will display any backlinks when we are looking at blog posts or bookmarks. For the final step, we will enable our new block.

Click on the **Structure | Blocks** link, or navigate to `admin/structure/block`.

We named this block when we adjusted the **Block** settings as shown in the preceding screenshot by section **3**. The value of the **Display** name, which we set to **conversations**, is part of the name of the block.

To display the block, use the drop-down menu to select the desired **REGION**.

BLOCK	REGION	OPERATIONS
Disabled		
Calendar Legend	- None -	configure
Main menu	- None -	configure
Management	- None -	configure
Recent comments	- None -	configure
Recent content	- None -	configure
Shortcuts	- None - Header Help Highlighted Featured Content Sidebar first Sidebar second Triptych first Triptych middle Triptych last Footer first column Footer second column Footer third column Footer fourth column Footer	configure
Syndicate		configure
User menu		configure
View: assignment_calendar		configure
View: assignment_calendar: Upcoming		configure
View: bookmarks_all		configure
View: conversations: conversations	- None -	configure
Who's new	- None -	configure
Who's online	- None -	configure

Select **Sidebar second**, and then click on the **Save** blocks button at the bottom of the page to save the settings.

> Blocks, and their role in creating an intuitive navigational structure, are covered in more detail in *Chapter 14, Theming and User Interface Design*.

Seeing it work

In this chapter, we have built the framework for the student blog, and started to build out the functionality that will support various types of interaction and discussion between people on the site. Now that we have built out this functionality, it's time to see how it fits together.

> The backlinks functionality uses the site's **search index** to track links. The search index gets updated when cron jobs are run. We will discuss how to automate cron jobs in *Chapter 15, Backup, Maintenance, and Upgrades*. Until cron jobs are automated, you can run a cron job manually by navigating to admin/reports/ status and clicking on the **run cron manually** link under **Cron maintenance tasks**. If your backlinks are not showing (or any time search gives you unexpected results) triggering a cron job manually can help resolve the issue.

In this section, we will add some sample content to illustrate the functionality we have just built. To start, add some sample student users as described in *Chapter 5, Enrolling Students*. For this example, we will add two new students — lucy and helen.

We will then log in as **helen** and create two new blog posts. Helen's first post is shown in the following screenshot:

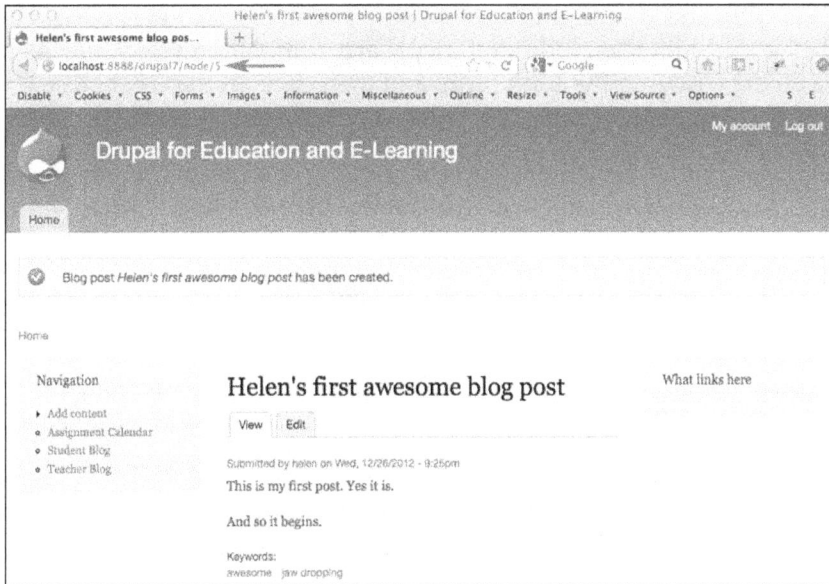

Copy the URL into your clipboard, and then, while still logged in as **helen**, create another blog post. When creating this second post, add a link to Helen's first awesome blog post as follows:

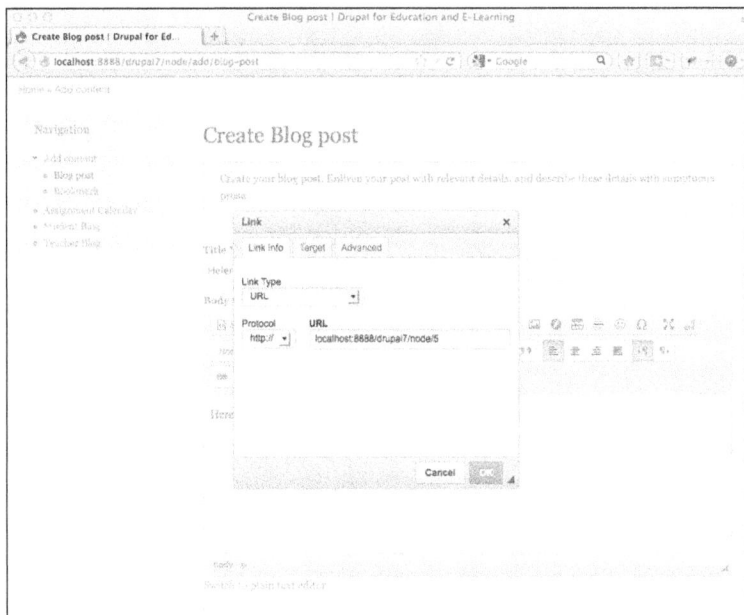

- To add the link, highlight the text you want to be the hyperlinked. Then click on the link icon, indicated by the arrow in the previous screenshot. Paste the URL into the **Link** form, and then click on the **OK** button.

- Finally, submit the post.

- Next, log out, and log back in again as `lucy`. As shown in the following screenshot, Lucy will click on the **Student blog** link to see what her classmates have been writing.

Lucy will read Helen's first awesome blog post, and after being inspired or motivated by Helen's post, Lucy will create her own post where she links back to Helen's first awesome blog post.

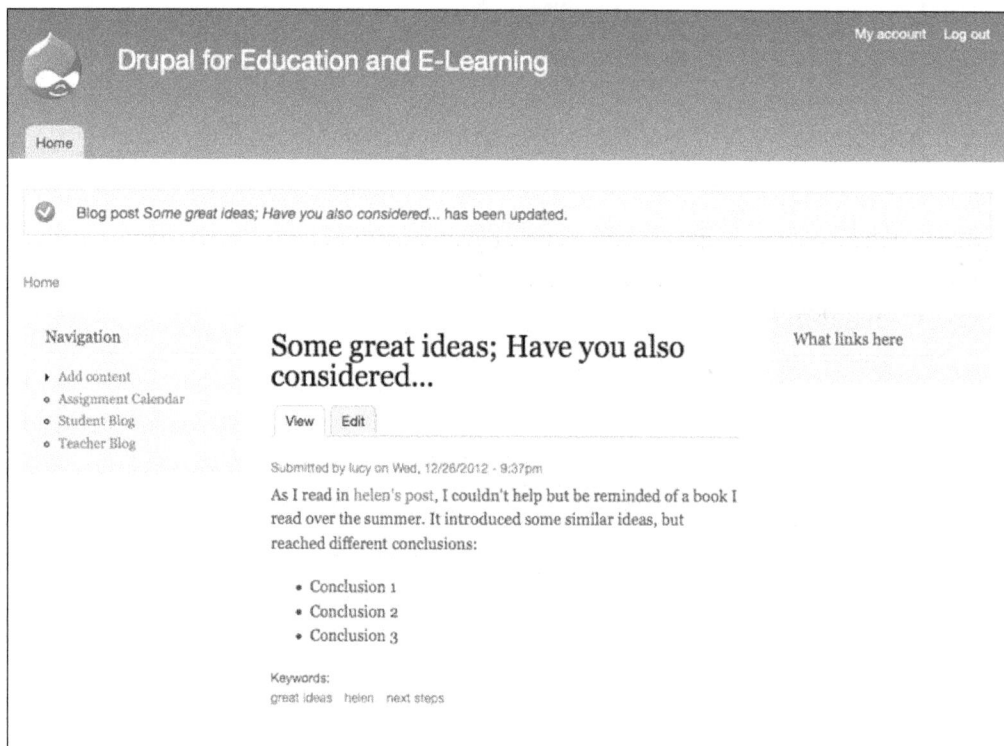

At this point, both Helen and Lucy have linked to Helen's first post. When we run the cron and then navigate to this, we will see a screen which looks like the following screenshot:

The **What links here** block that we created earlier in the chapter shows all posts within the site that link back to this blog post. This allows site members to communicate with one another through comments, or through their own blogs.

Summary

In this chapter, we created the foundation that will support both teacher-led and student-led interaction. The instructor blog, appearing on the home page of the site, can give structure to the class and provide guidance to students. The student blogs, collected and displayed via the view we created, provides a place for students and teachers to see each other's work, and to provide feedback via comments.

In the upcoming chapters, we will learn how to use the blog to share audio, video, and pictures. The upcoming chapters will also demonstrate how these different media types can be used in concert to provide support for organized, structured, and student-led inquiry.

7
Bookmarks

Bookmarks, at their most basic, allow site users to store, categorize, and share links to websites. The bookmarks can also be used as a tool for focusing student discussions and to teach media literacy and critical evaluation of sources. In this chapter, we will:

- Discuss how to store bookmarks on your website
- Describe some activities that incorporate bookmarks into the daily work of the class

In *Chapter 3, Getting Started*, we created a bookmark content type using the Link module. In *Chapter 4, Creating a Teacher Blog*, when we created the teacher blog, we set up the view that collects the teacher blog posts to include bookmarks. In *Chapter 6, Creating the Teacher Blog*, when we set up the student blog, we configured the views that collect student blog posts and backlinks to include bookmarks. To complete the process, we need to assign rights to users in the student role to create bookmarks.

Assign rights to use bookmarks

In order to use bookmarks effectively, we need to allow users with the student role to use the bookmark content type. To do so, follow these steps:

1. Click on **People** | **Permissions** | **Roles** or navigate to `admin/people/permissions/roles`. Click on the **edit permissions** link for the student role. Scroll down to the rights for the node module; assign students the right to **create content**, **delete own content**, and **edit own content** for the bookmark content type.

> Assigning privileges is covered in more detail in *Chapter 3, Getting Started.*

2. Click on the **Save permissions** button to save the updated permissions for the student role.

Now, both students and teachers have the rights to create bookmarks, and all stored bookmarks will show up in user's blogs.

Using bookmarks in the classroom

The most traditional use of bookmarks in the classroom involves storing a link to a useful resource and categorizing that link with descriptive keywords.

While bookmarks are a useful tool on their own merit, they can also be used to support other methods of teaching and learning. The bookmarks can be used to focus online and face-to-face conversations, as an extended tool to support note taking and as a tool for teaching media literacy.

Depending on the context, a bookmark can range from an online Post-it® to a more formal resource used as a central point in structured lessons. In this chapter, we will examine some methods of using bookmarks within a class setting. In future chapters, we will discuss how bookmarks can provide a useful starting point for research as a part of larger projects.

Sharing a bookmark

To share a bookmark, we really just need to create a bookmark node by following these steps:

1. To add a bookmark to the site, click on **Add content | Bookmark** or navigate to `node/add/bookmark`. For this example, we will add a link to a wiki article on *Moby Dick*, as shown in the following screenshot:

Create Bookmark

Add a bookmark that points to an external website.

Title *

Background on Moby Dick

Body (Edit summary)

| Source | ✂ | 📋 | 📋 | 📋 | ↶ | ↷ | 🔍 | ⁵ᵃ | 🔖 | 𝐼ₓ | 🖼 | ⊘ | ⊞ | ≡ | ☺ | Ω | ⤢ | ⬒ |

| Normal ▾ | **B** | *I* | U̲ | S̶ | xₐ | x² | ⅟≡ | ∷ | ⊣≡ | ⊢≡ | 99 | ≡ | ≡ | ≡ | ≡ | ⟩¶ | ¶⟨ |

| 🔗 | 🚫 | 🏳 |

This Wikipedia article on Moby Dick gives a solid overview of the novel. While this article lacks detail, it is accurate.

It also contains information on the basic themes of the novel, some historical context, and a character list.

body p

Switch to plain text editor

Text format   Filtered HTML ▾   More information about text formats ⓘ

- Web page addresses and e-mail addresses turn into links automatically.
- Allowed HTML tags: <a> <b> <blockquote>
 <caption> <center> <code> <col> <colgroup> <dd> <del> <div> <dl> <dt> <em> <font> <h1> <h2> <h3> <h4> <h5> <h6> <hr> <i> <img> <li> <ol> <p> <span> <strong> <sub> <sup> <table> <tbody> <td> <tfoot> <th> <thead> <tr> <u> <ul>
- Lines and paragraphs break automatically.

Link to Source

http://en.wikipedia.org/wiki/Moby-Dick

Enter a link to an external web site. Most links will start with http://

Keywords

Moby Dick, background, historical context, character list, themes ○

Enter keywords to describe your post.

Revision information
New revision

Comment settings
Open

Revision log message

Provide an explanation of the changes you are making. This will help other authors understand your motivations.

Save   Preview

2. Once you have entered the appropriate title, link, keywords, and body description, click on the **Save** button. The following screenshot shows the saved link:

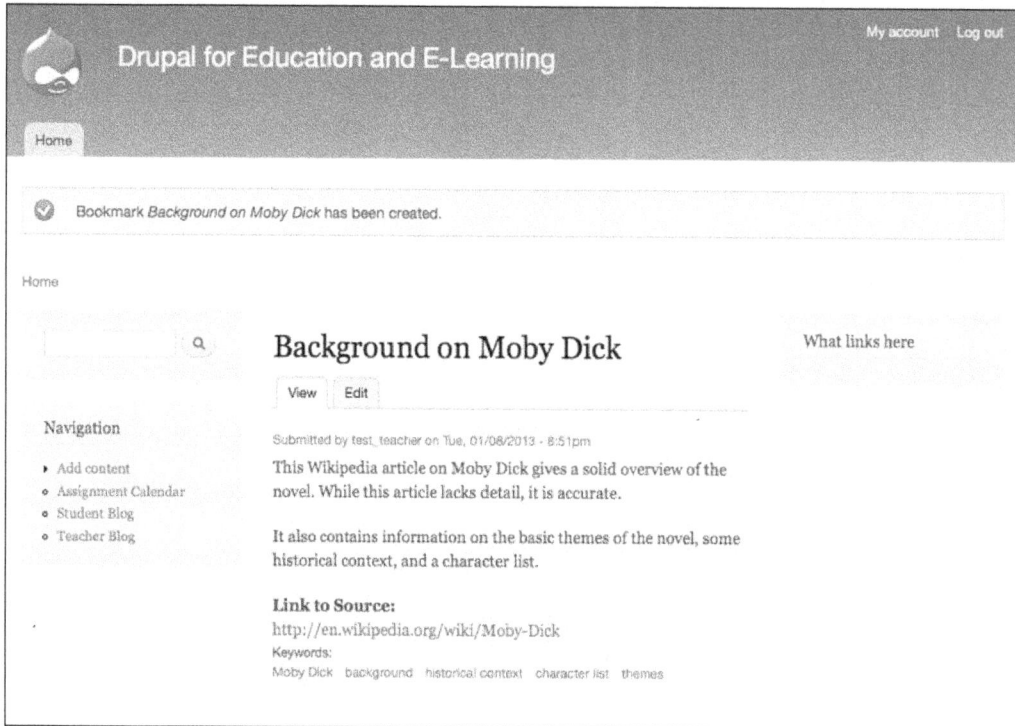

Bookmark to blog

Bookmarks can also be used as a starting point for student conversations via the student blog. By providing students a link to a common resource, you can use bookmarks as tools to structure preteaching or to support student-directed inquiry through content.

To get started, log in as a user in the teacher role. Create a bookmark, as described earlier, pointing to `http://www.greatwhatsit.com/archives/18405`. This site gives very general instructions to readers starting *Moby Dick*.

Use these keywords to describe the post: `Moby Dick, Reading Moby Dick, evaluating bookmarks`.

> When we use these keywords to describe a post, we are using Drupal's core taxonomy functionality. When we add keywords to a post, we will also refer to it as "tagging a post" or "categorizing a post".

Then, create an assignment (by clicking on **Add content | Assignment** or by navigating to `node/add/assignment`) that links to the newly created bookmark.

In the **Body** field, ask the following questions:

- What elements of this site help create the impression that the author is a reliable source of information?
- What elements of this site detract from the author's reliability?
- Does the author appear to have any biases?
- In order of importance, list the criteria you use to rate a site's/author's credibility? For example, do you look at spelling before looking at the date a page has been updated? What elements of a site do you examine in evaluating the information you are reading?
- Is this page a useful resource? For whom? Explain and support your opinion.

Create a blog post where you respond to these five questions. Tag your blog post with the keyword `evaluating bookmarks`.

Now, if we look at the original bookmark, we will see the assignment alongside it.

Some general advice on reading Moby Dick

View	Edit

Submitted by test_teacher on Tue, 01/08/2013 - 9:06pm

A general resource on reading Moby Dick.

Link to Source:

http://www.greatwhatsit.com/archives/18405

Keywords:

evaluating bookmarks   Moby Dick   Reading Moby Dick

What links here

- Media Literacy:
  Evaluating sources
  Post date: 01/08/2013 -
  9:02pm
  Type: Assignment
  Name: test_teacher

> In *Chapter 13, Tracking Student Progress*, we will describe how to track responses to assignments. Also, as noted earlier, the backlinks functionality requires cron jobs to be set up. The cron jobs are covered in detail in *Chapter 15, Backup, Maintenance, and Upgrades*.

Learning goals

This exercise accomplishes the following goals:

- Students gain an increased sense of how to use keywords/tags to organize their work and connect with the work/thoughts of others.

- Students begin or continue to develop the habit of thinking critically about websites.

- Students gain an increased familiarity with a vocabulary focused on media literacy and critical evaluation of resources. In many cases, these topics will dovetail with existing teaching practice within English and history curricula: identifying authorial bias and intent, identifying the target audience, identifying best practice with citation, and so on.

- Students and teachers begin to see how the different tools can be connected to support learning activities. Using the technique of a bookmark to lead into a reflective blog post can be used to support an almost limitless number of teaching and learning activities. The context of the student response is set by the subject of the initial bookmark, and follow-up questions can be used to provide a context for a focused blog response. If activities such as this are used as part of a homework assignment, a teacher can read these assignments prior to class with an increased sense of what the class understands and where they need additional support.

Bookmarks and media literacy

Bookmarks can also be used, as in this example, as a tool for developing media literacy. Focused questions that guide students to analyze the various elements of a web page help students develop the critical thinking skills and vocabulary needed to articulate the strengths and weaknesses of the content they encounter online.

Bookmarks as part of the ongoing student research

Bookmarks could also be used as a tool within an ongoing research. For example, in a unit covering *Moby Dick*, students need to include a bookmark per chapter that explains an allusion or symbol from the reading. For lower-level classes or classes needing more structure, the students could be assigned specific allusions. For upper-level classes, the students could select the allusions they want to research based on personal interest. In a text such as *Moby Dick*, the students could be assigned allusions/symbols based on specific topic areas; for example, one set of students could be assigned to store bookmarks referencing Biblical allusions, while another set of students could be assigned to allusions about American politics, and so on. As the course unfolds, the student bookmarks will provide a repository of categorized links. As a teacher, you can refer to these links during class discussions or even plan lessons around the links shared by your students. If you have students submit links as part of their homework assignments, you can open the class by having an icebreaker conversation where students explain why they chose to include a specific link.

Learning goals

By incorporating the student-generated links into your classroom plan, you can achieve several goals:

- As students create resources that become incorporated into the daily work of the class, they get the opportunity to view themselves (and their peers) as active participants in their learning environment.

- By using student-generated links to spark discussion, you reinforce the notion that all participants in the course (students and teacher) have a role to play in creating course content.

- By requiring ongoing research and providing a structure within which students can share items they find during this research, you help students develop the skills needed for self-directed learning.

- Sharing resources allows another venue for students to contribute to the course discussion. Frequently, students who do not enjoy class discussions can use online tools such as blogs and bookmarks to contribute to the discussion in a less direct way. Successful online interactions within the course space can lead to more active participation within the face-to-face class meetings.

Summary

In this chapter, we learned that bookmarks are an informal way for students to contribute material into the course space. The informal nature of the bookmark can be less daunting to students learning how to work in an online environment. Additionally, bookmarks provide a means of supporting other types of learning within the site. In future chapters, we will build on the strategies described in this chapter to use the different content types within a Drupal site to support student inquiry.

8
Podcasting and Images

Podcasting allows you to share audio or video files over the Internet. In recent years, as podcasting has increased in prominence and popularity, there has been an almost overwhelming amount of information about how to get started with podcasting: the technical requirements, the hardware, the software, and so on.

Sharing images creates a variety of ways for students to get involved in the class. In some classes, such as Photography or other Fine Arts courses, images provide a way for students to showcase their work. In other courses, online image sharing can be used to enhance the curriculum.

In this chapter, we will:

- Set up your site to work as a podcasting and image sharing platform
- Break down the technical aspects of publishing audio and images
- Discuss ways to integrate podcasting into your class

Getting Started with Podcasts

To create a podcast, you will need the following:

- An MP3 file
- A place to store the MP3 file

At the risk of stating the obvious, a good podcast requires thought and planning before you make the actual recording. Later in the chapter, we will discuss some of these general mechanics. From a technical perspective, once you have uploaded your audio file you will have published a podcast.

The AudioField module

The **AudioField** module supports the playback of audio files that have been uploaded to your site.

Installing and Enabling the AudioField module

Download the AudioField module from `http://drupal.org/project/audiofield`. Upload the module to your `sites/all/modules directory`, and enable it by clicking on the **Modules** link or by navigating to `admin/modules`.

Select the AudioField module. Click on the **Save configuration** button to submit the form and enable the modules.

Configuring the Audio module

Now that we have installed the AudioField module, we need to configure the module to support our needs. Click on **Configuration | Audio Field** link, or navigate to `admin/config/media/audiofield`.

The players

The AudioField module comes with support for several different players that can be used to play your audio files. You can use the settings on this page to choose your preferred player. The "best" player will largely be determined by your aesthetic preference; all of the players do a great job playing audio stored on your site.

Home » Administration » Configuration » Media

Audio Field ⚙

MP3 Audio Players

○ WordPress Audio Player

◉ Google Reader MP3 Player

Audio Players Directory

sites/all/libraries/player

Download and extract audio players in this directory

Download and install audio players

- Download XSPF Slim Player
- Download XSPF Button Player
- Download SoundManager2 360
- Download jPlayer

Save configuration

By default, the **Audio Field** module comes with **Google Reader MP3 Player**. Instructions for installing other supported players can be found at `http://drupal.org/node/973194`.

After you have chosen a player, click on the **Save configuration** button to save your preference.

Assigning rights to the AudioField module

Now that we have installed, enabled, and configured the AudioField module, we need to assign rights to it. Click on **People | Permissions | Roles**, or navigate to `admin/people/permissions/roles`.

PERMISSION	ANONYMOUS USER	AUTHENTICATED USER	ADMINISTRATOR	TEACHER	STUDENT
AudioField					
Download Own Audio Files Let the users download their own audio files.	☐	☑	☑	☑	☑
Download All Audio Files Let the users download any audio files.	☐	☑	☑	☑	☑

Edit the permissions for the **AUTHENTICATED USER** role, and give it the **Download Own Audio Files** and **Download All Audio Files** permissions.

Creating the podcast content type

The easiest way to organize our podcast within a Drupal site is to create a content type specifically for podcasts, as described in the following steps:

1. Click on **Structure | Content types | Add content type**, or navigate to `admin/structure/types/add`.

2. Enter `Podcast` for the **Name** field, and add the following in the **Description** field: An audio file. The audio file could be used for adding music, podcasts, or audio clips to your site.

Home » Administration » Structure » Content types

Content types ○

Individual content types can have different fields, behaviors, and permissions assigned to them.

Name *

Podcast

The human-readable name of this content type. This text will be displayed as part of the list on the *Add new content* page. It is recommended that this name begin with a capital letter and contain only letters, numbers, and spaces. This name must be unique.

Description

An audio file. The audio file could be used for adding music, podcasts, or audio clips to your site.

Describe this content type. The text will be displayed on the *Add new content* page.

Submission form settings	**Title field label** *
Title	Title
Publishing options	
Published	**Preview before submitting**
Display settings	○ Disabled
Display author and date information.	⦿ Optional
Comment settings	○ Required
Open, Threading , 50 comments per page	
Menu settings	**Explanation or submission guidelines**

This text will be displayed at the top of the page when creating or editing content of this type.

Save content type   Save and add fields

3. Under **Publishing** options, uncheck the box next to **Promoted to front page**, then click on **Save and add fields** to save your progress.

Adding an audio field to the podcast content type

Once we have set up the basic content type, we will have to add an audio field to it.

1. Add a new field called `Audio File`, select **File** as the **FIELD TYPE**, and select **Audio Upload** as the **WIDGET** type. Click on **Save** to add the field and continue configuring the field.

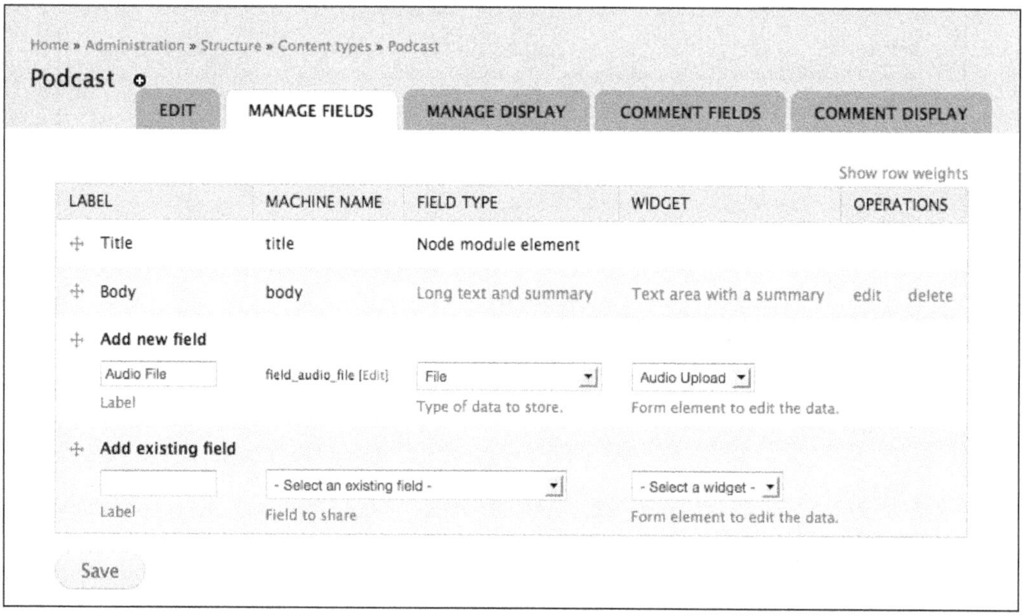

2. The options on the next screen allow you to add files to a podcast node without displaying it to the user viewing the node. For our purposes, it is fine to click on the **Save field settings** button to continue configuring the field.

3. On the next screen, check the **Required** field box, and then add some help text for your users. The other options can be left on their defaults.

> Adding and configuring content types is covered in *Chapter 3, Getting Started.*

Assigning rights to the podcast content type

After we have added the audio field, we will have to assign permissions for the content type. Let's assign permissions:

1. The possible rights that can be assigned are shown in the following screenshot:

PERMISSION	ANONYMOUS USER	AUTHENTICATED USER	ADMINISTRATOR	TEACHER	STUDENT
Podcast: Create new content	☐	☐	☑	☑	☑
Podcast: Edit own content	☐	☐	☑	☑	☑
Podcast: Edit any content	☐	☐	☑	☐	☐
Podcast: Delete own content	☐	☐	☑	☐	☐
Podcast: Delete any content	☐	☐	☑	☐	☐

2. We will need to assign rights for the **TEACHER** role, the **STUDENT** role, the **AUTHENTICATED USER** role, and possibly the **ANONYMOUS USER** role.
3. For the **STUDENT** role, assign rights to **Create new content** and **Edit own content** for podcasts.
4. For the **TEACHER** role, assign rights to **Create new content** and **Edit own content** for podcasts.
5. For the **ANONYMOUS USER** role, assign the rights you think are appropriate. In most cases, if you are allowing anonymous users to see content, allowing them the rights to download audio and play audio is appropriate.
6. Each time you assign rights to an individual role, click on the **Save permissions** button to save the rights for the role.

Adjusting the existing views

Currently, three views are being used to display student-created and teacher-created content. We will need to edit these views so that they return any podcast nodes created within the site. Let's start editing the views:

1. To edit these views, click on **Structure | Views**, or navigate to `admin/ structure/views`.

2. We need to edit three views: the **teacher_blog** view created in *Chapter 4, Creating a Teacher Blog* and the **student_blog** and **conversation** views created in *Chapter 6, Creating the Student Blog*.

3. As shown in the following screenshot, these views can be edited by using the **edit** link on the main Views administration page:

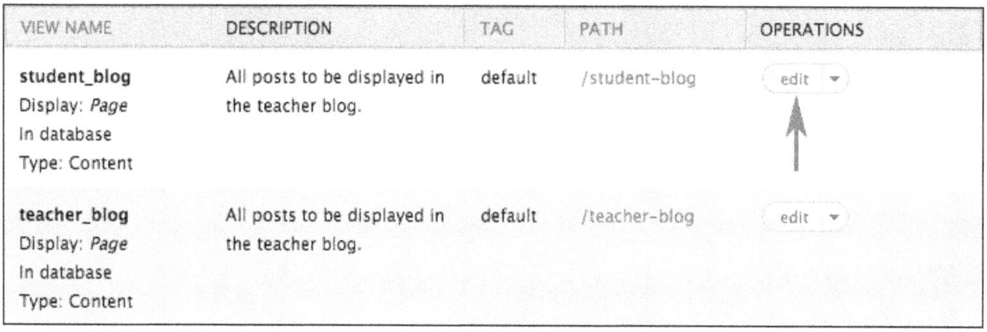

VIEW NAME	DESCRIPTION	TAG	PATH	OPERATIONS
student_blog Display: *Page* In database Type: Content	All posts to be displayed in the teacher blog.	default	/student-blog	edit ▼
teacher_blog Display: *Page* In database Type: Content	All posts to be displayed in the teacher blog.	default	/teacher-blog	edit ▼

Editing the student_blog view

Click on the **edit** link as shown in the preceding screenshot. Then, in the defaults display, under **Filters**, click on the **Node: Type** link.

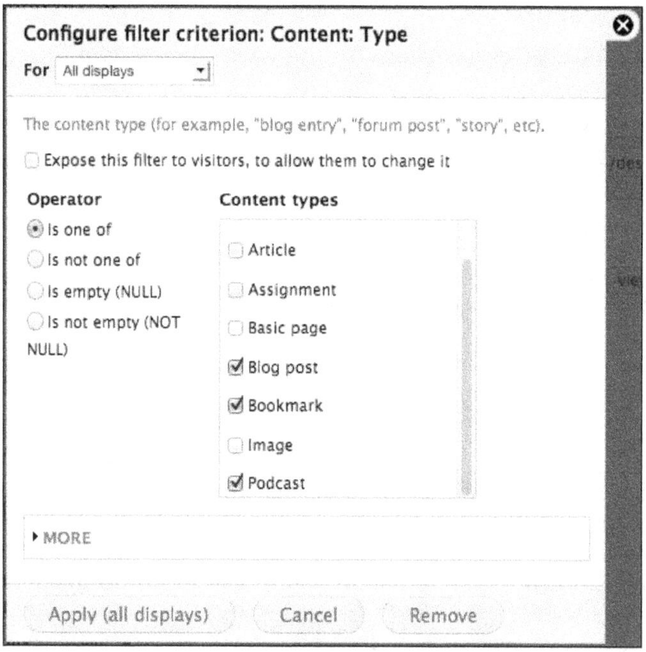

As shown in the preceding screenshot, add **Podcast** to the node types returned in this view. Click on the **Update** button to store this change, and then click on the **Save** button (not pictured in the preceding screenshot) to save the view.

Editing the teacher_blog view

To edit the **teacher_blog** view, repeat the same steps for the **student_blog** view.

To get a clear overview of the differences between the **student_blog** and the **teacher_blog** view, see *Chapter 6, Creating the Student Blog*, for a description of how we created the **student_blog** view by cloning the **teacher_blog** view.

Editing the conversations view

Click on the **edit** link for the **conversations** view. Then, in the defaults display, under **Arguments**, click on the **Search: Links to** link.

As shown in the preceding screenshot, add **Podcast** to the list of node types where this view will be validated. Click on the **Apply (this display)** button to store this change, and then click on the **Save** button to save the view.

As we add additional content types into the site, we will need to update these views to account for the newly-added content types.

Uploading an audio file

The instructions for uploading an audio file is shown in the following screenshot:

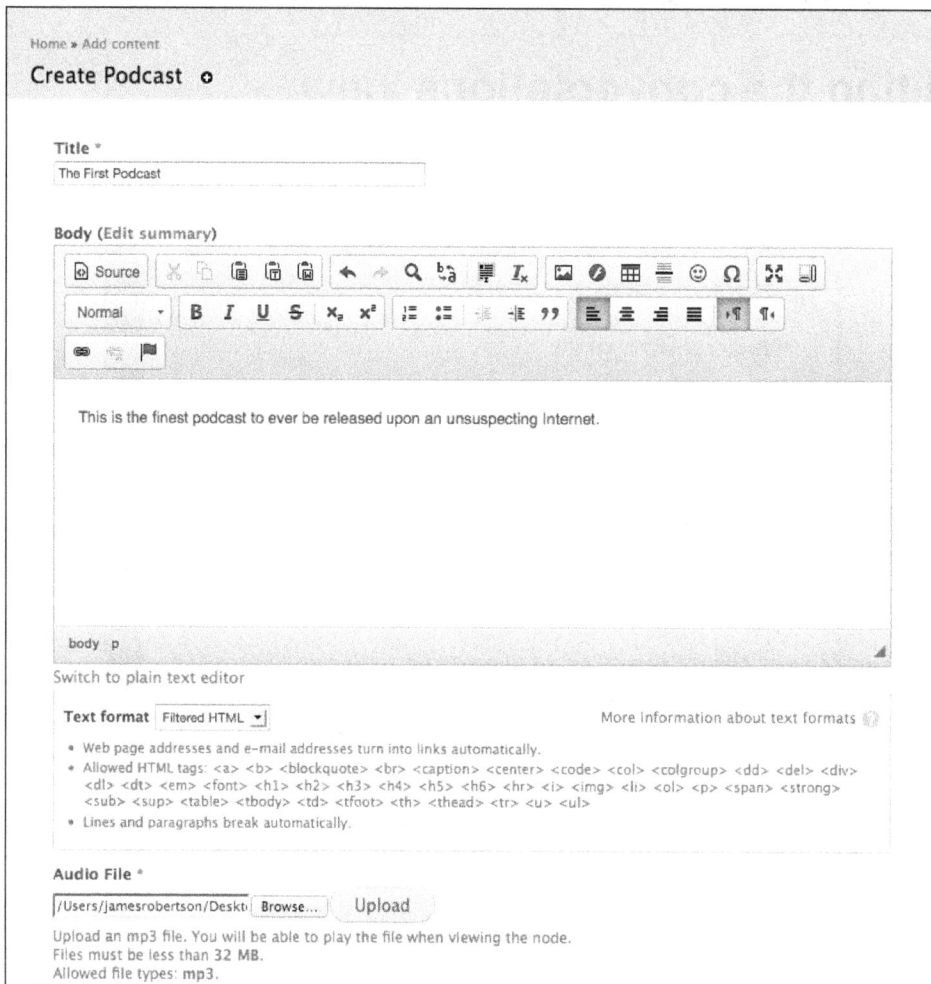

Home » Add content

Create Podcast ○

Title *

The First Podcast

Body (Edit summary)

This is the finest podcast to ever be released upon an unsuspecting Internet.

body p

Switch to plain text editor

Text format Filtered HTML ▾   More information about text formats

- Web page addresses and e-mail addresses turn into links automatically.
- Allowed HTML tags: `<a> <b> <blockquote> <br> <caption> <center> <code> <col> <colgroup> <dd> <del> <div>`
  `<dl> <dt> <em> <font> <h1> <h2> <h3> <h4> <h5> <h6> <hr> <i> <img> <li> <ol> <p> <span> <strong>`
  `<sub> <sup> <table> <tbody> <td> <tfoot> <th> <thead> <tr> <u> <ul>`
- Lines and paragraphs break automatically.

Audio File *

/Users/jamesrobertson/Deskt Browse...   Upload

Upload an mp3 file. You will be able to play the file when viewing the node.
Files must be less than 32 MB.
Allowed file types: mp3.

To create a new audio file, click on **Create Content | Podcast**, or navigate to `node/add/podcast` and follow these steps:

1. Give a title to the post.
2. Enter a description.
3. Click on the **Browse** button to select the audio file you want to upload.
4. Click on the **Save** button.

Once you have submitted your podcast, you will be able to play it back as shown in the following screenshot:

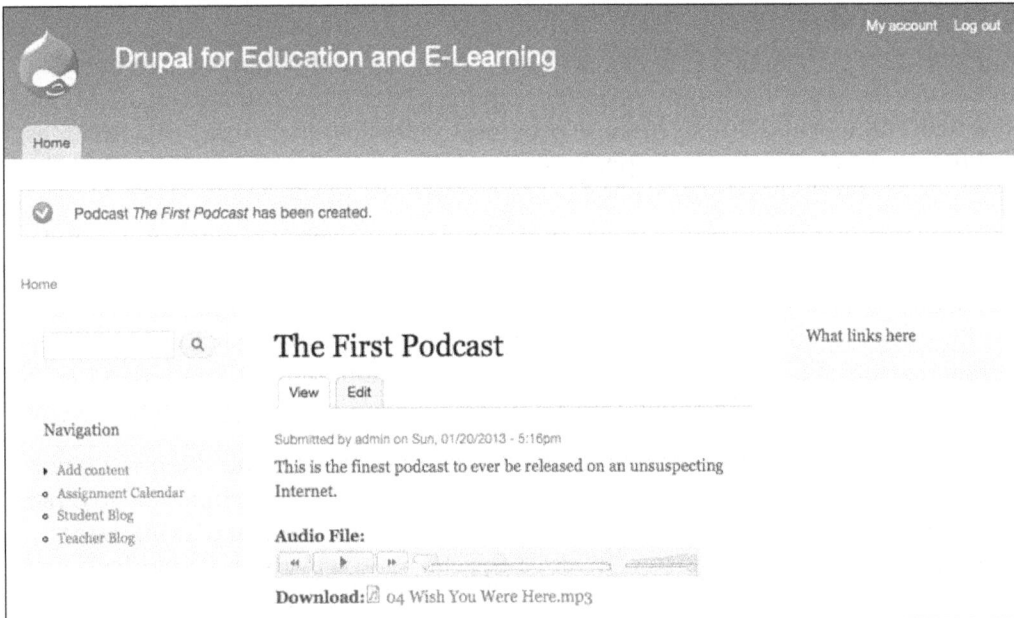

Using Podcasts in the Class

Podcasts can be used in a variety of ways to support learning in the classroom. Some of these uses require extensive planning, but there are a range of ways that podcasts allow both students and teachers to share material quickly and easily.

Creating podcasts – notes on hardware and software

Many podcast tutorials focus a large amount of attention on specialized hardware and software required for podcasting. If you are looking to create complex podcasts involving live music, complex transitions between scenes, or professional-quality production, then you will probably need to invest in specialized equipment to help create your podcast. However, most podcasts require very little specialized software and hardware.

Software

Audacity (`http://audacity.sourceforge.net/`) can be downloaded for free, and works on Mac, PC, or Linux-based computers. Mac users can also create MP3 files with Garageband. Either of these programs will allow the editing of audio files, and the export of these files as a podcast.

Hardware

Podcasters can use handheld audio recorders to capture sound during interviews. Additionally, handheld or lavalier microphones (a microphone that attaches to a person's clothing, also called a lav or a lapel microphone) can be purchased to improve the sound quality when making original recordings.

However, great podcasts require great content, and the best technical tools will not help overcome weak content. In this way, podcasts are directly comparable to other classroom activities: a good product requires thought, planning, and a clear sense of what the podcast is designed to achieve. Special audio effects and other bells and whistles are best left to the final part of the process, if at all.

In short, you can create great podcasts with a handheld recorder and a single computer but you need to focus on your content first.

Everyday uses of podcasts

At the simplest level, teachers can use podcasts to create a body of resources for students; in a foreign language course, for example, a teacher can publish a podcast with a dialog that emphasizes vocabulary, or that gives pronunciations for verb conjugations. In an English or history course, a teacher can publish speeches or literary readings. These primary source materials can be used to augment the curriculum.

For people looking to create a library of primary source materials, YouTube and Google Video can provide an amazing array of resources. Using a free online service such as `http://vixy.net`, you can extract the audio from videos hosted on YouTube and Google video. Of course, you will need to make sure that you are not infringing on any licensing restrictions when you republish the content, but the amount of content available for reuse within these sites can be overwhelming. Extracting the audio also helps avoid any issues with content from these sites being eliminated by firewalls or content filters.

The Internet Archive, at `http://www.archive.org/details/audio`, also offers a rich variety of freely-available primary source material.

Additionally, students can create podcasts as a form of audio blog—this can be an especially powerful tool for students who are visually impaired, or for students with learning differences who have difficulty expressing themselves in writing.

Using podcasts as a tool in project-based learning

Podcasts can also be used as part of a project-based lesson. In this context, creating a good podcast requires a blend of skills used in virtually all academic work, as outlined in the following steps:

1. Initial research leading to an outline/storyboard. This initial storyboard can be rough, but it should give a clear idea of the point/goals of the podcast.

2. Additional research/editing. At this stage, the point that was laid out in the original storyboard should be examined. Is it logical? Is it entertaining/interesting enough to be the subject of a podcast? Are there any counterarguments that need to be addressed?

3. Finalizing the storyboard.

4. Drafting a script.

5. Practicing and revising the script.

6. Recording the podcast.

7. If necessary, adding sound effects.

8. Saving the recording as an MP3 (usually by using Audacity or Garageband, as described earlier in this chapter).

9. Uploading the podcast to your site as an audio file.

As students progress through the various steps of creating a podcast, they can use the tools within the site to support their work. Initial research can make use of bookmarks; various drafts of the storyboard and script can be published as blog posts, and students can provide feedback via comments.

Additionally, students can use their blog (or quick podcasts) as a reflective tool to assess the effectiveness of their creative process.

Ideas for podcasting projects

Using the general structure described earlier, you can work with students on a variety of projects.

Some general examples

Following are some general examples for podcasts:

- In a literature class, you could have your students work in a group to distill scenes from a novel into a series of radio plays.
- In a history course, you could have students do news stories as embedded reporters.
- In an art history course, you could use the body of the audio post to display a series of paintings, and use the podcast to discuss them.
- For a physics course, students could prepare a series of podcasts on sound, ranging from the physics of musical instruments to everyday phenomena such as the Doppler Effect.

The podcast is a flexible medium capable of storing many different varieties of work by students. For this reason, novice podcasters will benefit from a clear structure that supports them as they develop their podcast. Podcasts are a useful tool because, if you believe the anecdotal stories concerning podcasts and student motivation, students tend to care more about a podcast than they do about a paper or a poster. Given that creating a podcast requires comparable research and analysis skills as summary projects delivered in other mediums, podcasts can provide a less traditional mechanism for reinforcing some more traditional learning goals.

iTunes or not

iTunes and iPods are frequently connected to the topic of podcasting. While the iTunes store is a useful place to find podcasts, and can help increase the visibility of your podcast, you do not need to use iTunes as part of your podcasting regimen. In general, if the purpose of your podcast is to reach an audience outside of your school community, and/or you are creating a series of podcasts over time, then iTunes could be a good way to extend the reach of your podcast.

In situations where the podcasts are informal in nature, or where podcasts are more of a regular means of communication, iTunes is an additional step that adds little value to the teaching and learning involved in creating podcasts.

If you want to add your podcast to the iTunes store, Apple has laid out the process on their website. Navigate to `http://www.apple.com/itunes/podcasts/creatorfaq.html`, and follow the link provided in the **How do I submit my podcast?** section.

Images and image galleries

In previous versions of Drupal, sharing images required many different modules and lots of configuration options. In Drupal 7, some of the functionality provided by image-related modules from the community has been moved into the core and simplified.

> Features from the **Imagefield** module, the **Image API** module and the **Imagecache** module have been moved into core.

Configuring your site to use images

To set up your site to use images, we will follow these steps:

1. Creating an image style (optional).
2. Creating gallery taxonomies.
3. Creating the image content type.
4. Editing the display (optional).

5. Assigning permissions to create and edit images.

6. Creating galleries.

7. Adjusting the student_blog, teacher_blog, and conversations views (optional).

Step 1 – creating an image style (optional)

Image styles allow you to process an image before it is displayed. The most common use for an image style is to create a thumbnail of an image.

Drupal provides three image styles by default:

- A thumbnail that scales an image to 100x100 pixels
- A medium size image that scales an image to 220x220 pixels
- A large size image that scales an image to 480x480 pixels

Click on **Configuration** | **Image styles**, or navigate to `admin/config/media/image-styles`, and click on the **Add style** link.

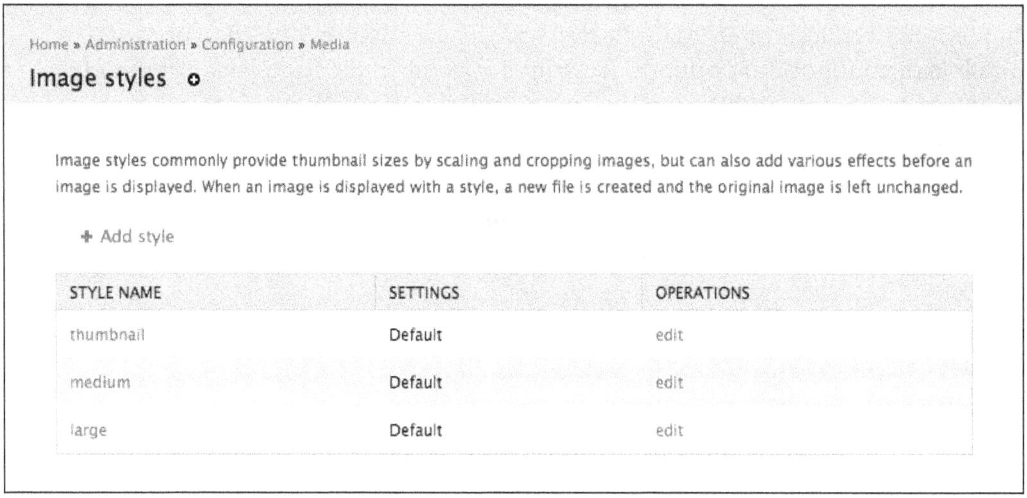

Home » Administration » Configuration » Media

Image styles ⚙

Image styles commonly provide thumbnail sizes by scaling and cropping images, but can also add various effects before an image is displayed. When an image is displayed with a style, a new file is created and the original image is left unchanged.

✚ Add style

STYLE NAME	SETTINGS	OPERATIONS
thumbnail	Default	edit
medium	Default	edit
large	Default	edit

On the next screen, give the style a name. The next screen also gives options to add to the image style. You can select one or many of these effects. If you have added multiple effects, you can drag-and-drop them into the order you wish.

Home » Administration » Configuration » Media » Image styles

Edit *really_big* style ⚙

✓ The image effect was successfully applied.

Preview

original (view actual size)   really_big (view actual size)

600px   540px

800px   720px

Image style name *

really_big

The name is used in URLs for generated images. Use only lowercase alphanumeric characters, underscores (_), and hyphens (–).

Show row weights

EFFECT	OPERATIONS	
✛ Scale 720x720	edit	delete
✛ Select a new effect ▾ Add		

Update style

After adding an effect, the example images will be updated, which allows you to see how the image will be processed by the effects you selected. When you are done, click on the **Update style** button to save your image style.

Step 2 – creating gallery taxonomies

In order to create a gallery, we will need a taxonomy to categorize all the images that should go in that gallery.

1. Click on **Structure | Taxonomy**, or navigate to `admin/structure/taxonomy`.
2. Click on the **Add vocabulary** link, and give the vocabulary the name `Image Galleries`, and a description if you wish.

3. On the next page, click on the **add terms** link next to the Image Gallery vocabulary. Fill in the **Name** field with the name of the first gallery, and a description if you wish.

4. Click on the **Save** button to save the term, and you will be redirected to the same form to add another term. Add a term for each gallery you want.

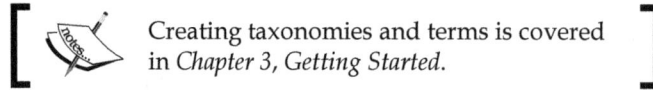

> Creating taxonomies and terms is covered in *Chapter 3, Getting Started*.

Step 3 – creating the image content type

When you are done adding terms, click on **Structure | Content types**, or navigate to admin/structure/types.

1. Click on the **Add content type** link, and name the new content type Image.

2. Uncheck the box next to **Promoted to front page** under the **Publishing options**, and uncheck all boxes under the **Menu** options. You can set the other options according to your own preferences, and then click on the **Save and add fields** button to continue.

3. Unless you need a place to write longer text than a caption, you can delete the **Body** field for this content type. In most cases, the **Title** of the node is sufficient to serve as a caption for the image.

4. By default, Drupal creates an **Image** field and attaches it to the article content type. We can use this field again in the **Image** content type. Under the **Add existing field** section, choose **Image: field_image (Image)**.

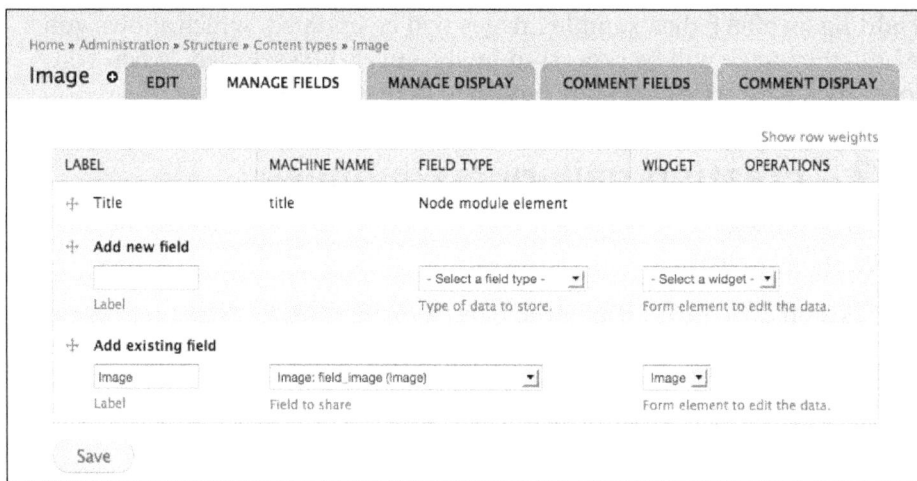

5. Check the box next to **Required**, and add some help text if you wish.

6. While you could use the default settings for all the other options, it would be a good idea to set at least the **Maximum image resolution** fields to be no larger than the widest section of your website. This would prevent large images from breaking the layout of your website. For Drupal's default theme with one sidebar, this width is 720 pixels.

Maximum image resolution

720   x   720   pixels ◀━━━━━

The maximum allowed image size expressed as WIDTHxHEIGHT (e.g. 640x480). Leave blank for no restriction. If a larger image is uploaded, it will be resized to reflect the given width and height. Resizing images on upload will cause the loss of EXIF data in the image.

Minimum image resolution

  x   pixels

The minimum allowed image size expressed as WIDTHxHEIGHT (e.g. 640x480). Leave blank for no restriction. If a smaller image is uploaded, it will be rejected.

Maximum upload size

Enter a value like "512" (bytes), "80 KB" (kilobytes) or "50 MB" (megabytes) in order to restrict the allowed file size. If left empty the file sizes will be limited only by PHP's maximum post and file upload sizes (current limit *32 MB*).

☐ Enable *Alt* field

The alt attribute may be used by search engines, screen readers, and when the image cannot be loaded.

☐ Enable *Title* field

The title attribute is used as a tooltip when the mouse hovers over the image.

Preview image style

thumbnail ▾ ◀━━━━

The preview image will be shown while editing the content.

---

7. You could also set **Preview image style** to a style that you created in step 1.

8. When you are finished setting options, click on the **Save settings** button to save your field.

9. After you have finished editing the **Image** field, add a new **Term Reference** field called **Image Gallery**. Choose **Select list** for **Widget Type**.

10. On the next page, select the **Image Gallery** vocabulary. Add some help text if you wish, and click on the **Save settings** button when you are ready.

11. Using the same method, add the **Term reference: field_keywords (Keywords)** field, with an **Autocomplete term** widget.

Step 4 – edit the display (optional)

If you created an image style in *Step 1 – creating an image style (optional)*, you may want to edit the display of the uploaded image when you view it in the **Image** node.

To do this, click on the **MANAGE DISPLAY** tab on the Image content type edit page. On this screen, you can hide the label for the **Image** field, and edit how the image displays.

To hide the label, select **<Hidden>** under the **Label** column. To update the image display, you can click on the gear button. Select the **Image style** you wish to display.

You can also choose whether to link the image to anything. For our purposes, leave it at the default of **Nothing**. Click on the **Update** button, and then the **Save** button to save your preferences.

Step 5 – assigning permissions to create and edit images

Click on **People | Permissions**, or navigate to `admin/people/permissions`. Under the **Node** section, for the **Image** node add the following rights:

- Assign the **student** role the rights to create images and edit own images
- Assign the **teacher** role the rights to create images and edit own images
- Assign the **administrator** role all the rights

Finally, under the **Taxonomy** section, give the **administrator** and **teacher** roles the permission to **edit terms** and **delete terms** in the **Image Gallery** vocabulary.

Step 6 – creating galleries

Drupal provides a Views template for image galleries, which we will use to create galleries on our site.

Click on **Structure | Views | Add view from template**, or navigate to `admin/structure/views/add-template`, and click on the **add** link next to the **Image Gallery** template.

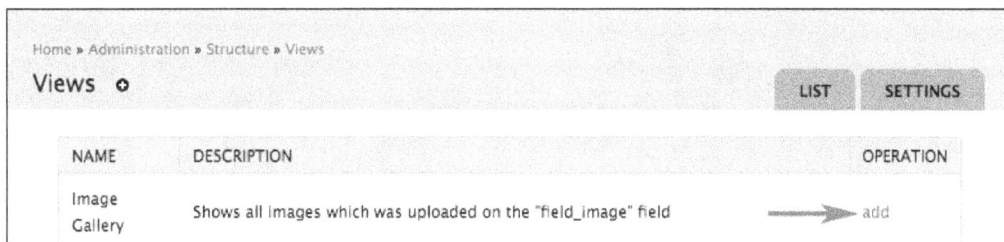

We will need to edit a few of the options as follows:

- Add the **Title** field
- Add **Sort Criteria**

- Add **Content: Taxonomy terms on node** relationship
- Change **Contextual Filter** to **Taxonomy term: Name**

Displays

Gallery page	+ Add		edit view name/description ▾

▾ Gallery Page details

Display name: Gallery page   (view gallery page ▾)

TITLE

Title: Image gallery

FORMAT

Format: Grid | Settings
Show: Fields | Settings

⊘ **FIELDS**   (add ▾)

Content: Image
1 Content: Title
(author) User: Name (Author)

⊘ **FILTER CRITERIA**   (add ▾)

Content: Image:fid (not empty)
Content: Published (Yes)

⊘ **SORT CRITERIA**   (add ▾)

2 Content: Post date (desc)

PAGE SETTINGS

Path: /gallery
Menu: No menu
Access: Permission |
View published content

⊘ **HEADER**   (add)

⊘ **FOOTER**   (add)

PAGER

Use pager: Full |
Paged, 24 items
More link: No

▾ Advanced

⊘ **CONTEXTUAL FILTER**   (add ▾)

4 (term) Taxonomy term: Name

⊘ **RELATIONSHIPS**   (add ▾)

Content: Author
3 Content: Taxonomy terms on
node

NO RESULTS BEHAVIOR   (add)

EXPOSED FORM

Exposed form in block: No
Exposed form style: Basic |
Settings

OTHER

Machine Name: page_1
Comment: No comment
Use AJAX: No
Hide attachments in summary: No
Hide contextual links: No
Use aggregation: No
Query settings: Settings
Field Language:
Current user's language
Caching: None
CSS class: None
Theme: Information

Adding the title field

Click on the **add** button in the **FIELDS** section, add the **Content: Title** field, and uncheck the box next to **Create a label**. Rearrange the fields so the **Title** field is second in the list. Then, click on the **Apply (all displays)** button to continue.

Adding the sort criteria

Click on the **add** button in the **SORT CRITERIA** section. Add the **Content: Post date** criteria, then choose the **Sort descending** radio button. Click on the **Apply (all displays)** button to add the sort criteria and continue.

Adding content relationship

Click on the **add** button in the **RELATIONSHIPS** section. Add the **Content: Taxonomy terms on node** relationship. Click on the checkbox next to the **Image Galleries** vocabulary. Finally, click on the **Apply (all displays)** button to continue.

Changing the contextual filter to taxonomy term

First, remove the **Content: Has taxonomy term ID** filter. Next, add the **Taxonomy term: Name** filter. Select the **Display all results for the specified field** radio button, if it is not already selected. Check the box next to **Override title**, and enter %1 in the text field below it. Click on the **Apply (all displays)** button to continue.

Click the view's **Save** button to save your changes. Now, if you visit http://yoursite.org/gallery you will see an image gallery that contains all the **Image** nodes on the site, with the newest ones displayed first.

When we changed the contextual filter, we made the view accept terms from the **Image Gallery** vocabulary as arguments. So, if you visit http://yoursite.org/gallery/[gallery name], you will see all the images in that specific gallery, and the title of the page will match that term. This feature allows you to add more galleries without having to add a new view each time!

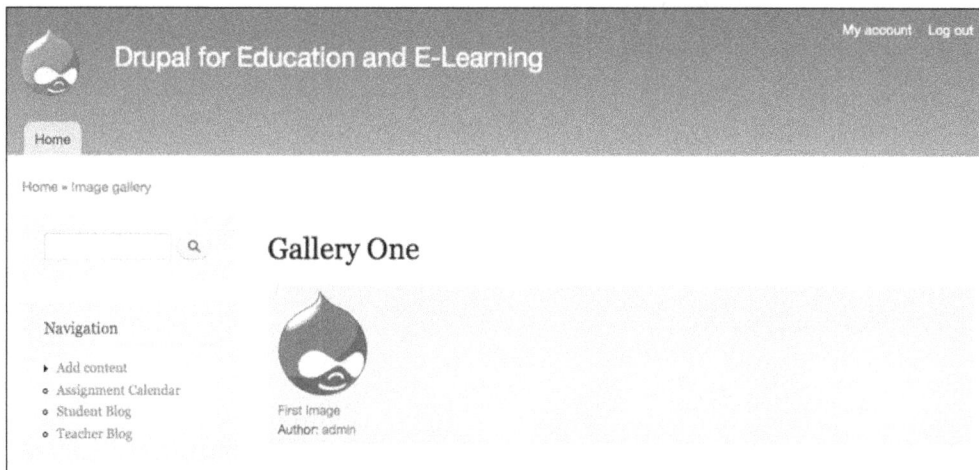

Step 7 – adjusting views (optional)

As was covered earlier in this chapter, we need to adjust the views for the teacher blog, the student blog, and the conversations view to ensure that images get included in these different views. The steps used to add **Audio** nodes to these views—covered earlier in this chapter—can be replicated to add **Image** nodes.

Creating images

Now that the image module has been enabled and configured, we need to upload a photo onto the site. To add an image, navigate to **Create content | Image**, or `node/add/image`.

As shown in the following screenshot, give the image a title, add it into an **Image Gallery**, categorize it using a **Keyword**, and then **Browse** and select the image. Click on the **Save** button to upload the image:

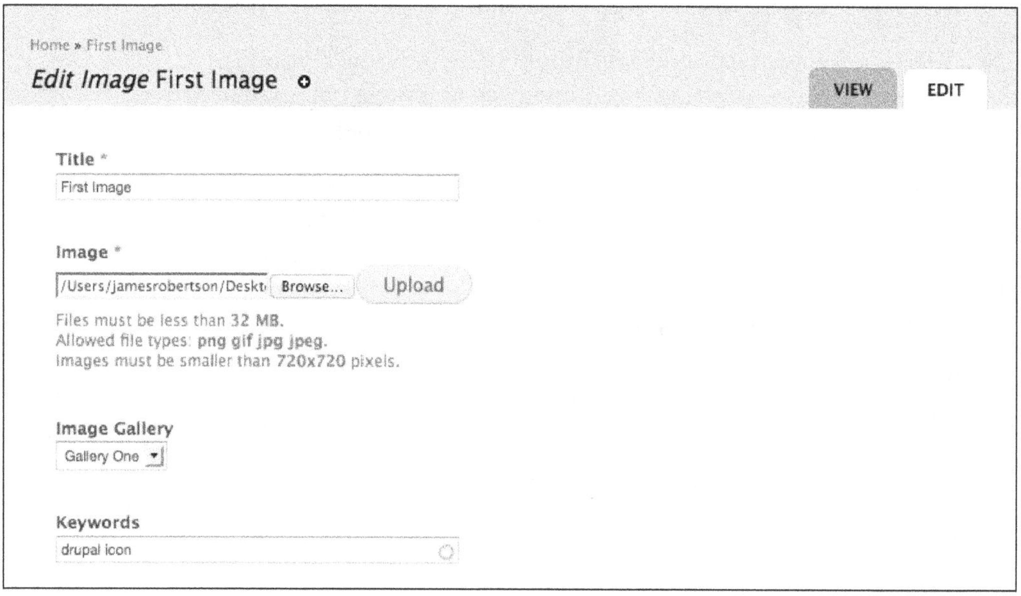

Home » First Image

Edit Image First Image

VIEW   EDIT

Title *

First Image

Image *

/Users/jamesrobertson/Deskt [Browse...] Upload

Files must be less than 32 MB.
Allowed file types: png gif jpg jpeg.
Images must be smaller than 720x720 pixels.

Image Gallery

Gallery One

Keywords

drupal icon

Summary

Depending on the educational goals, podcasts can range from spontaneous acts of creation, such as an audio blog, to a crafted production like a radio play. Creating podcasts uses a range of academic skills that can be addressed explicitly in the process of creating the podcast. The flexibility of the podcast as a medium for expression can be leveraged in support of many different learning goals. However, the most important element of podcasting involves removing barriers between learners and publishing content. At the most basic level, a podcast is just an MP3 file you upload to your site. By remaining focused on the content within a podcast—as opposed to the bells and whistles of unnecessarily complex production of podcasts—you ensure that podcasts remain an accessible tool for daily learning and extended projects.

While the goals and uses of sharing images will vary from class to class, the ability for students to share images creates an additional means by which students can contribute. The technique covered in this chapter provides a flexible, adaptable tool that can be used to organize images for a variety of different educational needs.

In the next chapter, we will add the ability to host video to the site, which can be used to create video podcasts or as another resource to enhance the learning experience in the classroom.

9
Video

Using video in the classroom can be as simple or as complex as you want to make it. As with any use of technology in the classroom, effective planning will help ensure that the technology supports a specific educational goal.

When using video as part of a student project, you can organize the project into these general areas:

- **Clarify the concept**: Frequently, the assignment will provide the context within which the student will work. If the assignment is open-ended, the students should be able to articulate the goal of their video and a specific outline of the action before they begin the next step.

- **Assemble the media**: The media will support, demonstrate, or explain the concept developed in the first step. The media can be a new video that is recorded using screen capture, video camera, or existing freely available media from a variety of online sources.

- **Edit/Organize the media**: Cut unnecessary scenes, add transitions, and clean up the audio. In many cases, this step is not essential, as not every project requires flawless production values.

- **Save**: Save the video in a web-friendly format.

- **Upload**: Upload the video to the Web.

The purpose of this chapter is not to document the skills to make you an award-winning film maker. However, the goal of this chapter is to give you a solid overview of how to create and share informative videos. As with podcasts, the content of your video is the most important thing. If you have compelling content, you have made the most important step toward creating compelling video.

Setting up the video content type

In this chapter, we will cover how to share video using the Embedded Media Field module, available at `http://drupal.org/project/emfield`. There are other methods available for processing, storing, and sharing video that we will cover later in the chapter. For general use, however, we recommend the use of Embedded Media Field, as it balances ease of use and flexibility.

Installing the embedded media field module

Download the Embedded Media Field module from `http://drupal.org/project/emfield` and the Media module from `http://drupal.org/project/media`. Upload these modules into your `sites/all/modules` directory, as described in *Chapter 3, Getting Started*.

The Embedded Media Field module also requires a separate module for each video-hosting service you wish to be able to use on your site. The available modules are listed on the Embedded Media Field project page at `http://drupal.org/project/emfield`. We'll start by downloading and installing the Media: YouTube module (`http://drupal.org/project/media_youtube`).

> You can also use Media API to provide access to services not listed on the project page. Guidance on how to create your own module can be found at `http://drupal.org/node/367359`.

Click on the **Modules** link or navigate to `admin/modules`. Enable the **Embedded Media Field**, **File entity**, **Media**, **Media Internet Sources**, and **Media: YouTube** modules, as described in *Chapter 3, Getting Started*.

Click on the **Save configuration** button at the bottom of the page to save your changes.

Creating the video content type

When creating the video content type, we will refer to the process outlined in *Chapter 3, Getting Started*. When creating a content type, you will need to:

1. Create the content type.
2. Add fields to the content type. In this case, we will add the field that will contain the embedded video.

3. Assign a taxonomy to the content type. In this case, we will allow the video content type to be organized or described using the Keyword taxonomy.

4. Assign permissions to the content type. In our example, both the student and teacher role will be assigned permissions over videos.

Step 1 – creating the content type

Click on **Structure** | **Content types** or navigate to admin/structure/types. Click on the **Add content** type link. In the **Identification** section, use the following values:

- **Name**: Video
- **Type**: Video
- **Description**: Embed video in your site
- In the **Submission form** settings section, the **Explanation or submission guidelines** option can be set to

Click on the **Select media** button to upload a video, embed a video from a video-sharing service (YouTube, Google Video, and so on), or select a video that is already uploaded on the site:

- In **Publishing options**, set the default to **Published**
- In the **Comment settings** section, set the default to **Read/Write**
- Configure the comment displays as described in *Chapter 3, Getting Started*
- In **Menu settings**, uncheck all the options

Click on the **Save and add fields** button to create the content type.

Step 2 – adding the Video field

After you save the **Video** field as described earlier, you will be redirected to the **Fields** page for the Video content type at **Structure** | **Content types** | **Manage fields** or admin/structure/types/manage/video/fields.

In the **add field** administrative screen, enter the following values:

- **Label**: Video location
- **Field type**: File
- **Widget**: Media file selector

Click on the **Save** button to move to the configuration screen for this field.

Configuring the field

The field settings are broken into two sections: the **Video** and the **Field** settings.

Configuring the Video settings

Check the box next to the **Required** field.

For the help text, you can use: `For some video providers, you will be able to simply enter the URL where you see the video. For other providers, you will need to use the embed code. If one method doesn't work, please try the other.`

Uncheck the box next to **Image** and check the option next to **Video**.

In the textbox under **Allowed file extensions for uploaded files**, enter: `mp3 mov m4v mp4 mpeg avi ogv wmv`.

Check all the boxes you need under **Allowed URI schemes**. The **youtube://** option refers to YouTube videos (provided by the Media: YouTube module), and the **public://** option refers to files uploaded to your site.

The final two fields, **File directory** and **Maximum upload size**, are optional.

Configuring the Field settings

In the **Field** settings, set the **Number of values** option to **1**. Then, click on the **Save settings** button to save your settings.

Ordering the fields

After you save the field settings, you will be returned to the **MANAGE FIELDS** admin screen for the Video content type.

Drag the fields into the order in which you want them to be displayed and then click on the **Save** button to save your changes.

Step 3 – assigning a taxonomy

Add the **Term reference: field_keywords (Keywords)** field to the content type, as described in *Chapter 8, Podcasting and Images*.

Step 4 – assigning permissions

Click on **People** | **Permissions** or navigate to `admin/people/permissions`.

As described in *Chapter 3, Getting Started*, assign the teacher role and the student role permissions to **create video content**, **delete own video content**, and **edit own video content**.

Additionally, you need to give the student role the import media files from the local filesystem permission and the **View media** permission. Give the teacher role the same permissions and also the **Edit media** permission.

Click on the **Save permissions** button to save the permissions assigned to both roles.

Embedding videos

Now that we have created the Video content type, it's time to start sharing some video. Log in using one of the test accounts created earlier. As both the student and teacher role have rights to add video, a test account in either the student or teacher role will suffice.

Embedding from an external site

Embedding video from an external site allows you to easily share videos uploaded to other video hosting sites with your classes. As of this writing, 72 hours of video is uploaded to YouTube every minute. Using video from external sites allows you to harness the potential of millions (or even billions) of hours of educational videos these sites offer to the public for free. Follow these steps:

1. Click on **Create Content** | **Video** or navigate to `node/add/video`.

2. Complete the form, as shown in the following screenshot, by filling in the appropriate values for **Title**, **Keywords**, and **Body**:

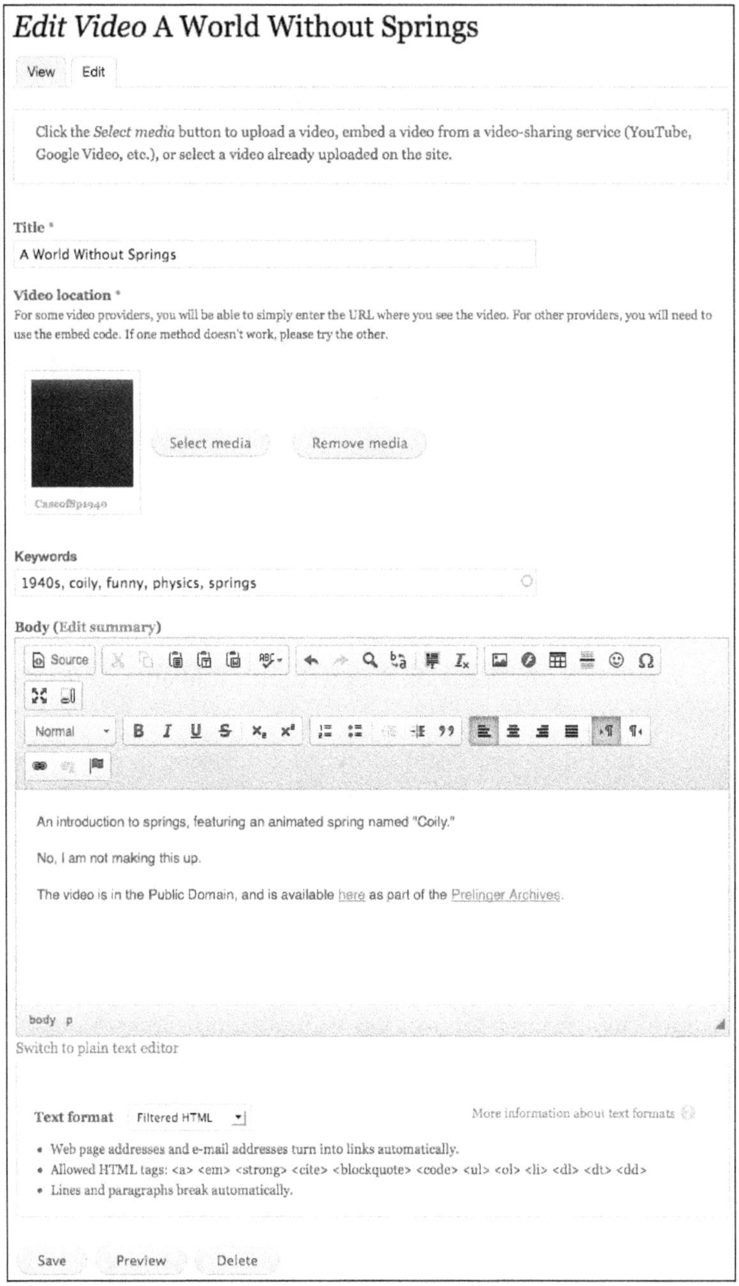

Edit Video A World Without Springs

View   Edit

Click the *Select media* button to upload a video, embed a video from a video-sharing service (YouTube, Google Video, etc.), or select a video already uploaded on the site.

Title *

A World Without Springs

Video location *

For some video providers, you will be able to simply enter the URL where you see the video. For other providers, you will need to use the embed code. If one method doesn't work, please try the other.

Select media   Remove media

CaseofSp1940

Keywords

1940s, coily, funny, physics, springs

Body (Edit summary)

Source

Normal

An introduction to springs, featuring an animated spring named "Coily."

No, I am not making this up.

The video is in the Public Domain, and is available here as part of the Prelinger Archives.

body p

Switch to plain text editor

Text format   Filtered HTML   More information about text formats

- Web page addresses and e-mail addresses turn into links automatically.
- Allowed HTML tags: <a> <em> <strong> <cite> <blockquote> <code> <ul> <ol> <li> <dl> <dt> <dd>
- Lines and paragraphs break automatically.

Save   Preview   Delete

3. Click on the **Select media** button and a pop up will open. Click on the **Web** tab and enter the URL or embed code of a YouTube video in the **URL or Embed code** field.

> The value you enter in the **URL or Embed code** field will vary on a site by site basis due to differences in how sites store and share video. In most cases, you will be able to enter the URL of the page where the video plays, but in some cases, such as for the Internet Archives, you will need to enter the specific URL to the video file. For other sites, you may need to use the provided embed code.

4. Click on the **Submit** button and you will see your video, as shown in the following screenshot:

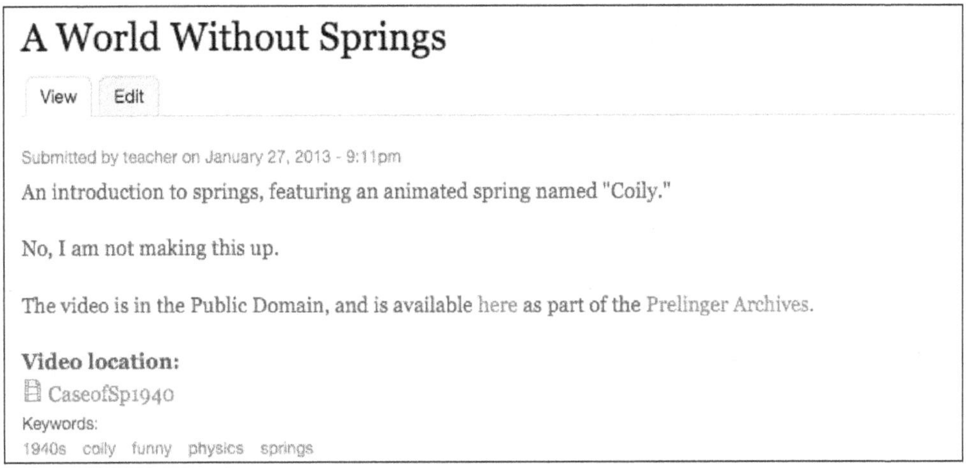

A World Without Springs

View   Edit

Submitted by teacher on January 27, 2013 - 9:11pm

An introduction to springs, featuring an animated spring named "Coily."

No, I am not making this up.

The video is in the Public Domain, and is available here as part of the Prelinger Archives.

Video location:
CaseofSp1940

Keywords:
1940s coily funny physics springs

Embedding from the local site

Follow these steps to embed from the local site:

1. Click on **Create Content | Video** or navigate to `node/add/video`. Complete the form as described earlier by filling in the appropriate values for **Title**, **Keywords**, and **Body**.

2. Click on the **Select media** button and a pop up will open. Click on the **Browse** button to navigate to the video you want to upload.

3. Click on the **Submit** button to save your video.

Sharing video that has been uploaded to your site can require a significant amount of server resources. If a small number of videos are shared in this way, it will not have a significant impact. If, however, video sharing becomes a widespread need, you should look to storing your videos on an external service and streaming them from there, or setting up your site to process and compress videos, as mentioned later in this chapter.

Additionally, sharing video by uploading it to the site can run into file size upload limits. To adjust these limits, navigate to **Structure** | **Content types** | **manage fields** | **edit** or `admin/structure/types/manage/video/fields/field_video_location`.

Adjusting the student and teacher blogs

Now that we have added the Video content type to the site, we need to adjust the student and teacher blogs to display video posts. Editing the view that generates the teacher blog is covered in *Chapter 4, Creating a Teacher Blog*, and *Chapter 6, Creating the Student Blog*.

Additionally, the conversations view, created in *Chapter 6, Creating the Student Blog*, will also need to be updated.

The necessary steps for updating all three of these views are covered in *Chapter 8, Podcasting and Images*.

Hardware and software to create videos

The complexity of producing videos can vary widely. As an easy option, videos can be shot by one person in natural light using a cell phone and uploaded directly to the Web; a complex option would be a video shoot requiring a large crew, specialized cameras, microphones, lighting equipment, video editing software, and dedicated computers for video editing and rendering. The variables for more complex setups are beyond the scope of this book, and fortunately, largely unnecessary for most video production.

In short, if you are starting a video program or just getting into video, you don't need to spend thousands of dollars on specialized equipment and software. As a general rule, specialized equipment adds complexity. As with most classroom usage of technology, you want to make sure that you are emphasizing the learning supported by the technology, as opposed to the technology itself. To that end, a simpler production environment can help support your video program by making it easier and faster to publish videos.

Hardware

Before spending any money on hardware or software for producing videos, talk to people within your organization. If your school offers a course in video production, speak with the instructors and students of that course. In addition to getting good recommendations on equipment, you also might be able to enlist support and assistance if you need it.

Cameras and video capturing equipment

Video cameras range from simple, inexpensive web cams to complex, expensive, professional-quality digital video cameras. Additionally, many computers now come with built-in webcams. If you are unsure about the quality of the camera you need, talk to anyone doing video work within your school, spend some time researching online, and then go down to a local store and try out some cameras before you buy. Depending on the needs of your project, there are many inexpensive options when it comes to capturing video, ranging from the video cameras on many cell phones to flip video cameras.

Microphones and audio quality

Some mid-level to high-end video cameras have a jack where you can record audio directly from a microphone. In some cases, you might also want to use an external microphone (as described in *Chapter 8, Podcasting and Images*) to capture your audio tracks or to capture ambient noise to use during transitions. Capturing a separate audio track will require more work during the production and editing of your video, but it will generate better sound quality. However, it adds a level of complexity that will not be necessary for many video projects.

Lighting equipment and editing stations

For many classroom use, specialized lighting equipment and editing stations are not necessary. Obviously, if the videos are being produced as part of a course on video production, part of the curriculum will likely include the effective use of lighting.

Editing stations can be useful when creating and editing longer videos, as a computer specifically configured for processing video will be faster and more efficient and will therefore save time. However, for many classroom uses, a specialized editing station is not necessary, and it adds a level of technical complexity that can slow down students.

Copying videos from YouTube/Google video

The following websites will download videos from most video hosting sites onto your local hard drive:

- `http://keepvid.com/`
- `http://keep-tube.com/`
- `http://www.videodownloadx.com/`

Additionally, you can download and install the Video Download Helper browser extension for Firefox from `https://addons.mozilla.org/en-US/firefox/addon/3006`. This browser extension allows you to download videos from most video sharing sites; as such, this can be useful if you want to show a video from a site that happens to be blocked by your organization's firewall. Download the video from a location outside the firewall and upload it to your site, as described earlier in this chapter. Then, you can display this video from within the firewall.

> Before you download video from a website, make sure that downloading the video does not violate the licensing terms for reusing the video. If you are ever unsure of the licensing terms for a video, check with the author or copyright holder of the video before using the video.

Software to create and edit videos

As mentioned earlier, for some video projects, no real editing is required. If you need to edit video, however, you have a range of options from free to fairly expensive.

Desktop software

The following list provides some of the options for desktop-editing software:

- **Windows Movie Maker**: This is a video-editing utility installed with Microsoft Windows
- **iMovie**: This is a video-editing utility installed on Mac
- **Quicktime Pro**: This is a relatively inexpensive cross-platform video editing tool
- **Camtasia**: This is a PC-only tool used for screencasts

- **CamStudio**: This is a free, cross-platform tool used for screencasts
- **Wink**: This is a free, cross-platform tool used for screencasts
- **Adobe Premiere**: This is a cross-platform tool. It is a part of Adobe's Creative Suite and is fairly expensive, but is a powerful video-editing tool
- **Final Cut Pro**: This is a Mac-only powerful video production tool, which is fairly expensive

Online tools

Many online tools can be used to create videos and many sites allow you to add clips, edit them down, add audio, and then compile the completed video. Additionally, some sites, such as Google Video and YouTube, allow video to be uploaded directly from mobile phones and other handheld devices. Alan Levine has compiled a list of over 50 options at `http://50ways.wikispaces.com/`.

In addition to these tools, the Jing project at `http://www.techsmith.com/jing.html` is an online tool that lets you collate media into a completed video.

Also, although it isn't specifically an online tool, many mobile phones allow you to take videos and upload them directly to Google Video or other video-sharing sites. Once your video is online, you can download it as described earlier in this chapter.

Using videos in the classroom

The subject matter will play a role in determining how to use video and how much detail (if any) to pay to production values.

Using video effectively requires good planning and some specific ideas about the goals you would like to achieve. In addition to the actual video, students should be expected to learn from the process of making the video. During video-based projects, students should be blogging about their process and their progress, sharing bookmarks on their research, and even constructing short audio podcasts about the project. These points of reflection will provide a more complete picture of the student's work over the course of the project, and will also help to reinforce one of the most important lessons of video production; people get better at something by thinking about how they want to achieve their goals, and the means that they are using to achieve them.

Student projects

If we look at the video from a storytelling or a documentary perspective, we can structure projects within and across curricular boundaries.

Some brief examples:

- **Language learning**: Students can write and film plays that demonstrate vocabulary usage, the use of new grammar, the incorporation of dramatic elements, and so on. These plays can be used in acquiring a foreign language or in studying literature.

- **Videotape field trips**: Prior to a field trip, form your class into several groups. Each group is responsible for producing a documentary of the trip. The specific goals of the documentary can be tailored to support specific educational goals.

- **Video bookends**: Each student produces a video about themselves at the beginning and the end of the school year. This type of project can be used within a specific course as part of a portfolio or across courses as part of a holistic assessment of student growth.

- **Videotape labs**: By adding a video element to labs, students can document their steps and process more clearly. Additionally, in the process of planning and creating the video, students will generate a traditional lab report. Over time, videos can reveal a more clear and compelling portrait of student involvement in a course.

None of these projects have complex production needs, and all can be produced using inexpensive equipment and without specialized hardware or software.

Teaching with video

This section does not address the use (or lack thereof) of feature films in education. Instead, this section addresses how to use primary source material found on the Web to support teaching and learning. Brief clips from video archives that illustrate a clearly defined topic can be used to provide context, introduce a key idea, or provide a point of reference.

Given the range of video available on the Web, we have a wide range of opportunities open to us.

A brief list of sources that contain public domain or Creative Commons licensed video includes:

- `http://wiki.creativecommons.org/Content_Curators`
- `http://commons.wikimedia.org/wiki/Category:Video`
- `http://ourmedia.org/`
- `http://open-video.org/`
- `http://www.archive.org/details/movies`

These video repositories all contain a wealth of freely available content. However, many of these repositories also contain video that would be inappropriate for younger students.

Teachers can create video to achieve specific educational goals. In one of the best examples of effective video use I have seen, a math instructor named Dan Meyer filmed a series of events that can be measured over time: distance, elevation, speed, and so on. Then, he showed these videos to his students and made the graph of what was shown in the videos. The full description, including the videos he created for his lesson, are available on his blog at `http://blog.mrmeyer.com/?p=213`.

Although creating new videos as part of a curriculum is time-consuming, it can also be a useful tool for modeling how to use video effectively for students.

Drupal as a video hosting and processing platform

Drupal can be configured to work as a fully functional YouTube or Google Video clone, by combining video processing modules, such as Video (`http://drupal.org/project/video`) or Media Mover (`http://drupal.org/project/media_mover`) and other modules, such as Views. Setting up the environment to serve video requires some familiarity with setting up Linux-based servers and an open source video conversion utility called FFmpeg. The advantage of building your own video-processing site is that it gives you full control over all aspects of your material with none of the privacy concerns, or concerns over inappropriate content that you may have with YouTube or Google Video.

Additionally, if your academic program needs to support the hosting of large amount of video, using either Video or Media Mover, will have performance benefits. As noted earlier, using Video or Media Mover requires a more robust server environment, but the benefits of hosting your own video processing (that is, onsite conversion of different video formats to Flash files) can justify the additional time needed to set up the server infrastructure.

Although the complete details of setting up such as server environment are beyond the scope of this book, you can read more details of how to set these systems up in the documentation for the Media Mover and the Video modules.

Summary

If you are interested in learning more about communicating with video, the Web is filled with incredible resources. The two sites that have particularly useful information include:

- `http://www.youtube.com/video_toolbox`
- `http://chris.pirillo.com/50-youtube-and-online-video-tips-and-tricks/`

However, the most important thing to remember about video is that it doesn't need to be technologically complex. If you keep the focus on what can be learned through making the video, in addition to the actual video, you can use the process of creating video to help your students learn more efficiently. In the next chapter, we will cover how to use Drupal's core forum functionality, and compare and contrast it with the blog functionality we have already created.

10
Forums and Blogs

In this chapter we will explore the relationship between blogs and forums. These tools support communication between site members but each tool offers different capabilities, and using them effectively requires a clear understanding of how these tools relate to one another. Depending on the goals of your course, you can choose the tool that matches your instructional goals, and your students' learning styles.

The first half of this chapter covers how to install and configure the **Forum** module. The second half gives a brief overview of the relationships between forums and blogs.

Installing the Forum module

Drupal comes with a core Forum module. To install this module, click on **Modules**, or navigate to admin/modules. Select the checkbox next to **Forum**, and then click on the **Save configuration** button at the bottom of the page to enable the module.

Configuring forums

After enabling the Forum module, we need to configure it. To begin this process, navigate to **Administration** and select the **Index** tab, or navigate directly to `admin/index`.

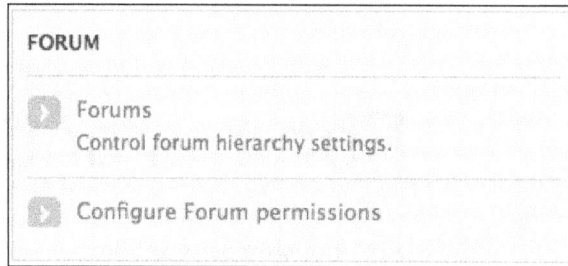

```
FORUM

    Forums
    Control forum hierarchy settings.

    Configure Forum permissions
```

Click the link for **Forums,** by navigating to **Administration | Structure | Forums** or `admin/structure/forum` page.

Containers and forums

When configuring forums, we can organize our forums using top-level containers and individual forums.

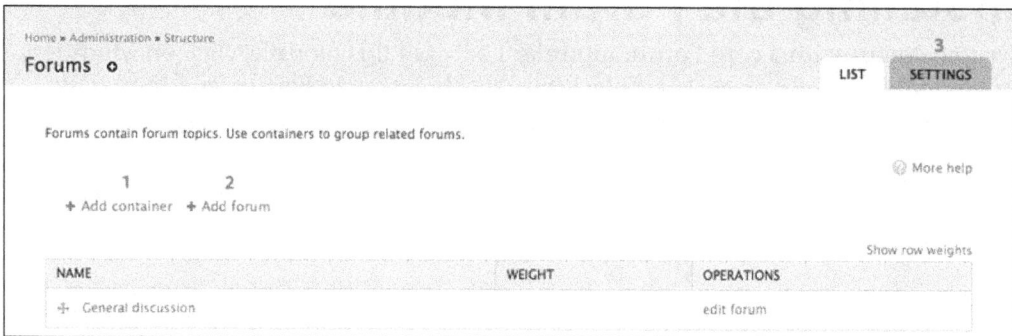

```
Home » Administration » Structure                                                     3
Forums  ○                                                      LIST    SETTINGS

  Forums contain forum topics. Use containers to group related forums.
                                                                        ⑦ More help
            1            2
    + Add container   + Add forum
                                                                    Show row weights
  NAME                              WEIGHT           OPERATIONS

  ╬  General discussion                              edit forum
```

To add a container, click on the **Add container** button as shown in the preceding screenshot by section **1**.

To add a forum, click on the **Add forum** button as shown in the preceding screenshot by section **2**.

Forums do not need to be in containers. If you have more than one forum, a container is a useful tool to organize your forums. However, in setting up forums, it is recommended that you start as simple as possible, as you can always create additional forums and containers as the need for them arises. In the early stages of building community, you want your site to look busy; multiple forums can fragment user interaction, which makes your site appear less busy. Multiple forums can also overwhelm users as they are attempting to learn how to navigate around your site. Too many options (in the form of multiple forums) can feel overwhelming.

For an example of containers, and forums within that container, visit http://drupal. org/forum. Here, **Support** is a container; **Post installation**, **Before you start**, **Installing Drupal**, and **Upgrading Drupal** are all forums inside the **Support** container.

Drupal

Get Started   Community   Documentation   Support   Download & Extend   Marketplace   About

Drupal Homepage   Log In / Register

Refine your search ▾

Community

Community Home   Getting Involved   Chat   Mailing Lists   Member Directory   Forum

Login to post new content in the forum.

Forum	Topics	Posts	Last post
★ Support Try searching the site or a specific project's bug reports first. Remember all support on this site is on a volunteer basis, so please visit the forum tips for posting hints.			
Post installation Drupal is up and running but how do I ...?	156933	560331	41 sec ago by chukkitty
Before you start Is Drupal a viable solution for my website? Please see the documentation Getting Started before posting.	6814	28563	4 hours 41 min ago by nicoz
Installing Drupal Installing Drupal? Please see the documentation in the handbook and the video resources for Drupal 5 and Drupal 6 for additional installation resources.	14517	61494	15 min 1 sec ago by cosmospie
Upgrading Drupal Questions regarding upgrading an existing Drupal site. Don't forget to read the UPGRADE.txt that comes with evey Drupal download.	5888	22823	3 hours 1 min ago by rchan001

New forum topics

Account Pending Approval

File Attachments

Updating module's schema: Best practice?

Theme development detail

Unexpected Error Please Help

Creating a gallery and allowing authenticated users to upload photos that need Moderator approval

Form api states on selectbox with multiple

question about devel_themer

How to uninstall a module?

Dragable Views - issue with exposed filters?

more

The final step in configuring forums involves adjusting the **Settings**, as indicated by section **3** in the screenshot featuring adding new forums and modules, and as shown in the following screenshot:

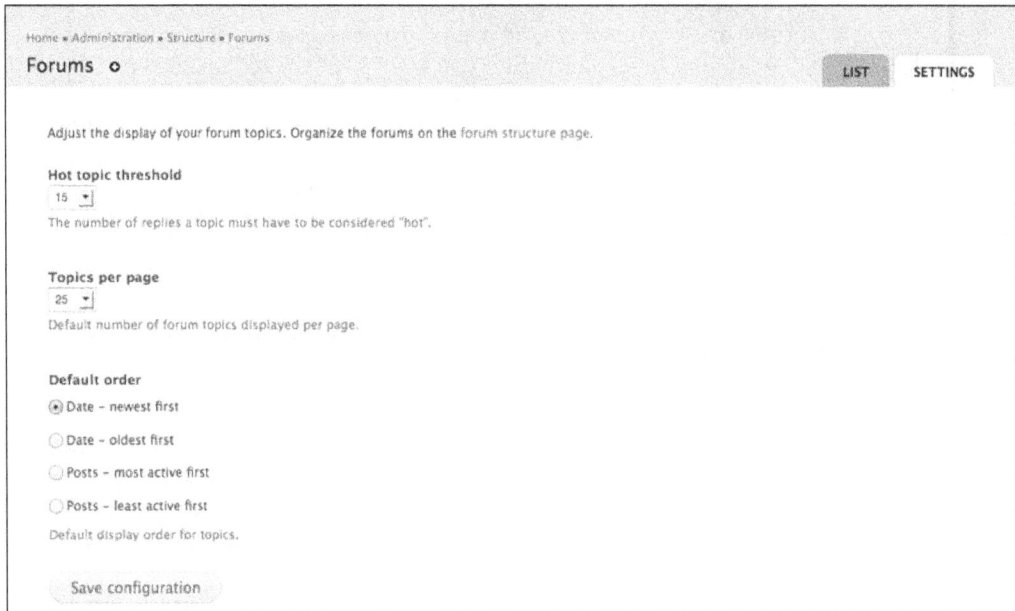

The forum settings consist of three options:

- **Hot topic threshold**: This indicates the number of comments in a thread required for a post to be considered more active than others. These posts can be displayed in the **Active forum topics** block, which can be enabled by clicking on **Structure | Blocks**, or by navigating to `admin/structure/block`.

- **Topics per page**: This indicates the number of posts displayed on the forum overview page. The default (**25**) makes sense, as 25 posts can be displayed on a single screen on most monitor resolutions.

- **Default order**: This indicates the order in which posts are displayed. Although the best setting is subjective, displaying the newest posts first allows the more recent conversations to be highlighted, which can help discussions on a site gather and maintain momentum over time.

After you have made all necessary adjustments to the settings, click the **Save configuration** button to save your settings.

Displaying multiple content types in a forum

Within Drupal, forums are actually organized using **taxonomy**. When the Forum module is enabled, a new Forums vocabulary is created. This vocabulary can be edited in the usual way, as described in *Chapter 3, Getting Started* by clicking on **Structure | Taxonomy**, or by navigating to admin/structure/taxonomy.

You can set which content types are added to forums by adding a **Term reference** field that uses the Forums vocabulary.

This feature can be very useful in a site that manages a single class, or in a site where forums are the primary vehicle for organizing communication. However, if we use a combination of forums, blogs, and groups alongside each other, it can become confusing for site users.

Assigning permissions to forums

To assign permissions for forums, click on the **People | Permissions** tab, or navigate to admin/people/permissions. We will be adjusting permissions for the **Teacher** and **Student** roles.

PERMISSION	ANONYMOUS USER	AUTHENTICATED USER	ADMINISTRATOR	TEACHER	STUDENT
Forum topic: Create new content	☐	☑	✓	✓	✓
Forum topic: Edit own content	☐	☑	✓	✓	✓
Forum topic: Edit any content	☐	☐	☑	☑	☐
Forum topic: Delete own content	☐	☐	☑	☑	☐
Forum topic: Delete any content	☐	☐	☑	☑	☐

The forum module has six permissions:

- **administer forums**
- **Create new content**
- **Edit own content**
- **Edit any content**
- **Delete own content**
- **Delete any content**

Of these six permissions, only one, **Create new content**, is a must assign for site users. Additionally, most users will probably want to be able to **Edit own content**. However, it's worth considering that if a user edits a forum post after a comment has been made, the context of the comment and the subsequent discussion will be lost. For this reason, we generally recommend only assigning the ability to **Edit any content** — and either of the **delete** privileges — to very trusted users.

Once you have assigned the desired rights to both the **Student** and **Teacher** roles, click on the **Save permissions** button to save the settings.

The relationship between forums and blogs

Forums and blogs both support interactive, threaded discussions between users. However, many users report that conversations within blogs feel different than conversations within forums. In general terms, forums feel more group centric, and blogs feel more individual centric.

Within Drupal, however, these paradigms can be shifted. For example, the taxonomy module and use of keywords allows blog posts to be organized in the same way as forum posts; within groups (discussed in *Chapter 12, Supporting Multiple Classes*), blog topics can feel more like a forum. In the rest of this chapter, we will look at some of the ways in which these modes of discussion differ, with an eye towards helping clarify how and when to use each tool for the greatest effect.

Forums

Forums are among the oldest of the online communication tools, as they have their roots in tools that have been around since the 1970s. Traditionally, forums provide a place for group members to come together to discuss specific issues and questions; within a classroom, this provides their greatest strength and greatest weakness.

For more information on the history of online forums and discussion boards, Wikipedia provides an excellent overview at `http://en.wikipedia.org/wiki/Bulletin_board_system`.

Strengths

As discussed in this chapter, forums provide a place for people to go to ask questions. Because forums are usually organized around specific topics, when you're there, you have context about what you are supposed to be discussing. Particularly with younger students, or less tech-savvy students, this level of structure can be both comforting and useful.

Forums can be very useful as a place for offering support, or for posting announcements. Because these needs are largely recurring, the structure of a forum provides an ideal place to publish and store such information.

Additionally, because discussions in forums typically play out over time, the discussion can be more gradual. This offers the potential for more thoughtful discussions.

Concerns

In an online course, forums can feel repetitive when used alongside blogs. Traditionally, forums existed as part of a larger website, or as the primary means of communication within a course. When other methods of communication exist, the multiplicity of options can become confusing for the end user, and can end up fragmenting the conversation. This is particularly true when using blogs, groups, and forums within the same site.

Blogs

When compared to forums, blogs are relatively new, having risen to prominence and popularity in the 1990s. For an overview of how blogging has developed over time, refer to the History of Blogging Timeline at `http://en.wikipedia.org/wiki/History_of_blogging_timeline`.

Strengths

Blogs are ideally suited as a tool for personal reflection, as blogs feel more centered around a person and their ideas. Additionally, other classroom activities can be used to transition into reflective blog postings; for example, ideas raised in response to a chat prompt can be explored fully within a blog post.

Concerns

When compared to forums, the decentralized nature and individual focus of blogs feels less conducive to community building. Within a Drupal-based course site, however, where some blogging occurs within a course, and blogs can be tagged with community-generated keywords, this is mitigated to some extent.

Forums versus blogs

Blogs and forums both support communication. The differences between blogs and forums are fairly subjective, and the best choice often revolves around issues more closely attached to style than substance. Because of these similarities, using blogs and forums within the same site can get confusing.

If you have multiple courses on one site (which we will cover in *Chapter 12, Supporting Multiple Classes*), you might want to use forums for more general discussions across all the courses, and use blogs as the means for managing discussions for a single course. In this situation, people know that to communicate for a specific course, they use a blog, and to communicate outside of the context of a specific course, they use a forum.

However, in the absence of a clear distinction between blogs and forums, we recommend using either a blog or a forum. This can lead to a site that is easier to use, which in turn contributes to a better learning experience. Whatever choice you make in structuring your course, be sure that you can explain the rationale behind it to your students.

For those of you who want additional information and insight on using blogs and forums, Donna Cameron and Terry Anderson published the results of an academic research study entitled Comparing Weblogs to Threaded Discussion Tools in Online Educational Contexts, in the International Journal of Instructional Technology and Distance Learning. The full text of the article is available at `http://www.itdl.org/Journal/Nov_06/article01.htm`.

Summary

In this chapter we discussed how to set up forums using Drupal's built-in Forum module. We also discussed how to determine whether forums or blogs will be the best choice for fostering communication on our site. In the next chapter, we will learn how to further open up communication among students by setting up user profiles and adding other social networking features.

11

Social Networks and Extending the User Profile

The term social network means different things to different people. However, the starting point of any network is the individuals within it. A user profile provides a place for site members to describe themselves and for other site members to find out about one other. In this chapter, we will:

- Examine how to create a user profile that is aligned with the goals of your site
- Learn how to add fields to the user profile
- Learn how to organize fields in a more meaningful way
- Learn how to set permissions for individual fields

Identifying the goals of user profiles

User profiles can be used for a range of purposes. On one end of the spectrum, a profile can be used to store basic information about the user. On the other end of the spectrum, a user profile can be a place for a user to craft and share an online identity. As you create the functionality behind your user profile page, you should know the type of profile you want to create for your users.

Drupal ships with a core User module. This module is a great starting point, and for many sites, it will provide all of the functionality needed.

If, however, you want more control over who will see certain parts of a profile, you will probably need to take the next step: adding modules to control the field-level permissions.

The most suitable approach to user profiles will be determined by the goals of your site. Using Drupal's core User module provides some simple options that will be easy to set up and use. Adding permissions modules requires more time to set up.

In this chapter, we will begin by describing how to set up profiles using the core User module. Then, we will look at how to use the Field Permissions module.

Using the core User module

You can see a user's profile information by navigating to `http://example.com/user/UID`, where UID is the user's ID number on the site. To see your own user profile, navigate to `http://example.com/user` when you log in or click on the **My account** link.

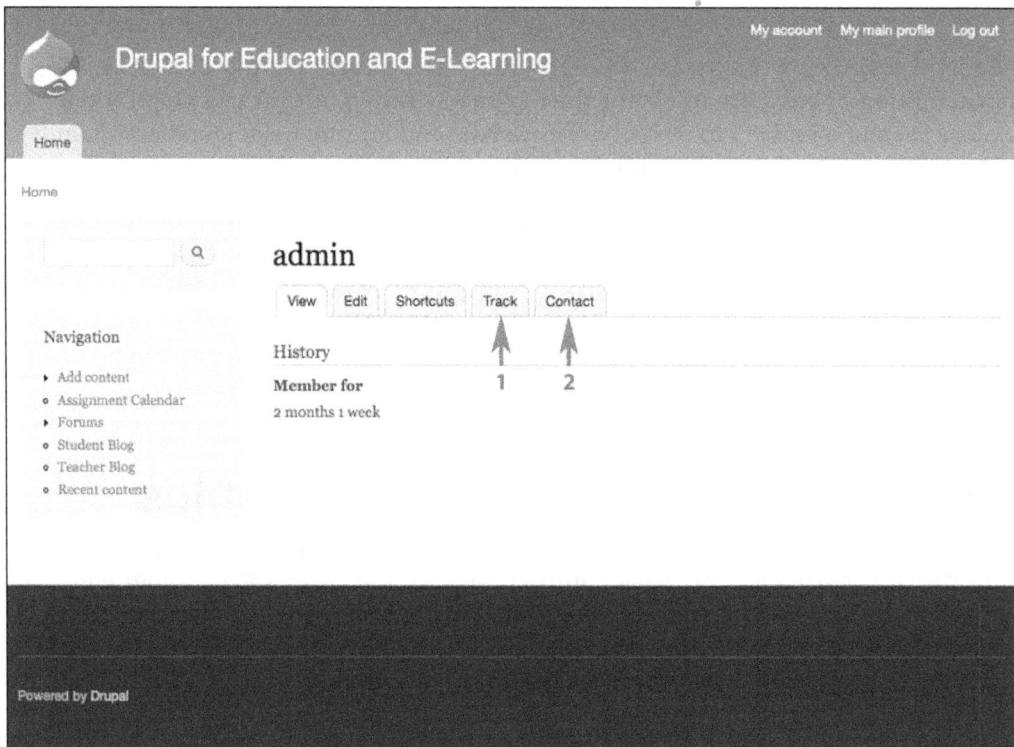

The default user profile page exposes some useful functionality. First, it shows the user's profile, and secondly, it provides the **Edit** tab that allows a user to edit their profile. The **Edit** tab will only be visible to the owner of the profile or to administrative users with elevated permissions.

Other modules can add tabs to the core profile page. As shown in the preceding screenshot by section **1**, the core Tracker module adds a **Track** tab; this tab gives an overview of all the posts to which this user has participated. The Tracker module is discussed in more detail in *Chapter 13, Tracking Student Progress*.

As shown in the preceding screenshot by section **2**, the **Contact** tab has been added by the core Contact module. The Contact module allows users to contact one another via the site.

Customizing the core profile

The first step in customizing the user profile requires us to plan what we want the profile to show. By default, Drupal only requires users to create a username and provide an e-mail address. From a user privacy perspective, this is great. However, for a teacher trying to track multiple students across multiple classes, this can be less than useful.

For this sample profile, we will add two fields using the core User module: a last name and a birthday.

The admin features for the core profile module are accessible via **Configuration | Account settings | Manage Fields** or you can navigate to `admin/config/people/accounts/fields`.

As seen in the preceding screenshot, the core profile module offers the same possibilities for customization as nodes.

In our example profile—adding a last name and a birthday—our last name will be a text field; our birthday will be a date field.

Adding a last name

Let's start by clicking on **Configuration | Account settings | MANAGE FIELDS** or by navigating to admin/config/people/accounts/fields and then adding a text field.

For reasons of clarity, we will break up the administrative form used for adding profile fields. The first half is shown in the following screenshot:

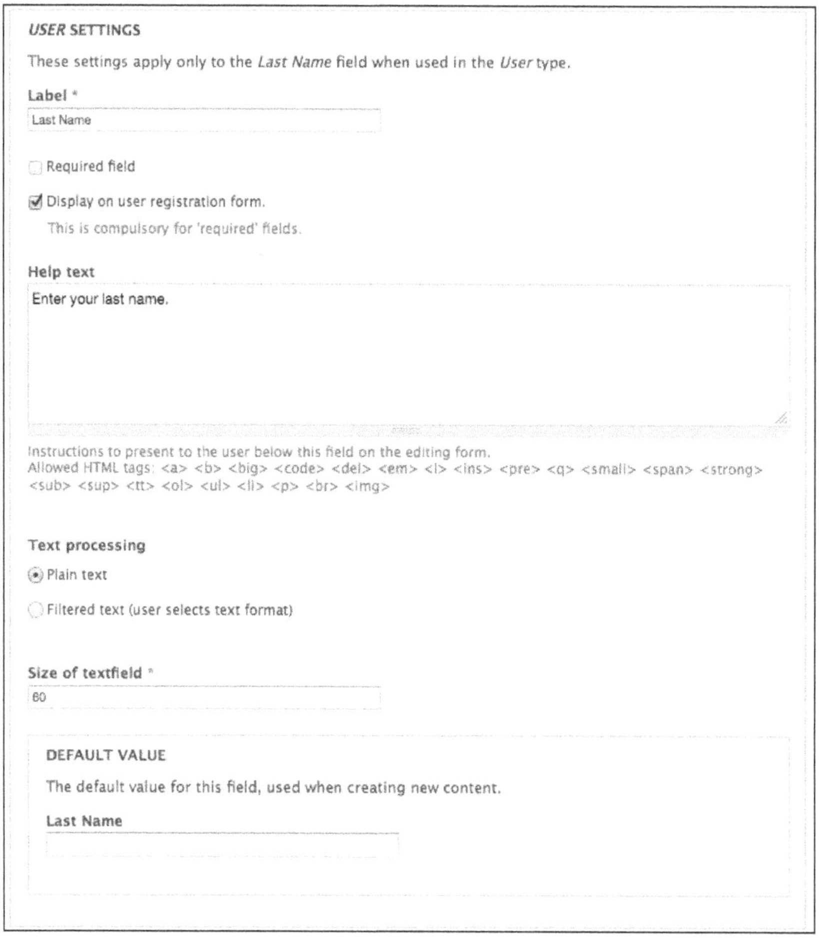

USER SETTINGS

These settings apply only to the *Last Name* field when used in the *User* type.

Label *

| Last Name |

☐ Required field

☑ Display on user registration form.
   This is compulsory for 'required' fields.

Help text

| Enter your last name. |

Instructions to present to the user below this field on the editing form.
Allowed HTML tags: `<a> <b> <big> <code> <del> <em> <i> <ins> <pre> <q> <small> <span> <strong> <sub> <sup> <tt> <ol> <ul> <li> <p> <br> <img>`

Text processing

◉ Plain text

○ Filtered text (user selects text format)

Size of textfield *

| 80 |

DEFAULT VALUE

The default value for this field, used when creating new content.

Last Name

| |

The following is the description of the options present in the previous screenshot:

- **Label**: The **Label** section will be presented to the user when they are completing the profile form. The value here should be short and should make sense.

- **Required field**: This checkbox makes the field required for all users.

- **Display on user registration form**: This checkbox adds the field to the user registration form, so users can enter a value when they create an account. As noted, if the field is required, this checkbox will turn on automatically.

- **Help text**: The help text is presented to the person as they are completing or editing the form. It is optional.

- **Text processing**: These radio buttons select whether the field should accept plain text or if it should accept filtered text. Text filters can be set on **Administration | Configuration | Text formats** or at `admin/config/content/formats`.

- **Size of textfield**: By default, the size of the text field is 60 characters. You can make it shorter if you wish.

- **DEFAULT VALUE**: While it doesn't make sense for this specific use, you can set the default value for a text field here.

The following screenshot shows the remaining options on the form:

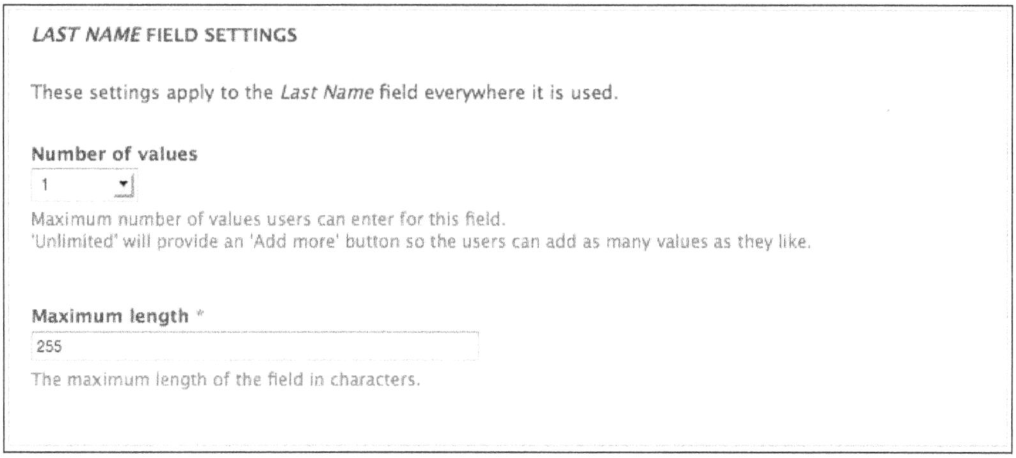

LAST NAME FIELD SETTINGS

These settings apply to the *Last Name* field everywhere it is used.

Number of values

1

Maximum number of values users can enter for this field.
'Unlimited' will provide an 'Add more' button so the users can add as many values as they like.

Maximum length *

255

The maximum length of the field in characters.

The following is the description of the remaining options :

- **Number of values**: This is set to **1** by default
- **Maximum length**: This is set to 255 characters by default

For the last name field, the previous values should be set as shown in the last two screenshots. These values are also listed as follows:

- **Label**: **Last name**
- Check the **Display on user registration form** checkbox
- **Help text**: Enter your last name
- Plain text
- **Size of textfield: 60**
- **Default value**: Leave this blank
- **Number of values: 1**
- **Maximum length**: 255

When you have adjusted these settings to your desired preferences, click on the **Save settings** button to submit the form and save your changes.

Adding a birthday

Adding the birthday field is nearly identical to adding the last name field.

Let's start by clicking on **Configuration | Account settings | MANAGE FIELDS** or by navigating to `admin/config/people/accounts/fields`, and then adding a date field.

Set the **Date** field's **Form Options** as follows:

- **Label**: **Birthday**
- **Date attributes to collect**: **Year**, **Month**, and **Day**
- Check **Display on user registration form** checkbox
- **Help text**: **Please enter your date of birth**
- All other options can be left at their defaults

When you have adjusted these settings to your desired preferences, click on **the Save settings** button to submit the form and save your changes.

Managing your profile fields

When you have created your profile fields, you can manage them by clicking on
Configuration | Account settings | MANAGE FIELDS or by navigating to `admin/config/people/accounts/fields`, as shown in the following screenshot:

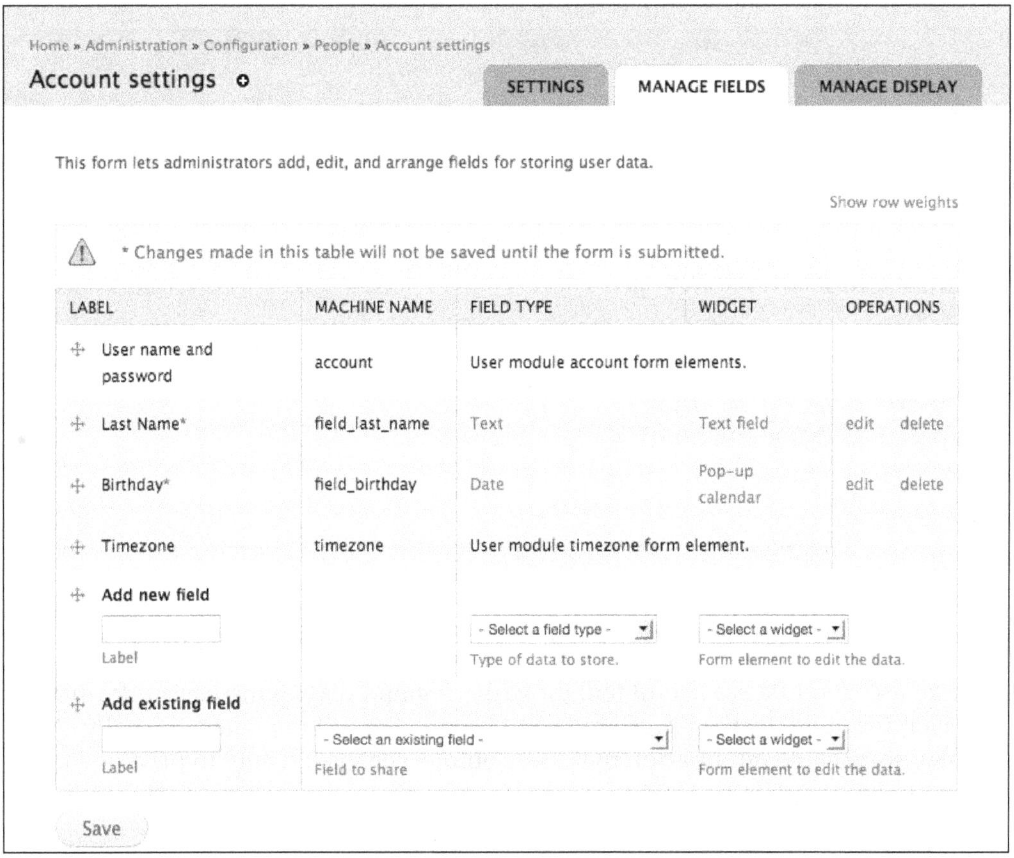

Home » Administration » Configuration » People » Account settings

Account settings ⚙

| SETTINGS | MANAGE FIELDS | MANAGE DISPLAY |

This form lets administrators add, edit, and arrange fields for storing user data.

Show row weights

⚠ * Changes made in this table will not be saved until the form is submitted.

LABEL	MACHINE NAME	FIELD TYPE	WIDGET	OPERATIONS
✛ User name and password	account	User module account form elements.		
✛ Last Name*	field_last_name	Text	Text field	edit delete
✛ Birthday*	field_birthday	Date	Pop-up calendar	edit delete
✛ Timezone	timezone	User module timezone form element.		
✛ **Add new field**				
Label		- Select a field type - ▾ Type of data to store.	- Select a widget - ▾ Form element to edit the data.	
✛ **Add existing field**				
Label		- Select an existing field - ▾ Field to share	- Select a widget - ▾ Form element to edit the data.	

Save

The **edit** link allows you to adjust the settings of the individual fields, and the order of the fields can also be rearranged by dragging-and-dropping.

Adding content to a profile created using the core User module

Users can edit their profile by clicking on the **My account** link and the **Edit** tab, as shown in the following screenshot:

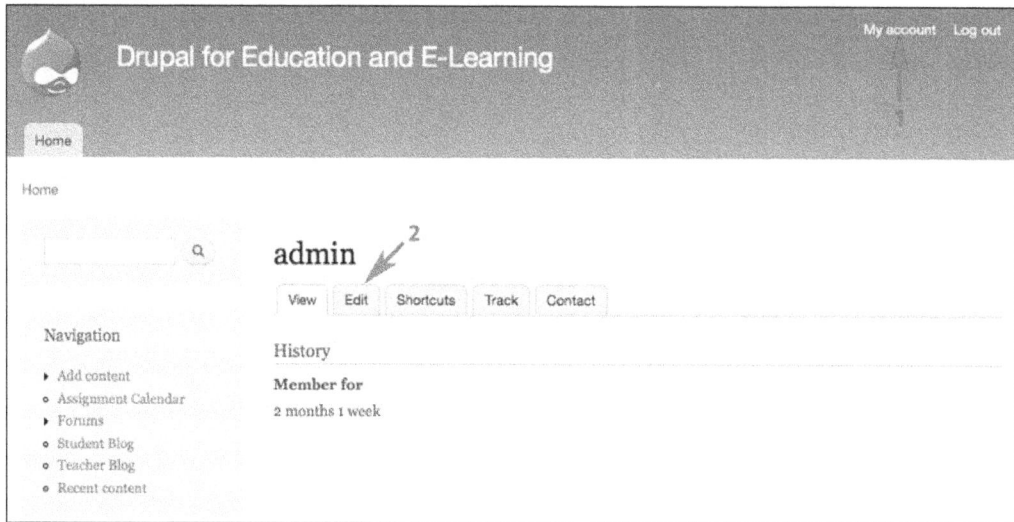

Moving beyond the core profile module

The core user module is a useful tool for gathering and displaying basic information. However, for more detailed profiles it can become difficult to manage visually. Also, you may want some information that users enter to be visible only to privileged users or to be completely private.

When to look beyond the profile module

There are multiple options for how to extend user profiles; to the extent that there is an entire group devoted to discussing it at http://groups.drupal.org/profiles-as-nodes. You may want to consider other modules that extend user profiles if:

- You want to organize the fields in a more meaningful way
- You want to have a blend of public and private information and you want the public information to be searchable

- You want more flexibility in what your users can share and display, and you want to set up pages where people can find other people based on interests, likes, dislikes, and so on

Extending profiles using the field group and field permissions modules

To extend user profiles, we will use the Field group module available at `http://drupal.org/project/field_group` and the Field Permissions module available at `http://drupal.org/project/field_permissions`.

To begin, install the Field group and Field Permissions modules as described in *Chapter 3, Getting Started*. Once these modules are installed, we are ready to begin building our extended profile.

Building the profile

We need to complete a few additional steps to make our profile fully functional:

1. Add fields to the profile.
2. Add taxonomy terms to the profile.
3. Create field groups.
4. Add fields to field groups.
5. Assign rights to view and edit fields.

Adding fields to the profile

For this example, we want to add a long text and summary field and a taxonomy to the profile.

Create a **Long text and summary** field with the name Bio with the following values:

- **Label: Bio**
- **Display on user registration form**
- **Help text: Enter a short biography. You may add a summary of your biography by clicking on the Edit summary link. Otherwise, the summary will be taken from the beginning of your full biography and shortened to a certain number of characters**

- **Filtered text**
- **Summary input**
- All other options can be left to their defaults

After clicking on **Save settings**, add a new taxonomy called **Interests**, as you did in *Chapter 10, Forums and Blogs*.

Next, add a **Term reference** field called **Interests** with an **Autocomplete** widget. Use the newly created **Interests** vocabulary and set the other options as follows:

- **Label: Interests**
- **Display on user registration form**
- **Help text: Enter a comma-separated list of your interests.**
- **Number of values: Unlimited**

Creating field groups

If you navigate to **Configuration | Account settings | MANAGE DISPLAY** or to `admin/config/people/accounts/display`, you will see there is now an option to add new group.

The Field group module allows you to create many different user interface elements to help organize fields in your profile, including HTML field sets, vertical tabs, horizontal tabs, accordions, and multipage tabs.

For our profile, we will create a horizontal tab group to mimic the functionality of the core profile module in Drupal 6.

First, navigate to **Configuration | Account settings | MANAGE DISPLAY** or to `admin/config/people/accounts/display`. Here you will see a new option: **Add new group**.

To create a horizontal tab group, first we have to create a **Horizontal tabs group** item, which will represent the container to hold all of the tabs. Next, we will create individual **Horizontal tab items** and drag-and-drop them to be children of **Horizontal tabs group item**. Finally, we will add our fields as children of those **Horizontal tab items**.

Create a **Horizontal tabs group** field with a field name of **Tabs** and a label of **group_tabs**.

Create a **Horizontal tab item** field called **Personal Information** with the label **group_personal_info** and drag it under **Tabs**.

Create a **Horizontal tab item** field called **About Me** with the label **group_about_me**. Click-and-drag it so it is a child field of **Tabs**. When you are finished, the **MANAGE DISPLAY** screen should look like the following screenshot:

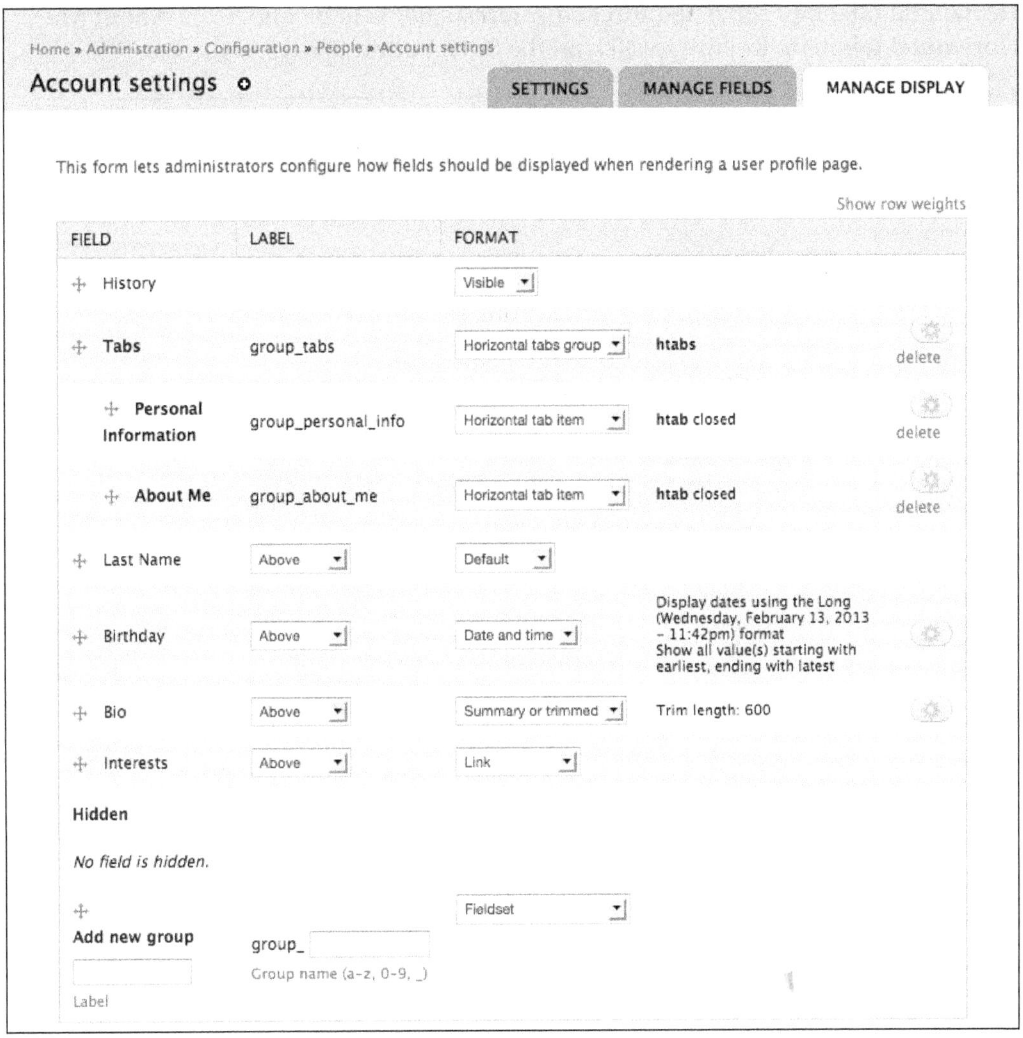

Adding fields to the field groups

Fields can be added to field groups by clicking on the crossed arrow icons and dragging them where you want them to be in the hierarchy, much like you did with the field groups.

Move the **Last Name** and **Birthday** fields to be under the **Personal Information Horizontal tab** item. Move the **Bio** and **Interests** fields to be under the **About Me Horizontal tab** item. Be sure to click on the **Save** button to save your changes.

Assigning permissions to view and edit fields

The Field Permissions module makes it possible to show and hide certain fields based on who has permission to view them. For our example, we will make the **Last Name** and **Birthday** fields private and the **Bio** and **Interests** fields public.

To change the permissions for a field, click on the **edit** link next to the field on the **Manage Fields** screen. You can set the permissions on the field under the field-level settings at the bottom of the page, under the heading **Field visibility and permissions**.

LAST NAME FIELD SETTINGS

These settings apply to the *Last Name* field everywhere it is used.

Field visibility and permissions

○ Public (author and administrators can edit, everyone can view)

◉ Private (only author and administrators can edit and view)

○ Custom permissions

Number of values

| 1 | ▾ |

Maximum number of values users can enter for this field.
'Unlimited' will provide an 'Add more' button so the users can add as many values as they like.

Maximum length *

255

The maximum length of the field in characters.

Assigning rights to view profiles

You can control which roles are able to see user profiles by navigating to **People | PERMISSIONS** or admin/people/permissions. In general, you probably only want users with accounts on the site to see each other's profiles, so give the authenticated user role the permission to **View user profiles**.

Additionally, you can give trusted users the ability to see the contents of protected fields by giving them **Access other users' private fields permission**.

Creating an extended profile

Now that we have made all of the necessary adjustments to the profile, we are ready to have users populate their profiles.

Users can fill out their profiles by navigating to their profile page, either by clicking on the **My account** link or by navigating to `http://example.edu/user` when they are logged in. Clicking on the **Edit** tab will direct the user to the edit page for their profile.

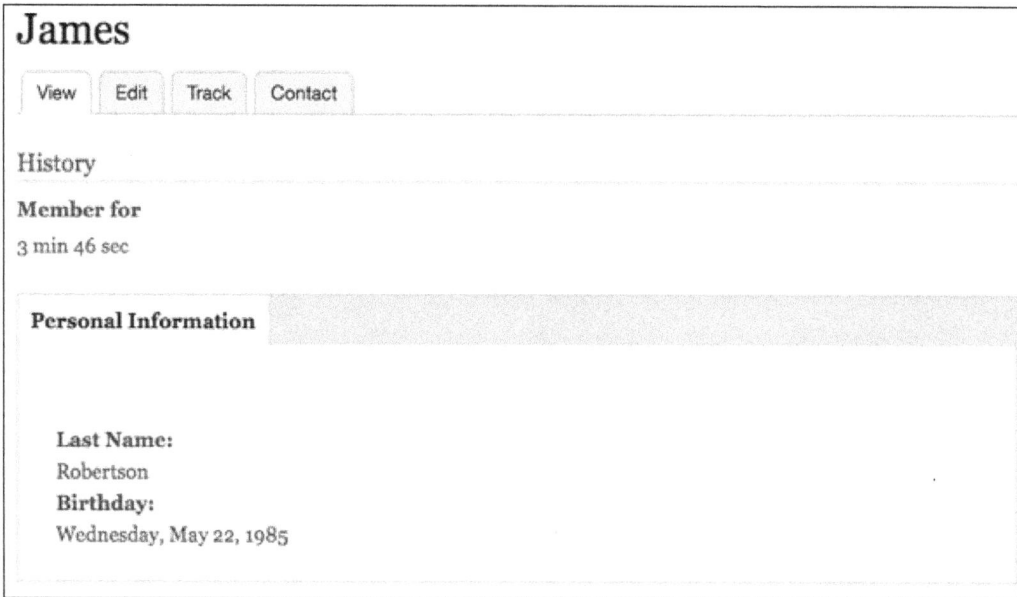

James

| View | Edit | Track | Contact |

History

Member for

3 min 46 sec

Personal Information

Last Name:
Robertson
Birthday:
Wednesday, May 22, 1985

This screenshot is taken from the perspective of the profile owner; that is, this profile is owned by user *James*, and this screenshot was taken while the user was logged in as *James*.

As shown in the preceding screenshot, the **Last name** and **Birthday** fields we created earlier in this chapter are visible.

In the following screenshot, you can see our profile contains text areas for the **Bio (Edit Summary)** section , as well as a vocabulary for **Interests**:

Last Name

Robertson

Enter your last name.

Birthday

Date

05/22/1985

E.g., 02/13/2013

Please enter your date of birth.

Bio (Edit summary)

[Source | X | toolbar icons]

[Normal | B I U S x₂ x² | toolbar icons]

I am the author of *Drupal for Education and E-Learning*.

body p em

Switch to plain text editor

Text format | Filtered HTML ▾   More information about text formats

- Web page addresses and e-mail addresses turn into links automatically.
- Allowed HTML tags: <a> <b> <blockquote>
 <caption> <center> <code> <col> <colgroup> <dd> <del> <div> <dl> <dt> <em> <font> <h1> <h2> <h3> <h4> <h5> <h6> <hr> <i> <img> <li> <ol> <p> <span> <strong> <sub> <sup> <table> <tbody> <td> <tfoot> <th> <thead> <tr> <u> <ul>
- Lines and paragraphs break automatically.

Enter a short biography. You may add a summary of your biography by clicking on the Edit summary link. Otherwise, the summary will be taken from the beginning of your full biography and shortened to a certain number of characters.

Interests

cars, photography, programming, hockey

Enter a comma-separated list of your interests.

When you have entered the appropriate values, click on the **Save** button to create the extended profile.

Additional options for social networking and user profiles

In many social networking sites, people often want to allow users to become friends with one another. Although the advisability of this type of interaction in a classroom setting is a matter of much debate, this functionality can be delivered through the User Relationships module, available at `http://drupal.org/project/user_relationships`.

There are several modules that provide streams of what users are doing on the site or import activity from other social networks. Some of these modules include Activity Stream (`http://drupal.org/project/activitystream`), Follow (`http://drupal.org/project/follow`), and Heartbeat (`http://drupal.org/project/heartbeat`).

Additionally, if you want to work directly with the theming layer, the possibilities for user profiles are virtually limitless. For more information on using the theming layer, refer to *Chapter 14, Theming and User Interface Design*. Additionally, you can find excellent information in the theming section of the Drupal handbook at `http://drupal.org/theme-guide` and the handbook page on overriding user profiles at `http://drupal.org/node/35728`.

Summary

In this chapter, we looked at how to build user profiles using the core User module and then how to extend the user profile using the Field group and Field Permissions modules. The best solution for you will certainly be determined by the goals that you want to achieve in your site.

A well-constructed user profile allows people to express areas of personal interest and learn details about other site members. While this is not necessary in all class settings, in contexts where this is appropriate, a detailed user profile can provide a starting point for site members to have more personal investment in the site.

The techniques covered in this chapter allow you to build effective user profiles that address a broad range of needs. Through judicious use of the theming layer or by using other contributed modules shared on Drupal.org, more can be done with user profiles. In short, building an effective user profile allows your users to have some fun, and learn about one another in the process. In the next chapter, we will learn how to support multiple classes in one site, using the Organic Groups module.

12
Supporting Multiple Classes

In Drupal, group functionality comes with the Organic Groups module. This module, along with related modules that extend its functionality, allow us to set up focused workspaces within a website.

Unless you are blessed with a large salary for a light teaching load, at some point it will become necessary to support more than one class within your site. In Drupal, courses can be organized as teacher-centered groups or as less-hierarchical learning communities. Moreover, by creating different types of groups, we can support both types of learning within the same site.

Installing and configuring Organic Groups

To get started with Organic Groups, we will download and install three modules: Organic Groups, OG Vocabulary, and OG Extras, available at `http://drupal.org/project/og`, `http://drupal.org/project/og_vocab`, and `http://drupal.org/project/og_extras` respectively. The Organic Groups module also requires the Entity API (`http://drupal.org/project/entity`) and Entity Reference (`http://drupal.org/project/entityreference`) modules. The Organic Groups UI module, which is part of the Organic Groups project, also requires the Views Bulk Operations module (`http://drupal.org/project/views_bulk_operations`). Download these modules and upload them to your server as described in the *Installing modules and themes* section of *Chapter 3, Getting Started*.

> Throughout this chapter, we will abbreviate **Organic Groups** to **OG**. This abbreviation occurs frequently in discussions of Organic Groups that occur on `drupal.org`.
>
> The OG module works closely with many other modules. In this book, we will focus on the base OG module and the OG Vocabulary module. However, other modules worth examining in connection with OG include the Panels module and the Notifications module, available at `http://drupal.org/project/panels` and `http://drupal.org/project/notifications` respectively. For a full list of the modules that extend OG, see `http://drupal.org/project/modules?f[0]=im_vid_3%3A90`.

OG comes with a suite of modules. To get started, we need to enable some of these modules, along with the OG Vocabulary module.

As shown in the preceding screenshot, you should enable the following modules:

- **Entity Reference**
- **Organic groups**
- **Organic groups access control**
- **Organic groups context**
- **Organic groups register**
- **Organic groups UI**
- **Organic groups vocabularies** (this module is provided by the OG Vocabulary module, whereas all the other modules are part of the Organic groups module)
- **Entity API**
- **Views Bulk Operations**

Click on the **Save configuration** button to save your settings.

Upon enabling the Organic groups access control module, you will be prompted to rebuild the content access permissions, as shown in the following screenshot:

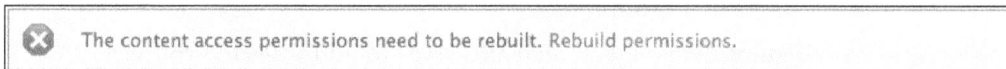

> ❌ The content access permissions need to be rebuilt. Rebuild permissions.

Follow the link provided and rebuild the permissions. Organic Groups is now installed and ready to be configured.

Useful links for Organic Groups

OG interacts with many different areas of your site. As a result, some options are spread around other administrative areas.

Administrative links

The following is a list of useful places to know about when using OG:

- **Reports | Status report | Rebuild permissions** or `admin/reports/status/rebuild`: This admin screen exposes the button to rebuild the access permissions. Occasionally, it might be necessary to rebuild these permissions. The ability to rebuild access permissions is useful when using any access control module.

- **Structure | Content types** or `admin/structure/types`: This is the administrative page for content types; now that OG is enabled, the main edit page for each content type has an OG fieldset. The options contained in this fieldset are discussed at greater length later in this chapter when we cover working with content types while using OG.

- **Configuration | Organic Groups** or `admin/config/group`: This admin screen contains five fieldsets. These options are discussed in greater detail later in the chapter but in brief are:

    - **OG field settings**, which allows us to add OG-related fields to different sections of the site. We will be modifying this section to allow users to join a group when they join the site.

    - **OG membership types**, which allows us to set different options for different types of memberships. For example, we could set up membership types for teachers and students, in addition to the roles we set up earlier. The student membership type could be set up to expire after the school year is over, while the teacher membership type would not expire.

    - **OG permissions overview**, which allows us to easily set permissions for users of a group.

    - **OG roles overview**, which allows us to add roles to groups.

    - **OG settings**, which allows us to set default behaviors for groups.

Adjusting your site to work with Organic Groups

Now that we have installed OG, we need to make some configuration changes to use the group functionality effectively. As we make this shift, it will help if we adjust our perspective to think about the content differently. Before we installed OG, content was created within the site and generally displayed via a view or a menu. Now, with OG installed, content is obviously still posted within the site, but it can also be contained within one or more groups.

In the Drupal 6 version of OG, groups were created by creating nodes of designated content types. In the Drupal 7 version, groups can be created using any entity.

> Entities are chunks of content in Drupal 7. Nodes, users, and taxonomy terms are all entities. Bundles are implementations of entity types. For example, the content types are bundles of node entity types. You can learn more about these terms (and many other Drupal terms) at `http://drupal.org/glossary`.

Since it is still possible to use content types and nodes as a way to create groups and this method is probably the easiest to understand, we will use this method for our site. As we configure OG, we will separate our content types into three distinct categories:

- Content types that can be used to create groups
- Content types that can be posted into groups
- Content types that are never posted into groups

Once we have configured our content types to work with OG, we will examine the options for configuring individual groups.

Creating group types

Once you have installed OG, you need to create content types for your groups. Click on **Structure** | **Content types** or navigate to `admin/structure/types`.

> Creating content types is covered in detail in *Chapter 3, Getting Started*.

We are going to create two new content types that we will use as groups: Class and Club. Functionally, these two content types will be identical. In this example, we will allow only the teacher role to create classes and will allow both students and teachers to create clubs. Depending on how responsibilities are organized at your school or organization, both the names of your groups and the ability to create them can be adjusted to fit within your learning context.

Creating the Class content type

While at **Structure | Content types** or `admin/structure/types`, click on the **Add content type** link.

For the **Identification** section, use the following values:

- **Name**: **Class**
- **Title field label**: **Name**
- **Description**: **Create a class**
- In the **Submission form settings** section, the **Explanation or submission guidelines** can be set to **Describe your class. Use this section to link to a syllabus, or to other relevant information.**
- In **Publishing options**, set default settings to **Published**
- In **Display settings**, uncheck **Display author and date information**
- In the **Comment settings** section, set the default to **Hidden**
- In **Menu settings**, if you want to be able to add Class nodes to any menu, check its box; menus are covered in more detail in *Chapter 14, Theming and User Interface Design*

The Organic Groups fieldset

As mentioned earlier, enabling OG creates an OG fieldset on the various edit screens for individual content types at **Structure | Content types** or `admin/structure/types`. The options in this fieldset allow us to define how content types interact with groups.

Submission form settings Title	Specify how OG should treat content of this type. Content may behave as a group, as group content, or may not participate in OG at all.
Publishing options Published , Promoted to front page	☐ Group Set the content type to be a group, that content will be associated with, and will have group members.
Display settings Display author and date information.	
Comment settings Open, Threading , 50 comments per page	☐ Group content Set the content type to be a group content, that can be associated with groups.
Menu settings	
Organic groups	

The description of options is given as follows:

- **Group**: This option allows you to specify a content type that will be used to create groups.

> When creating the Class and Club content types, we will select **Group** node because these node types will be used to create groups.

- **Group content**: This setting allows you to specify that a content type can be used within a group. If the **Group** checkbox is checked or there are no groups created yet, this setting will disabled.

Once the new node type has been configured appropriately, click on the **Save content type** button to create the new node type.

Creating the Club content type

Creating a Club node type is identical to creating the Class node type, as described earlier. The only elements that will differ are laid out later.

For the **Identification** section, use the following values:

- **Name: Club**
- **Type: club**
- **Description: Create a club**
- In the **Submission form settings** section, **the Explanation or submission** guidelines can be set to **Describe your club. Once you create your club, you can begin inviting other members.**

> In some cases, you might want to require approval for groups. If you want to do this, you can set the default **Publishing options** to unpublished, that is, with all options unselected. This way, people can create groups, but a site administrator will need to publish the groups before they become active.

Click on the **Save content type** button to create the Club node type.

Assigning permissions to group nodes

Now that we have created our node types that will create our groups, we need to assign permissions to allow users to create groups. In this example, we will allow teachers to create classes and both teachers and students to create clubs. To set these permissions, click on **People | Permissions link** or navigate to `admin/people/permissions`.

To assign rights to specific roles, scroll down to the options for the Node module.

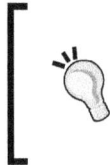

> Once you have installed OG on your site, you will probably want to create a Site Maintainer role with expanded rights to administer content. For more information on creating roles and assigning rights via roles, refer to *Chapter 3, Getting Started*, and *Chapter 5, Enrolling Students*.

Class nodes

You should set the permissions for class nodes as follows:

- The *Teacher* role should be assigned rights to **Create new content** and **Edit own content for the Class content type**

- The *Site Maintainer* role (assuming one has been created) should be assigned rights to **Create new content** and **Edit any content for the Class content type**

> Deleting rights for group nodes should be assigned very carefully. Deleting a group deletes all the posts within the group, and while there is a variety of screens and checks that a user will see before they can delete a group, these permissions should only be assigned to very trusted users.

Club nodes

You should set the permissions for club nodes as follows:

- The *Teacher* and *Student* role should be assigned rights to **Create new content** and **Edit own content for the Club content type**

- The *Site Maintainer* role (assuming one has been created) should be assigned rights to **Create new content** and **Edit any content for the Club content type**

After assigning the appropriate rights to each role, click on the **Save permissions** button to save your settings.

Setting the options for content types

So far, we have:

- Installed OG and created group nodes
- Assigned rights to be able to create and edit group nodes

Now, we need to configure the OG-specific content type settings. Click on **Structure | Content types** or navigate to admin/structure/types. We will have to set the OG options for each content type individually by clicking on the **edit** link and then navigating to the **Organic groups** fieldset, much as we did when adding group types.

Click on the **edit** link next to **Assignment**. Click on the **Organic groups** field and then check the box next to **Group content**.

Submission form settings Title	Specify how OG should treat content of this type. Content may behave as a group, as group content, or may not participate in OG at all.
Publishing options Published	☐ Group
Display settings Don't display post information	Set the content type to be a group, that content will be associated with, and will have group members.
Comment settings Hidden, Threading , 50 comments per page	☑ Group content
Menu settings	Set the content type to be a group content, that can be associated with groups.
Organic groups	**Target type** Node ▾ The entity type that can be referenced thru this field.
	Target bundles Class Club
	The bundles of the entity type that can be referenced. Optional, leave empty for all bundles.

As seen in the previous screenshot, two fields will appear. Since we have only created node-based groups, only Node will be available in the **Target type** field, which can be ignored in our case.

The next field, **Target bundles**, determines if the content type can be posted to a group type. In the multiple select box, choose **Class**. This means Assignment nodes will only be able to be posted to the **Class** group type, which makes sense for our site. Click on the **Save content type** button to save your changes. Follow the same procedure for the Bookmark content type as well.

For the Blog post, Image, Podcast, and Video content types, you can follow much of the same procedure but do not select any options in the **Target bundles** select box. This will make these content types available to both Class and Club groups.

> The OG Forum D7 module (`http://drupal.org/project/og_forum_D7`) allows you to confine forums to groups. You can install and configure it if you wish, but for now we will exclude Forum topics from being available to groups by leaving both boxes in the **Organic groups** section unchecked.

Assigning OG fields to group and content types

By adding group types and making content types available to groups, we are simply connecting the two entities. To take advantage of some of the more advanced features of OG, we need to enable them manually. For our site, we would like to allow users to join a group when they register for an account and optionally create private groups that are not visible to all users on the site.

To enable the features, we add the OG fields to the content or group types. Click on **Configuration | OG field settings** or navigate to `admin/config/group/fields`.

Home » Administration » Configuration » Organic groups

OG field settings ⚙

Bundles

| Class | ▾ | 1 |

Fields *

| Group visibility | ▾ | 2 |

Determine access to the group.

| Class – Node entity |
| Club – Node entity |
| Assignment – Node entity |
| Blog post – Node entity |
| Bookmark – Node entity |
| Image – Node entity |
| Podcast – Node entity |
| Video – Node entity |

FIELD	DESCRIPTION	OPERATIONS
Group	Determine if this should be a group.	Delete
Group visibility	Determine access to the group.	Delete
Group register	Add Group register field group types.	Delete

Add field

As you can see in the previous screenshot, this screen looks pretty complex. The section marked **1** is a select box that contains all the bundles available on the site. We will primarily be concerned with the Node options.

The section marked **2** lists all the OG fields available that can be added to each bundle.

When we created the group types, the OG module automatically added Group fields to our Class and Club group types, and Group audience fields to each of the content types we made available to the group types.

The OG fieldset on the content type edit screen is a Group field. It determines whether a content type should be a Group or Group content. A Group audience field allows the creator of a post to determine to which group the post should belong.

In order to allow users to join a group when they register on the site, we will have to add a Group register field to our Class and Club bundles, and make a Groups audience field visible on the user registration page.

To set the visibility of a group to public or private, we need to add a Group visibility field to our Class and Club bundles.

Adding fields

To add a Group register field to the Class bundle, choose **Class** from the **Bundles** select box and **Group register** from the **Fields** select box. Click on the **Add field** button. Repeat this step, but choose **Club** from the **Bundles** select box instead.

If your site needs both public and private groups, also add a Group visibility field to the Class and Club bundles, much as you did with the Group register field.

Setting field names and visibility

When you add fields through the **OG field settings** page, the fields also become visible on the individual content type's **MANAGE FIELDS** and **MANAGE DISPLAY** pages. Click on **Structure | Content types** or navigate to admin/structure/types to access the links to the **MANAGE FIELDS** and **MANAGE DISPLAY** pages.

For the Class and Club content types, we want to hide the output of the Group visibility and Group register fields. Click on the **manage display** link next to **Class** and choose **<Hidden>** in the **Format** select boxes for the Group visibility and Group register fields. Click on the **Save** button to save your changes.

FIELD	LABEL	FORMAT		
⊹ Group	Above ▼	OG subscribe link ▼	No field selected (best matching)	⚙
⊹ Body	<Hidden> ▼	Default ▼		
Hidden				
⊹ Group visibility	Above ▼	<Hidden> ▼		
⊹ Group register	Above ▼	<Hidden> ▼		
⊹ Add new group	group_	Fieldset ▼		
Label	Group name (a-z, 0-9, _)			

On the **User** page, we want to make the Group membership display on the registration form. Click on **Configuration | Account settings | MANAGE FIELDS** or navigate to `admin/config/people/accounts/fields`. Click on the **edit** link next to the Group membership field and check the box next to the **Display on user registration form** option. Click on the **Save settings** button at the bottom of the page.

OG fields in action

Click on **Content | Add content | Class** or navigate to `node/add/class`. You will see the **Group visibility** and **Group register** fields on the page.

If you are signed in to the site, click on the **Log out** link and then click on the **Create new account** link in the **User login** block. You will see the **Group membership** select box at the bottom near the **Create new account** button.

Editing OG roles and permissions

By default, OG creates three roles for each group: nonmember, member, and administrator member. These roles are different from the overall site's roles, in that they only apply to group-specific content.

You can add more roles by clicking on **Configuration | OG roles overview** or by navigating to `admin/config/group/roles`. Each group type is listed on this screen and you can add roles and edit permissions for these roles by clicking on the **edit** link.

For a larger overview of a group type's roles and permissions, you can click on **Configuration | OG permissions overview** or navigate to `admin/config/group/permissions` and click on an **edit** link next to the group type:

GROUP TYPE	OPERATIONS
Node – Class	edit
Node – Club	edit

Home » Administration » Configuration » Organic groups
OG permissions overview

We will use this page to edit the permissions for each group type all at once. Set the permissions for both the Class and Club group types to the following:

- For the nonmember role, the default permissions should suffice for our site. You can optionally allow nonmembers to join a group without approval by giving them the **Subscribe to group (no approval required)** permission.

- For the member role, give the **create**, **edit own**, and **delete own** permissions for each node type. For Class groups, you may want to revoke the permission to **Unsubscribe from group**.

- For the administrator member, give all permissions.

Click on **Configuration | OG settings** or navigate to admin/config/group/ settings. Most of the defaults should be fine here but we need to change **GROUP MANAGER DEFAULT ROLES**. Choose the **administrator member** option for both select boxes and then click the **Save configuration** button:

Navigation links

The navigation links are added into the main navigation menu by the OG extras integration module; if this module is not enabled, these menus will not exist.

Enable the **Organic groups extras** and **Organic groups context** modules by navigating to **Modules** or `admin/modules`.

The screenshots in this section are taken with content already added to the site. OG does not ship with content already installed. Although the menus and pages here exist in the default installation, you need actual groups and group content to see how they work. Over the course of this chapter, we will add content that will flesh out these pages.

Finding groups and navigating group content

The `Groups` directory can be accessed by clicking on the **Groups** menu (shown in the following screenshot) or by navigating to `groups`:

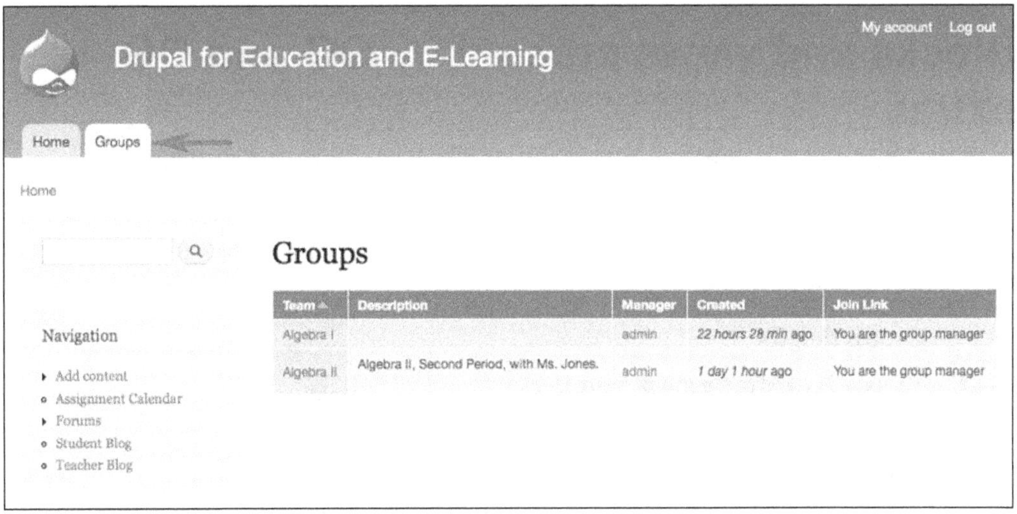

The **Groups** tab provides a list of all groups that are visible in the directory. As discussed earlier in the chapter, groups can be included in or excluded from the directory at the discretion of the site administrator or the group manager.

The **Group membership** field on a user's profile page contains a list of a user's groups.

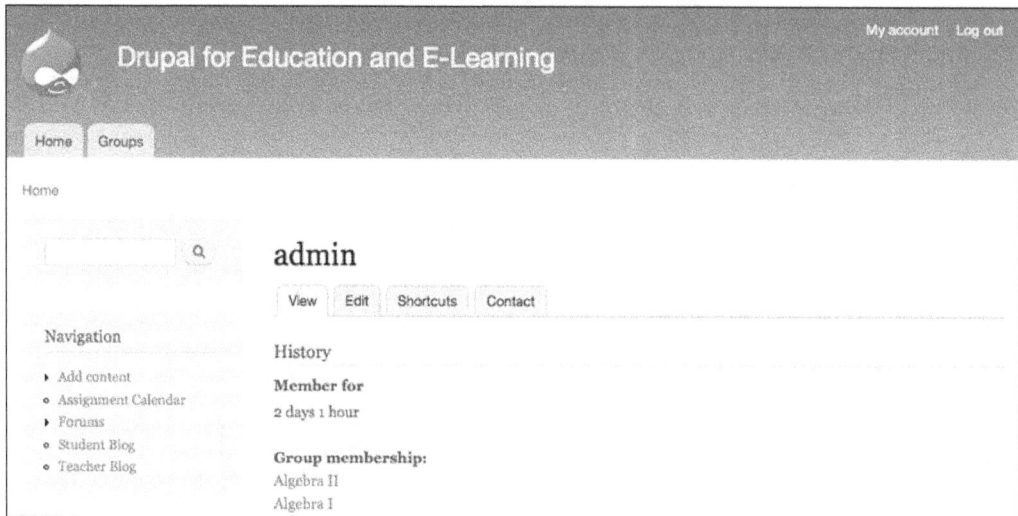

Blocks and views created by OG and OG extras

Both the OG and OG extras modules provide blocks and views that display OG-related information.

Click on **Structure** | **Blocks** or navigate to `admin/structure/block` to see the blocks created by OG and OG extras, including:

- **Group details**
- **View: OG Extras group members**
- **View: OG members**
- **Node content links**

Disabled

✛	Active forum topics	- None - ▾	configure
✛	Calendar Legend	- None - ▾	configure
✛	Group details ⬅——	- None - ▾	configure
✛	Main menu	- None - ▾	configure
✛	Management	- None - ▾	configure
✛	New forum topics	- None - ▾	configure
✛	Node content links ⬅——	- None - ▾	configure
✛	Recent comments	- None - ▾	configure
✛	Recent content	- None - ▾	configure
✛	Shortcuts	- None - ▾	configure
✛	Syndicate	- None - ▾	configure
✛	User menu	- None - ▾	configure
✛	View: OG Extras group members ⬅——	- None - ▾	configure
✛	View: OG members ⬅——	- None - ▾	configure
✛	View: assignment_calendar	- None - ▾	configure
✛	View: assignment_calendar: Upcoming	- None - ▾	configure
✛	View: bookmarks_all	- None - ▾	configure
✛	Who's new	- None - ▾	configure
✛	Who's online	- None - ▾	configure

Click on **Structure** | **Views** or navigate to `admin/structure/views` to see the views created by OG and OG extras. Each view created by the modules is tagged with og or OG Extras. Not all of these views provide pages or blocks but you can clone and modify the views, so they will do so. Just remember to disable the original view!

OG all user group content None In code Type: Content	Show the content from all the group the current user belongs to	og		edit ▾
OG content None In code Type: Content	Show all content (nodes) of a group.	og		edit ▾
OG Extras content Display: *Feed* In code Type: Content	Show all content (nodes) of a group.	OG Extras	/node/%/feed	edit ▾
OG Extras group members Displays: *Block, Page* In code Type: User	Group members.	OG Extras	/node/% /members	edit ▾
OG Extras Groups Display: *Page* In code Type: Content	A listing of all node groups.	OG Extras	/groups	edit ▾
OG members Display: *Block* In code Type: User	Newest group members.	og		edit ▾
OG members admin None In code Type: User		og		edit ▾
OG User groups None In code Type: OG membership	Show groups of a user.	og		edit ▾

Creating a menu for groups

Once you have created the Class and Club content types, you can increase the usability of your site by moving the links for creating classes and clubs into their own menu.

Although this step is not necessary, confusion can arise because groups are also content types. A look at the default navigation menu, pictured in the following screenshot, helps illustrate why:

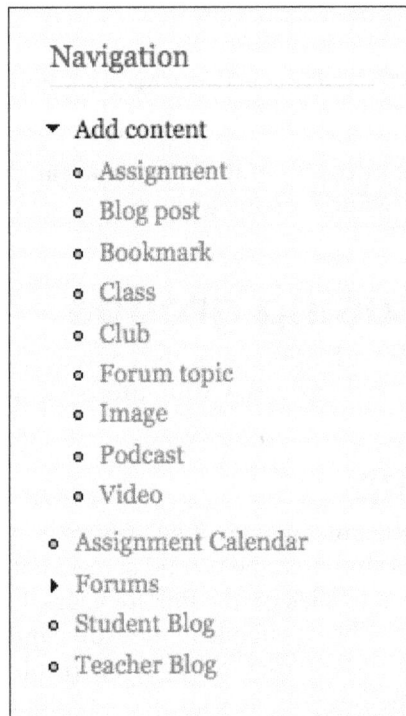

Navigation

▾ Add content
  - Assignment
  - Blog post
  - Bookmark
  - Class
  - Club
  - Forum topic
  - Image
  - Podcast
  - Video
- Assignment Calendar
▸ Forums
- Student Blog
- Teacher Blog

In the default navigation menu, all content types are grouped together in the same area. This can be confusing; although Club and Video are both content types, they do very different things from the other content types.

Separating Group nodes into a separate menu and then displaying that block—as shown in the following screenshot—can help eliminate some of this confusion:

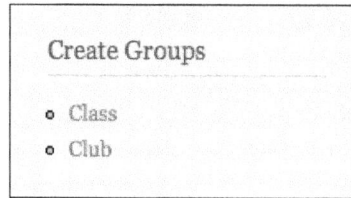

Create Groups

○ Class
○ Club

The process of creating custom menus is described in detail in *Chapter 14, Theming and User Interface Design*.

By separating Group nodes into a separate menu, you can provide a distinct place for people to go when they want to create groups.

Creating and using groups

Now that we have set the default options for the content types that can be used in groups and the privacy levels of groups, we are prepared to create the groups.

Creating a group

To create a group, click on the link created when you created the content type. If you created the custom menu, as shown in the second screenshot under Create a Menu for Groups, you will simply need to click on the link for Class. If you did not create this custom menu, then the link will be available in the **Add content** menu as shown in the screenshot under Create a Menu for Groups under heading the **Navigation** links. In all cases, regardless of whether you have created a custom menu or not, you can create groups by navigating to node/add/[group-type].

Drupal for Education and E-Learning

My account   Log out

Home   Groups

Home » Add content

Navigation

- ▾ Add content
  - ○ Assignment
  - ○ Blog post
  - ○ Bookmark
  - ○ Class
  - ○ Club
  - ○ Forum topic
  - ○ Image
  - ○ Podcast
  - ○ Video
- ○ Assignment Calendar
- ▸ Forums
- ○ Student Blog
- ○ Teacher Blog

Create Groups

- ○ Class
- ○ Club

Create Class

Describe your class. Use this section to link to a syllabus, or to other relevant information.

Name *

Algebra II

Body (Edit summary)

Algebra II, Second Period with Ms. Jones.

body   p

Switch to plain text editor

Text format   Filtered HTML ▾   More information about text formats

- Web page addresses and e-mail addresses turn into links automatically.
- Allowed HTML tags: <a> <b> <blockquote>
 <caption> <center> <code> <col> <colgroup> <dd> <del>
  <div> <dl> <dt> <em> <font> <h1> <h2> <h3> <h4> <h5> <h6> <hr> <i> <img> <li> <ol> <p> <span>
  <strong> <sub> <sup> <table> <tbody> <td> <tfoot> <th> <thead> <tr> <u> <ul>
- Lines and paragraphs break automatically.

Group visibility *

◉ Public - accessible to all site users

○ Private - accessible only to group members

Group register *

○ Do not show on registration page

◉ Show on registration page

Save   Preview

- **Title**: The group title will be seen frequently throughout the site; a good title is short and descriptive enough to give an idea of the purpose of the group. In the case of courses as groups, if you have multiple sections of the same course, the title should help differentiate between the various sections.

- **Body**: The body will show up in the group directory.

- **Group register**: These settings allow you to control if users can join this group when registering for the site.

- **Group visibility**: This setting allows you to control whether or not your group is automatically listed along with other groups on the site in the group directory.

Once you have set up your group, click on the **Save** button to create your group.

Enabling group-specific blocks

The OG module, in conjunction with the OG extras integration module, creates several OG-specific blocks. These blocks are only displayed when viewing groups or content posted into groups.

To see these blocks, click on **Structure** | **Blocks** or navigate to `admin/structure/block`.

The best way to get a sense of what blocks you should enable is by experimentation. To begin, enable **Group details**, **Node content links**, and either of the **Group members** blocks.

Adding users/Managing subscriptions

Once you have enabled the group-specific blocks, navigate to your new group.

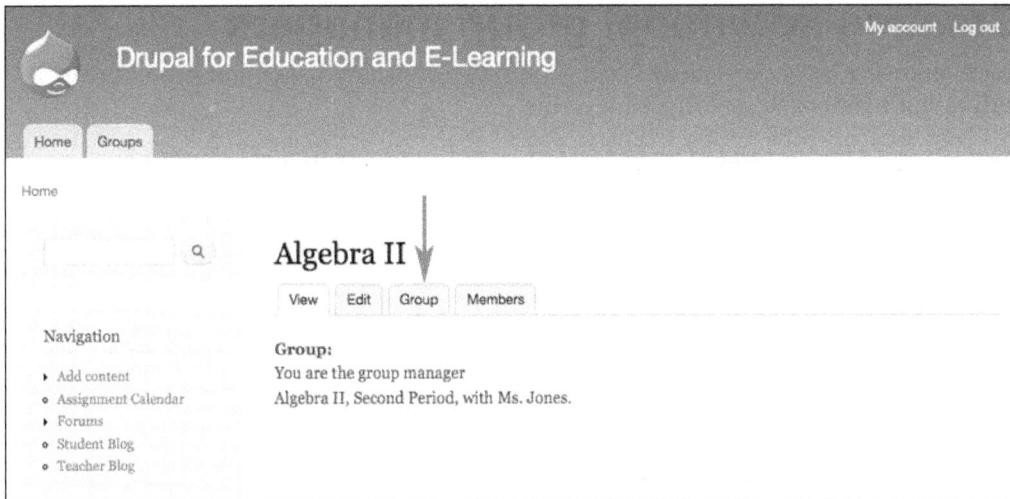

To add users to the group, click on the **Group** tab as shown in the preceding screenshot. This brings us to the Group administration page.

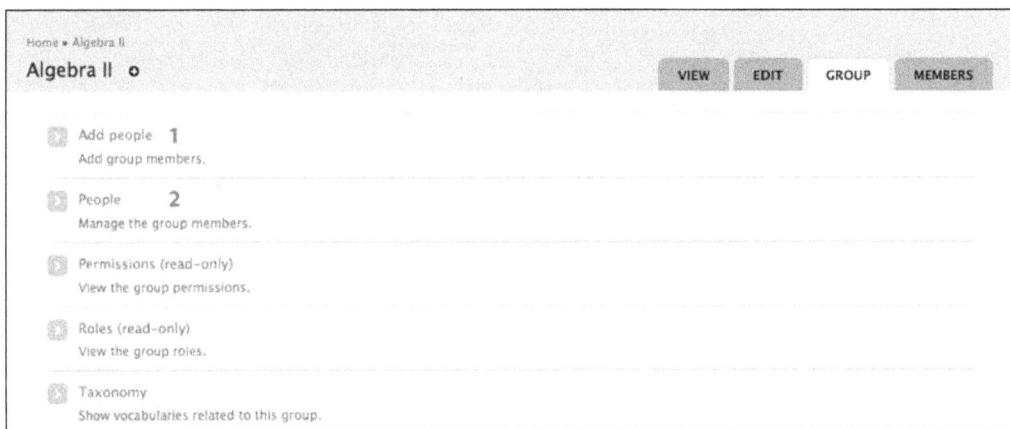

To add members, click on the **Add people** link identified in the preceding screenshot, indicated by section **1**.

To add members, list their usernames and separate each username with a comma. When you have entered all of the usernames, click on the **Add users** button to add the users to the group. All users to be added must be pre-existing site members.

Creating additional group managers

Once members have been added to a group, the group manager can promote any individual member to a group admin role.

As can be seen in the previous screenshot, indicated by section **2**, additional group managers can be created by using the **People** link.

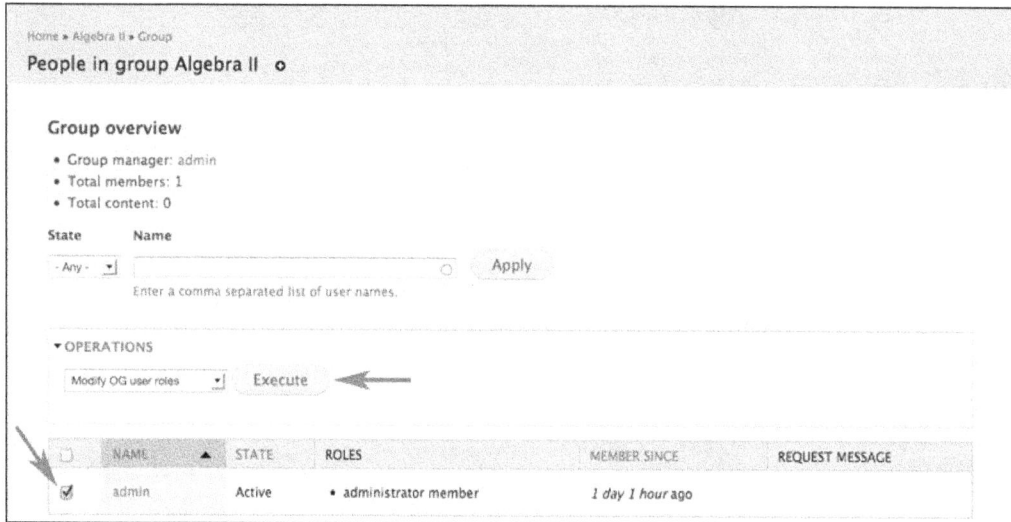

You can change the user's role by selecting the users you want to promote, choosing the **Modify OG user roles** option under the **Operations** fieldset and clicking on the **Execute** button. On the next screen. you can add or remove roles and then click on the **Next** button. Click on **Confirm** (on the next page) and you will see that the role has been added to the user.

Group administrators have the same rights as the group manager; if two teachers are working together in the same class, both teachers should be group managers.

Also, a person can be a group manager in one course and a regular participant in another course. This allows, for example, teaching assistants to be given extended rights in the group for which they are a TA.

Adding group-specific taxonomies

Using the Organic groups vocabularies module, we can set up unique vocabularies for each group. This allows each group to have separate ways of categorizing content. This can be useful for different classes, as an English class will have different needs and categories than a Biology class.

Group managers and group administrators have the rights to create new vocabularies. To create a specific vocabulary for a group, click on the **Group** tab. Then, click on the **Taxonomy** link:

Home » Taxonomy
Taxonomy ⚙

Name *

Assignment Type   Machine name: assignment_type [Edit]

Description

NODE – ASSIGNMENT

☑ Enable

    Show term reference in Node – Assignment add and edit form

Widget type *

Autocomplete (Tags style) ▼

The type of form element you would like to present to the user when creating this field in the *Video* type.

☐ Required field

Number of values

Unlimited ▼

Maximum number of values users can enter for this field.

From here, the process of creating a vocabulary is identical to creating all other vocabularies in the site, as described in *Chapter 3, Getting Started.*

For this example, we will create a vocabulary to categorize Assignment nodes and assign the following values:

- **Vocabulary name**: **Assignment type**
- **Description**: Leave this blank; the description is only shown to group managers and should be obvious from the context
- **Help text**: **Select the appropriate term**
- Check the box next to **Node, Assignment** (three new fields will appear)
- Select **Autocomplete (Tags style)** from the **Widget type** select box
- The remaining options can be left to their defaults

Click on the **Submit** button to save your vocabulary.

Once you have created your vocabulary, use the **add terms** link to populate it with specific terms. For the Assignment type vocabulary, the terms should be the different types of assignments used in the course.

Creating content in a group

For this example, we will create an assignment for the group.

To create an assignment, click on **Add content | Assignment link** or navigate to node/add/assignment:

When you create the assignment, tag it with a term from the Assignment type vocabulary.

In the **GROUPS AUDIENCE** section, you can add the Assignment to a group. This section shows the different groups to which you belong.

Click on the **Submit** button to create your assignment.

Summary

Using groups allows you to support classes, clubs, extracurricular activities, study groups, and other activities. Moreover, different groups can be used to support different types of learning.

The Organic Groups module provides you with a range of options for configuring groups. The best options for your site will likely vary widely based on teacher and student preference. For example, some teachers might want to use private groups, whereas others will want more public interactions. With this in mind, the optimal group settings — finding the balance between group privacy, user privacy, free interactions, connections between groups, and so on — will evolve over time as people work in the site and begin to understand how to use the different features. So, while you may get it right the first time, don't count on it. Fine-tuning group configurations requires talking with and listening to people using your site.

Finally, effective group use also requires some training for group managers to help them understand the different options they have available to them. Periodic training also provides the opportunity for people to provide feedback about the different features of the site. Groups play a central role in the growing community around a site; fine-tuning the technical aspects of how they work should be seen as both a technical and community-building exercise.

In the next chapter, we will build upon the blogging and assignment features we built earlier in the book by discussing several ways to track student progress.

13
Tracking Student Progress

As more people post more content into your site, you will need some simple ways to keep track of their work. This chapter outlines some techniques for organizing student work to allow you to effectively monitor student progress and learning.

Getting an overview of student work

Drupal offers several methods for tracking student work. The simplest method uses Drupal's core Tracker module. The Tracker module will work very well for sites with a small number of users. For sites with larger numbers of users and more complex tracking needs, we can use the Views module. We will discuss various methods of using the Views module later in this chapter.

Using the core Tracker module

To start, make sure that the Tracker module is enabled. Click on **Administer | Site building | Modules** or navigate to admin/build/modules. In the **Core** section, make sure that the **Tracker** module is enabled.

The Tracker module tracks the posts of all users. To see a list of all content created on the site, click on the **Recent content** link—generated by the Tracker module—in the main navigation menu or navigate to `http://yoursite.org/tracker`. While this is a useful way to see a quick list of recently created content, it isn't the most useful way of tracking posts from large numbers of users.

The core Tracker module also tracks the posts of individual users. To see these individual user pages, navigate to a user's profile page (usually by clicking on their username) and click the **Track** tab:

However, this quickly becomes tedious, particularly if you are working with many students.

Replacing the Tracker module with Views

The core Tracker module, while useful in a general sense, can feel insufficient in sites with large numbers of students and in sites using groups to support multiple classes.

To use Views instead of the core Tracker module, you need to do two things. First, disable the Tracker module by clicking on the **Modules** link or by navigating to admin/modules.

Second, you need to enable the tracker view that ships with the Views module. To enable this view, click on **Structure | Views** or navigate to admin/structure/views.

Click on the **enable** link to activate the view.

The tracker view that ships with the Views module replicates the functionality of the core Tracker module, and is visible at the same URL: http://yoursite.org/tracker. The main difference is that the Views-based solution removes the **Track** tab on the user profile page, as shown in the screenshot before the preceding one.

A reasonable person might ask why we use the Views module to deliver functionality when the Tracker module does exactly the same thing. Using the Views module allows us to modify the fields returned in our view; for example, the core Tracker module does not show any taxonomy terms connected to a post. Using the Views module, we can modify the default view that is provided to display all taxonomy terms.

> For a detailed overview of adding new views, refer to *Chapter 3, Getting Started*. For a detailed overview of modifying a view that ships with the Views module, refer to *Chapter 4, Creating a Teacher Blog*.

The Views module also allows us to filter the results in ways that are not possible using the core Tracker module. Later in this chapter, we will highlight techniques and strategies for building flexible solutions using views.

Using code snippets to track student progress

Code snippets are small chunks of PHP code that can be embedded in a page. Using PHP snippets offers a great deal of flexibility, but they should also be used with extreme care. To start, the right to embed PHP snippets should only be given to trusted users who actually know PHP. A poorly formed PHP snippet has the potential to bring down a site; a malicious user with the rights to use PHP snippets can also wreak havoc. However, when used appropriately, the PHP snippets are a powerful tool.

Enabling PHP snippets

To enable selected users to embed PHP snippets, we first need to enable the PHP filter module. To enable this module, click on the **Modules** link or navigate to admin/modules. In the **Core** section, enable the PHP filter module. Click on the **Save configuration** button to save the changes.

Then, click on **Configuration** | **Text formats** or navigate to `admin/config/content/formats`.

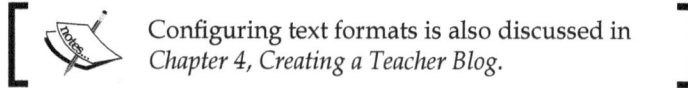

> Configuring text formats is also discussed in *Chapter 4, Creating a Teacher Blog.*

Click on the **configure** link for the PHP code input filter; this brings you to the admin screen, as shown in the following screenshot:

Home » Administration » Configuration » Content authoring » Text formats

PHP code ⚙

A text format contains filters that change the user input, for example stripping out malicious HTML or making URLs clickable. Filters are executed from top to bottom and the order is important, since one filter may prevent another filter from doing its job. For example, when URLs are converted into links before disallowed HTML tags are removed, all links may be removed. When this happens, the order of filters may need to be re-arranged.

Name *

PHP code   Machine name. php_code

Roles

☐ anonymous user

☐ authenticated user

☑ administrator ⬅——

☐ teacher

☐ student

Enabled filters

☐ Limit allowed HTML tags

☐ Display any HTML as plain text

☐ Convert line breaks into HTML (i.e.
 and <p>)

☐ Convert URLs into links

☑ PHP evaluator

   Executes a piece of PHP code. The usage of this filter should be restricted to administrators only!

☐ Convert Media tags to markup

   This filter will convert [{type:media...]] tags into markup.

☐ Correct faulty and chopped off HTML

Filter processing order

                                    Show row weights

  + PHP evaluator

Filter settings

Save configuration

As mentioned earlier in this section, access to the PHP input format should only be given to highly trusted users. As seen in the preceding screenshot, we are only giving users with the administrator role the rights to use this input format.

Embedding a PHP snippet in a page

For users with the rights to use the PHP input format, code snippets can be embedded in any post.

The next code snippet gives a listing of all students in the site, with links to each user's tracker page. This snippet assumes that you have created a last name field in the user profile, as described in *Chapter 11, Social Networks and Extending the User Profile*.

The snippet works as follows:

- When an anonymous user views the page, they are directed to log in
- When users who do not belong to the teacher role view the page, they are presented with a link to their profile
- When users in the teacher role view the page, they are presented with a list of all users in the student role, sorted by last name, with a link to their tracker page

For this example, we will embed the PHP snippet in a page. To create the page, click on **Add content** | **Basic page** or navigate to node/add/page. Type the snippet into the body and do not use the text editor, as the editor will strip out the PHP code.

```php
<?php
global $user;
$instructor_role_id = 4;
$student_role_id = 5;
$per_page = 50;
if ($user->uid == 0) {
  print l(t('You must log in to view this page'), 'user');
  return;
}
```

```
else if (!array_key_exists($instructor_role_id, $user->roles)) {
  print l(t('View your profile'), 'user/'. $user->uid);
    return;
}


$query = db_select('users','u')->extend('PagerDefault');
$query->fields('u',array('uid','name'));
$query->join('users_roles','ur','u.uid = ur.uid');
$query->fields('ur',array('rid'));
$query->leftJoin('field_data_field_last_name','ln','u.uid =
ln.entity_id');
$query->fields('ln',array('field_last_name_value'));
$query->condition('rid',$student_role_id);
$query->orderBy('field_last_name_value');
$query->limit($per_page);
$results = $query->execute();
foreach ($results as $account){
  $items[] = l($account->name, 'tracker/'. $account->uid,array()) .' |
'.$account->field_last_name_value;
}
$output['list'] = array(
  '#theme'=>'item_list',
  '#items'=>$items,
  '#title'=>'',
  '#type'=>'ul',
  '#attributes'=>array()
);
$output['pager'] = array('#theme'=>'pager');
print drupal_render($output);
?>
```

Home » List of site users

Edit Basic page List of site users ⚙

VIEW   EDIT   DEVEL

Title *

```
List of site users
```

Body (Edit summary)

```php
<?php
global $user;
$instructor_role_id = 4;
$student_role_id = 5;
if ($user->uid == 0) {
    print l(t('You must log in to view this page'), 'user');
    return;
}
else if (!array_key_exists($instructor_role_id, $user->roles)) {
    print l(t('View your profile'), 'user/'. $user->uid);
    return;
}
$query = db_select('users','u')->extend('PagerDefault');
$query->fields('u',array('uid','name'));
$query->join('users_roles','ur','u.uid = ur.uid');
$query->fields('ur',array('rid'));
$query->leftJoin('field_data_field_last_name','ln','u.uid = ln.entity_id');
$query->fields('ln',array('field_last_name_value'));
$query->condition('rid',$student_role_id);
$query->orderBy('field_last_name_value');
$results = $query->execute();
```

Text format `PHP code ▾`   More information about text formats ⓘ

- You may post PHP code. You should include <?php ?> tags.

Menu settings
Not in menu

☐ Provide a menu link

Revision information
No revision

URL path settings
No alias

Comment settings
Closed

Authoring information
By admin on 2013-02-26 22:36:58
-0500

Publishing options
Published

Save   Preview   Delete

When saving a post with an embedded code snippet, always use the **Preview** button, as shown in the previous screenshot. This way, if there are any issues with your snippet, you will discover them on preview before any PHP errors do any damage.

When you are done entering the PHP snippet, select PHP code as the text format. Then click on the **Preview** button to ensure that your snippet works as intended. Once you have ascertained that your snippet works as you need, click on the **Save** button to save the node.

Once the page has been saved, you will see a page as shown in the following screenshot:

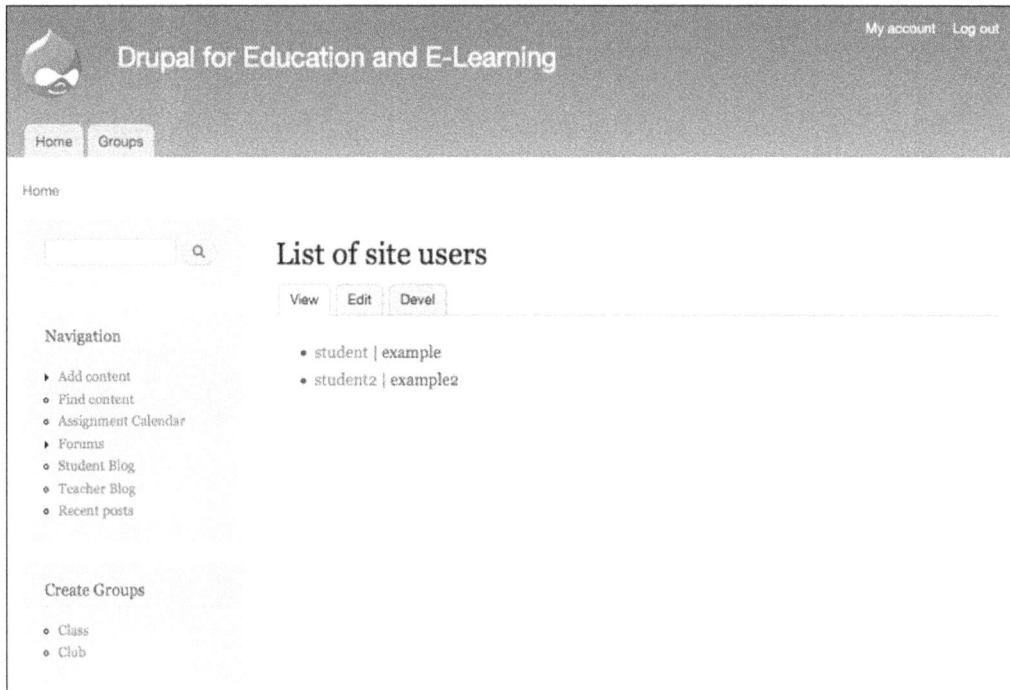

Explaining the snippet

The username links to the user's tracker page. The snippet displays a person's username followed by their last name.

The snippet loads a PHP object that describes the currently logged in user. It checks to see if the user is an authenticated user or has the teacher role. If the user is not an authenticated user, the snippet prints a message asking the user to log in and quits. If the user has any other role than teacher, it prints a link to the user's profile page and quits.

To find the role ID of the teacher and student roles, click on **People | Permissions | Roles** or navigate to admin/people/permissions/roles. Hover over the **edit role** link next to a role and look in the bottom left of your browser, as shown in the next screenshot. The number at the end of that URL is the role ID. Change the numbers for the $instructor_role_id and $student_role_id variables to match the ones for your site.

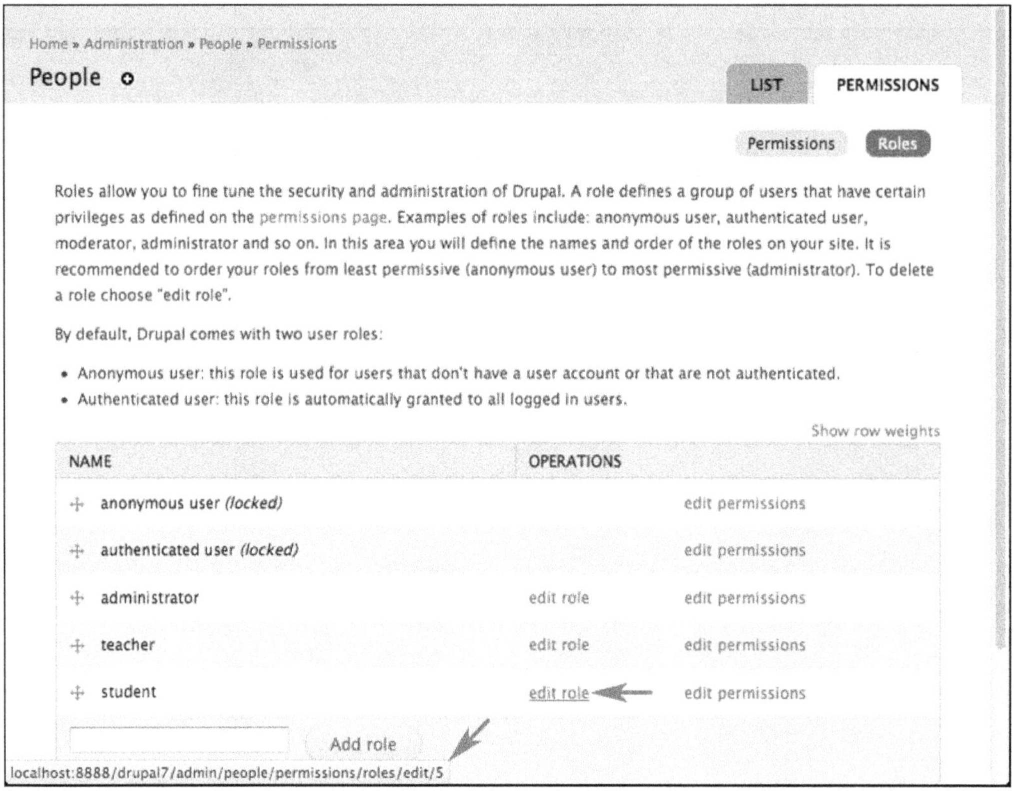

The next few lines of the snippet set up a database query via Drupal's database abstraction layer. If the query returns more items than the number set in the $per_page variable, it creates a pager.

After the query returns results, the snippet creates a link to a user's tracker page and stores it in an array. This array is used in a renderable array to output the list of users.

Drupal 7 makes use of structured arrays (called renderable arrays) and functions to more easily control and override the site's output. You can learn more about renderable arrays in *Chapter 14, Theming and User Interface Design* or at http://drupal.org/node/930760.

Although the PHP code can be embedded in any node, it is a very powerful and therefore, very dangerous tool. As discussed earlier, you should exercise very careful control over who can access the PHP input format through the administrative controls via **Configuration | Text formats** or by navigating to admin/config/content/formats.

Using Views and PHP snippets together

Individually, both the Views and PHP snippets let us do some amazing things; when used together, we have even more options. In this section, we will cover one technique that uses a snippet to pass arguments to a view. This technique can be adapted to different contexts to provide some very powerful methods of creating dynamic navigation paths through content.

This can be very useful when tracking posts in a site that uses Organic Groups. In our example, we will create a view that takes two arguments: the group ID and the user ID. These two arguments will allow us to display all of the posts created by a specific user in a specific group.

Our PHP snippet will display a list of groups to which the currently logged in user belongs. The membership of each group will also be listed and clicking on a username will pass the arguments—the group ID and the user ID—to the view.

Creating the view

To create this view, we will clone the Tracker view that ships with the Views module. We enabled this view earlier in this chapter.

Cloning views is covered in detail in *Chapter 4, Creating a Teacher Blog,* and *Chapter 6, Creating the Student Blog.*

To clone the view, click on **Structure | Views** or navigate to admin/structure/ views. Click on the **clone** link for the **Tracker** view. This brings us to the **Clone view** admin screen. Enter byuser_bygroup as **View name**.

After entering values for the field, click on the **Continue** button to proceed. To complete cloning the view, we will need to edit some values in the **Page** display.

Adjusting the display

To customize the view, we will need to add fields and also add a contextual filter.

Displays

Page*   + Add   edit view name/description ▾

▾ Page details

Display name: Page   view page ▾

TITLE	PAGE SETTINGS	▾ Advanced
Title: Recent posts	Path: /bygroup	CONTEXTUAL FILTER add ▾ 2
FORMAT	Menu: No menu	Content: User posted or commented
Format: Table	Settings	Access: None	
FIELDS 1 add ▾	HEADER add	OG membership: Group ID
Content: Type (Type)	FOOTER add	RELATIONSHIPS add ▾
Content: Title (Title)	PAGER	Content: Author
(author) User: Name (Author)	Use pager: Full		NO RESULTS BEHAVIOR add
Content: Comment count (Replies)	Paged, 25 items	EXPOSED FORM
Content: Last comment time (Last Post)	More link: No	Exposed form in block: No
Content: Has new content		Exposed form style: Basic	Settings
Content: New comments		OTHER
Content: Groups audience (Groups)		Machine Name: page
Content: All taxonomy terms (All taxonomy terms)		Comment: No comment
FILTER CRITERIA add ▾		Use AJAX: No
Content: Published (Yes)		Hide attachments in summary: No
SORT CRITERIA add ▾		Hide contextual links: No
Content: Last comment time (asc)		Use aggregation: No
		Query settings: Settings
		Field Language: Current user's language
		Caching: None
		CSS class: None
		Theme: Information

The previous screenshot shows the view after the edits described in this section have been completed.

To add fields, click on the **add** icon as indicated in the preceding screenshot by section **1**. To add contextual filters, click on the **add** icon as indicated in the preceding screenshot by section **2**.

Adding fields

Add the **Organic Groups: Group** and **Taxonomy: All terms** fields. After configuring the fields, click on the **Apply (all displays)** button to save the changes.

Adding an argument

Add the **OG membership: Group ID** argument. Once we have added the argument, we need to configure it to refine its behavior. Refer to the following screenshot:

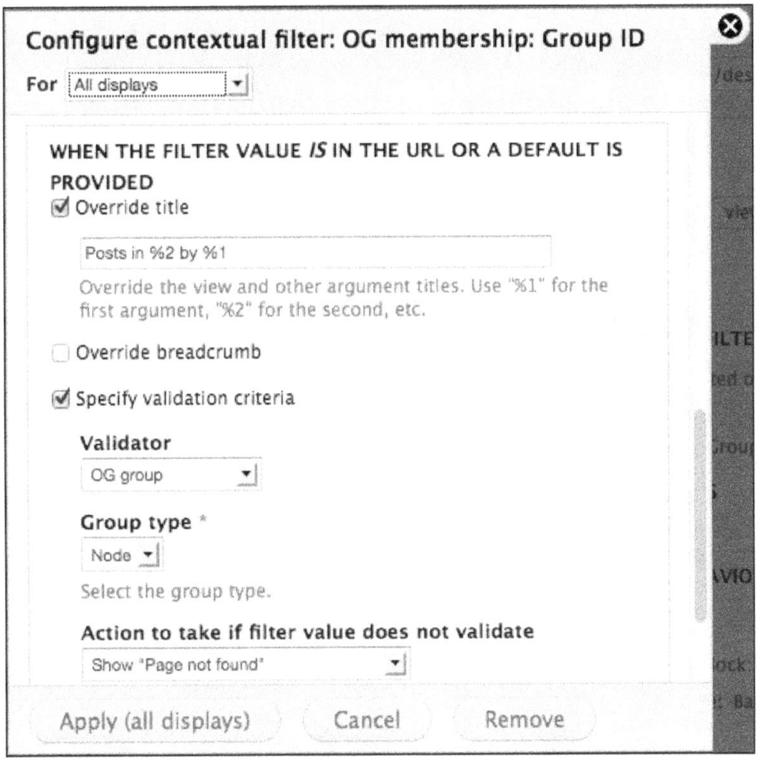

First, we need to change the title. Enter Posts in %2 by %1. This title contains two placeholders—%1 and %2—that will pull their values from the arguments. As marked by section **2** in the screenshot prior to this one, this view is configured to take two arguments; the first (%1) for a user ID and the second (%2) for a group ID. When this title is created, it will substitute the username for %1 and the group name for %2.

Next, click on the **Specify validation criteria** checkbox. Choose **OG group** in the **Validator** select box. This will allow the Views module to substitute the group name for the group ID in the page title.

Click on the **Apply (all displays)** button to save the argument configuration, then click on the **Save** button to save these edits. Now, we can move on to adjusting the page settings.

Adjusting the page settings

We will need to change the path and delete the menu item. Changing the path helps with site navigation and prevents the cloned view from overriding the original one. Deleting the menu item removes the **Recent posts** link from the left-hand menu. Both of these settings are controlled in the **Page Settings** section.

For this example, we will set the path to bygroup. Click on the link next to **Menu** and then select the **No menu entry** radio button. Click on the **Apply** button, then the **Save** button to save the view.

Embedding the snippet

The view that we created, visible at http://example.edu/bygroup, takes two arguments: one for user ID and the second for the group ID. To make this work manually, we would need to know the numerical ID of both users and groups. To state the obvious, this is less than useful. However, a code snippet can create these links for us and present them to us in a usable format.

On a class site using organic groups, teachers and students will likely belong to multiple groups. Teachers, in particular, will want to be able to take a look at the work completed by individual students within their groups. The following PHP snippet lists the groups that a user belongs to and lists all of the users within those groups. Then, it creates a link off the username that feeds the user ID and the group ID to the view created earlier.

Embed the snippet in a page by clicking on **Add content | Basic page** or by navigating to node/add/page.

```php
<?php
drupal_add_library('system','drupal.collapse');
function _my_group_snippet_print_groups($heading, $gids) {
  global $user;
  if (empty($gids)) {
    return;
  }
  $separator = ' | ';
  $output['heading'] = array(
    '#type' => 'html_tag',
    '#tag' => 'h2',
    '#value' => t($heading)
  );
  foreach ($gids as $gid){
    $node = node_load($gid);
    $output['fieldset'.$gid] = array(
      '#type' => 'fieldset',
      '#title' => t($node->title),
      '#attributes' =>
        array('class'=>array('collapsible'))
    );
    //get all users in group $gid
    $query = db_select('users','u');
    $query->join('og_users_roles','ogr','u.uid = ogr.uid');
    $query->
    leftJoin('field_data_field_last_name','ln','u.uid=ln.entity_id');
    $query->fields('ln',array('field_last_name_value'));
    $query->fields('u',array('name','uid'));
    $query->condition('ogr.gid',$gid);
    $results = $query->execute()->fetchAll();
    $links = array();
    foreach ($results as $result){
      if ($result->uid != $user->uid){
        $links[] = l($result->name,'bygroup/'. $result-
>uid.'/'.$gid,array()) .$separator . $result->field_last_name_value;
      }
    }
```

```
      if ($links){
        $output['fieldset'.$gid]['list'] = array(
          '#theme'=>'item_list',
          '#items'=>$links,
          '#title'=>'',
          '#type'=>'ul',
          '#attributes'=>array()
        );
      } else {
        $output['fieldset'.$gid]['empty_message'] = array(
          '#markup'=>t('You are the only user in the group.')
        );
      }
    }
    print drupal_render($output);
  }
  global $user;
  $groups = og_get_groups_by_user();
  foreach ($groups['node'] as $gid){
    $roles = og_get_user_roles('node',$gid);
    $groups_and_roles[$gid] = $roles;
  }
  $admin_groups = array();
  $other_groups = array();
  foreach($groups_and_roles as $gid => $roles){
    if (in_array('administrator member',$roles)){
      $admin_groups[] = $gid;
    } else {
      $other_groups[] = $gid;
    }
  }
  _my_group_snippet_print_groups(t('Groups I manage'), $admin_groups);
  _my_group_snippet_print_groups(t('My groups'), $other_groups);
  ?>
```

Once you have entered the snippet into the page and tested it by using the **Preview** button, create the page by clicking on the **Save** button.

Explaining the snippet

This snippet starts by getting the user ID of the user viewing the page. It uses this user ID to generate a list of groups to which the user belongs and then uses the group IDs to get a list of users within each group.

A closer examination of a section of the snippet helps show how this snippet works:

```
$links[] = l($result->name, 'bygroup/' . $result->uid . '/' . $gid,
array()) . $separator . $result->field_last_name_value;
```

This section of the snippet helps generate the output that creates the links to the view and displays the last name from the user profile:

- `bygroup`: This is the identical path that we set to the view; if you have used a different path when creating your view, then you will need to adjust this section of the snippet.

- `field_last_name_value`: This is the field name of the custom profile field we created in *Chapter 11, Social Networks and Extending the User Profile*. To use a different field, adjust this name accordingly.

Once the page containing the snippet has been saved, it will resemble the following screenshot:

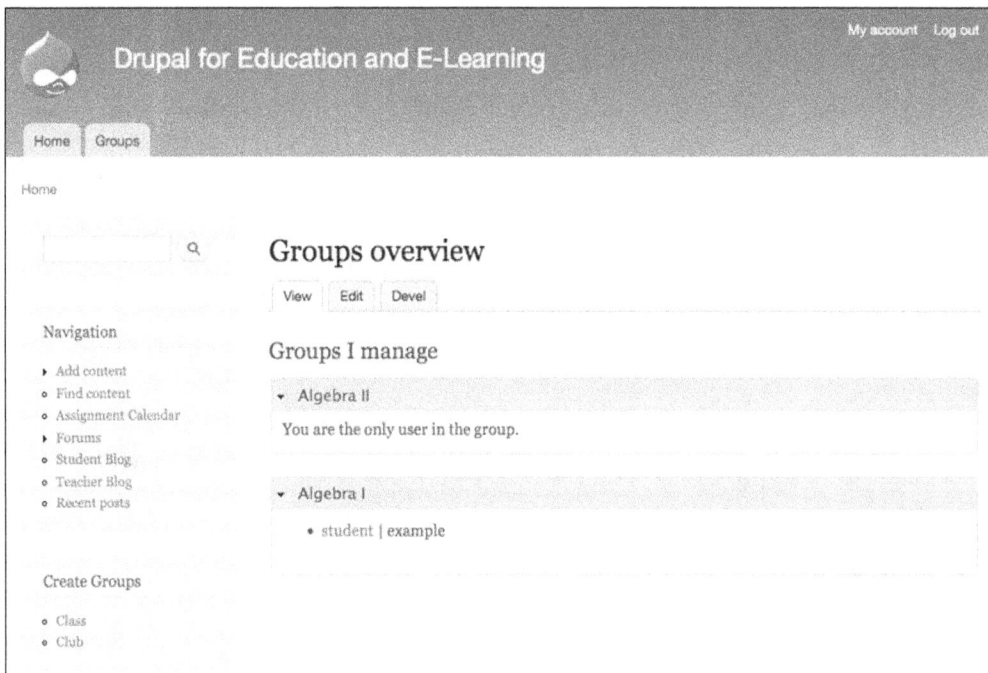

The actual groups and members within those groups, will obviously vary depending upon the user viewing the page.

Clicking on a username brings you to the view, as shown in the following screenshot:

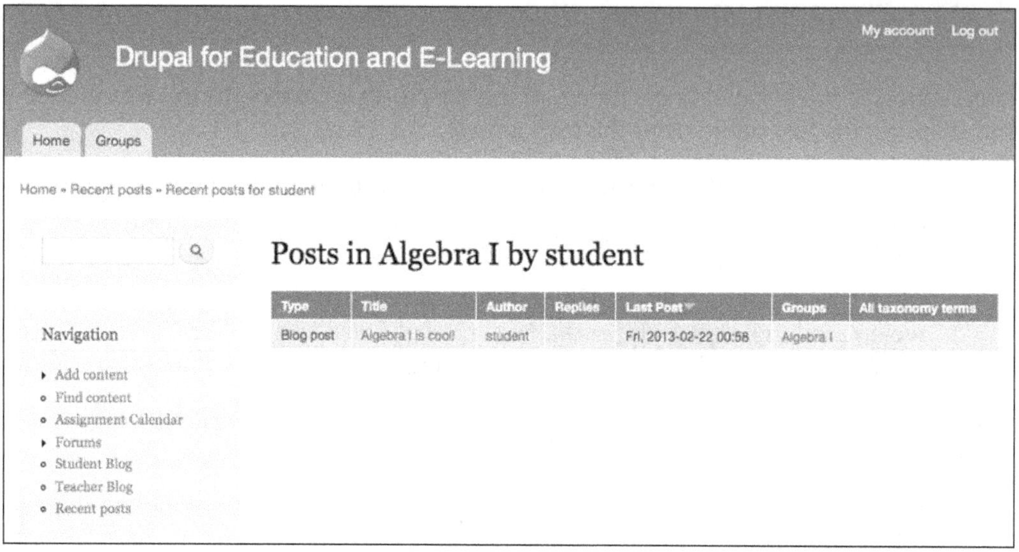

In the preceding screenshot, the title of the view (**Posts in Algebra I by student**) is pulled from the arguments we set up earlier in this section when we modified the tracker view.

Tracking responses to specific assignments

In some cases, an assignment will be answered by students online. This section covers how to track student responses to specific assignments. In *Chapter 6, Creating the Student Blog*, we cloned the default backlinks view that comes with the Views module as a way of showing links between blog posts. We will use the same technique to see student responses to specific assignments.

Chapter 6, Creating the Student Blog, describes the steps we need to follow. Depending on how you want your view to look, you can add fields, modify the display style, and experiment with other options as described in the different sections of this book. However, the primary changes we need to make with this view concern modifying the argument and the access to the view.

All of the edits we will make will be to the **Page** display.

Editing the argument

We only want this view to return posts that link to assignments. To make this happen, we need to edit the existing argument of the view to only validate for assignments.

Click on the **Search: Links to** link. This brings up the configuration options, as shown in the following screenshot.

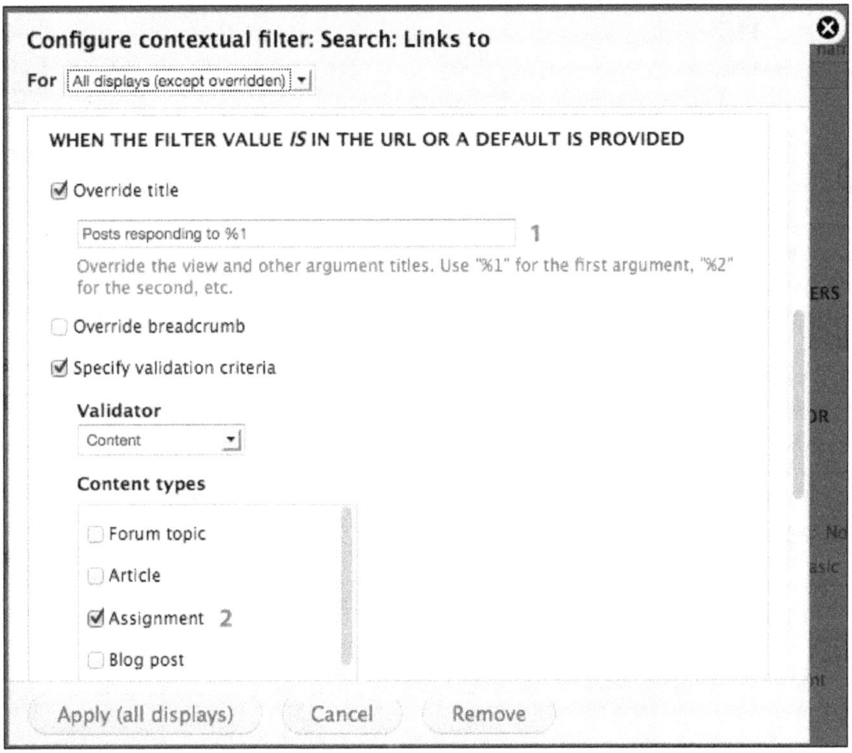

Then, as indicated by section **1**, change the title to `Posts responding to %1`. Lastly, as indicated by section **2**, select **Assignment** as the node type. Click on the **Apply (all displays)** button to save these changes.

Restricting access

Views provide you with several options for restricting access. As this view collects student responses to work, we will limit access to it by only allowing users with the rights to create assignments to see it.

Click the link next to **Access**. This brings up the **Page: Access restrictions** options. Select **Permission** as indicated and then click on the **Apply (all displays)** button.

Page: Access restrictions

For [All displays ▾]

○ None
○ OG permission
⦿ Permission
○ Role

You may also adjust the settings for the currently selected access restriction.

[Apply (all displays)]   [Cancel]

From the **Permission** drop-down menu, select **Assignment: Create new content**. Selecting this option means that any user with the rights to create assignments can see the view. Also, make sure you change **For** options to **All displays (except overridden)**.

Page: Access options

For [All displays (except overridden) ▾]

Permission

[Assignment: Create new content ▾]

Only users with the selected permission flag will be able to access this display. Note that users with "access all views" can see any view, regardless of other permissions.

[Apply (all displays)]   [Cancel]

Click on the **Apply (all displays)** button to save the changes and the **Save** button to save the view.

How it works

When a student is responding to an assignment, they need to include a link to the assignment in their response. By including the link to the assignment, the site will automatically detect the backlink and register it as a response.

> As described in *Chapter 6, Creating the Student Blog*, the list of backlinks is created during cron runs. For information on setting up cron, refer to *Chapter 15, Backup, Maintenance, and Upgrades*.

In the preceding screenshot, we can see the **Responses** page. In addition to the edits described in this chapter, this view contains some additional fields, including **created on date**, **username** (that is, the person responding to the assignment), and **user picture**. Adding fields to views is covered in *Chapter 3, Getting Started, Chapter 4, Creating a Teacher Blog*, and *Chapter 6, Creating the Student Blog*.

Private communication with students

Throughout a course, teachers may want to keep private notes on students' progress, or create an online space where they can communicate directly with students regarding their progress. By using the *Node access user reference* module, teachers and students can create posts and then single out individual users who can see and/ or edit these posts. Additionally, posts can also be private, in which case they are only visible to the author, making this method suitable for maintaining a journal or private notebook.

Getting started

Download the Node access user reference module from `http://drupal.org/ project/nodeaccess_userreference`. Install this module as described in *Chapter 3, Getting Started*.

Then, click on **Structure | Content types** or navigate to `admin/structure/types`. Create a content type named `Notes`, and in the **Publishing options** settings, make sure that you enable **Create new revisions**.

Next, click **People | Permissions** or navigate to `admin/people/permissions`. Assign rights to the **Notes** content type: both the **Teacher** and **Student** roles should be able to create notes and edit own notes.

Configuring Node access user reference

In order to use the Node access user reference module, we need to add some fields to the **Notes** content type. Click on **Structure | Content types** or navigate to `admin/ structure/types` and then click on the **edit** link for the **Notes** content type.

First, add an entity reference field called **Editors** with an **Autocomplete (Tags style)** widget. Click on the **Save** button.

On the next screen, choose **User** in the **Target type** select box. In the **Sort by** select box, choose **A field attached to this entity**, and for the **Sort** field, select **Last Name (column value)**. Click on the **Save field settings** button to continue editing the field.

On the next screen, we will primarily be concerned with the **Node Access User Reference** fieldset; click on the link to expand it. Under the **Grants for referenced users on the node** options, check the boxes next to **View** and **Update**. Under the **Grants for referenced users to create content** options, check the **Notes** box. And, under the **Grants for author** options, select the **View** and **Update** boxes. Further down the page, set **Number of values** to **Unlimited**. Click on the **Save settings** button to save the field.

After saving the field, the content access permissions will need to be rebuilt. Follow the link and then navigate back to the **Manage Fields** screen for the **Notes** content type.

Add another entity reference field called **Viewers** to the **Notes** content type. Most of the options will be the same, except for the permissions. For this field, only give the **View** permissions under **Grants for referenced users on the node**. Click on the **Save settings** button, then rebuild the permissions again.

> The Node access user reference module (as the name implies) is an access control module. In earlier versions of Drupal, using multiple types of access control on the same piece of content could result in behavior that looks unpredictable to the end users. While a lot of these issues have been addressed in Drupal 7, using multiple access control modules can still be unpredictable. To prevent this, any content type that is governed by Node access user reference should not be used inside an OG, as this is also an access control module.

Using Node access user reference

To use Node access user reference, create a note by clicking on **Add content | Note** or by navigating to node/add/note.

To add editors and viewers, type the username into the **Editors** or **Viewers** field. The username fields will autocomplete as names are added.

Then, after you have added all desired viewers or editors, save the node. Note that if no viewers or editors are added, the post will function like a private journal.

Summary

In this chapter, we learned several methods for keeping track of student work and for providing feedback on that work. Over time, as you experiment with different options, you will find the method that aligns cleanly with your teaching and web-browsing style. As you build different methods of tracking student work, it's okay to have two or more pages offering similar content. Experimenting with different options accomplishes two important things: first, it allows you to experience different methods of working within the site and second, the process of experimenting gets you more familiar with the tools at your disposal. In the next chapter, we will learn how to modify the look and feel of the site or the theme, and discuss strategies for making the site easier to navigate.

14
Theming and User Interface Design

In this chapter, we will examine how to make your site easier to use, and how to customize its look and feel.

Discussions of design can get tricky. If you ask 10 people to define what they mean by design, you run the very real risk of getting a dozen answers.

To simplify and focus the conversation, we will concentrate on a subset of design elements:

- Navigational and menu structure, including setting up a home page
- General design elements (for example, the logo, text color, background colors, or graphics, and so on)

By focusing on these elements, we will seek to maximize the effect of the time spent designing your site. When working on the site design, we need to remember that the point of design is to make things easier and more enjoyable for people using your site.

Basic principles

Two basic principles will guide our design work:

- Make things as simple as possible
- Hide unnecessary options

Keeping it as simple as possible

If you look at the Google homepage at `http://google.com`, you won't see much.

And that's precisely the point. You're not presented with a huge number of options because the people designing that page have made some decisions about why people are navigating to `http://google.com`—they have arrived there to search. The screen is remarkably uncluttered. Nothing gets in the way of what the user is there to do: type in a search string, click on submit, and then browse away.

The minimalistic design—with a splash of color in the logo—supports the main activity people engage in at Google.

To look at it in another way, there is nothing on the page to distract or impede users from what they are there to do.

This brings us to the second main principle of creating an easily navigated site —hide unnecessary options.

Hiding unnecessary options

Frequently, people designing educational portals attempt to create a landing page that links to the full range of activities within the site. While creating such a detailed and useful landing page is a worthwhile goal, it often results in a page that is visually cluttered and text-heavy. For an example of what I describe, navigate to virtually any page built within Ning. An example of such a page is shown in the following screenshot:

In order to conserve space, we are only showing the top half of the page. The text-heavy layout makes it difficult for users to find content. Imagine how a user with any spatial processing issues would fare with a page such as this.

By paying attention to how you build your menus and how you organize your site, you can avoid this problem. A series of well organized menus allows you to group related options together and create a site that is intuitive to navigate. By keeping your pages as uncluttered as possible, with simple, well organized menus, you will create a site that is far easier to use than the site shown in the previous screenshot.

These ease-of-use issues are particularly important when you are working with students learning a language or with adult language learners. Additionally, sites with uncluttered pages will be easier to use for students with learning difficulties.

Setting the home page

Create a page that gives an overview of your site. As shown in the following screenshot, enter `home` in the **URL alias** text box.

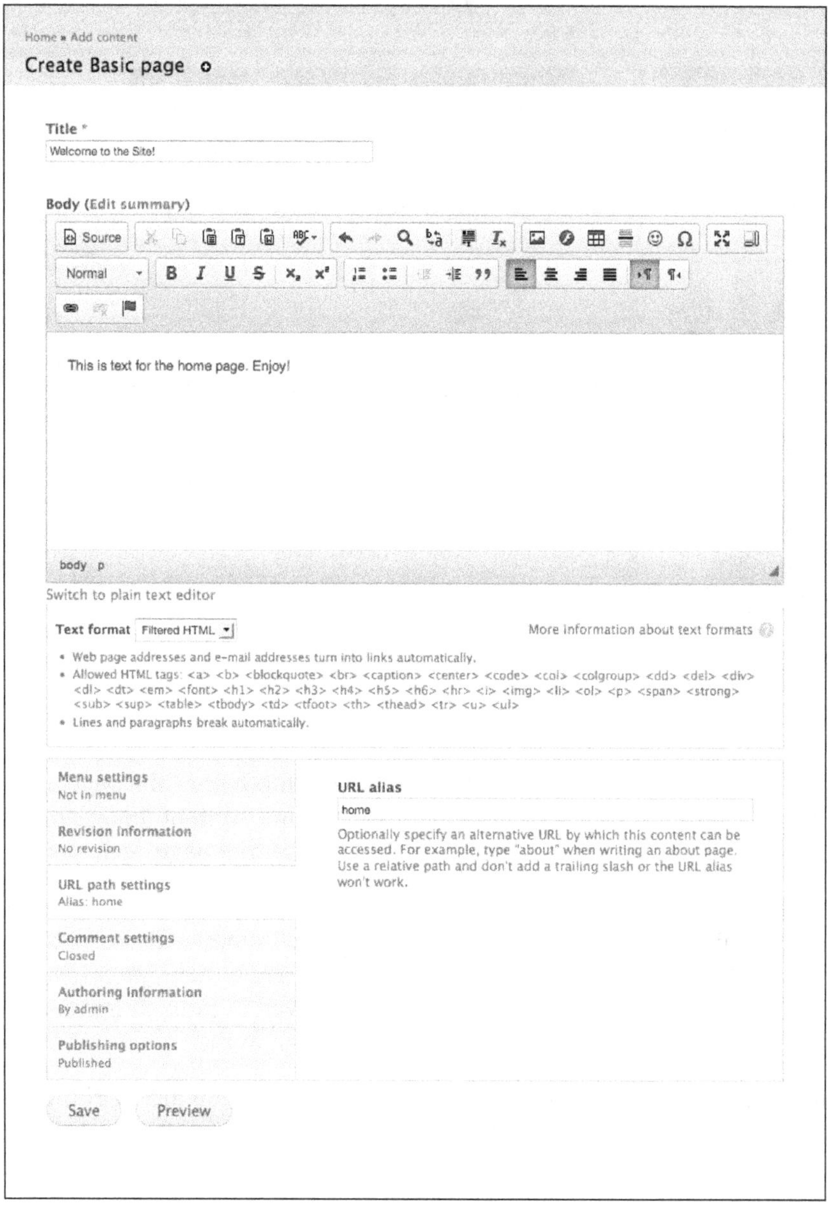

Home » Add content

Create Basic page ✪

Title *

Welcome to the Site!

Body (Edit summary)

| Source | ✂ | ⎘ | ⎗ | ⎘ | ⎙ | ᵃᵇᶜ▾ | ↶ | ↷ | 🔍 | ᵇᵃ | 🖉 | *Iₓ* | 🖼 | ⊘ | ▦ | ═ | ☺ | Ω | ⤢ | ⬗ |

| Normal ▾ | **B** | *I* | U̲ | S̶ | x₂ | x² | ⅛ | ⅜ | ⅞ | ⅞ | 99 | ▤ | ▥ | ▦ | ▦ | ᵔ¶ | ¶ᵔ |

| 🔗 | ✂ | 🚩 |

This is text for the home page. Enjoy!

body p

Switch to plain text editor

Text format [Filtered HTML ▾]   More information about text formats ⓘ

- Web page addresses and e-mail addresses turn into links automatically.
- Allowed HTML tags: `<a>` `<b>` `<blockquote>` `<br>` `<caption>` `<center>` `<code>` `<col>` `<colgroup>` `<dd>` `<del>` `<div>` `<dl>` `<dt>` `<em>` `<font>` `<h1>` `<h2>` `<h3>` `<h4>` `<h5>` `<h6>` `<hr>` `<i>` `<img>` `<li>` `<ol>` `<p>` `<span>` `<strong>` `<sub>` `<sup>` `<table>` `<tbody>` `<td>` `<tfoot>` `<th>` `<thead>` `<tr>` `<u>` `<ul>`
- Lines and paragraphs break automatically.

Menu settings
Not in menu

Revision information
No revision

URL path settings
Alias: home

Comment settings
Closed

Authoring information
By admin

Publishing options
Published

URL alias

home

Optionally specify an alternative URL by which this content can be accessed. For example, type "about" when writing an about page. Use a relative path and don't add a trailing slash or the URL alias won't work.

(Save)   (Preview)

Then, click on the **Configuration | Site information** link, or navigate to admin/config/system/site-information. As shown in the following screenshot, set the **Default front page** setting to home.

Home » Administration » Configuration » System

Site information ⚙

SITE DETAILS

Site name *

    Drupal for Education and E-Learning

Slogan

How this is used depends on your site's theme.

E-mail address *

    james@jamesgrobertson.com

The *From* address in automated e-mails sent during registration and new password requests, and other notifications. (Use an address ending in your site's domain to help prevent this e-mail being flagged as spam.)

FRONT PAGE

Number of posts on front page

    1 ▾

The maximum number of posts displayed on overview pages such as the front page.

Default front page
http://localhost:8888/drupal7/ home ⬅━━━━

Optionally, specify a relative URL to display as the front page. Leave blank to display the default content feed.

Click on the **Save configuration** button to save the default front page settings. The other items on the **Site information** page are covered later in this chapter.

Menus, blocks, and primary links

Menus and blocks are the central elements used to build a navigational structure. A **menu** is a collection of links; **blocks** have many uses, but for this discussion, we will focus on how they are used to display menus.

At its most basic, designing a navigational structure can be reduced to the following simple process:

1. Create a list of places that you want your users to go and/or of things they will need to do. For example, if you want your students to be able to see a list of assignments, your blog, and other student blogs, you could place links to these pages in a custom menu, which would automatically generate a block.

2. Then, via the block display settings, enable the block and place it where you want it to appear on the page.

Main menu

The main menu is a unique type of menu in which most Drupal themes are set up to format and display them in a specific way. The main menu is usually displayed across the top of your site; it is useful for presenting your users with a consistent set of links across all the pages on the site.

The main menu can be set and configured through the menu settings accessible by clicking on **Administration | Structure | Menus** or by navigating to `admin/structure/menu`.

If you are looking to extend the functionality of primary and secondary links, you should look at the **Nice Menus** module at `http://drupal.org/project/nice_menus`. This module allows you to display nested menus in a block. While primary links are excellent for displaying a small number of important links, they are not good at showing more than a couple of options below that primary menu. The **Nice Menus** module solves that problem.

Creating customized menus

As is usually the case with Drupal, you have several viable ways of doing something. In this instance, we need to get back to our goal—creating a clean, easy-to-use navigation structure. Toward the end, we want to complete the following two tasks:

- Separate the content-creation links into a separate menu, and display the resulting block
- Create the primary links

Within Drupal usability studies, many respondents point to confusion when it comes to adding content within a site. To help reduce this confusion, we will separate out the links to add content into a separate block. This step helps distinguish the process of adding content from the other possibilities in the site.

> In *Chapter 12, Supporting Multiple Classes*, we mention another menu customization: separating all the content types that can be used to create groups into their own menu. The steps used for creating a custom add content menu can be used to create a custom create groups menu.

To add new menus, we will follow these four steps:

1. Add a new menu (or use an existing menu).
2. Enable the block associated with the menu.
3. Add menu items into the menu.
4. Fine-tune the block settings, including the block name and the visibility settings.

Adding new menus

Click on **Structure | Menus** or navigate to `admin/structure/menu`. We will use the **Add menu** link to add two new menus: **Add New Content** and **Holding Tank**.

As the name implies, we will use the **Add New Content** block to hold the links for adding new posts.

When creating the **Add New Content** block, use the following values:

- **Title**: `Add New Content`
- **Description**: `This menu contains links for adding content. It replaces the default "Add Content" menu.`

We will use the **Holding Tank** as a place to store links we are not going to use. Although we could just disable these menu items, moving them to the **Holding Tank** menu also simplifies the menu administration.

When creating the **Holding Tank** block, use the following values:

- **Title**: `Holding Tank`
- **Description**: `This menu is a storage tool for links we do not need or want to use`

Once the two new menus have been created, we will enable the block for **Add New Content**.

> Whenever you create a new menu, Drupal automatically creates a block to display that menu. In order for your new menu to be displayed, you need to enable the block.

Enabling blocks

To enable the new block, browse to the block administration section by clicking on **Structure | Blocks**, or by navigating to `admin/structure/blocks`.

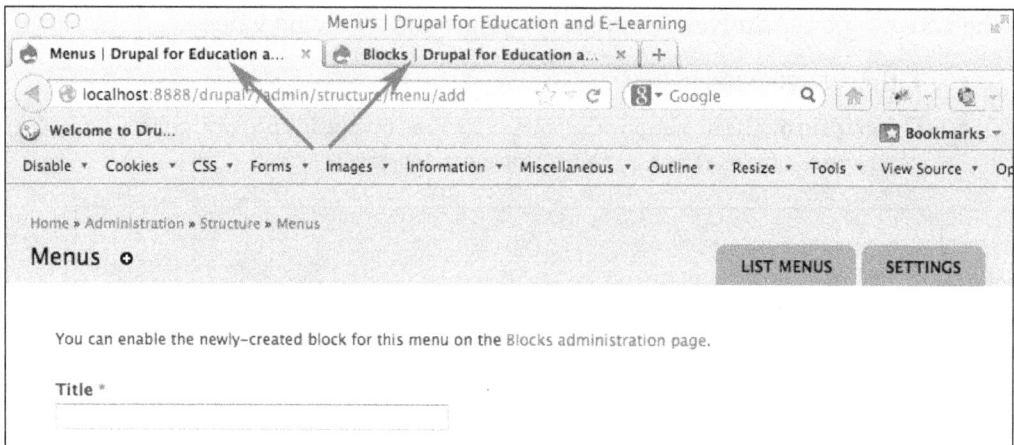

> Open up the block menu in a new tab. Because of the close relationship between menus and blocks, having both tabs open at the same time allows you to switch between them quickly; press the *F5* key from your keyboard to refresh the screen and see the effects of any changes.

Enable the **Add New Content** block on **Sidebar first**. Drag and drop the blocks in the order you want them.

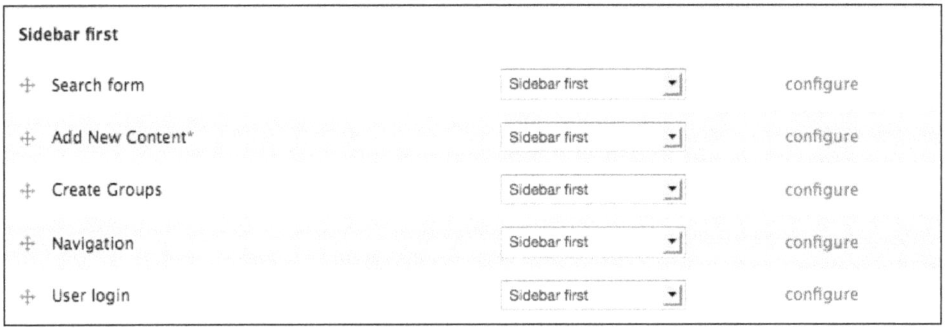

Sidebar first			
⊹ Search form	Sidebar first ▾		configure
⊹ Add New Content*	Sidebar first ▾		configure
⊹ Create Groups	Sidebar first ▾		configure
⊹ Navigation	Sidebar first ▾		configure
⊹ User login	Sidebar first ▾		configure

Adding menu items into the menu

To begin with, return to the menu administration screen by clicking on **Structure | Menus,** or by navigating to admin/structure/menu. Click on the **List Links** item next to **Navigation** to edit the navigation menu, and then click on the **edit** button for the **Add content menu** item. As shown in the following screenshot, move the **Add content menu item** to the **Add New Content** menu.

Once you have moved the menu item into **Add New Content**, click on the **Save** button to submit the form and save your changes.

Edit menu link ○

Menu link title *

Add content

The text to be used for this link in the menu.

Path

Add content

Description

Shown when hovering over the menu link.

☑ Enabled

Menu links that are not enabled will not be listed in any menu.

☑ Show as expanded

If selected and this menu link has children, the menu will always appear expanded.

Parent link

<Add New Content>

The maximum depth for a link and all its children is fixed at 9. Some menu links may not be available as parents if selecting them would exceed this limit.

Weight

-50

Optional. In the menu, the heavier links will sink and the lighter links will be positioned nearer the top.

Save

If you wish, you can move items into **Holding Tank**. If you do not want to use **Holding Tank**, you can disable the individual menu items. The only real difference is that moving the unused menu items to holding tank reduces visual clutter for people administering the menus.

When you are done, your users will have a distinct menu to use when they need to add content.

Populating the main menu

In this step, we will add some useful links into the main menu. As you populate the main menu, think about the work your site members will be performing. You want your main menu to act as doorways to their most commonly performed tasks.

The process for adding menu items into the main menu is just the same as for moving them into other menus. As shown in the following screenshot, when editing an existing menu item, select **Main menu** under Default parent item.

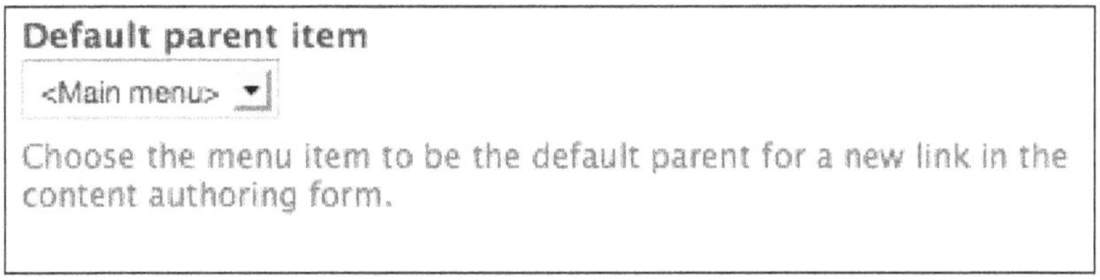

Default parent item

<Main menu> ▾

Choose the menu item to be the default parent for a new link in the content authoring form.

Adding a post directly to a menu

Users in a role with administer menu privileges can assign new posts directly into existing menus, if the content type **Menu settings** allow it. To make a content type available to a certain menu, click on **Structure | Content types** or navigate to admin/structure/types. For each Content type, click on the **edit** link and then on the **Menu settings** tab at the bottom of the page. You will see each menu listed and can check the boxes next to the menus to select which content types are available to each menu.

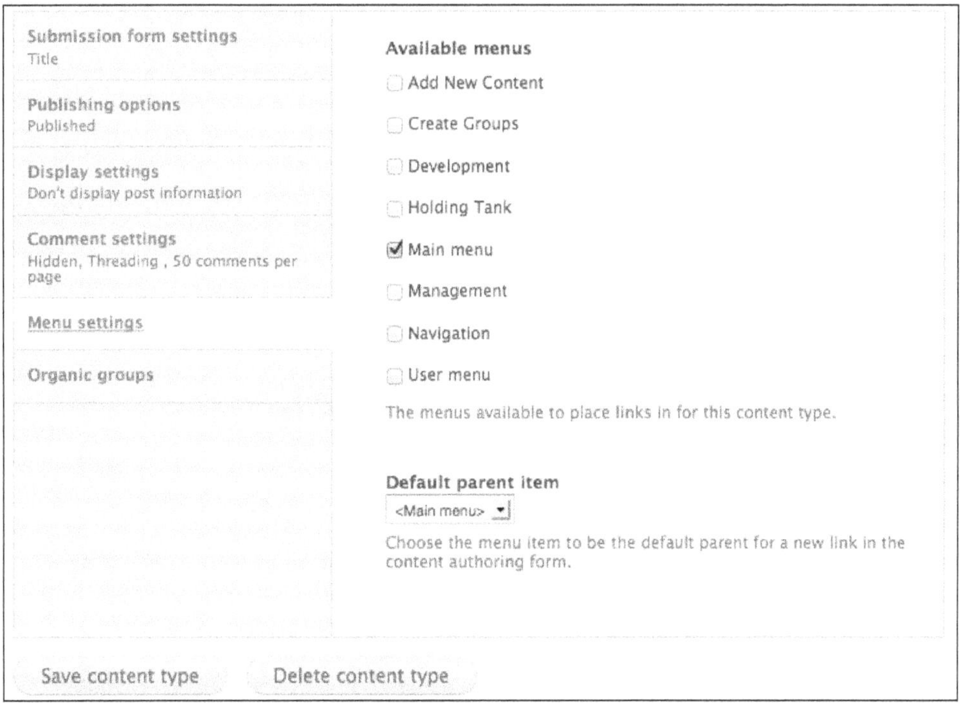

Submission form settings
Title

Publishing options
Published

Display settings
Don't display post information

Comment settings
Hidden, Threading , 50 comments per page

Menu settings

Organic groups

Available menus

☐ Add New Content

☐ Create Groups

☐ Development

☐ Holding Tank

☑ Main menu

☐ Management

☐ Navigation

☐ User menu

The menus available to place links in for this content type.

Default parent item

<Main menu> ▾

Choose the menu item to be the default parent for a new link in the content authoring form.

Save content type   Delete content type

As shown in the following screenshot, the **Menu settings** (**Provide a menu link**, **Menu link title**, **Description**, **Parent item**, and **Weight**) are at the bottom of the page.

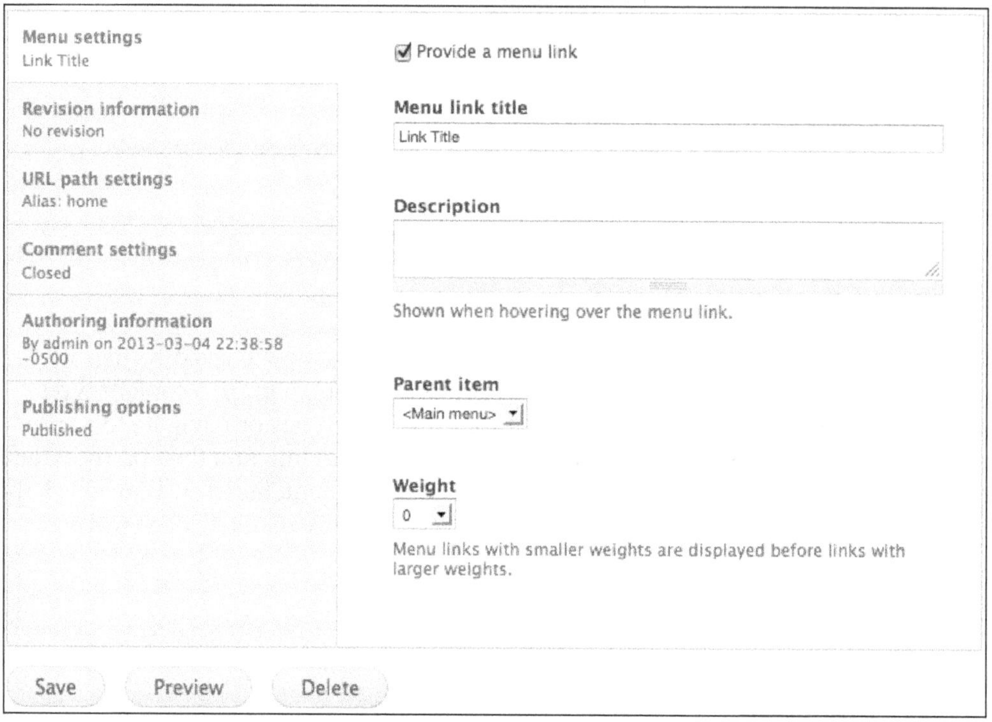

The main menu appears in the top left corner of the screen as tabs. Drupal's default theme, **Bartik**, automatically creates a tab for the home page, which updates as the home page setting on the **Site information** page updates.

As noted above, different themes present the main menu in different ways. For example, some themes display the main menu as links or buttons. For a complete look at contributed themes and how they display the primary links, visit http://drupal.org/project/themes.

Adding a new menu item

In some cases, such as creating a menu item that links to an external site, you will need to add a new menu item into an existing menu — for example, you might want to link to your main school site from the class website.

For this example, we will add a link to http://drupal.org. At the risk of stating the obvious, you can use the same steps to place a link to any site in any menu.

1. To begin with, return to the menu administration screen by clicking on **Structure | Menus**, or by navigating to `admin/structure/menu`. Click on the **List Links** tab next to the name of the menu you want to edit. For this example, click on the link next to **Main menu**.

2. To add a menu item, click on **Add link**.

3. For each new menu item, you need to specify the following:
   - **Menu link title**: This text will be displayed in the menu
   - **Path**: This can be internal or external
   - **Description**: This text will be displayed when hovering over a menu item
   - **Parent link**: To determine where the new menu item will be displayed

Home » Administration » Structure » Menus » Main menu

Main menu ○

LIST LINKS   EDIT MENU

Menu link title *

Drupal

The text to be used for this link in the menu.

Path *

http://drupal.org

The path for this menu link. This can be an internal Drupal path such as *node/add* or an external URL such as *http://drupal.org*. Enter *<front>* to link to the front page.

Description

The main website of Drupal

Shown when hovering over the menu link.

☑ Enabled

Menu links that are not enabled will not be listed in any menu.

☐ Show as expanded

If selected and this menu link has children, the menu will always appear expanded.

Parent link

<Main menu>

The maximum depth for a link and all its children is fixed at 9. Some menu links may not be available as parents if selecting them would exceed this limit.

Weight

0

Optional. In the menu, the heavier links will sink and the lighter links will be positioned nearer the top.

Save

4. Click on the **Save** button to submit the form and create the new menu item. After the menu item has been saved, you are redirected to a page where you can reorganize the menu items via drag-and-drop.

Blocks and block-placement FAQ

Due to their relationship with menus, the full range of functionality offered by blocks can remain unclear. This section addresses some commonly asked questions about using blocks.

What is a block? How is it different from a menu?

Blocks and menus complement each other. Menus provide a way to create, group, and organize links. Blocks then display those menus.

What is a region?

Regions are specific places on the page that can be used to display content. Regions can be used in conjunction with blocks, as blocks can be dropped into any predefined region. Most of Drupal's core themes have nine regions enabled: **Left sidebar**, **Right sidebar**, **Content**, **Header**, **Footer**, **Highlighted**, **Help**, **Page Top**, and **Page Bottom**. If you navigate to admin/structure/block you can see the default location of these regions. These regions are identified in the following screenshot:

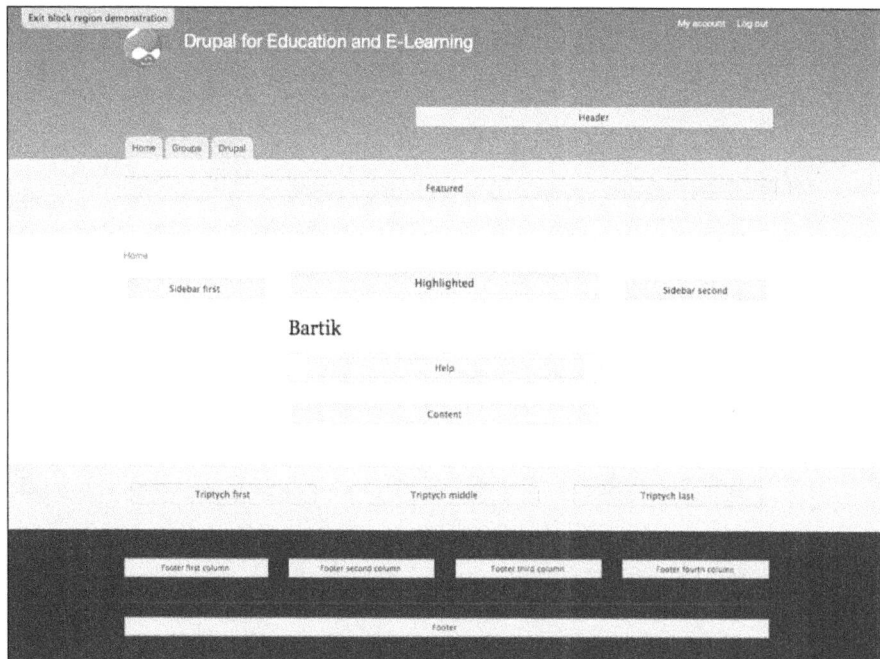

What else can I do with a block?

A lot can be done with blocks! You can create custom blocks that use HTML markup, or blocks that use PHP code. You can limit block visibility by user role, and by path. To get a sense of the full range of what can be done with blocks, check out the options available when you add a new block at `admin/structure/block/add`. Fully exploiting the power of blocks requires a working knowledge of PHP. In this book we explore some of these options in context. The Drupal handbook includes a selection of PHP snippets related to blocks at `http://drupal.org/node/21867`. However, when using a snippet from the handbook, you should always check two things:

- Make sure that the snippet is for the correct version of Drupal, as snippets for Drupal 5 or 6 will not work for Drupal 7.
- Test your snippet in a page first by using the **Preview** option. This allows you to make sure that the snippet works as advertised, as blocks do not have a preview option.

Can I make a block visible to specific roles or on specific pages?

Yes, you can make a block visible to specific roles or on specific pages. Every block has customizable block visibility settings. To access these settings, click on **Structure | Blocks**, or navigate to `admin/structure/blocks`.

Visibility settings

Pages
Not restricted

Content types
Not restricted

Roles
Not restricted

Users
Not customizable

Show block on specific pages

- All pages except those listed
- Only the listed pages
- Pages on which this PHP code returns TRUE (experts only)

Specify pages by using their paths. Enter one path per line. The '*' character is a wildcard. Example paths are *blog* for the blog page and *blog/** for every personal blog. *<front>* is the front page. If the PHP option is chosen, enter PHP code between *<?php ?>*. Note that executing incorrect PHP code can break your Drupal site.

Save block

As shown in the preceding screenshot, block visibility can be set by URL path, content type, or role. You can also decide whether to allow users to show or hide the block themselves. So, for example, a block could be made to disappear whenever content is being added or edited by using the **Pages** tab under **Visibility settings**. Set the block to **All pages except those listed**, and enter the following URLs:

- `node/add/*`
- `node/*/edit`

As the above example implies, you can use wildcards in the path name.

Changing settings via the admin menu

Between creating custom menus and blocks, and the various options available through the administrative screens, you have a fair amount of control over the look and feel of your site. In this section, we will look at these options.

The Site information page

Navigate to the **Site information** page by clicking on **Configuration | Site information**, or by navigating to `admin/config/system/site-information`.

This page contains some basic options that can be customized for your site.

Home » Administration » Configuration » System

Site information ⚙

SITE DETAILS

Site name *

Drupal for Education and E-Learning

Slogan

How this is used depends on your site's theme.

E-mail address *

james@jamesgrobertson.com

The *From* address in automated e-mails sent during registration and new password requests, and other notifications. (Use an address ending in your site's domain to help prevent this e-mail being flagged as spam.)

FRONT PAGE

Number of posts on front page

1 ▾

The maximum number of posts displayed on overview pages such as the front page.

Default front page

http://localhost:8888/drupal7/ home

Optionally, specify a relative URL to display as the front page. Leave blank to display the default content feed.

ERROR PAGES

Default 403 (access denied) page

http://localhost:8888/drupal7/

This page is displayed when the requested document is denied to the current user. Leave blank to display a generic "access denied" page.

Default 404 (not found) page

http://localhost:8888/drupal7/

This page is displayed when no other content matches the requested document. Leave blank to display a generic "page not found" page.

Save configuration

As you can see in the preceding screenshot, **Site name** and **Slogan** appear on every page of the site.

Default front page has been covered earlier in this chapter.

Much like you did with the **Default front page**, you can create pages that users will see when a page can't be found, or when a user is not allowed to see the page under the **Error Pages** section.

Theme settings

Theme settings can be set globally and also individually within a theme. If you want, you can allow users to choose their own theme. As the site administrator, you get to specify which themes are allowed. Global settings can be set site-wide among all themes, for use. However, you can also override these settings within the individual themes.

In this section, we will look at enabling themes, adjusting Global settings, and then adjusting the settings for the Bartik theme, one of Drupal's core themes.

Enabling themes

To view the list of installed themes, click on the **Appearance** link or navigate to `admin/appearance`. On this page, you will see a list of all of the installed themes, as shown in the following screenshot:

To install a theme, refer to the instructions given in *Chapter 3, Getting Started*. To enable a theme, click on the **Enable** button under the theme heading. To set a theme as a site-wide default, click on the **Enable and set default** option. On most sites, you will only need to have one theme enabled.

Global theme settings

To access the global theme settings, click on the **SETTINGS** tab as indicated by **Item 1** in the preceding screenshot, or navigate to `admin/appearance/settings`, and then select **Global settings**.

The global theme settings have three different sections: **Toggle display**, **Logo image settings**, and **Shortcut icon settings**.

All three sections can be set within the individual themes, and if a setting is set within a theme, it will override the global setting.

Toggling the display

This section lets you toggle the display of information collected from various areas of the site configuration.

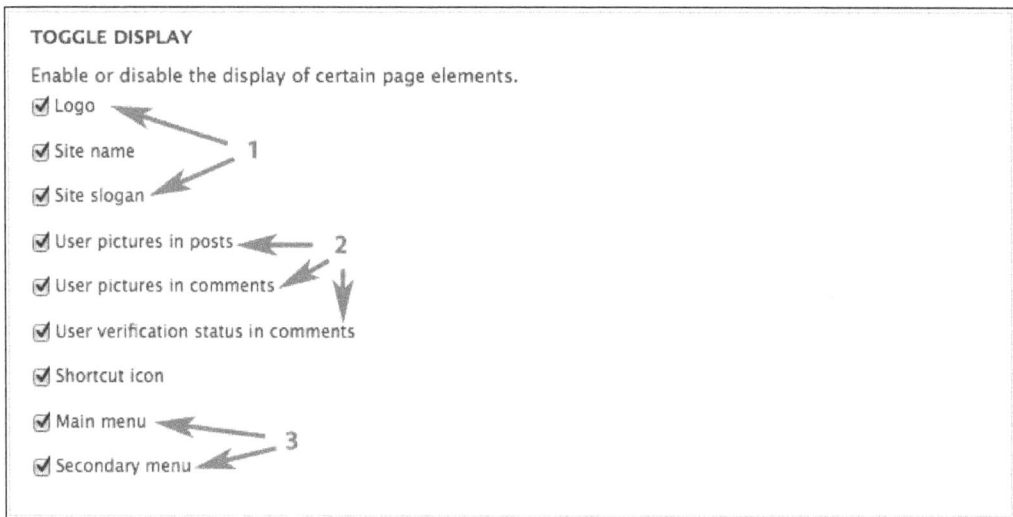

Items in section **1** can be set by clicking on **Configuration | Site information**, or by navigating to `admin/config/system/site-information`. These settings were covered in detail earlier in this chapter.

Items in section **2** can be set by clicking on **People | Account settings**, or by navigating to `admin/config/people/accounts`.

Items in section **3** can be set within the menu system by clicking on **Structure | Menus**, or by navigating to `admin/structure/menu`. These settings were covered in detail earlier in this chapter.

The shortcut icon is covered later in this section.

Once you have adjusted the settings to how you want them, save your choice by clicking on the **Save configuration** button.

Logo image settings

The logo and shortcut (as shown in the next section) icons allow you to customize the logo displayed on the site's pages and the shortcut icon (also called the favicon) displayed in the browser address bar and favorites.

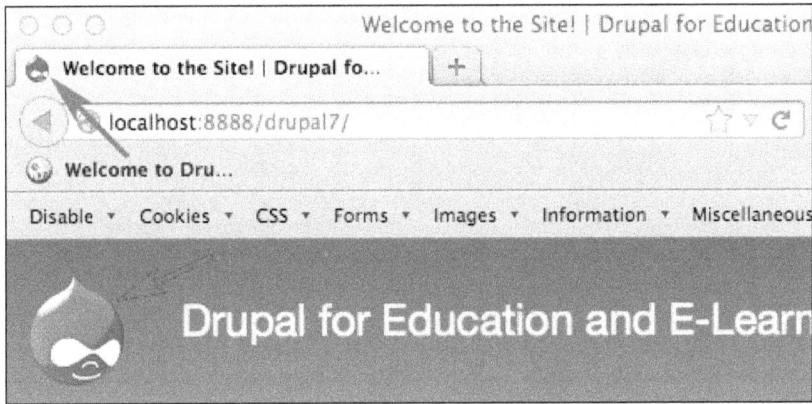

A new logo can be uploaded via the form, pictured in the following screenshot. Note that an oversized logo can break a site layout!

Once you've adjusted the settings to how you want them, save your choices by clicking on the **Save configuration** button.

Shortcut icon settings

You can upload a custom shortcut icon, also called a favicon, using the form shown in the following screenshot:

SHORTCUT ICON SETTINGS

Your shortcut icon, or 'favicon', is displayed in the address bar and bookmarks of most browsers.

☐ Use the default shortcut icon.

Check here if you want the theme to use the default shortcut icon.

Path to custom icon

The path to the image file you would like to use as your custom shortcut icon.

Upload icon image

[Browse...]

If you don't have direct file access to the server, use this field to upload your shortcut icon.

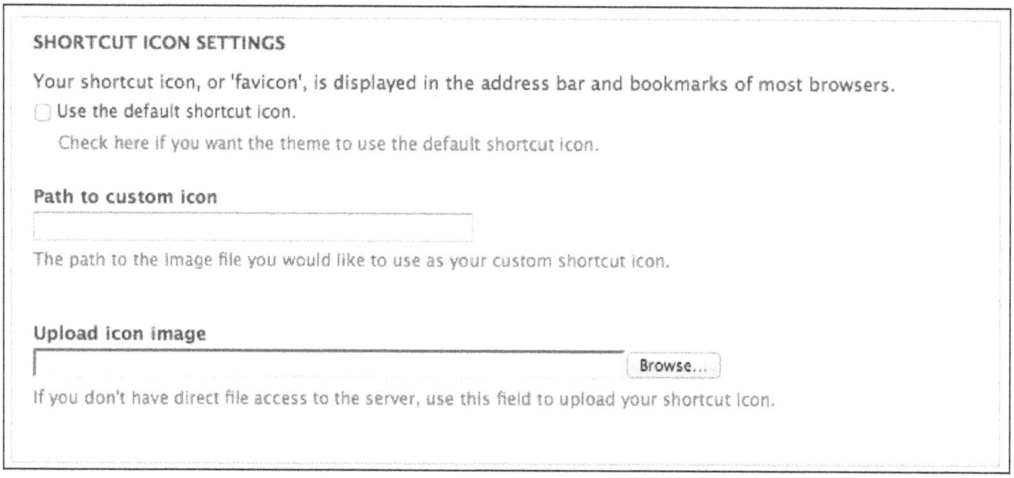

You can create favicons using most graphic software, but it is easier to use one of the free online favicon creators. My personal favorite is `http://www.chami.com/html-kit/services/favicon/` – this site will automatically generate a favicon from a picture.

Once you've adjusted the settings to how you want them, save your choices by clicking on the **Save configuration** button.

Theme-specific settings

As stated above, adjusting the theme-specific settings will override the global settings.

In this tutorial, we are configuring the options for the Bartik theme. This theme includes a color picker, which allows you to choose specific colors for the different elements of your theme.

The color picker, shown in the following screenshot, provides a way of selecting colors for specific theme elements via the web browser:

Using the color picker, you can select new colors via drag-and-drop, and redefine the text color, the link color, and the general color scheme.

Once you have selected a color scheme, save your choices by clicking on the **Save configuration** button.

Looking under the hood

Like most Drupal-related things, you have an overwhelmingly broad range of options available to you if you want to tinker with the code that makes your site run. While this holds an incredible amount of appeal to those with a do-it-yourself spirit, it's a bit much for most people.

If, however, you are one of the statistical minority inclined to roll your sleeves up and start messing with such things, this section is for you.

Additionally, the Drupal handbook has an excellent overview of the theming system for Drupal 7 at `http://drupal.org/documentation/theme`.

Drupal's theme structure

At the outset, I want to make a couple of things clear. First, a detailed analysis of Drupal's theming system is beyond the scope of this book. Second, Drupal offers a lot of flexibility for those who want to mess around with the code; however, just because you can doesn't mean you should.

Additionally, developing a theme is not complete without checking to see how the theme displays in different browsers. This means looking at your site in at least the following browsers: Internet Explorer 6 through 9, Google Chrome, Firefox, Safari, and Opera. For each browser, it is also helpful to look at the site in as many of the browser's supported operating systems as possible. The cross-browser compatibility checking can be incredibly time-consuming, particularly when trying to get a complex page to render cleanly in Explorer and all the other browsers listed. Often, adjusting a value to get a clean display in one browser causes a new problem to arise in another. When you edit your theme via the settings described earlier, you minimize the risk of creating more complex issues. However, leveraging the full power of design within Drupal requires the editing of theme files.

With that said, the following screenshot gives an overview of the directory structure of the Bartik theme:

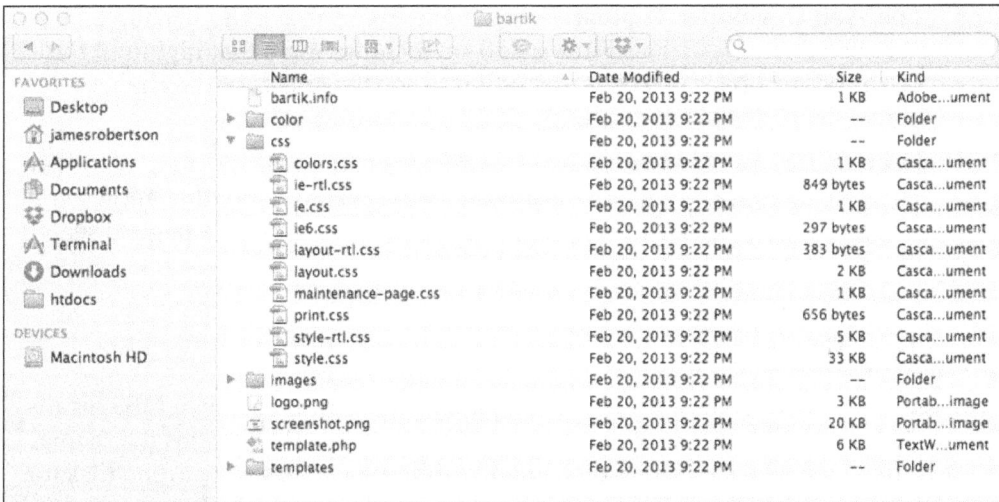

CSS files

CSS is an abbreviation for Cascading Style Sheets. Style sheets contain information about how the content within your site should be displayed. For background information on style sheets, visit `http://en.wikipedia.org/wiki/Cascading_Style_Sheets`.

> When working with your theme's CSS files, *always* back up a working copy of your theme before making any changes.

The first place to get started when modifying a theme is within the theme's CSS files. In the preceding screenshot you can see the ten CSS files that are included with the Bartik theme. Of these 10 files, we are mostly interested in `style.css`, as that is where the bulk of the information concerning the look and feel of the Bartik theme is stored.

A full exploration of CSS is beyond the scope of this book, but for those interested in learning more, the following resources are indispensable and freely available online:

- **The W3 school's CSS tutorial**: (`http://www.w3schools.com/css/`) This website gives a top-to-bottom tutorial on CSS. Great for beginners looking to learn and CSS gurus who don't want to remember every single detail.

- **The Web Developer Toolbar**: (`https://addons.mozilla.org/en-US/firefox/addon/60`) This Firefox add-on includes tools that highlight the CSS used on a page, and lets you edit it to see the effects of the changes in real time.

- **Firebug**: (`https://addons.mozilla.org/en-US/firefox/addon/1843`) This Firefox add-on is a more technical web-developer tool that allows you to (among many other things) highlight specific sections of a page to see the CSS in use on that section.

tpl.php files

If you have edited the CSS files of your theme and still haven't achieved the results you wanted, you still have another option: editing the code that creates the theme. The code that creates the theme is contained within the various `*.tpl.php` files for your theme. Additionally, many themes have a `template.php` file that contains functions used by the theme.

> When working with your theme's' `*.php` files, always back up a working copy of the files before changing them.

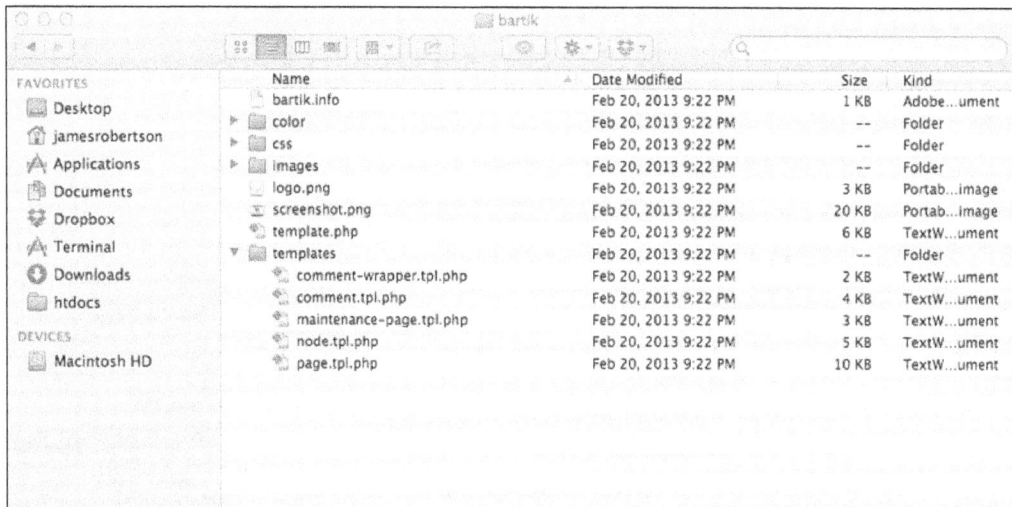

If you look at the preceding screenshot, you will see several `tpl.php` files; for example: `comment.tpl.php`, `node.tpl.php`, and `page.tpl.php`.

In general terms, the `page.tpl.php` collects all of the information passed to it by the other `tpl.php` files. This makes the `page.tpl.php` file of singular importance within the theme, as it controls the general layout of every page rendered on your site.

To effectively work with these files, you need to have some familiarity with PHP. In short, by working with these files you have a great degree of control over how your site looks. The downside of this power is that, if you make a mistake in editing one of these files, you can cause your entire site to crash.

As I said earlier, a full discussion of Drupal's theming system is beyond the scope of this book. However, some quick highlights will serve as a starting point for people looking to learn more about building custom themes in Drupal.

Custom tpl.php files

To create custom pages, make a copy of your original `page.tpl.php` (or `comment.tpl.php`, or `node.tpl.php`) file and rename it as described:

- You can build custom pages based on the node id by creating a `page--node--x.tpl.php` (where x is the node id of the specific page you want to theme) file.

- You can create a custom home page for your site by creating a `page--front.tpl.php` file.

- You can theme blocks differently by region by creating a `block--regionname.tpl.php` file—so, if you created `block--footer.tpl.php` then this file would control how any block placed in the footer region appears.

- You can theme separate content types differently by creating a `node--contenttype.tpl.php` file. For example, `node--blog.tpl.php` can be used to customize how blogs are displayed.

CSS and JavaScript aggregation

Drupal 7 comes with the ability to aggregate your CSS and JavaScript files. Aggregating these files can improve the performance of your site, and it can also help eliminate some bugs in Internet Explorer. Turn on aggregation after you have configured your site to its desired settings. Developing your site with aggregation enabled can cause delays in seeing the results of changes and tweaks, which can complicate the design process.

To aggregate your CSS and JavaScript files, click on **Configuration | Performance**, or navigate to `admin/config/development/performance`, and select the appropriate options in the bandwidth optimizations settings.

Additional resources

The Drupal handbooks contain a wealth of good information on developing and customizing themes. Two good places to start in the handbooks are:

- The theme snippets page at `http://drupal.org/node/45471` — this page contains user-submitted theme modifications

- The theme HowTos page at `http://drupal.org/node/22803` — a collection of solution based on CSS and PHP for a variety of theme-related issues

Additionally, there is a **Theme developer** module available as part of the **Devel** module. This module can be used by advanced designers to help develop custom themes. For more details, visit `http://drupal.org/project/devel_themer`.

Summary

In this chapter, we discussed some of the tools available to customize the look and feel of your site. The discussion examined how to use menus and blocks effectively, and how to use different administrative options to alter the basic design elements of your site.

Finally, for the intrepid souls who are not content to use only the options given to them via the admin screens, we made a brief examination of how to customize a theme via the style sheets and the actual PHP code that generates the theme. In the next chapter, we will learn some of the best practices for backing up and maintaining your site.

15
Backup, Maintenance, and Upgrades

Backup and maintenance procedures are among the more onerous tasks of maintaining a website. These procedures are detail oriented, and they require a level of geek-like work that many people simply don't enjoy. Additionally, many users have the expectation that a website, once set up, will run by itself.

Unfortunately, just about everything in life—a car, a computer, a relationship, or a website—requires work to run smoothly. In this chapter, we will go over the steps that you need to take to keep your site safe and secure.

The instructions in this chapter are intended for teachers running a site to support their classes, or for a technology department at a small school—for example, for people running under ten sites overall. For larger Drupal installations, or for people developing applications using Drupal, I strongly recommend a more complex support structure using a version control system (CVS, svn, git, bazaar, and so on).

In this chapter, we will cover:

- Setting up periodic maintenance tasks called cron jobs
- Site backups
- Site upgrades
- Setting up a backup and test environment

Setting up cron jobs

In Drupal, **cron** jobs are used to schedule and perform various maintenance tasks on your site. Within a Drupal site, cron jobs trigger several important tasks, such as building the search index for your site, and generating and updating log files. Frequently, other modules will also set up actions that are triggered by cron jobs.

The name cron job comes from the Linux utility cron. It is an automated scheduling program installed on Linux systems. For an overview of cron, visit `http://en.wikipedia.org/wiki/Cron`.

Drupal 7 now ships with a module for automating cron jobs. To configure the module, click on **Configuration | Cron**, or navigate to `admin/config/system/cron`.

Home » Administration » Configuration » System

Cron

Cron takes care of running periodic tasks like checking for updates and indexing content for search.

Run cron

Last run: *1 min 7 sec* ago.

Run cron every

3 hours

Save configuration

The configuration options allow you to specify how frequently cron should run. For most learning sites, cron should run every two to three hours. Since Drupal's default setting is 3 hours, no further configuration is necessary!

If you need to run cron jobs more frequently than the module allows, you can also configure cron jobs to run from the command line. Some web hosting companies have utilities that simplify the creation of cron jobs. For information about setting up cron jobs within different hosting environments, refer to the Drupal handbook at `http://drupal.org/cron`.

Backup and maintenance overview

Drupal sites run as a result of an interaction between four components:

- The database
- The core codebase
- The contributed modules and themes directory, along with the `settings.php` file
- The files directory

In practice, we will back up the **module**, **theme**, and **file** directories together, as they all reside in the `sites` directory. However, when it comes to updating the site, it is helpful to think of them as separate from one another. When upgrading sites, we treat the core codebase, contributed modules, and contributed themes in different ways.

Also, as part of your backup and maintenance strategy, you should create a document that lists all of the critical usernames and passwords for your site.

This list of critical data includes:

- Username and password of UID1 on your site
- Username, password, and database name of your database
- Username and password for FTP (or preferably SFTP) access to your site
- Username and password for SSH (or shell) access to your site

At the risk of stating the obvious, this document should be stored in a very secure place. For a more secure setup, you should use a tool such as Password Gorilla, available at `https://github.com/zdia/gorilla`.

Backing up the codebase

In order to create a back up of the codebase, use your FTP client to connect to your server. Ideally, for reasons of download speed and stability, this should not be done over a wireless connection.

When the download is complete, you will have a full copy of your working codebase saved on your computer.

Later in this chapter, we will cover how to use the command line to speed up this process, but, for those of you who want to avoid the command line, you can make adequate backups of your codebase using FTP.

> While using FTP to back up your site will work, it will certainly get unwieldy over time, particularly as people store files on your site.

Automating backups using backup and migrate

The **Backup and Migrate** module simplifies the process of backing up your site by automating the key steps of site maintenance. To get started, download the 7.x-2 Version of the module from `http://drupal.org/project/backup_migrate`, and install it as described in *Chapter 3, Getting Started*. Also download and install the latest version of the **Backup and Migrate Files** module, found at `http://drupal.org/project/backup_migrate_files`.

Once you have the modules installed, click on **Configuration | Backup and Migrate**, or navigate to `admin/config/system/backup_migrate`.

As you work with your site over time, you will fine-tune the settings for the Backup and Migrate module. As we cover how to configure this module, we will discuss how to tune the settings. The Backup and Migrate module performs two related maintenance tasks:

- Backing up the database
- Backing up the files directory

Once the database and files have been backed up, they are compressed and stored on the server, and, optionally, a site administrator is sent an e-mail about the backup.

Configuring the database and file backup options

For the Backup and Migrate module to work, a private files directory must be set up. Click on **Configuration | File system**, or navigate to `admin/config/media/file-system`.

Home » Administration » Configuration » Media

File system ○

Public file system path

sites/default/files

A local file system path where public files will be stored. This directory must exist and be writable by Drupal. This directory must be relative to the Drupal installation directory and be accessible over the web.

Private file system path

sites/default/files/private

An existing local file system path for storing private files. It should be writable by Drupal and not accessible over the web. See the online handbook for more information about securing private files.

Temporary directory

/Applications/MAMP/tmp/php

A local file system path where temporary files will be stored. This directory should not be accessible over the web.

Default download method

◉ Public local files served by the webserver.

○ Private local files served by Drupal.

This setting is used as the preferred download method. The use of public files is more efficient, but does not provide any access control.

Save configuration

> The Drupal documentation contains tips for placement of the private files directory, available at `http://drupal.org/documentation/modules/file#access`. In short, if your hosting allows, put your private files directory outside your Drupal installation. If not, you can put it in another folder under the public files directory. Make sure to test whether the private files directory is really private!

Enter the path of your private directory in the **Private file system path** field, and then click on the **Save configuration** button. If the parent directory of the path you entered is writeable by Drupal, the directory will automatically be created if it doesn't already exist.

Return to the Backup and Migrate settings page by clicking the **Configure | Backup and Migrate** link, or by navigating to `admin/config/system/backup_migrate`.

When using the Backup and Migrate module to back up your database and files, you can set different backup intervals for each item. Therefore, configuring the module will take a few steps:

1. Modify the default profile to enable e-mail notifications for backups
2. Schedule the database backups
3. Schedule the files directory backups

Modifying the default profile

Click on the **Profiles** tab, and then the **override** link next to the **Default Settings** profile. Expand the **ADVANCED OPTIONS** accordion. Check the boxes next to **Send an email if backup succeeds** and **Send an email if backup fails**, and enter the e-mail address of a trusted user in the corresponding boxes.

▾ ADVANCED OPTIONS

☑ Send an email if backup succeeds

Email Address for Success Notices

`james@jamesgrobertson.com`

☑ Send an email if backup fails

Email Address for Failure Notices

`james@jamesgrobertson.com`

☑ Take site offline

Take the site offline during backup and show a maintenance message. Site will be taken back online once the backup is complete.

Site off-line message

Drupal for Education and E-Learning is currently under maintenance. We should be back shortly. Thank you for your patience.

Message to show visitors when the site is in off-line mode.

Description

Add a short description to the backup file.

Save profile   Cancel

It would be a good practice to check the **Take site offline** box. This prevents data loss and corruption in the backup, as it prevents users from writing to the database after the backup has started. Users won't be able to log into the site, and will see a page with the **Site off-line** message.

Click on the **Save profile** button when you are finished. You will be redirected back to the main Backup and Migrate configuration page.

Scheduling database and file backups

Click on the **Schedules** tab, and then the **Add Schedule** link. Change **Schedule Name** to Daily Database Backup. In general, the database should be backed up daily, and since that is the module's default we will not change it.

Home

Edit Schedule ○

☑ Enabled

Schedule Name

Daily Database Backup

▼ BACKUP SOURCE

Backup Source

Default Database ▼

Choose the database to backup. Any database destinations you have created and any databases specified in your settings.php can be backed up.

Settings Profile

Default Settings ▼

Create new profile

Backup every 1   Days ▼

Number of Backup files to keep

0

The number of backup files to keep before deleting old ones. Use 0 to never delete backups. Other files in the destination directory will get deleted if you specify a limit.

Destination

Scheduled Backups Directory ▼

Choose where the backup file will be saved. Backup files contain sensitive data, so be careful where you save them.
Create new destination

Save schedule   Cancel

The only other option you may want to change on this page is the **Number of Backup files to keep** option. If you have a limited amount of space on your hosting account, you may want to limit this to five or ten backups. Click on **Save schedule** to save your changes.

Repeat these steps again, with the following values:

- **Schedule Name**: `Weekly Files Directory Backup`
- **Backup Source**: **Public Files Directory**
- **Backup every**: **1 Weeks**
- Again, if you have limited space in your hosting account, limit the **Number of Backup files to keep** option.
- Click on the **Save schedule** button to save your changes.

Summary – using backup and migrate to automate backup and maintenance

The Backup and Migrate module automates the process of backing up those elements of your site that change on a regular basis. The database and file backups, when used in conjunction with a backup of your working codebase, is all you need to run your site securely.

At this point, your site will be running securely if you have:

- A backup of your core codebase.
- A backup of all contributed modules and themes, and a copy of your `settings.php` file (that is, a copy of the sites directory).
- A configured Backup and Migrate module that is taking copies of your database and files directory. These files will be retrieved from the server by a trusted and responsible site administrator.

These three things make up the core of your backup plan. If you have completed these elements, your site is now running securely.

Caring for your database

The database containing your site's data is the single most important piece of your site. It contains all of the configuration options you have put into your site, as well as the countless hours of work completed by your students. In short, it needs to be treated with care. Taking care of your database ensures that your site will run smoothly over time.

As you use your site, your database tables will benefit from optimization. This step, although not technically necessary in most cases, can help prevent errors over time. Optimizing tables can be compared to giving a car a tune-up, or with defragmenting a computer's hard drive.

Table optimization can be automated by using the DB Maintenance module, which can be downloaded from http://drupal.org/project/db_maintenance. Download and install this module as described in *Chapter 3, Getting Started*.

Automating table optimization using DB maintenance

The DB maintenance module provides several options for optimizing your database, which can be configured by clicking on **Configuration | DB maintenance**, or navigating to admin/config/system/db_maintenance.

To start, as shown in the preceding screenshot, you should use the following options:

- Select the **Log OPTIMIZE queries** option
- Select **Bi-Weekly** in **Optimize tables**
- For **Tables in the drupal7 database**, select all of the tables listed

When you are initially setting up your site, you should always choose to optimize all tables, and always log what tables get optimized. By setting your site to optimize tables bi-weekly, you will be able to use your log files (available at **Reports | Recent log messages** link, or by navigating to admin/reports/dblog) to see which specific tables need to be optimized over time. You can then select to optimize only those tables, which will make your site more efficient. At that point, you might also want to adjust the frequency with which the tables are optimized.

If you choose not to use the DB maintenance module you have other tools at your disposal.

Using phpMyAdmin as a maintenance and backup tool

phpMyAdmin comes with some useful, browser-based tools for backing up and optimizing your database.

Optimizing tables using phpMyAdmin

As shown in the following screenshot, phpMyAdmin contains a great utility for optimizing tables and also shows when these tables need optimizing:

Table ▲	Action						Rows ⑦	Type	Collation	Size	Overhead
actions						✕	17	InnoDB	utf8_general_ci	16 KiB	-
advanced_help_index						✕	0	InnoDB	utf8_general_ci	32 KiB	-
authmap						✕	0	InnoDB	utf8_general_ci	32 KiB	-
backup_migrate_destinations						✕	0	InnoDB	utf8_general_ci	16 KiB	-
backup_migrate_profiles						✕	0	InnoDB	utf8_general_ci	16 KiB	-
backup_migrate_schedules						✕	2	InnoDB	utf8_general_ci	16 KiB	-
☑ batch						✕	0	InnoDB	utf8_general_ci	32 KiB	-
block						✕	66	InnoDB	utf8_general_ci	48 KiB	-
blocked_ips						✕	0	InnoDB	utf8_general_ci	32 KiB	-
block_custom						✕	0	InnoDB	utf8_general_ci	32 KiB	-
block_node_type						✕	1	InnoDB	utf8_general_ci	32 KiB	-
block_role						✕	2	InnoDB	utf8_general_ci	32 KiB	-
☑ cache						✕	17	InnoDB	utf8_general_ci	1.4 MiB	-
☑ cache_block						✕	0	InnoDB	utf8_general_ci	32 KiB	-
cache_bootstrap						✕	6	InnoDB	utf8_general_ci	176 KiB	-
cache_entity_og_membership						✕	0	InnoDB	utf8_general_ci	32 KiB	-
cache_entity_og_membership_type						✕	0	InnoDB	utf8_general_ci	32 KiB	-
cache_field						✕	4	InnoDB	utf8_general_ci	176 KiB	-
☑ cache_filter						✕	0	InnoDB	utf8_general_ci	32 KiB	-
☑ cache_form						✕	0	InnoDB	utf8_general_ci	32 KiB	-
cache_image						✕	0	InnoDB	utf8_general_ci	32 KiB	-
cache_media_xml						✕	0	InnoDB	utf8_general_ci	32 KiB	-
cache_menu						✕	53	InnoDB	utf8_general_ci	512 KiB	-

Select the checkbox to the left of all of the tables that you want to optimize, and then choose the **Optimize table** option as shown in the following screenshot:

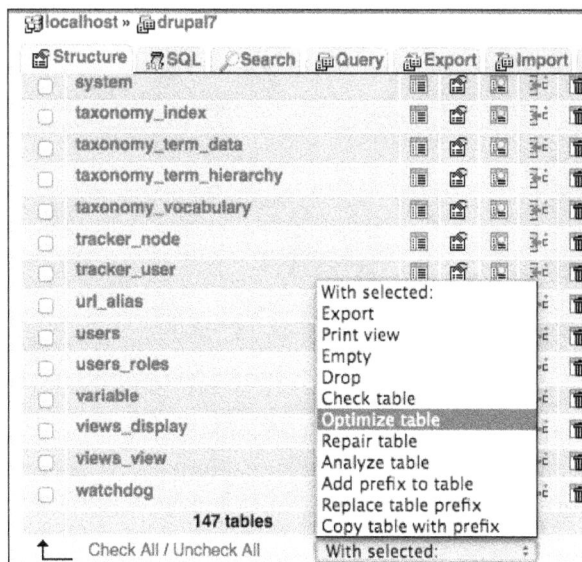

Although you can optimize tables using the command line, doing so requires more technical skills than using phpMyAdmin. MySQL syntax can change between versions. phpMyAdmin is a useful and easy tool for these types of maintenance procedures.

Manually backing up the database

The Backup and Migrate module automates database backups for you. However, there are still times when you might want to or need to back up your database manually, such as before a site upgrade.

Before you back up your database, you should optimize the tables in the database.

Backing up the database via phpMyAdmin

phpMyAdmin has an export utility that can be used to back up your database. As shown in the following screenshot, you can access it by clicking on the **Export** tab:

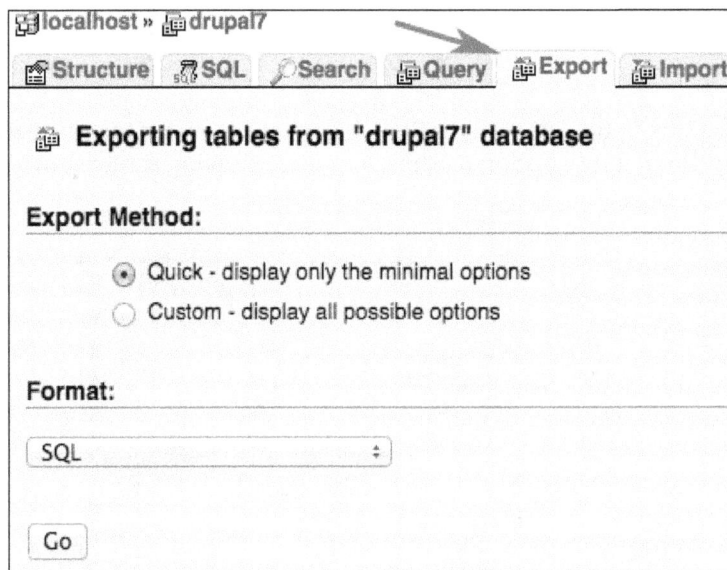

The **Export** screen contains two options: **Quick** and **Custom**. A quick export will output a text representation of the database in the format you select with the **Format** select box. Clicking on the **Custom** radio button displays all the other options available:

Let's the options available for the Custom radio button:

- **Table(s)**: By default all tables are selected, which is what we want.

- **Output**: Choose the **Save output to a file** option. In the **File name template** option, enter a descriptive filename. I recommend a name that combines the name of the database with the date of the backup. This naming convention simplifies the process of finding your most current backup if you need it. So, for a database named drupal7 that is backed up on January 15, 2013, the name of the backup file would be drupal7_15jan2013. Also, note that in this section, we have selected **gzipped** as the file type. Selecting this option reduces the size of your backed up database.

- **Format**: By default, phpMyAdmin selects **SQL**, which is what we want.

- **Format-specific options**: In general, we can leave these set on their defaults.

Click on the **Go** button to download the file.

> For database files that are too large to be backed up using phpMyAdmin, both the DB maintenance module (covered earlier in this chapter) and command-line backups (covered in the next section) sidestep this issue.

Backing up your database via the command line

In this section, we provide instructions that eliminate the need to use the command line. However, knowing how to use the command line can save you time. Using the command line can be confusing, as the command line is not intuitive; you need to know the precise commands and syntax to use. However, for clearly-defined tasks, knowledge of the command line can be very useful.

When working from the command line on your server, you should create a staging directory. You will use this directory as a place to upload files, to store backups, and as a place to extract any files prior to moving them into your site. Ideally, this staging directory is outside of the web root.

> The **web root** is the highest-level directory on your server that can be accessed via a web browser. Any files or directories within this directory are said to be within the web root. Placing a file or directory outside the web root means that it cannot be accessed via a web browser, but that it can be accessed via FTP or SSH.

To use the command line, you will need shell access to SSH into your web server. On Mac and Linux machines, you can use the **terminal** application. On PC's, you can use **Putty**, available at `http://www.chiark.greenend.org.uk/~sgtatham/putty/download.html`.

For an overview of working via the command line, see the Linux command line tutorial at `http://www.tuxfiles.org/linuxhelp/cli.html`. There are numerous other comparable online tutorials available.

Command-line database backups – the short version

If you are familiar with the command line, here are the commands you will need once you have SSH'ed into your server:

- `mkdir backup`: This creates the staging directory that you will use to store your backups. You will only need this command once. This directory should be outside of the web root.

- `cd backup`: This moves you into the backup directory.

- `mysqldump --skip-lock-tables -u databaseuser -pdatabasepassword databasename > filename.sql`: This command is used to back up your database.

Command-line database backups – the full explanation

1. After logging in to your server, use the `ls -al` command to list the contents of the directory that you are currently in:

```
[jamesgrobertso@p3nlh023 ~]$ ls -al
total 304
drwx---r-x  7 jamesgrobertso inetuser    4096 Mar 16 12:55 .
drwxr-xr-x 11              0          0    4096 Mar 15 18:30 ..
-rw-------  1 jamesgrobertso inetuser      21 Mar 16 12:55 .bash_history
-rwx---r-x  1 jamesgrobertso inetuser     100 Dec  8 2008 .bash_logout
-rwx---r-x  1 jamesgrobertso inetuser     176 Dec  8 2008 .bash_profile
-rwx---r-x  1 jamesgrobertso inetuser     124 Dec  8 2008 .bashrc
-rwx---r-x  1 jamesgrobertso inetuser      29 Dec 18 2010 .cgi_auth
-rw-r--r--  1              0          0     496 Mar 15 17:22 .disk_usage
-------r--  1              0          0       0 Nov  6 11:14 .htaccess
lrwxrwxrwx  1 jamesgrobertso inetuser       8 Dec  8 2008 cgi -> html/cgi
-rw-r--r--  1 jamesgrobertso inetuser       0 Jan 14 2009 cron.php
-rw-r--r--  1 jamesgrobertso inetuser  255847 Jan 14 2009 cron.php.1
-rw-------  1 jamesgrobertso inetuser      79 Apr 12 2009 crontab
-rw-------  1 jamesgrobertso inetuser      19 Apr 12 2009 crontab.disabled
drwx---r-x  2 jamesgrobertso inetuser    4096 Dec  8 2008 data
drwx---r-x  2              0          0    4096 Oct 10 2011 error_logs
drwx---r-x  2 jamesgrobertso inetuser    4096 Oct 14 15:57 htconfig
drwx---r-x 23 jamesgrobertso inetuser    4096 Nov 11 11:05 html
drwx---r-x  2 jamesgrobertso inetuser    4096 Oct  3 2011 scc
[jamesgrobertso@p3nlh023 ~]$
```

2. Use the `mkdir` command to create a directory named `backup`: `mkdir backup`.

3. Use the `ls -al` command to see your newly-created directory, and the `cd` command to move into your newly-created directory. Refer to the following screenshot for more detail:

```
ls -al
cd backup
```

```
 ◯ ◯ ◯        ⌂ jamesrobertson — jamesgrobertso@p3nlh023:~ — ssh — 100×24

[jamesgrobertso@p3nlh023 ~]$ mkdir backup
[jamesgrobertso@p3nlh023 ~]$ ls -al  ◀──
total 308
drwx---r-x  8 jamesgrobertso inetuser   4096 Mar 16 12:59 .
drwxr-xr-x 11              0         0   4096 Mar 15 18:30 ..
-rw-------  1 jamesgrobertso inetuser     21 Mar 16 12:55 .bash_history
-rwx---r-x  1 jamesgrobertso inetuser    100 Dec  8 2008 .bash_logout
-rwx---r-x  1 jamesgrobertso inetuser    176 Dec  8 2008 .bash_profile
-rwx---r-x  1 jamesgrobertso inetuser    124 Dec  8 2008 .bashrc
-rwx---r-x  1 jamesgrobertso inetuser     29 Dec 18 2010 .cgi_auth
-rw-r--r--  1              0         0    496 Mar 15 17:22 .disk_usage
-------r--  1              0         0      0 Nov  6 11:14 .htaccess
drwxr-xr-x  2 jamesgrobertso inetuser   4096 Mar 16 12:59 backup  ◀──
lrwxrwxrwx  1 jamesgrobertso inetuser      8 Dec  8 2008 cgi -> html/cgi
-rw-r--r--  1 jamesgrobertso inetuser      0 Jan 14 2009 cron.php
-rw-r--r--  1 jamesgrobertso inetuser 255847 Jan 14 2009 cron.php.1
-rw-------  1 jamesgrobertso inetuser     79 Apr 12 2009 crontab
-rw-------  1 jamesgrobertso inetuser     19 Apr 12 2009 crontab.disabled
drwx---r-x  2 jamesgrobertso inetuser   4096 Dec  8 2008 data
drwx---r-x  2              0         0   4096 Oct 10 2011 error_logs
drwx---r-x  2 jamesgrobertso inetuser   4096 Oct 14 15:57 htconfig
drwx---r-x 23 jamesgrobertso inetuser   4096 Nov 11 11:05 html
drwx---r-x  2 jamesgrobertso inetuser   4096 Oct  3 2011 scc
[jamesgrobertso@p3nlh023 ~]$ cd backup  ◀──
```

4. Now that we have created and moved into our backup directory, we can actually back up the database using the `mysqldump` command. See the highlighted section in the following screenshot for a detailed example.

```
 ◯ ◯ ◯        ⌂ jamesrobertson — jamesgrobertso@p3nlh023:~/backup — ssh — 100×25

[jamesgrobertso@p3nlh023 ~]$ ls -al
total 312
drwx---r-x  8 jamesgrobertso inetuser   4096 Mar 16 12:59 .
drwxr-xr-x 11              0         0   4096 Mar 15 18:30 ..
-rw-------  1 jamesgrobertso inetuser    780 Mar 16 14:21 .bash_history
-rwx---r-x  1 jamesgrobertso inetuser    100 Dec  8 2008 .bash_logout
-rwx---r-x  1 jamesgrobertso inetuser    176 Dec  8 2008 .bash_profile
-rwx---r-x  1 jamesgrobertso inetuser    124 Dec  8 2008 .bashrc
-rwx---r-x  1 jamesgrobertso inetuser     29 Dec 18 2010 .cgi_auth
-rw-r--r--  1              0         0    496 Mar 15 17:22 .disk_usage
-------r--  1              0         0      0 Nov  6 11:14 .htaccess
drwxr-xr-x  2 jamesgrobertso inetuser   4096 Mar 16 14:19 backup
lrwxrwxrwx  1 jamesgrobertso inetuser      8 Dec  8 2008 cgi -> html/cgi
-rw-r--r--  1 jamesgrobertso inetuser      0 Jan 14 2009 cron.php
-rw-r--r--  1 jamesgrobertso inetuser 255847 Jan 14 2009 cron.php.1
-rw-------  1 jamesgrobertso inetuser     79 Apr 12 2009 crontab
-rw-------  1 jamesgrobertso inetuser     19 Apr 12 2009 crontab.disabled
drwx---r-x  2 jamesgrobertso inetuser   4096 Dec  8 2008 data
drwx---r-x  2              0         0   4096 Oct 10 2011 error_logs
drwx---r-x  2 jamesgrobertso inetuser   4096 Oct 14 15:57 htconfig
drwx---r-x 23 jamesgrobertso inetuser   4096 Nov 11 11:05 html
drwx---r-x  2 jamesgrobertso inetuser   4096 Oct  3 2011 scc
[jamesgrobertso@p3nlh023 ~]$ cd backup
[jamesgrobertso@p3nlh023 backup]$ mysqldump -h ▓▓▓▓▓▓▓▓▓▓▓▓▓▓▓▓▓▓▓▓▓▓▓▓▓▓▓▓ -u dru
pal7education -pEdu4Drupal! drupal7education > drupal7_16mar2013.sql▯
```

The `mysqldump` command accepts the following switches (options):

- `--skip-lock-tables`: Although this option won't be necessary on every server, including it can help avoid error messages that will impede your progress.

- `-h`: This option specifies the hostname of the MySQL server. You will not need this option if your MySQL server is on the same system as your web server.

- `-u`: This option specifies a user with rights to your database. This user should be the same as the user specified when you created your site as described in *Chapter 2, Installing Drupal*.

- `-p`: This option specifies the password of your database user. Do not include a space between the `-p` and the actual password.

5. The next option in the `mysqldump` command is the database name; in the example used in the preceding screenshot the database name is **drupal7education**. The user, password, and database name will all be the same as what you used when installing your site.

   The `> filename.sql` option specifies the name of your backup file.

6. To verify your backup, use the `ls -al` command to list the contents of the backup directory. See the highlighted section in the following screenshot for details:

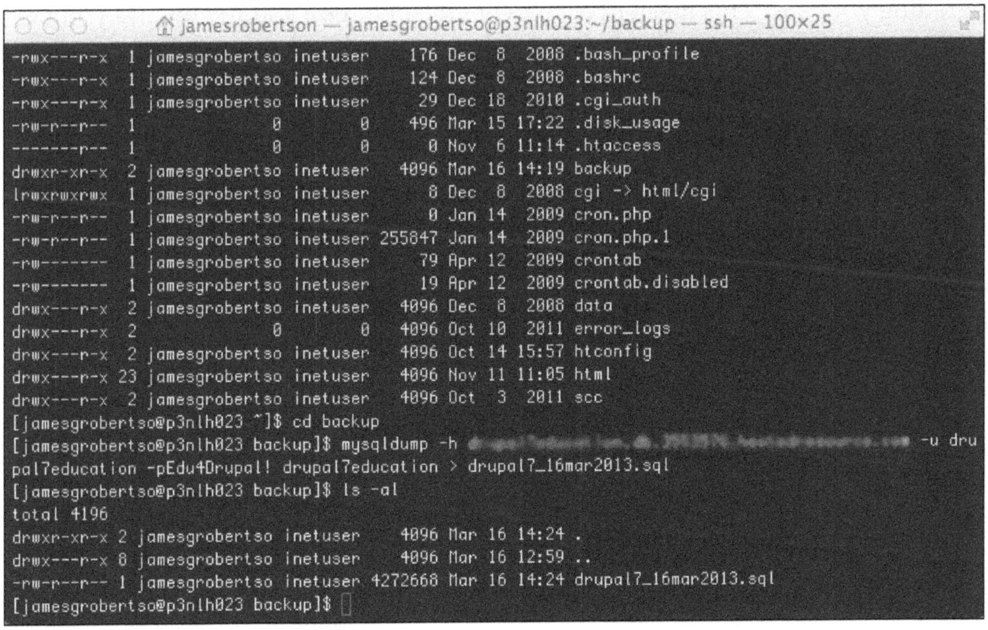

Later in this chapter, we cover how to test your backup by recreating your database on a different server.

Command-line backups of core codebase, contributed modules, and files

Earlier in this chapter, we took a full backup of the codebase by downloading a copy of the codebase via FTP. In this section, we will cover how to make code and file backups via the command line. We will also break our backup into three separate sections:

- The core codebase
- Contributed modules, contributed themes, and the `settings.php` file
- The files directory

These distinctions will be useful later in the chapter when we go over how to upgrade your site.

The master backup

You should perform a master backup when you launch your site, and again after upgrading your site. This master backup contains the code and the themes you need to run your site. To perform the master backup, you need to copy and archive the web directory running your Drupal install.

In this example, we will back up the site in the `drupal7` directory.

1. Log in to your server and `cd` to the staging directory. For more information on creating a staging directory, refer to the instructions in the *Backing up your database via the command line* section.

2. Enter `cp -pr /var/www/html/drupal7 site_date`. Replace `site_date` with the site name and the date of the backup

> For the `cp` command, you will need to specify the path to your Drupal install.

3. Enter `tar cvf site_date.tar site_date`.

4. Enter `gzip site_date.tar` — this creates a file named `site_date.tar.gz`, which contains a compressed version of your entire codebase.

5. FTP into your site, and download the codebase and the backup of database created earlier in the chapter.

Details on the command line

The `tar` command compresses files to allow us to store backups using less space.

The `cvf` options stand for:

- `c`: create a tarred file
- `v`: verbose — list all the files and directories included in the tarred file
- `f`: the filename of the tarred file will be the next option in the command

As with the database backup, you should give the backup a descriptive filename. Including the site and the date in the filename will help you keep track of your backups over time.

The path to the directory to be backed up. If you have access to the folders above your web root, then you can use your FTP client to determine the directory locations. Frequently, using your FTP client in conjunction with your SSH client simplifies the maintenance tasks you need to perform.

The `gzip` command compresses the tarred file further, which saves storage space for backups.

Backing up the contributed modules and themes

Log into your server via SSH and `cd` to your staging directory.

> In this description, we are using the path `/var/www/html/drupal7`, where `drupal7` is the name of the directory from which our Drupal site is accessed. When you are doing your backups, you will need to substitute this with the path to your site.

To tar only the modules and the themes, we will need to point specifically to the `/var/www/html/drupal7/sites/all/` directory, using the following command:

```
tar cvf mod_themes_date.tar /var/www/html/drupal7/sites/all/
```

Alternatively, we could grab a copy of the entire sites folder; this would create a backup up copy of all contributed modules and themes used on the site, as well as any files uploaded by site members, as well as the `settings.php` file. To tar the entire `sites` directory, use this command:

```
tar cvf entire_sites_dir_date.tar /var/www/html/drupal7/sites/
```

Whether you have copied only the contributed modules and themes, or the entire sites directory, `gzip` the folder as described earlier, and download it from your server.

File backups

To back up the files directory, you need to change the path to the directory you want to tar.

For the master backup, we tarred the `/var/www/html/drupal7/` directory. To tar the files directory, we would need to use the following command:

```
tar cvf files_date.tar /var/www/html/drupal7/sites/default/files/
```

Then, `gzip` the file as described earlier and download it from your web server.

Putting it all together

The process of using the command line can be daunting, as the command line doesn't give us much in the way of feedback. However, getting familiar with the command line can save us time, and help us perform important work quickly.

To put this into perspective, once we have SSH'ed into our server, the following commands are all we need to create our master backup:

```
cd backup
mysqldump --skip-lock-tables -u databaseuser -pdatabasepassword
databasename > filename.sql
tar cvf site_date.tar /path/to/your/site/
gzip site_date.tar
```

Once you have created the master backup, the following commands will create snapshots that will allow you to restore the site in the case of a server crash:

```
cd backup
mysqldump --skip-lock-tables -u databaseuser -pdatabasepassword
databasename > filename.sql
tar cvf files_date.tar /path/to/your/site/default/files
gzip files_date.tar
```

Although working from the command line is unfamiliar territory, learning the commands described in this chapter can allow you to backup your site quickly and easily.

It is also worth noting that the DB maintenance module automates the process of backing up the database and the files directory, making these command line steps unnecessary.

What should I backup and when should I do it?

At the start of this chapter, we described the four elements that need to be backed up:

- The database
- The core codebase
- The contributed modules and themes directory, along with the settings.php file
- The files directory

Of these four elements, only two—the database and the files directory—change on a regular basis.

From a practical perspective, this means that we only need to back up the core codebase and the contributed modules and themes directory after we have upgraded, or installed a new module.

The files directory and the database, however, change as a result of user activity. Therefore, they should be backed up on a more regular basis.

Verifying that your backup works

Going through the steps required to back up your site is an excellent first step, but for a backup to provide a true peace of mind you need to know it works. To test your backup, you need to use it to recreate your site in a different location. This process involves three steps, and is similar to the install process described in *Chapter 2, Installing Drupal*:

1. Creating your backup database

2. Uploading your codebase to the backup server

3. Editing the `settings.php` file to point to your database

Before we begin – web space for testing your backup

To verify that your backup works, you need to test that you can recreate your site. This step requires server space that is usually obtained in one of three ways:

* **Buy an additional test domain**: If you do a lot of work with websites and want a place to learn, a test domain can be a great resource. If you want to teach your class and spend as little time possible dealing with maintenance, then one of the other options will be a better fit.

* **Create a subdomain in your existing account**: For example, if your site is accessible at `http://www.yoursite.org`, the subdomain would be at `http://test.yoursite.org`. The advantage of the subdomain is that it is probably the easiest to set up, as most web hosts will help you to do this, and some will even do it for you. The disadvantage of using a subdomain is that if your server goes down, you will lose both your backup site and your main site.

* **Set up a test site on your computer using XAMPP or MAMP** (refer to `http://drupal.org/node/75545` for XAMPP or `http://drupal.org/node/66187` for MAMP): This is a useful step if you want to learn more about running a server, but it can be too much technical work for many people.

Creating the backup database

You can use either phpMyAdmin or the command line to recreate your database. Although phpMyAdmin provides an easier interface to work with, it has some limitations, especially when it comes to restoring larger databases.

First, create a database and a user for that database, as described in *Chapter 2, Installing Drupal*.

> Make sure that you keep the username, password, and database name of this database in a convenient place, as you will need to specify these values in your `settings.php` file, and you could also need them if you need to populate this database via the command line.

Recreating the database via phpMyAdmin

Let's see how to recreate database via phpMyAdmin. Refer to the following screenshot for details.

1. Click on the **Import** tab on the top-level navigation.

2. On the **Import** screen, use the **Browse** button to select your database.

3. Note the upload size limit, shown in the following screenshot by section **3**. (If your database backup is larger than this, you need to use the command line.)

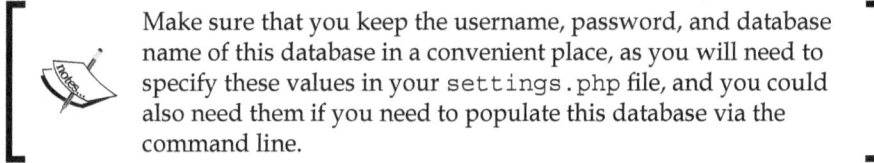

4. Select the correct file, and click on the **Go** button.

Recreating the database via the command line

To recreate the database using the command line, you will need to FTP the file containing your backed-up database into your staging directory. Then, log into your server via SSH, and cd to your staging directory.

Populate your database using the following command:

```
mysql -u username -p databasename < backupfilename.sql
```

Once you have completed these steps, you can view the database using phpMyAdmin to verify that the database has been created correctly.

Uploading the backup codebase

In this chapter, we have covered two ways of backing up the codebase: using your FTP client or by tarring and gzipping the file via the command line. If you used your FTP client to download the codebase, then simply upload the codebase to the appropriate location on your server. If you backed up the codebase via the command line, use your FTP client to upload the backup tar.gz file into your staging directory.

Then, SSH into your server and cd to your staging directory. Untar the codebase using this command:

```
tar -xzvf backup_codebase.tar.gz
```

The tar command extracts the codebase. From here, you can use the cp command to copy the codebase into your web directory.

```
cp -pr backup_codebase /path/to/web/directory
```

The actual path to your web directory will vary from server to server. If you don't know the path to your web directory, you can use your FTP client to figure this out.

Editing the settings.php file

Once you have moved the codebase into the web directory, you will need to edit the settings.php file so that it points at the correct database. The settings.php file is located in the sites/default directory. You can edit this file using any text editor, or any more-advanced authoring tool, such as Dreamweaver or Zend.

> Even though you can open the settings.php file using a word processor, don't do it! Word processors add in spaces and formatting that will render the settings.php file useless.

As shown in the highlighted section in the following screenshot, you will need to edit three values:

- Database name
- Username
- Password

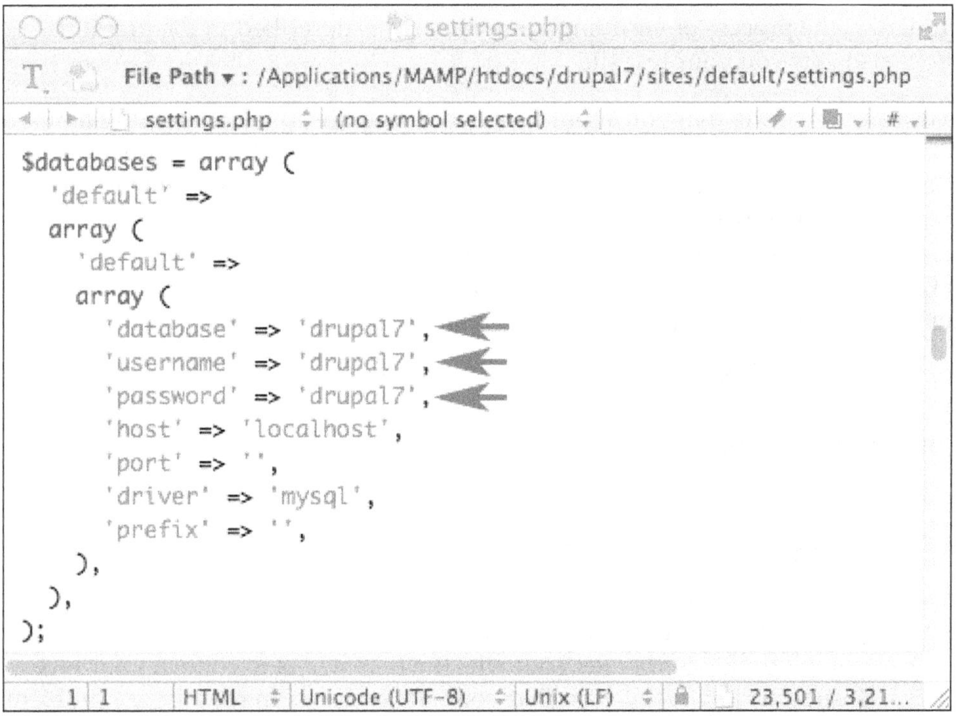

settings.php
File Path ▾ : /Applications/MAMP/htdocs/drupal7/sites/default/settings.php
settings.php
(no symbol selected)
$databases = array (
'default' =>
array (
'default' =>
array (
'database' => 'drupal7',
'username' => 'drupal7',
'password' => 'drupal7',
'host' => 'localhost',
'port' => '',
'driver' => 'mysql',
'prefix' => '',
),
),
);
1 1
HTML
Unicode (UTF-8)
Unix (LF)
23,501 / 3,21...

Edit these values, save your changes, and then replace the old `settings.php` file with the new file, and your backup is complete. You can test the backup by navigating to the homepage of your new site. You will see an exact replica of your existing site.

Congratulations! You are now running your website with the security of a solid backup procedure.

The test site

If you want to experiment with Drupal by installing additional modules, a test site provides a safe place to do this. For all of the obvious reasons, your live class site is not the place to experiment or take chances. Although installing a test site is additional work, it provides you with a safe place to learn and experiment without fear of consequences.

Fortunately, the process of verifying your backup, as described in the previous section, also gets you your test site.

The test site is the site that you should use when you are trying something new, from evaluating a new module or theme, to testing an upgrade procedure. Using the test site allows you to take chances you would not otherwise be able to take. For example, if you want to try a new module, you can install it and experiment with the functionality and settings on your test site. If the module does what you need, then you can deploy it on your live site. If, however, the module does not meet your needs, you can just wipe out the database and start from scratch.

Your test site is also the place where you should test all upgrades before you perform them on your live site. Even though upgrades almost always occur seamlessly, you are in a much better place if you spot the problem on your test site.

Disaster recovery

By using the backup strategy described in this chapter, you can recover your site relatively quickly using your most recent backups. If your server crashes, or if some other technological disaster befalls your site, the first step is to contact your web host or tech support to inform them that your site is down. In most cases, problems involving a website going down (and this applies to all sites, not just Drupal sites) has nothing to do with the site, but with the hosting infrastructure. Fixing the issues with the web server, or the connection to the web server, usually fixes the problems with the site.

However, should your actual site become compromised, here is how to recover:

* Retrieve your most recent backup of the files directory
* Retrieve your most recent backup of your database
* Retrieve your most recent master backup
* Within your master backup, replace the files directory at sites/default
* Replicate your site as described in the previous section

Updating your site

Drupal sites require periodic upgrades. These upgrades should be considered part of the maintenance process, and Drupal includes a core module called **Update manager** that simplifies this process. The Update manager module provides an overview of the modules installed on your site, and informs you if they are out of date.

> Make sure that the Update manager module is enabled by clicking the **Modules** link, or by navigating to admin/modules.

The Update manager module informs you of two main types of upgrades:

* Maintenance
* Security

A security upgrade patches a security hole, and requires an immediate upgrade. A maintenance release adds functionality, or fixes non-critical bugs. Whenever there is a new core Drupal release, you should upgrade your site to the new release. For contributed modules, maintenance releases should eventually be included, but, unlike security releases, they are not an immediate priority.

The updates page is available at **Reports | Available updates**, or http://yoursite.org/admin/reports/updates.

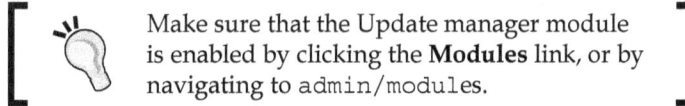

Upgrading core

Before upgrading core, you should do two things:

- Back up your database, and test this backup by copying into an empty database.
- Back up the `sites` directory. The `sites` directory contains the `files` directory, the `modules` directory, the `themes` directory, and your `settings.php` file—all of which are critical elements of your site.

Once you have completed these steps, you are ready to proceed with your upgrade.

Upgrading core – the short version

When performing a core upgrade, we will replace the old version of Drupal core with the updated version. This process involves five steps:

1. Log into the new site as UID1; place the site in maintenance mode, and run `update.php`.
2. Download the new codebase from `http://drupal.org/project/drupal`.
3. Extract the Drupal codebase.
4. Delete the `sites` directory from the freshly downloaded codebase; replace it with the `sites` directory from your existing site.
5. Replace the existing codebase with the new codebase.

Upgrading core – the detailed version

These more-detailed directions expand on the short version, and provide step-by-step instructions on how to upgrade via the command line. In these detailed instructions, the new site is prepared on the web server. For people who don't want to work on the command line, the new site can be prepared on your local computer, and then uploaded to the web server via FTP.

Preparing the upgraded site

Before we start the upgrade, there are a few tasks we need to complete to stay organized:

1. In the same directory as your existing site, create a folder named `upgrade_temp`.

2. Download the latest version of core Drupal from `http://drupal.org/project/drupal`. Once you have downloaded the `tar.gz` file, use your FTP client to upload it to the `upgrade_temp` directory.

3. SSH into your server and `cd` to the `upgrade_temp` directory.

4. Using the command line, extract the Drupal codebase:

   ```
   tar -xzvf drupal_release.tar.gz
   ```

5. Delete the `sites` directory from the newly-extracted Drupal codebase:

   ```
   rm -r path/to/new/codebase/sites
   ```

6. Using the command line, copy the sites directory from your existing site into the new codebase:

   ```
   cp -pr /path/to/livesite/sites path/to/new/codebase/sites
   ```

> On some operating systems, the command will need to be `cp -pR`.

At this point, the new codebase should be ready for the upgrade. To verify that all files have been copied to the right places, examine the `upgrade_temp` directory using `ls -al` at the command line or by navigating to the `upgrade_temp` directory using your FTP client.

Preparing the codebase – additional notes

In some cases, your site will have a custom `php.ini` file, or a modified `.htaccess` file in the root of your Drupal install. If you have either of these modifications in your site, be sure to copy the modified files to your upgraded codebase.

Also, in very rare instances, the upgrade will include changes to the `settings.php` file. In this rare case, you will need to copy over the database name, database user, and database password from your old `settings.php` file. Editing the `settings.php` file is covered earlier in this chapter, where we described how to test your backup.

Bringing the upgrade live

Now that we have updated the codebase, we need to complete the following steps to finish the upgrade:

1. Log in to your site as UID1.

2. Click on **Configuration | Maintenance mode,** or navigate to `admin/config/development/maintenance`, and put your site into maintenance mode.

3. Using your FTP client, navigate to the web directory on your server. Rename the folder containing the codebase for your existing site from `foldername` to `foldername_old`.

4. Using the command line, copy the `upgrade_temp` directory (which contains the new codebase) into the web directory, and rename it to match the folder name that was edited in step 3.

> In some cases, there may be additional files stored within the web directory. If this is the case, you will need to delete the full Drupal codebase from the web directory, and copy the upgraded codebase into this directory. Both methods work perfectly well; however, one advantage of renaming the directories is that you have a working codebase on your server to roll back to if something goes awry during the upgrade process.

5. Navigate to `http://yoursite.org/update.php`. You will be presented with a wizard with four steps: **Overview**; **Review updates**; **Run updates**, and **Review log**. Click on the **Continue** button.

Drupal database update

Use this utility to update your database whenever a new release of Drupal or a module is installed.

For more detailed information, see the upgrading handbook. If you are unsure what these terms mean you should probably contact your hosting provider.

✓ Verify requirements

▸ Overview

Review updates

Run updates

Review log

1. **Back up your database.** This process will change your database values and in case of emergency you may need to revert to a backup.
2. **Back up your code.** Hint: when backing up module code, do not leave that backup in the 'modules' or 'sites/*/modules' directories as this may confuse Drupal's auto-discovery mechanism.
3. Put your site into maintenance mode.
4. Install your new files in the appropriate location, as described in the handbook.

When you have performed the steps above, you may proceed.

Continue

6. At the **Review updates** screen, click on the **Apply pending updates** button. The update process will continue through without the need for additional input.

7. Once the upgrade process has completed, test your site by logging in as different users, adding sample content, and so on. Even if the upgrade process was generally uneventful, a little extra time verifying a clean upgrade is never a bad thing.

8. A best practice for upgrades involves a series of tests for users in different roles. For example, users in the teacher role would create an assignment in a group, view a student's assignments, and add a note about a student.

9. Once you have verified a clean upgrade, delete the `foldername_old` directory, and the `upgrade_temp` directory.

10. Click on **Configuration | Maintenance mode**, or navigate to `admin/settings/site-maintenance`, and take your site out of maintenance mode.

11. Perform a master backup of your site as described earlier in this chapter.

Upgrading contributed modules

Upgrading contributed modules is considerably easier than upgrading Drupal core.

To update a contributed module, download the latest copy of the module and read the upgrade instructions. For most modules, these instructions are found in a `readme.txt` or in a separate `upgrade.txt` file.

Follow any module-specific instructions found in this file. In the overwhelming majority of cases, though, the following steps will work for a clean upgrade:

1. Log in as UID1; click on **Administer | Site configuration | Maintenance**, or navigate to `admin/settings/site-maintenance`, and put your site into maintenance mode.

2. In your `sites/all/modules` directory, delete the old version of the module.

3. Upload the new version of the module.

4. In your browser, navigate to `http://yoursite.org/update.php` and run through the upgrade wizard.

5. Click on **Administer | Site configuration | Maintenance**, or navigate to `admin/config/development/maintenance`, and take your site out of maintenance mode.

6. Perform a master backup of your site, as described earlier in this chapter.

If you have multiple contributed modules to upgrade, you should run the upgrades one at a time. This way, if one module has an issue with the upgrade, you will know exactly where the problem lies.

Upgrading your theme

Theme upgrades occur very infrequently, and are rarely required for security reasons. The Upgrade manager module will tell you if there is a new version of your theme available. However, if you have made changes to your theme by modifying the actual files or style sheets within the theme, note that an upgrade will eliminate your changes unless you specifically preserve them. In short, although the theme should be upgraded if there is a security problem (which is extremely rare), themes generally don't require upgrades.

Should your theme require an upgrade, you should download the new version of the theme, and look for any upgrade instructions within a `readme.txt` file or an `upgrade.txt` file. In the absence of any other instructions, delete the old theme directory, and upload the new theme in its place.

Summary

The work involved in setting up a backup strategy, and in maintaining your site through security upgrades, can feel overwhelming. However, one thing worse than struggling through setting up a backup strategy is attempting to recover your site after a server crash without a backup strategy.

A backup strategy, combined with a test site, allows you to run your site with fewer worries. The test site also provides a place in which you can experiment with new options without fear of consequences.

Drupal is not a static program. It is constantly changing and updating, and keeping up with those changes is important to keeping your site secure and working well.

In the next chapter we will learn some tips and tricks for working with the Drupal community, including how to troubleshoot and research issues and best practices for giving and receiving help.

16

Working Effectively in the Drupal Community

Using an open source tool has many benefits and the Drupal community offers a wealth of knowledge and experience. The Drupal community is an international group with a diverse base of users. However, making your way in the community, especially if you are new to Drupal in particular and open source software in general, can be daunting. The guidelines in this chapter will help you get acquainted with how to work effectively in the world of Drupal.

In this chapter, we will learn the following:

- Researching Drupal using the handbooks and issue queues available on `Drupal.org`
- How and where to ask questions
- Tips on how to contribute back to the community

Getting started

Numerous support venues exist within the Drupal community. Experience has shown that if you show some effort toward researching a problem before asking a question, it is more likely to receive a meaningful response.

One of Drupal's main strengths is the depth of knowledge and experience of the user community; by asking questions and answering the questions of others, you become a member of the community. As you participate in the community, over time, you gain more credibility. However, people new to Drupal bring fresh perspectives to the project, and there is no need to feel like an expert before answering a question.

Researching on Drupal.org

When looking for information from the Drupal community, you should generally start by searching through the information that has already been created. Reading the handbooks and searching on `Drupal.org` can help you answer many questions quickly, with minimal effort.

Searching effectively

The Drupal community search feature is available at `http://drupal.org/search` and can often yield good results. The advanced search, as shown in the following screenshot, allows you to narrow the scope of your search and focus on specific subjects or content types:

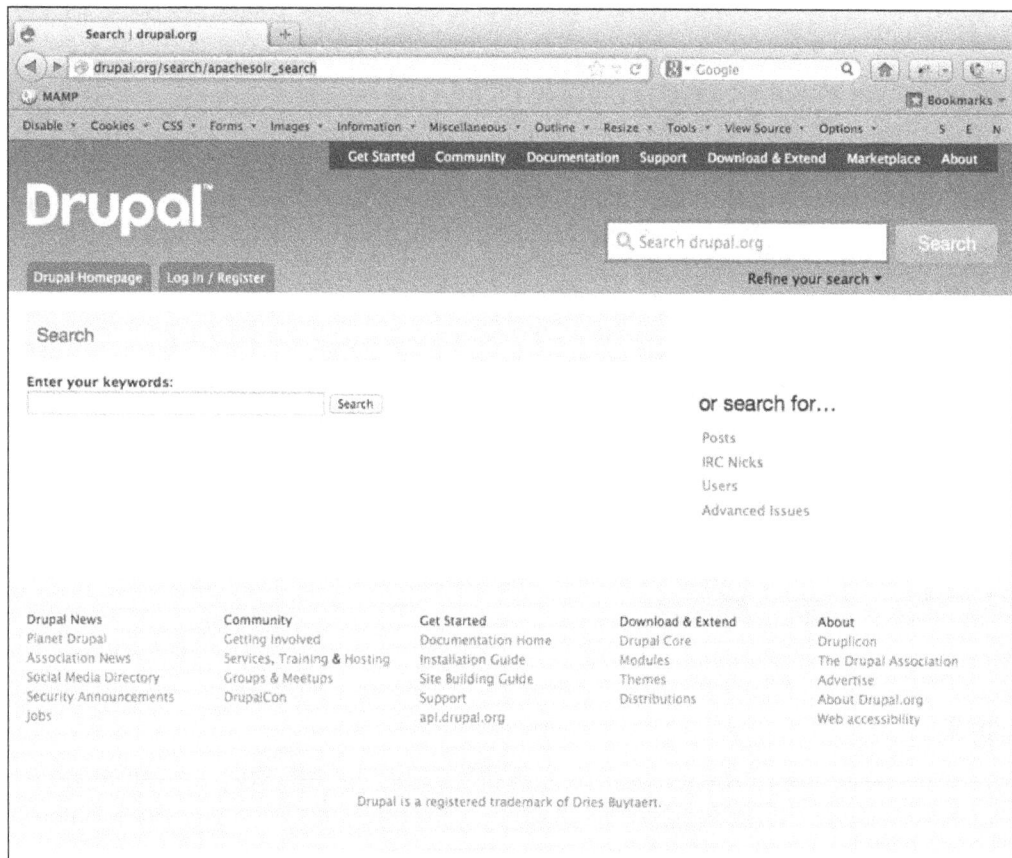

You can also use Google's site-specific search feature by adding the text **site:drupal. org** to the beginning of your search string. This focuses your search onto `Drupal.org` itself and is often the most effective way to start finding an answer to your question.

Handbooks

The handbooks contain a blend of generalized information and more specialized information. Browsing the handbooks can often yield unexpected gems and ideas and they contain a wealth of information. For example, this page on videocasts contains some amazing resources: `http://drupal.org/videocasts`.

Reading the handbooks is a great way to start researching an issue in Drupal, and the process of reading the handbooks can help you learn many details quickly. However, for precise answers to specific questions, you have other resources at your disposal.

Browsing the issue queue

Every module on `Drupal.org` has a project associated with it, and every project has an issue queue. The complete issue queue can be found at `http://drupal. org/project/issues`. The issue queue allows you to filter on specific modules. The projects associated with each module are used to track potential bugs and questions about the specific module. If you are having problems/issues with a specific module, you can often find other users reporting similar issues.

If you end up needing to post a question about a module, you should include the fact that you looked at the issue queue before asking; the fact that you have searched the issue queue shows a level of research and attention to detail that gives you more credibility.

Asking questions

If your research doesn't get you what you need, then it's time to start asking questions. To begin unraveling your issue, read through the FAQ at `http:// drupal.org/troubleshooting`. If your answer is not covered here, then it's time to start asking questions.

Support forums

The support forums, available at `http://drupal.org/forum`, are a good place to start asking for help when you need it.

When asking questions in the forum (or really, in any of the support areas for Drupal) you can take the following measures to make it easier for people to help you:

- Describe the research you undertook prior to asking the question. Did you search using Google? Did you look at the issue queue? Were there any other forum threads or handbook pages that seemed to give some of the information you need? If so, give links of those pages. The more detailed you can be in your question, the more specific people can be when responding.

- Ask, don't demand. The overwhelming majority of people responding to questions on `Drupal.org` are doing it in their own time. While it can be frustrating to ask a question and not get a response, nobody is required to answer questions on the forums. Generally, people who make demands often get reminded of the proper forum etiquette but they also get actual answers less frequently.

- If a response rubs you the wrong way, try not to escalate the tension. Drupal is an international community, and miscommunications can occur due to the language barrier. At times, people are just plain rude. If someone responds to you in a way that doesn't feel right, take the high ground. While you may feel justified at responding to a sharp exchange, it probably doesn't do much to get your question answered.

- Give your posts a meaningful, descriptive title. The more someone can glean from the title, the better the chance that they will read your full post and try to respond.

- If you asked a question that did not draw a response, don't take it personally. There is a lot of traffic on `Drupal.org`, and many questions get overlooked simply due to the vagaries of timing.

For the forums, all recent posts show up at `http://drupal.org/tracker`, and this is where most people look to answer questions or get a sense of activity in the forums. Putting a comment on your own post (a practice known as **bumping**) is generally frowned upon if done frequently or after a very short wait. However, if your question remains unanswered for one or two days, you should feel free to post a follow up response on your initial question to bump it back to the front page of the tracker.

Type	Post	Author	Replies	Last updated
Issue	breaks with localized links	RobKoberg	0	1 min 18 sec ago
Project	ClickBank Download	brycefisherfleig	0	1 min 19 sec ago
Forum topic	One large menu, or multiple smaller menus?	Toby Wild	1	1 min 39 sec ago
Issue	Convert config_admin_import_form to a new FormInterface implementation and routing definition.	Alan Evans	5	2 min 12 sec ago
Issue	Fatal error after switching from metatags to metatag	amirtaiar	4	3 min 3 sec ago
Issue	IPs deleted from hosting_ip_addresses table on server verify	omega8cc	15	3 min 11 sec ago
Issue	Convert book_outline to a new-style Controller	Crell	10	4 min 11 sec ago
Issue	Views Superglobals Default	ryan.armstrong	0	4 min 40 sec ago
Issue	Remove the "metatags" module	chriscalip	3	5 min ago
Issue	Link not closed on FAQ page	silverwing	2	5 min 13 sec ago
Issue	test with other modules & themes	mikeytown2	1	5 min 37 sec ago
Issue	tablebooker	johannesdr	18	5 min 42 sec ago

Finally, when someone does respond to your question, thank them. And, if no one responds to your question but you figure out an answer on your own, post back on your thread with your answer. You can be sure that someone else will have the same problem at some point and will find your thread and get the answer they need.

The Support mailing list

The support mailing list offers similar support to what you find in the forums, and the same rules regarding questions apply. Many people swear that they get better results on the mailing list, while others swear by the quality of support on the forums. In general, both resources are excellent places to get answers. You can subscribe to the *support* list at `http://drupal.org/mailing-lists`.

Groups.drupal.org

The Groups site, located at `http://groups.drupal.org`, contains affiliated groups organized by geographic location, area of interest, and functionality. For example, the site has a group for users from Portland, Oregon, several groups dedicated to education-related issues, and groups organized around building social networking sites. If you are working on a site to achieve a specific goal, you can often find people within a group working on a similar goal.

Additionally, the "Drupal in Education" group is, as the group name suggests, focused on different uses of Drupal in Education. This group can be found at `http://groups.drupal.org/drupal-education`.

Internet Relay Chat (IRC)

An additional resource for finding support and working within the Drupal community is **Internet Relay Chat (IRC)**. IRC is often the best option for finding answers in a hurry. It is also the best method to quickly develop a reputation within the Drupal community, as the subset of people found on IRC tends to be among the more active participants in the Drupal community.

You need an IRC client to join IRC; one of the easiest to install and use is an application called Chatzilla, available as a Firefox add-on at `https://addons.mozilla.org/en-US/firefox/addon/16`.

The Drupal handbook at `http://drupal.org/node/108355` has an excellent overview of using IRC.

The IRC channel for Drupal support is `#drupal-support` on Freenode at `http://freenode.net`.

Giving support

People who use Drupal for any length of time reach a point where they become capable of answering questions for other users. Helping out in the forums, writing up a case study describing how you used Drupal, or joining the documentation team and helping to write the handbooks are all ways that non-programmers can contribute to Drupal. By giving support to other users as time allows, you help to keep the project moving forward. Contributing back to the community also allows you to begin building a network of contacts within the community; these contacts can help you as your needs become more complex.

For a starting point on how you can get more involved in the Drupal community, see `http://drupal.org/contribute`.

Summary

When you have a question about using Drupal, the community contains resources that can help you out. By searching the existing resources and asking effective questions, you can lean on the community to help you when you need it. As you increasingly use Drupal, over time, you will also be able to help others who are in similar situations. And at that point it's only a matter of time before you come home with a Druplicon tattoo.

Index

B

backlinks view 153
backup
    codebase, uploading 342
    content 339
    contributed modules 338
    file backups 338
    overview 321
    settings.php file, editing 342, 343
    themes 338
    verifying 340
Backup and Migrate module
    database, configuring 322, 323
    database, scheduling 325, 326
    default profile, modifying 324, 325
    files backup options 322, 323
    files backups, scheduling 325, 326
    summary 326
    view 322
backup database
    creating 340
    recreating, via command line 342
    recreating, via phpMyAdmin 341
Backup module 322
backup verification
    site, testing ways 340
basic principles
    simple presentation 292
    unnecessary options, hiding 292, 293
block
    about 11, 295, 304
    activities 305
    comparing, with menu 304
    making, visible to specific pages 305
    making, visible to specific roles 305, 306
blog post content type
    about 111
    blog module 113
    fields, adding 112
    permissions, assigning 112, 113
    taxonomy, assigning 112
blog posts 152
blogs
    about 219
    and forum relationship 218
    concerns 220

strengths 219
versus forums 220
bookmarks
    about 152, 165
    and media literacy 171
    goals 170-172
    rights, assigning for use 165
    sharing 166, 168
    using, for blog 168-170
    using, in classroom 166
    using, in ongoing search 171
bumping 354
bundle 10

C

CamStudio 209
Camtasia 208
CANCELLATION section 144
class nodes 244
club node 244
codebase
    backing up 321, 322
code snippets
    PHP snippets, embedding in page 270-275
    PHP snippets, enabling 268, 270
    snippet 274
    used, for student progress tracking 268
Comment module 35, 137
Configuration administrative section 49
Configuration | Maintenance mode 349
Configuration | Performance 318
Configure site screen 31
content 304
Content administrative section 44, 45
Content: All taxonomy terms field 88
Content: Link to source field 87
content type options
    setting 245, 246
content types
    about 10
    Comment settings page 68
    creating 62, 63
    creating, summary 79
    Description section 65
    Display settings section 67, 68
    fields, adding 69-73

signatures 145
PHP Data Objects. *See* PDO
phpMyAdmin
    used, for table optimization 328-330
    using, as backup tool 328
    using, as maintenance tool 328
PHP snippets
    using, with Views 275
PHP version 14
podcast
    creating 184
    examples 186
    hardware requirements 184
    project ideas 186
    requirements 174
    software requirements 184
    uses 184
    using, in classroom 183
    using, in project-based learning 185
podcast content type
    audio field, adding 178
    creating 176
    rights, assigning to 179
podcasting 173
post 10
private communication, with students
    about 286
    node access user reference, configuring
        286, 287
    node access user reference, using 288
Putty 332

Q

questions
    groups.drupal.org 356
    support forums 354, 355
    support mailing list 355
Quicktime Pro 208

R

Recent content link 266
region
    about 11, 304
    content 304
    footer 304
    header 304

help 304
highlighted 304
left sidebar 304
page bottom 304
page top 304
right sidebar 304
registration process
    Account Settings page 143
    customizing 143
REGISTRATION section 144
Reports administrative section 50, 52
rights
    assigning 135, 136
    assigning, for student role 136-138
right sidebar 304
roles
    about 11, 135, 136
    creating 61, 62
RSS 84

S

sample content
    adding 122-124
Save configuration button 60
Save permissions button 36, 138, 166
Save profile button 325
search index 160
Search module 36
settings
    changing, via admin menu 306
site
    setting up, for image usage 187
    updating 345
Site information page
    about 306, 308
    themes, enabling 308, 309
    theme settings 308
social network 221
social networking
    additional options 236
software requirements, for video creating
    desktop software 208
    online tools 209
specific assignments
    argument, editing 283-285
    responses, tracking 282

configuring 60, 61
core modules 54
decompressing 57
directories 54
downloading 56, 57
enabling 58-60
files 54
installing 53
sites directory 55
upgrading 350
uploading 58
tpl.php files
about 316, 317
custom pages, creating 317
Type of Assignment 120

U

UID1 (User ID 1) 12
Update button 142
Update manager 345
user accounts
creating, additional modules used 148
User module 36, 138
user profile goals
identifying 221
user profiles
about 229
additional options 236
building 229
field, adding to field groups 232
field groups, adding 230
fields, adding to 229, 230
permission, assigning for field edit 233
permission, assigning for field view 233
rights, assigning for profile view 233
users
about 11
adding 120, 121
section summary 122

V

video content type
about 200
creating 201

embedded media field module,
    installing 200
video field, adding 201, 202
video field
permissions, assigning 203
taxonomy, assigning 203
video field configuration
field settings 202
video settings 202
videos
about 199
creating, hardware requirement 207
creating, software requirement 208
embedding 203
embedding, from external site 203-205
embedding, from local site 205, 206
using, in classroom 209
video settings
configuring 202
videos, using in classroom
about 209
language learning 210
student projects 210
used, for teaching 210
video bookends 210
Videotape field trips 210
videotape labs 210
view
about 80
adding 81
additional configuration options, setting 96
contextual filters, adding 92
contextual filters, editing 92
creating 80
creating, summary 102
data type, selecting 83
default values, overriding 98-100
describing 82
display format, editing 93-95
display format, setting 84
display type options, setting 83, 84
display type, selecting 83
editing 84
fields, adding 85-88, 92
fields, configuring 88-92
fields, editing 92

[PACKT] open source
PUBLISHING   community experience distilled

Thank you for buying
Drupal for Education and E-Learning Second Edition

About Packt Publishing

Packt, pronounced 'packed', published its first book *"Mastering phpMyAdmin for Effective MySQL Management"* in April 2004 and subsequently continued to specialize in publishing highly focused books on specific technologies and solutions.

Our books and publications share the experiences of your fellow IT professionals in adapting and customizing today's systems, applications, and frameworks. Our solution based books give you the knowledge and power to customize the software and technologies you're using to get the job done. Packt books are more specific and less general than the IT books you have seen in the past. Our unique business model allows us to bring you more focused information, giving you more of what you need to know, and less of what you don't.

Packt is a modern, yet unique publishing company, which focuses on producing quality, cutting-edge books for communities of developers, administrators, and newbies alike. For more information, please visit our website: www.packtpub.com.

About Packt Open Source

In 2010, Packt launched two new brands, Packt Open Source and Packt Enterprise, in order to continue its focus on specialization. This book is part of the Packt Open Source brand, home to books published on software built around Open Source licences, and offering information to anybody from advanced developers to budding web designers. The Open Source brand also runs Packt's Open Source Royalty Scheme, by which Packt gives a royalty to each Open Source project about whose software a book is sold.

Writing for Packt

We welcome all inquiries from people who are interested in authoring. Book proposals should be sent to author@packtpub.com. If your book idea is still at an early stage and you would like to discuss it first before writing a formal book proposal, contact us; one of our commissioning editors will get in touch with you.

We're not just looking for published authors; if you have strong technical skills but no writing experience, our experienced editors can help you develop a writing career, or simply get some additional reward for your expertise.

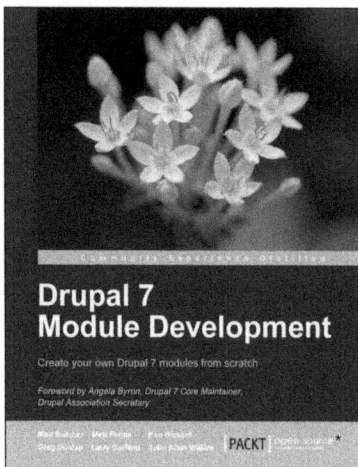

Drupal 7 Module Development

ISBN: 978-1-849511-16-2   Paperback: 420 pages

Create your own Drupal 7 modules from scratch

1. Specifically written for Drupal 7 development

2. Write your own Drupal modules, themes, and libraries

3. Discover the powerful new tools introduced in Drupal 7

4. Learn the programming secrets of six experienced Drupal developers

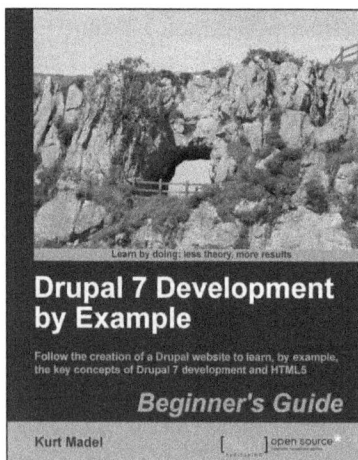

Drupal 7 Development by Example Beginner's Guide

ISBN: 978-1-849516-80-8   Paperback: 366 pages

Follow the creation of a Drupal website to learn, by example, the key concepts of Drupal 7 development and HTML 5

1. A hands-on, example-driven guide to programming Drupal websites

2. Discover a number of new features for Drupal 7 through practical and interesting examples while building a fully functional recipe sharing website

3. Learn about web content management, multi-media integration, and e-commerce in Drupal 7

Please check **www.PacktPub.com** for information on our titles

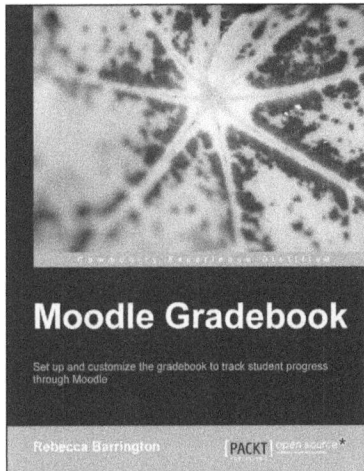

Moodle Gradebook

ISBN: 978-1-849518-14-7   Paperback: 128 pages

Set up and customize the gradebook to track student progress through Moodle

1. Use Moodle's powerful gradebook more effectively to monitor and report on the progress of your students

2. Customize the gradebook to calculate and show the information you need

3. Discover new grading features and tracking functions now available in Moodle 2

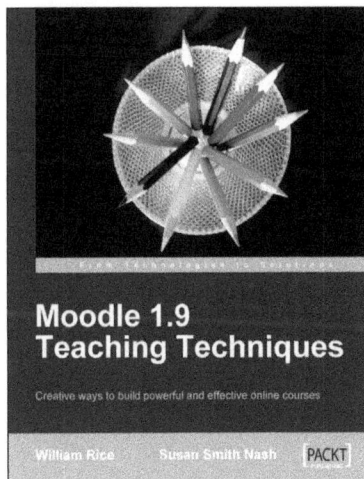

Moodle 1.9 Teaching Techniques

ISBN: 978-1-849510-06-6   Paperback: 216 pages

Creative ways to build powerful and effective online courses

1. Motivate students from all backgrounds, generations, and learning styles

2. When and how to apply the different learning solutions with workarounds, providing alternative solutions

3 Easy-to-follow, step-by-step instructions with screenshots and examples for Moodle's powerful features

Please check **www.PacktPub.com** for information on our titles

www.ingramcontent.com/pod-product-compliance
Lightning Source LLC
Chambersburg PA
CBHW080706220326
41598CB00033B/5327